The Creative Process in
the Autograph Musical Documents
of Hector Berlioz, c. 1818-1840

Studies in Musicology, No. 7

George Buelow, Series Editor
Professor of Musicology
Indiana University

Other Titles in This Series

The Creative Process in
the Autograph Musical Documents
of Hector Berlioz, c. 1818-1840

by
D. Kern Holoman

umi
RESEARCH PRESS

Produced and distributed by
UMI Research Press
an imprint of
University Microfilms International
Ann Arbor, Michigan 48106

Library of Congress Cataloging in Publication Data

Holoman, D   Kern, 1947-
   The creative process in the autograph musical
documents of Hector Berlioz, c. 1818-1840.

   (Studies in musicology series ; no. 8)
   Bibliography: p.
   Includes index.
   1. Berlioz, Hector, 1803-1869—Manuscripts. 2. Creation
(Literary, artistic, etc.)   I. Title. II. Series.

ML410.B5H6   780'.92'4   79-11879
ISBN 0-8357-0988-4
ISBN 0-8357-0989-2 pbk.

Contents

Facsimiles

Tables

Abbreviations

I. **Archival Location.** The system used in RISM has been adopted, thus:

A-Wg	Austria: Vienna, Gesellschaft der Musikfreunde in Wien
D-Bds	Germany: Berlin, Deutsche Staatsbibliothek
D-DS	Germany: Darmstadt, Hessische Landes- und Hochschulbibliothek, Musikabteilung
D-DT	Germany: Detmold, Lippische Landesbibliothek
F-G	France: Grenoble, Bibliothèque Municipale
F-Pan	France: Paris, Archives Nationales
F-Pc	France: Paris, Bibliothèque Nationale, fonds du Conservatoire
F-Pmeyer	France: Paris, private collection of André Meyer
F-Pn	France: Paris, Bibliothèque Nationale
S-Smf	Sweden: Stockholm, Stiftelsen Musikkulturens Främjande
US-NYpm	United States: New York, Pierpont Morgan Library

Several abbreviations have been devised specifically for use in this study:

F-CSA	France: La Côte-Saint-André, Musée Nationale Hector Berlioz
F-Pbuffetaud	France: Paris, private collection of Marie-Hélène and Eric Buffetaud (formerly collection of Léon Constantin)
F-Preboul	France: Paris, private collection of Mme Y. Reboul-Hector Berlioz, Berlioz's great-niece (by marriage)
GB-En H. B.	Scotland: Edinburgh, National Library of Scotland, Hopkinson Berlioz Collection
GB-TWmacnutt	England: Tunbridge-Wells, private collection of Richard Macnutt

Abbreviations

US-NYcu   United States: New York, Columbia University
Berlioz Collection Library, Berlioz Collection

US-NYkallir   United States: New York, private collection of
R. F. Kallir

II. Bibliographical reference. These abbreviations (in boldface type) are made up of three or four letters, depending on mnemonic strength, from the author's surname, followed by letters that suggest the title, for example:

A. *Books and articles*

BarzHB   Jacques Barzun, *Berlioz and the Romantic Century* (New York, 3rd edition, 1969), 2 volumes.

BosHB   Adolphe Boschot, *L'Histoire d'un romantique*, 3 volumes:

BosHB I   *La Jeunesse d'un romantique: Hector Berlioz, 1803-1831* (Paris, 1906);

BosHB II   *Un Romantique sous Louis-Philippe: Hector Berlioz, 1831-1842* (Paris, 1908);

BosHB III   *Le Crépuscule d'un romantique: Hector Berlioz, 1842-1869* (Paris, 1913).

HopBib   Cecil Hopkinson, *A Bibliography of the Musical and Literary Works of Hector Berlioz, 1803-1869* (Edinburgh, 1951).

MacSelf   Hugh Macdonald, "Berlioz's Self-Borrowings," *Proceedings of the Royal Musical Association*, no. 92 (1965-66), pp. 27-44.

B. *Writings of Berlioz*

BerCG   *Correspondance générale*, ed. Pierre Citron (Paris, 1972 -   ).

BerCG I   *1803-1832* (letters 1-273), ed. Pierre Citron (Paris, 1972).

BerCG II   *1832-1842* (letters 274-775), ed. Frédéric Robert (Paris, 1975).

BerCG III	*1842-1850* (letters 776-1367), ed. Pierre Citron (Paris, 1978).
BerCI	*Correspondance inédite de Hector Berlioz, 1819-1868*, ed. Daniel Bernard (Paris, 1879).
BerCSW	*Briefe von Hector Berlioz an die Fürstin Carolyne Sayn-Wittgenstein*, ed. La Mara (Leipzig, 1903).
BerMém	*Mémoires* (Paris, 1865; released 1870).
BerMemCairns	*The Memoirs of Berlioz*, trans. and ed. David Cairns (New York, 3rd edn, 1975. N.B. Norton paperpack edn., revised, corrected, and enlarged).
BerTG	*Lettres inédites de Hector Berlioz à Thomas Gounet*, ed. L. Michoud and G. Allix (Grenoble, 1903).

C. Music

OBE	"Old Berlioz Edition," i.e. *Hector Berlioz, Werke*, ed. Charles Malherbe and Felix Weingartner (Leipzig, 1900-07), 20 volumes.
NBE	*New Berlioz Edition*, gen. ed. Hugh Macdonald (London, etc., 1967-).

The abbreviation *aut.* refers to an autograph orchestra score, unless noted.

The first reference to a regularly cited work gives the complete bibliographical reference and the abbreviation; thereafter, only the abbreviation appears. Abbreviations used in the tables are explained in accompanying notes.

Acknowledgments

This study could not have been completed without the help of Hugh Macdonald, who allowed me unlimited use of the facilities of the New Berlioz Edition at the University of Oxford. Other scholars affiliated with the edition have provided no less valuable assistance: David Cairns, Ian Kemp, Richard Macnutt, and Julian Rushton. Special thanks are due Nicholas Temperley, who lent me a typescript from his edition of the *Symphonie fantastique* long before it was published.

I am grateful to Jacques Barzun; to Virginia Xanthos of Professor Barzun's staff; and to Kenneth Lohf and the staff of the Special Collections division of the Columbia University Library, who provided assistance with the collection of Berlioziana that Barzun has assembled.

My year of research in France was made possible by a Fulbright-Hays Grant administered by the Bureau of Educational and Cultural Affairs of the Department of State.

For granting access to the privately owned collections of Berlioz's autographs, I am grateful to Yvonne Reboul-H. Berlioz, to François Meyer and André Meyer, and to Philippe Gruss of the firm of Léon Constantin.

Further thanks go to Ruzena Wood of the National Library of Scotland; to Gerald Warfield and Joe Bailey Cole of the New York Public Library; to J. Rigbie Turner of the Pierpont Morgan Library; to Elisabeth Dunan of the Archives Nationales; to Geneviève Acker of the Franco-American Commission for Educational Exchange; to Françoise Chaumais of the Centre Universitaire International; to Thérèse Husson, Secrétaire-Générale of the Association Nationale Hector Berlioz; to Henriette Boschot of the Musée Nationale Hector Berlioz at La Côte-Saint-André; to Paul Vaillant, Conservateur-en-Chef of the Bibliothèque de Grenoble; to Francois Lesure; to Paula Morgan of the Princeton University Library, and finally to the staffs of the libraries in Grenoble, Nantes, Rouen, and in Paris at the Archives Nationales and the music division of the Bibliothèque Nationale.

My very special gratitude goes to my colleagues and advisers for their interest and assistance. Richard Swift arranged for the speedy acquisition of numerous relevant books and microfilms by the University of California, Davis, and lent valuable advice after reading the last draft of the study. William Drabkin, Thomas Hall, and Richard Sherr contributed their ideas, criticism, and friendship; Kenneth Levy, Edward Cone, and Arthur Mendel offered numerous suggestions; Peter Westergaard frequently discussed Berlioz's music with me. My wife Elizabeth's contributions were invaluable; without her knowledge, enthusiasm, and superb command of French, the project could never have been the exciting adventure it was.

Preface to the 1980 Edition

The results announced in the original edition of this study (March, 1974) remain fundamentally unchanged. Meanwhile, Berlioz scholarship has continued to advance at a respectable pace. Two new volumes of the *New Berlioz Edition* have been published, as well as volumes II and III of the composer's *Correspondance générale*. My own *Catalogue of the Works of Hector Berlioz* should appear at about the same time this book does; it contains descriptions of a very large corpus of manuscript sources discovered (or, rather, recovered) since the dissertation was completed. These advances and numerous less bulky ones have naturally suggested revisions to the original text of *Autograph Musical Documents*.

Citations of letters and musical sources, for example, have been modernized to refer to the new publications. I have revised the catalogue of sources in Chapter I such that the numeration is the same as in the forthcoming thematic catalogue. The new bibliography has been added. And of course I have corrected the errors of the original version to which my attention has since been drawn.

All the same, it has not seemed that rewriting the work extensively would change its basic thrust or usefulness. Now, perhaps, I would appoint Adolphe Jullien and Prod'homme to the Panthéon of Berlioz pioneers named in the Introduction; perhaps I would replace a portion of the last chapter with a study of the equally interesting and more far-reaching problems encountered in *Roméo et Juliette*. But in most particulars I am satisfied to leave the work as it was—satisfied, even, to leave the lengthy title, which does after all tell what comes inside.

Portions of the thesis have since 1974 reappeared in three published articles: "Reconstructing a Berlioz Sketch," *Journal of the American Musicological Society* 28 (1975), 125-30; "The Present State of Berlioz Research," *Acta Musicologica* 47 (1975), 31-67; and "Les Fragments de l'opéra 'perdu' de Berlioz: Les Francs-Juges," *Revue de Musicologie* 63 (1977), 77-88. A sentence here and there has appeared in my other writings on Berlioz.

The Bibliothèque Nationale and the Deutsche Staatsbibliothek have extended gracious permission to publish the facsimiles which appear within.

I would like to thank George Buelow for inviting me to undertake this publication, Richard T. Wood of University Microfilms International for arranging the technical details of my preparing the typescript while residing in France, Jean-Michel Nectoux for his help with recent acquisitions at the Bibliothèque Nationale, Eric Buffetaud for clarifying the new ownership of an important collection, Robert Maldonado for

Preface

recopying the musical examples, and, finally, three colleagues whose careful attention to the first edition has resulted in a number of sensible revisions in the second: David Cairns, Hugh Macdonald, and Caldwell Titcomb.

Introduction

This study examines the autograph sources for Berlioz's earlier works in order to reach some conclusions about his approach to musical composition. It has two specific goals: to establish a set of facts about the manuscripts such that conclusions may be drawn with confidence, and to reach from that evidence an understanding of how the composer worked.

The first is an empirical goal, and thus the first portion of the book concerns the number, nature, and location of Berlioz's autographs. Chapter I is a survey of the corpus of autograph documents through 1840, concluding with an inventory of works from that period and their sources. Chapter II deals with the non-musical considerations of manuscript study: papers, watermarks, copyists, and problems of identification and authenticity. The description of Berlioz's habits and procedures from the evidence of his autographs is mostly a matter of inference and implication; it cannot be undertaken without establishing a sound core of accurate factual data.

The second goal is to achieve a critical view of the composer at work. It is based on the assumption that analysis of autograph sources can lead to objective, provable conclusions about the composer's methods of work and that these conclusions accumulate to provide a convenient basis for formulating more general statements about his creative process. Chapter III, accordingly, is a study of Berlioz's methods of work, based on autograph evidence and the composer's own references to his work. Chapter IV consists of detailed studies of three works, the "lost" opera *Les Francs-Juges,* the *Symphonie fantastique,* and the *Requiem,* showing (insofar as the documents permit it) how they developed from first written ideas to definitive final version.

The evidence consists of a relatively small number of individual examples from which the general view must be developed. At first the task seems easy: compared with the more familiar autographs of Beethoven, those of Berlioz are notable at first for their legibility and the ease with which they can be identified. Only a few dozen sketches exist, however, and there is not a single "composing" score that resembles, say, the autograph of Beethoven's Fifth Symphony. Berlioz approached musical composition in a different way, and his markedly individual approach resulted in a unique array of sources and problems.

Modern studies of Berlioz are all indebted to—and must first contend with—three definitive secondary sources: the edition published by Charles Malherbe and Felix Weingartner, Julien Tiersot's *Berlioziana* [TierB'ana], and Adolphe Boschot's three-volume biography. The pronounced strengths and weaknesses of each call for brief review.[1]

The first complete edition was an impressive accomplishment coming so soon after the composer's death (the *Avertissement / Erläuterung* is dated 1 January 1900). It effectively combined the skills of the conductor with the more important work of the French librarian, and the result was a useful and reasonably accurate edition that has over the years been the only generally available reference for the musical texts and their sources. Today, however, some of the editors' decisions appear primitive, and there were inevitable but serious flaws. The edition attempted no critical catalogue of works, and after the first volumes it adopted a cavalier policy toward the description of sources and variants. The project collapsed after the publication of *Béatrice et Bénédict* in 1907, leaving *Benvenuto Cellini* and *Les Troyens* unpublished.

Julien Tiersot's *Berlioziana*, serialized weekly in *Le Ménestrel* from 1904 through 1906 (and, for brief runs, 1909-11), was the first comprehensive study of the sources for Berlioz's music. Tiersot examined and reported on all the familiar documents as well as many that had been previously unknown; *Berlioziana* is thus in some respects as significant as Gustav Nottebohm's *Beethoveniana*. Several of the documents Tiersot saw, including the unique sketchbook (1832-36), are now lost and known only from his descriptions. Yet the serialized format is so unwieldy that it is impossible to use the book efficiently for reference.[2] Tiersot's quarrel with Boschot over the origin of the *Marche au supplice* became a personal and ultimately embarrassing vendetta. The first series of studies (1904-06) ends abruptly, and in the later articles Tiersot never takes the opportunity to draw conclusions based on his decades of research.

Adolphe Boschot's *La Vie d'un romantique* (Paris: volume I, 1906; II, 1908; III, 1913) also gives detailed descriptions of certain documents, though the work is generally tedious and progressively unsympathetic to its subject. Unlike several later biographers (who relied heavily on his work) Boschot carefully examined various archives and described the most interesting manuscripts at length. The unabridged edition of his book, a treatise of over 1,900 pages, is still indispensable to a study of the autographs, and occasionally Boschot's narrative is the most illuminating account of Berlioz and his times ever written.

Together the three works constitute a formidable treatment of Berlioz and his music, one that in many respects cannot be surpassed. Since 1914, however, a few manuscripts have been lost while a considerable number have come to light. Some of the writers' assumptions about Berlioz have proved false. All three tended to regard the manuscript sources as mere curiosities, and only Tiersot seems to have had an inkling of the wealth of biographical and musical information that remained to be gleaned from the autographs.

The works treated here were written by Berlioz during his youth and early manhood. They run from the earliest songs (1818-19) to the completion of the *Grande Symphonie funèbre et triomphale* (July 1840). Eighteen-forty is a convenient and reasonably significant terminal date. It marks the beginning of what Boschot called the *années mystérieuses* (December 1840 to December 1842), which Berlioz suppressed from his *Mémoires* and during which there is a marked drop in his correspondence. More important, an uninterrupted sequence of masterworks comes to an end in 1840. The most likely explanation is that Berlioz had finished all the works conceived in Italy and directly based on his experience there: *Harold en Italie, Benvenuto Cellini,* the *Requiem,* and *Roméo et Juliette.* After *Les Nuits d'été* and the *Symphonie funèbre,* there is not another brilliant accomplishment until *La Damnation de Faust* of 1846. By that time Berlioz must have felt that he had mastered his craft, for the *Grand Traité d'instrumentation* (published 1843) is the work of a confident and accomplished musician. This temporary decline in his musical and literary productivity after 1840 is almost certainly connected with the crisis in Berlioz's domestic life; his affair with Marie Recio probably began in late 1841, and by 1842 the two had traveled to Belgium together.

Altogether there are roughly sixty different autograph sources (not including manuscript sources with autograph notation) for music composed through 1840, nearly three thousand pages. Although it may be true that a study of these documents is cumbersome in terms of the number of works and the multiplicity of problems involved therein, it offers the opportunity to solve some of the problems by taking the trends of the evidence—the similarities and differences among the sources when considered as a group—into account. So interpreted, the evidence permits some fundamental observations about Berlioz's techniques of composition: how plans were made, drafts executed, and works finished. It is a view of the whole, or in this case of one of its major divisions, that will afford significant new insights into the mind of the composer at work.

Chapter One

The Documents

As an investigation of sources for Berlioz's music, this study deals primarily with those of his autographs which contain musical notation. Thus it considers various types of documents: sketches, scores, orchestra parts, autograph revisions in proofs and published editions, and miscellaneous items. In the present chapter, those documents, now dispersed in collections from Paris to Leningrad and Tokyo, will be described and classified. A brief catalogue of Berlioz's works (c. 1818-40) and their autograph sources summarizes the present location of the autograph musical documents.

1. History and Present Location

Each of the several thousand autograph pages of music and prose that Berlioz produced during his lifetime has in just over a century met one of three fates. Most of the musical sources are now easily accessible in public collections. Private collectors own a smaller but still formidable number of documents. A dozen or so early compositions and worksheets of all kinds were destroyed by the composer himself.

The most extensive collections available to the public are those in the Bibliothèque Nationale in Paris. The *fonds du Conservatoire*, now housed there, is the single largest repository of Berlioz's manuscripts. It includes scores that became the property of the Conservatoire after competitions for the *prix de Rome*; the composer's *envois* from Rome; manuscripts willed by Berlioz to the Conservatoire (*Benvenuto Cellini*, both parts of *Les Troyens*, and *Béatrice et Bénédict*); and Charles Malherbe's magnificent collection of a dozen manuscripts including the *Symphonie fantastique*, the *Symphone funèbre et triomphale*, and *Tristia*.[1] The collection of the Bibliothèque Nationale proper includes the fragments of *Les Francs-Juges* and *La Nonne sanglante* as well as albumleaves, fragments, miscellaneous papers, and several first editions with autograph notation.

A large and vastly important collection of manuscript sources has recently been made available for consultation at the Bibliothèque Nationale after more than a hundred years of neglect. In 1863, Berlioz donated all the performance material collected for his tours of Germany and Russia to the Société des Concerts du Conservatoire, convinced that it was the "only musical institution in France whose future inspires the confidence of a composer."[2] ("Perhaps," he went on to remark, "these works will be valuable to the Société des Concerts someday.") During the many ensuing upheavals and reorganizations common to agencies of the French government the collection, which had evidently been in two trunks, became separated. Half stayed at the Conservatoire and awaited attention there through two World Wars and the removal first of the Conservatoire itself to the rue de Madrid and then of the library to the music division of the Bibliothèque Nationale. The parts were recovered in the mid-1960s by Hugh Macdonald and François Lesure,[3] but careful analysis of the thousands of pages haphazardly kept had to be postponed until the collection had been catalogued, a task not completed until the Spring of 1973.

A portion of the collection at the Conservatoire, however, became mixed with parts belonging to the *fonds du roi*, possibly because they were stored together in a leaky loft and had to be moved around during rainstorms. Thus some other parts are now housed at the Conservatoire itself and catalogued with the *fonds du roi*. Found there are parts for the 1833 version of the *Scène héroïque*, some published parts with autograph revision for the *Chant guerrier* and *Chant sacré* from *Neuf Mélodies irlandaises*, and a complete set of manuscript and lithographed parts of the *Requiem*. From after 1840 are parts for *La Damnation de Faust*, *L'Enfance du Christ*, the overture to *Benvenuto Cellini*, and Berlioz's arrangement of Schubert's *Erlkönig*.

The orchestra of the Société des Concerts has since become the Orchestre de Paris, and the other half of Berlioz's material remained in the library of the orchestra. A portion of that collection, including a set of autograph parts for *La Captive* (in E major, c. 1848), corrected engraved parts for the *Symphonie fantastique*, *Harold en Italie*, and *L'Enfance du Christ*, and a hitherto unknown autograph score of Berlioz's arrangement of Martini's *Plaisir d'amour* (orchestrated 1859), was generously donated to the Bibliothèque Nationale in 1975 (after the appearance of the first edition of this study).[4]

After a work had been published, Berlioz often presented the autograph score to the dedicatee or a close friend. He gave *Roméo et Juliette* to Georges Kastner,[5] *Harold en Italie* to Auguste Morel,[6] *Waverley* to an otherwise unknown Monsieur Brown,[7] *Le Roi Lear* to Armand Bertin (Berlioz's patron at the *Journal des Débats*),[8] and the *Te Deum*, at the request of Vladimir Stasov, to the Bibliothèque Impériale Publique at St. Petersburg for the Russian people.[9] The dedication of each makes it clear that the gift is permanent. The *Te Deum* is still in

Russia and *Le Roi Lear* still in a private collection, but the others were eventually donated to the library of the Conservatoire.[10]

Of the many manuscript and published scores given by Berlioz to his friend Humbert Ferrand (1805-68), only four have survived: copies of the *Resurrexit*, the *Scène héroïque, La Mort d'Orphée* and a manuscript copy of Gluck's *Iphigénie en Tauride.*[11] The three works by Berlioz himself were prepared and sent at about the same time, since each is in the hand of the same copyist and carries the same erroneous date, *"22 juillet 1828."*[12] Ferrand (pseudonym, Georges Arandas) died tragically in 1868 while awaiting the execution of an adopted son who had murdered Mme Ferrand, his foster mother. Upon Ferrand's own death his invaluable collection of letters and music was sealed by court order; there was no surer way, as Boschot remarks,[13] to guarantee its dispersement. The collection disappeared under mysterious circumstances. Two of the items, *La Mort d'Orphée* and the *Scène héroïque*, became the property of an N. Martin, director of the Conservatoire in Marseille. After his death they were sold at auction (November 1885)[14] and eventually came to Paris. Ferrand's score of the *Resurrexit* is now in the library at Grenoble.

The performance parts, a rehearsal score, and the incidental material required for production of *Benvenuto Cellini* are in the archives of the Opéra. The libretto originally submitted was transferred to the Archives Nationales in July 1932.[15] Three other poems submitted by Berlioz for consideration at the Opéra, two of which were seen there by Boschot, have since disappeared. They are in none of the groups of rejected libretti now stored in the Archives Nationales, probably having been sold or stolen between the time Boschot saw them and the removal of the older archives from the Opéra itself.

The miscellaneous papers kept by the composer in his apartment became the property of his heirs, the descendants of his sisters Adèle (Chapot family) and Nanci (Reboul–H. Berlioz family). A considerable part of the Chapot collection was donated (c. 1900) to the Berlioz museum in La Côte-Saint-André. The gift included one sketch, two pocket albums (which neither come from before 1840 nor contain substantive original music), and various other manuscripts.[16] No scholar ever made a systematic inventory of the Reboul collection while it was intact, and in the recent past some of the most valuable items were accidentally lost. Several items now in the library at Grenoble seem once to have belonged to the Reboul family, but an item indispensable to a comprehensive study of sources, Berlioz's Italian sketchbook, has completely disappeared.

The major private collections of Berlioziana consist largely of letters, albumleaves, and printed material, but there are a few important privately owned musical sources. An autograph copy of *Le Jeune Pâtre breton*, prepared by the composer in 1834 for Thomas Gounet, is in the Cecil Hopkinson Berlioz Collection, now a part of the National Library of Scotland in Edinburgh. Also in Hopkinson's collection are a partially autograph copy of the revised piano-vocal version of *Le Spectre de la rose* and an autograph transcription (c. 1850) of Dalayrac's *Quand le bien-aimé reviendra*. Richard Macnutt, of Tunbridge Wells, England, owns a portion of a manuscript draft (not in Berlioz's hand) of the libretto to *Benvenuto Cellini* and a remarkable score of excerpts from Gluck's operas *Iphigénie en Aulide* and *en Tauride*, copied by Berlioz in 1822 at the Conservatoire. An autograph copy of *Iphigénie en Tauride* was in the Alfred Cortot Collection and later the Robert O. Lehman Collection before coming to the Morgan Library. The largest private collection of autograph music documents is that of André Meyer,[17] which includes half the sketches for *Les Troyens*, some pages deleted and removed from an autograph of *Benvenuto Cellini*, and an autograph variant of the *Sanctus* from the *Requiem*.

It is difficult to know exactly what documents are owned by private collectors at any given time, since they continue to circulate as collections are sold and rebought. Certain manuscripts are known to exist from a single citation or facsimile in a dealer's catalogue; for example, a manuscript plan (c. 1833) for a version of the incomplete oratorio *Le Dernier Jour du monde* was sold by the firm of Charavay in 1957. A number of other "lost" documents may simply be in little-known private collections. The autograph of the *Ballet des ombres* that once belonged to the French pianist Raoul Pugno (1852-1914) and the Italian sketchbook, for example, have been in circulation so recently it is hard to imagine that they have been destroyed. In any case, there will continue to be exciting finds. Recently discovered were an important collection of letters to Léon Compaignon, the vocal score of *Roméo et Juliette* now in the Columbia University Library, and the Gluck pieces that Macnutt found in a shop in Paris.[18]

Autograph sources are gradually becoming more accessible, as private collections are opened to scholars or donated to public archives. More manuscript sources can be consulted now than at any other time since Berlioz's death. Three libraries, indeed, have become important repositories in the relatively recent past: the Columbia University Library (where part of the collection constitutes a memorial to Roland M. Baughman, a Columbia librarian), the Bibliothèque de Grenoble, and the National Library of Scotland. Each year public archives acquire more Berlioziana, and though certain documents are still lost, it is entirely possible that few important sources remain at large.

One circumstance that prohibits a comprehensive view of the sources is that Berlioz himself destroyed many of his manuscripts. As a young man he regularly tried to destroy works that on second thought appeared unsatisfactory or immature. In the *Mémoires* he describes burning early quintets (Chap. IV), a cantata, portions of an opera, and the *Messe solennelle* (Chap. VIII). He further states that he destroyed *Rob–Roy* (Chap. XXXIX), the *Scène héroïque* (Chap. XIX), and the *Resurrexit* (Chap. VIII, in a footnote); each of these three works is actually preserved in a second copy that Berlioz was unable to recover. (In BerCG 234, a letter of 3 July 1831, he asks Ferrand to destroy his copy of *Orphée* because a movement had been reused in the *Mélologue*. Ferrand disregarded the request, and his manuscript is now the single surviving source of the cantata.) Additionally, the composer very nearly succeeded in destroying the *Huit Scènes de Faust* (Chap. XXVI), of which only a dozen copies survive, and the *Ballet des ombres*. Two sources of the *Ballet* escaped Berlioz, the autograph that Pugno later acquired and a print[19] formerly in the library of the Vicomte Spoelberch de Lovenjoul in Chantilly,[20] but both have since disappeared. While writing a letter to Ferdinand Hiller (BerCG 156: 3 March 1830), Berlioz accidentally burned the manuscript of his *Elégie en prose*. He may also have been responsible for the near-complete disappearance both of a published guitar tutor for which he wrote the exercises and of a set of variations for guitar on Mozart's *Là ci darem la mano*. The loss of these early works makes assessment of his musical education and first compositional efforts practically impossible, as of course he intended.

Berlioz is known to have burned his papers at one other time. In the 1860s, as many of his friends died and as it became clear that he would never see a complete performance of *Les Troyens*, the composer convinced himself that his own death was imminent. He drew closer than ever before to the single surviving member of his family, his son Louis, then a captain in the French merchant marine.[21] On 29 June 1867, Berlioz was informed of Louis' death from yellow fever in Havana. Shortly thereafter, according to Boschot, he proceeded to the Conservatoire and burned all the papers in his office.[22] A porter at the Conservatoire named Fursey assisted him and later provided Boschot with an eyewitness account.[23] (Tiersot, in a more prosaic account also based on a conversation with the porter, says that the papers were burned when the Conservatoire was moved in 1860.[24]) The conflagration was fed primarily by administrative dossiers, letters, and memorabilia, but some miscellaneous musical sources may have been inadvertently tossed in.

Berlioz seems to have made no effort to preserve sketches, drafts, and other early plans. Several miscellaneous documents, however, were found among his papers: two measures of music possibly intended as a correction (**F-Pc** ms 1171), an anonymous fugue annotated by the composer (**F-Pc** ms 1521); incorrectly attributed to him and published in the **OBE** VI, 10-12), some counterpoint lessons c. 1845 (**F-Preboul**), and an item that might be a sketch for a song abandoned before completion (**F-Pc** Rés F 1040); altogether there is not much that can be considered of great significance to this study. What few sketches there are from the early period have been incidentally preserved in the orchestral scores themselves. Berlioz had little interest in the by-products of his compositions, so he simply threw the miscellaneous material away.

Further complicating an accurate assessment of the autograph sources has been the appearance in the recent past of forged autograph documents. These manuscripts surfaced in connection with the Berlioz centennial year in 1969, when the forger rightly suspected that the market for Berlioziana would be especially strong. Columbia University acquired (and returned) a forged sketchbook for the song *La Captive.*[25] Cecil Hopkinson published a description of two newly found autographs that he later had to retract.[26] Among what seem to be the most interesting items in the growing collection at Grenoble are forged sketchbooks and albumleaves. Collectors in the United States and England inadvertently acquired several forged letters. Their mistake was understandable, for the forger knew Berlioz's biography well and used both contemporaneous paper and iron-galled ink. His best forgeries are thus practically undetectable. A portion of Chapter II concerns the forger and his work.

2. Types of Musical Documents

The term "autograph musical documents" as used herein covers four types of manuscripts: sketches and drafts, scores, performance parts, and miscellaneous items (albumleaves, corrections and revisions in manuscript and published sources, and musical notation in letters).

A. Autograph Scores.

The most provocative manuscripts of Berlioz are his scores, for they are the best preserved and are most likely when reviewed to yield new biographical and musical information. Until a work was published Berlioz kept the autograph score himself, revised it, and conducted from it, seldom bothering to have a second copy prepared for his personal use.[27] An autograph of Berlioz can therefore be regarded as recording a series of individual events in the composing of the work: experiments with a given passage, for example, or revisions, or preparations for publication. Even the gift of a manuscript is a significant event in the chronology of a work, because it shows that the composer considered the work complete and the autograph obsolete.

At first glance the autographs seem strikingly similar in appearance. They are always easily legible and often beautifully copied. Few of the manuscripts suggest that a great deal will be gained from further study. Berlioz was proud of the neatness of his autographs, and in a letter to Georges Kastner referring to the manuscript of *Roméo et Juliette,* he apologized for its appearance (as he had already done in the dedication added to the title page): "Isn't it too bad that there were corrections, cuts, added leaves? It was so beautifully written, calligraphically speaking. The Trojans are even better; . . . I defy my copyist to do anything like it!"[28] (Boschot, who regarded the autographs as finished copy not likely to show the "secret and intimate genesis" of the work, was misled by this very neatness.)

Actually, the autographs may be divided into two groups: working copies (like *Roméo et Juliette,* with the corrections, cuts, and added leaves) and fair copies. The term "working copy" is preferable in Berlioz study to "composing score." Although many of his scores were repeatedly overhauled after the clean draft was finished, the first (or bottom) layer of ink draft in no way represents an experimental stage. Here we encounter the first of several fundamental differences in the attitudes and procedures of Beethoven and Berlioz. Beethoven used the paper of his composing scores for working out details in ink *during* the process of drafting; Berlioz, on the other hand, most often drafted an entire movement and later went back to work out specific problems encountered along the way. Since the term "composing score" is more commonly associated with Beethoven's manuscripts, it has not been used here.

The autographs of the major works treated in this study (the *Symphonie fantastique, Harold en Italie, Benvenuto Cellini,* the *Requiem,* and *Roméo et Juliette*) are working scores. Pasted-in revisions, deletions by cross-hatching, and various non-musical autograph notations are common. Parts for added instruments have been squeezed into several scores. Numbers are scattered throughout the manuscripts. (Usually these are page, folio, or measure numbers, useful in reconstructing the original structure of the manuscript, but occasionally there are figured bass symbols, as in the score of the *Requiem.*) Autograph *X*'s in the

Symphonie fantastique, movement I, are simply conductor's cues. Non-autograph numbers are usually those of the engraver.

As examples of autograph scores in working copy are three facsimiles. Facsimile I.1, from the second movement of *Harold en Italie* (mm. 146-54; aut. p. 123; **OBE** II, 72-73),[29] is a typical page of score for a larger work. It contains several editorial changes as well as a pencil sketch. Facsimiles I.2 and I.3 are from the autograph of the *Requiem.* The first of these pages, (*Quaerens me,* mm. 31-44; aut. p. 92; **OBE** VII, 51) seems, from its initial appearance, to be from the final, fairly-copied version of the work. A comparison with the last published version of the work (used by the **OBE**), however, shows that much of this page was eventually deleted.   Moreover, a careful look at the second page (*Lacrymosa,* mm. 111-16; aut. p. 116; **OBE** pp. 69-70) reveals two remarkable details. First, an autograph note in pencil can be seen at the bottom of the page, beneath the third measure;   *"Entrée des grosses caisses / tous les cuivres réunis"* ("Entry of the bass drums; all the brass together").   Second, several lines (staves 1-9 and 28-30) are in the hand of a copyist.   In short, the score is more than simply a fair copy of the final version.   Consideration of such markings as these provides the basic matter for Chapter III, the study of Berlioz's methods of work.

The scores in autograph fair copy include most of the songs as well as the two preserved autographs submitted for the *prix de Rome: Herminie* and *Cléopâtre.* (Facsimile I.4, the first page of *Herminie,* shows the elegant calligraphy of which Berlioz was proud.)   These scores were surely prepared from lost composing drafts. It is possible, of course, that among the fair copies of the songs (notably several autographs of *La Captive,* two of *Le Jeune Pâtre breton,* and the first version of *Les Nuits d'été*) is actually an original score or two, notated with the facility that must have been common for Berlioz. (The *Mémoires* indicate that *La Captive* was written in a single sitting on makeshift paper [Chap. XXXIX], though Tiersot describes sketches for the song in Berlioz's Italian sketchbook.) Although the fair copies are of little significance to a study of the composer's methods of work, they are nevertheless primary sources, often with variant readings important in reconstructing the chronology of a work.

Performance materials and an occasional copy of an autograph score were prepared as needed by professional calligraphers.   When Berlioz had parts for his *Messe solennelle* copied by amateur copyists (1825; see **BerMém**, Chap. VII), the disastrous results taught him a lesson; thereafter, he usually relied on professionals even though he could not always afford it.   Scribal copies prepared in Rome of the *Resurrexit,* the *Quartetto e coro dei Maggi,* and *Rob-Roy* are unique sources for those

Facsimile I. 1: *Harold en Italie,* aut. p. 123. Note the revisions in the viola line (staves 15, 22) and harp part (staves 13-14), as well as the pencil sketch (staff 21).

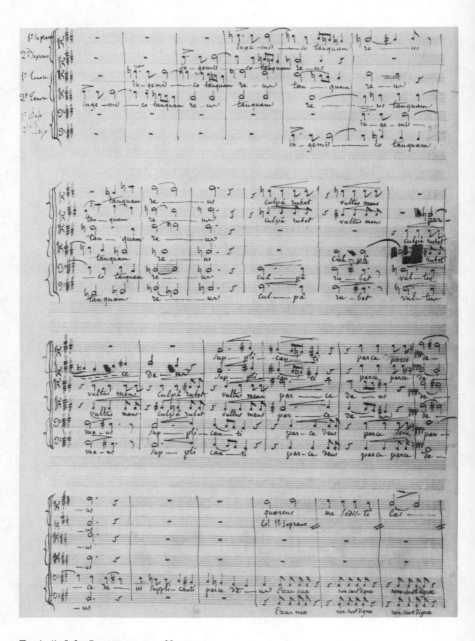

Facsimile I. 2: *Requiem,* aut. p. 92.

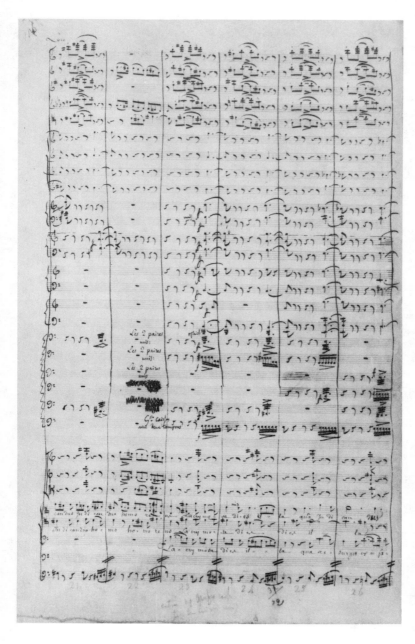

Facsimile I. 3: *Requiem,* aut. p. 116.

Facsimile I. 4: *Herminie*, aut. p. 1.

works. The material prepared by Berlioz's chief copyist, a certain Rocquemont, includes a number of significant sources. Rocquemont prepared vocal scores of the *Requiem* and *Roméo et Juliette*, portions of a conductor's score of the first version of *Benvenuto Cellini*, and the master parts for each instrument in several sets of orchestra parts. Berlioz left note-for-note recapitulations in his scores to be filled in by Rocquemont; in these cases he simply indicated with letters where his scribe could find the relevant passages in the preceding music. In general, the quality of the scribal copies is very high. The copyists were supervised by a competent director. Berlioz himself occasionally proofread orchestra parts and frequently went through them to make new changes in the musical text or phrase and dynamic markings. In the long run, then, certain scribal copies are nearly as useful sources as the autographs.

B. Performance parts.

Berlioz's gift of his performance materials to the Société des Concerts should have meant that the collection would be used and carefully guarded over the years. That, indeed, was the premise on which the gift was based. The parts for such popular works as the *Symphonie fantastique* and *Roméo et Juliette* seem to have been used after the composer's death, but the rest of the substantial collection was neglected. Better parts were soon published, and the collection had been unwieldy even for the composer. (He recounts in the *Mémoires* how keeping up with his trunks of music was the major problem of his travels; see BerMém, *"Premier voyage en Allemagne, 2ᵉ lettre, à M. Girard"*).[30] The historical value of these sources was simply overlooked. Now that a portion of the collection has been catalogued and shelved,[31] a large number of manuscript parts can finally be compared with autographs and published scores.

Half the collection, as it turns out, is of no real value to this study. Because the material was assembled expressly for Berlioz's German and Russian tours, much of it is for pieces or versions of pieces later than the period treated here. For these trips the composer used the recently published parts for the *Symphonie fantastique, Harold,* and *Roméo et Juliette.* The autograph parts for *La Captive* are, as the dated watermark shows, from no earlier than 1847.

A few of the parts are nevertheless from well before 1840. The most interesting documents in the entire collection, in fact, are the autograph parts for the *Mélologue* that Berlioz copied at La Côte-Saint-André on his way back to Paris from Rome (1832; see BerCG 284). He was able to attach the already existing parts for *La Tempête* (1830), which had

become the sixth movement of the *Mélologue*; thus among these parts
are some of the earliest known manuscript parts for a Berlioz work.
Since there are two versions of *La Tempête* (before and after its inclusion
in the *Mélologue*) visible in the parts, they permit an illuminating
comparison of revisions and their dates. (The versions can be separated
in the score as well, but there the distinction is not so clear.) The chorus
parts for *Roméo et Juliette* and all the parts for the *Requiem* are originals
prepared for the first performance, so underneath the many layers of
subsequent revision lies the first version of each work.

In 1972 the author and Julian Rushton, editor of the *Faust* settings
for the **NBE**, were able to separate from a huge set of manuscript parts
for *La Damnation de Faust* some of the original parts for three
movements of *Huit Scènes de Faust* (1829; now **F-Pc** ms 17466). Several
of the manuscripts are autographs of Berlioz, similar to the single
fragment that had previously been located.[32] Parts were prepared for
three movements instead of just the one (*Concert de sylphes*) that was
performed, suggesting the surprising conclusion that Berlioz actually
intended to perform all three at a concert of 1 November 1829, and for
some reason (probably the lack of rehearsals or performers) was
prevented from doing so.

A complete set of parts for the *Scène héroïque grecque*, arranged in
1833 for wind band and chorus, is preserved at the Conservatoire.
Tiersot knew of their existence but did not notice that there were major
differences between the parts and the existing score. The *Requiem* parts
that served for the first and subsequent performances are well preserved;
only a few wind parts are lacking. For the *Requiem, Roméo et Juliette,*
and the version of *Benvenuto Cellini* presented in London in 1853,
lithography was used to reproduce the dozens of necessary chorus parts
from manuscript originals. The parts for the *Requiem* and *Roméo et
Juliette*, prepared by a lithographer named Mme Boboeuf, can for
practical purposes be considered manuscript sources.

Berlioz organized his concerts carefully and took special pains to have
all the performance parts corrected and brought up to date. He and
Rocquemont went carefully through practically every part to be taken to
Germany and Russia, adding nuances, rehearsal letters, and the latest
revision in the musical text. Thus the parts often show the same
evolution of a musical text suggested by the autograph score, permitting
a helpful comparison of sources.

In spite of this vast improvement in our knowledge of sources, some
lacunae remain, particularly from the period before 1830. Although
frequently used published parts for the *Symphonie fantastique* have been
located, the original set of manuscript parts, no doubt copied by the

composer himself, would be the more interesting source; it has been lost. Not a trace remains of the original parts for the two early overtures or the *Messe solennelle*. All three works were performed, however, so separate parts must have been prepared. Berlioz's revelation (**BerCG 71**) that he copied parts for excerpts from *Les Francs-Juges* is tantalizing, for if they are ever found a reconstruction of the missing portions of the opera may be possible.

C. Sketches and Drafts.

Few sketches by Berlioz exist. There are roughly seventy pages for *Les Troyens*, published transcriptions of a few pages from the lost sketchbook, and descriptions by Boschot of some otherwise unknown items. A few random pages, including two for *Roméo et Juliette* and three for *Benvenuto Cellini* complete the corpus of commonly known plans for musical compositions. There are two possible explanations for this paucity of independently preserved sketches: either Berlioz did not prepare many sketches, or he destroyed them. It will be shown below that in fact both explanations are correct, that Berlioz neither sketched a great deal nor made any effort to save what sketches there were.

Clouding the entire issue has been loose employment of the term "sketch." Particularly in French (*esquisse*), it has been applied to any autograph notation whose relationship to the final text of the work is not readily apparent. (The same kind of confusion exists for the word "draft," Fr. *brouillon*.) Another offender in this regard is the English translator of the critical notes in the **OBE**, who offers dozens of translations like the following:

Original	Translation
Dans la première version de l'autographe, la partie de quatuor actuelle n'existait pas.	The part now entrusted to the quartet was not in the original sketch of the autograph (OBE II, ix).

Tiersot misuses the term now and then, and more recently Nicholas Temperley, in his edition of the *Symphonie fantastique* (**NBE 16**), has applied the word to two passages that are abandoned fair drafts, failing to apply it to other notations properly considered sketches. In this study the word "sketch" is employed with a more precise meaning: a passage of limited length in which the purpose of the composer is to plan what will take place in a section of music. The definition is without chronological implication. The composer can sketch while planning, drafting, or revising.

There are in the autograph scores various kinds of autograph notations in pencil and ink appropriately termed sketches. Altogether some sixty are preserved, many of which are only scraps preserved coincidentally with layers of revision. But this newly-identified repertoire of autograph items provides conclusive proof that at least some sketches did exist for the earlier works.

Similarly, there exists a heretofore neglected group of drafts. A draft may be defined as a document where the composer's purpose is to achieve a near-final version of his piece, particularly in terms of length, melodic and harmonic organization, and orchestration. Although there are no complete drafts of compositions by Berlioz, a few fragments show what drafts must generally have looked like. The plans for *Benvenuto Cellini* and *Roméo et Juliette* mentioned above seem to be fragments of longer drafts in ink, implying the possibility that for many works drafts in short score once existed. Several autographs reveal upon careful scrutiny a kind of draft in pencil where certain musical details are worked out. The presence of both sketches and drafts in the autograph scores confirms a premise of the present study, that the autograph documents are still an important source of unrecognized historical information.

Of the hundreds of new facts and insights suggested by analysis of the autograph musical sources, none has seemed so fundamental as the realization that these sketches and drafts, however limited their number, have been preserved. A significant aspect of the composer's approach to composition that might otherwise be overlooked emerges as a reality subject to analysis. A large portion of Chapter III is therefore dedicated to a study of those documents.

D. Miscellaneous Musical Documents.

Berlioz's works were seldom published immediately upon completion, but rather months or years later. Between the earliest performance and the publication, a piece might be revised in a few details (as was the *Marche de pèlerins* from *Harold en Italie*, with several different revisions of the same few details) or overhauled completely (as was the first movement of the *Symphonie fantastique*). Even the title can change; *Irlande, Lélio,* and *Le Jeune Pâtre breton* are all second titles. Before the score was sent to the engraver, however, the many variants had to be reconciled: the composer was required to adopt a definitive musical text, title, and opus number. His autograph would be returned with page proofs to be corrected.

A few of Berlioz's corrected proofs still exist, including those for the *Huit Scènes de Faust,* the *Symphonie fantastique, Harold en Italie,* the

Requiem, Roméo et Juliette, and the piano-vocal score of *Benvenuto Cellini.* Most of the autograph marks on these prints are simply corrections of typographical errors or oversights. The composer entered his changes carefully in pencil, ink, or occasionally editor's red chalk. Some changes in musical detail were usually made during the final retouching, reflecting the composer's determination that markings of nuance be as suggestive of the desired effect as possible. After a publication was released, Berlioz often discovered other typographical errors and corrected them in his own copy, and occasionally he made important revisions to be incorporated in later printings. As a general rule, however, the composer's last autograph notations for a work are in the corrected proofs.

Dozens of albumleaves by Berlioz are preserved (sometimes catalogued as "sketches" or "fragments"), over thirty with phrases from *Roméo et Juliette* alone. Berlioz usually inscribed passages from his most famous or recent works. Phrases from *Harold* and the *Requiem* predominate in the 1830s, melodies from *Faust,* in the late 40s and 50s. Because the leaves were prepared from memory, there are some inconsequential variants in musical text. Two leaves contain original material, a *Chansonette de M^r. de Wailly* (1835),[33] and a little song, *Nessun maggior piacere* (1841, 1847),[34] parodying Dante's famous words (*Nessun maggior dolore,* etc.); the *Chansonette* was eventually used in *Benvenuto Cellini.* The album *Souvenirs–Bêtises–Improvisations,* prepared (possibly for Marie Recio) during Berlioz's first journey to Belgium and Germany and now at La Côte-Saint-André, includes several original melodies still unpublished.

Berlioz includes passages of music in numerous letters, though in general the quotations are not important musical sources. One letter contains the only preserved autograph notation of a phrase from *Adieu, Bessy* (BerCG 148; the musical example, however, is incorrectly transcribed). An exchange of letters with Liszt (1852-53) contains extensive directions, with musical notation, for the production of *Benvenuto Cellini.*[35]

3. Other Sources

Evidence offered by the musical sources in manuscript, although in itself a useful core of information about Berlioz as composer, is most significant when interpreted in view of his own statements about his music in correspondence and the *Mémoires.* Contemporaneous accounts in newspapers and weekly journals of music provide related primary data, especially concerning first performances of new works. The press also reported on the composer's plans for future compositions. In early 1834, for example, the *Gazette musicale* announced that Berlioz would write a work called *Les Derniers Instants de Marie Stuart* for Paganini (see Table I, no. 68). This earlier idea for the work that became *Harold en Italie* is mentioned in neither the composer's correspondence nor his *Mémoires*.

Berlioz was a prolific writer of letters; approximately three thousand have been preserved, about one-third the number he must actually have written. (He wrote about five letters a week, some of them notes of only a few lines. Thus between 1828 and 1868 he would have turned out some 10,000 letters. Boschot eventually came to believe that a primary document could be found for every single day of the last decades of Berlioz's life; see **BosHB** I, 517-19 and III, 664-65.) Ascertaining the location, date, and authenticity of the letters is a gargantuan task. Tiersot began but did not complete a collected edition of Berlioz's letters.[36] More recently, a network of scholars set up during the Berlioz centenary year under the editorship of Pierre Citron has begun to publish a vastly improved *Correspondance générale*. To date, three volumes have appeared,[37] covering the years 1816-1850.[38]

For the period under consideration, the letters are useful for several reasons. First, they clarify dates of completion and first performance of certain works. Second, they depict the early stages of development of several compositions, as Berlioz describes his work in progress. Most important, the letters are probably honest. There is little reason to doubt the veracity or seriousness of most remarks Berlioz makes in letters to family or especially to such close friends as Thomas Gounet, Ferrand, and Ferdinand Hiller. Berlioz may well have exaggerated the reception accorded his works or romanticized slightly the circumstances surrounding their composition, but as a general rule he can be trusted when he mentions titles of works being composed, their chronology, and the problems and people so involved.[39]

The following excerpts can be cited as examples of how the correspondence aids in reconstructing the series of events that resulted in a completed work. These are passages concerning the composition of the *Mélologue* (later called *Lélio*), first from Italy and eventually from La Côte-Saint-André. Like Berlioz's later correspondence from foreign countries, the letters from Italy are especially detailed. The first letters about the *Mélologue* relate certain facts about its initial conception:

To his sister, Adèle (Rome, 6 June 1831):

Le dernier jour, je les* ai laissés dans la voiture et j'ai fait quinze lieues à pied en	The other day I left them* in the carriage and walked fifteen leagues while composing

composant un ouvrage moitié musique moitié poésie que j'écris dans ce moment (**BerCG** 230).

a half-musical, half-poetic work that I am now writing.

---

*Some "très bonnes gens extrêment polis."

*Some "very fine men, extremely polite."

To Thomas Gounet (Rome, 14 June 1831):

Je travaille beaucoup: j'achève dans ce moment un mélologue faisant suite à l'épisode de la vie d'un artiste; ce sera pour être exécuté après la symphonie et cela complètera un concert. J'ai fait les paroles en venant de St-Lorenzo à Rome, dans mon dernier voyage; j'avais laissé derrière moi la voiture et en cheminant j'écrivais sur mon portefeuille. La musique est faite aussi, je n'ai plus qu'à copier. Il y a six monologues et six morceaux de musique, chant seul, choeurs, orchestre seul, ou choeur et orchestre (**BerCG** 231).

I am working very hard; now I am finishing a melologue that comes after the scene from an artist's life. This will be played after the symphony and will complete a concert. I wrote the words while going from San Lorenzo to Rome during my last trip. I left the carriage behind and wrote on my portfolio while walking. The music is already done; I have nothing but the copying left to do. There are six movements of music: solo voice, chorus, orchestra alone, or orchestra and chorus.

To his parents (Rome, 24 June 1831):

J'attends pour partir d'ici d'avoir achevé d'écrire la musique d'un Mélologue en six parties *que j'avais composé en venant de Florence à Rome. Les paroles sont finies depuis longtemps, je n'ai plus qu'à mettre au net deux morceaux d'orchestre. C'est une composition sans modèle, d'un genre nouveau, dont l'idée m'a été donnée par une petite ébauche de Th. Moore qui se trouve à la fin des ses mélodies. Heureusement que tout était fini dans ma tête et sur mon portefeuille quand j'ai mis le pied dans la succursale de l' Académie, car je n'y ai pas une idée, pas une sensation; l'ennui y a établi sa demeure, et son sceptre de plomb me paraît cent fois plus lourd qu'ailleurs* (**BerCG** 232).

I am waiting to leave here until I finish writing the music for a *Mélologue en six parties* that I wrote while coming from Florence to Rome. The words have been finished for a long time; I have only to get two orchestral movements into shape. It's a work without a model, in a new genre, whose idea came from a little thing by Thomas Moore, found at the end of his melodies. Happily, all was finished in my head and on my portfolio by the time I set foot into the regional branch of the Académie, for here there is not an idea, not a sensation. Boredom has set up housekeeping here, and her lead scepter seems a hundred times heavier than elsewhere.

Berlioz does not say so, but the music for at least five and probably all six of the movements was already written. It had merely to be retouched or adapted for the new score. Evidently the sources for all the borrowings were with the composer in Rome, except for the one from *Orphée* (movt. V). The next letters reveal a concerted effort to have the proper page sent to Rome, plus the advice to Ferrand to destroy his own manuscript copy:

To Humbert Ferrand (Rome, 3 July 1831):

J'ai employé pour le chant de bonheur *une phrase de la* Mort d'Orphée, *que vous avez chez vous, et pour les* Derniers Soupirs de la harpe, *le petit morceau d'orchestre qui termine cette scène immédiatement après la Bacchanale. En conséquence, je vous prie de m'envoyer* cette page, *seulement l'adagio qui succède à la Bacchanale, au moment où les violons prennent les sourdines et font des tremolandi accompagnant un chant de clarinette lointain et quelques fragments d'accords de harpe; je ne me le rappelle pas assez pour l'écrire de tête, et je ne peux rien y changer. Comme vous voyez,* la Mort d'Orphée *est sacrifiée; j'en ai tiré ce qui me plaisait, et je ne pourrais jamais faire exécuter la* Bacchanale; *ainsi, à mon retour à Paris, j'en brûlerai la partition, et celle que vous avez sera l'unique et dernière, si toutefois vous la conservez; il vaudrait bien mieux la détruire, quand je vous aurai envoyé un exemplaire de la symphonie et du mélologue; mais c'est une affaire au moins de six cent francs de copie! n'importe, à mon retour à Paris, d'une manière ou d'une autre, il faudra que vous l'ayez.*

Ainsi, c'est convenu, vous allez me copier très fin ce petit morceau, et je l'attends dans les montagnes de Subiaco, où je vais passer quelque temps; adressez-le toujours à Rome (BerCG 234).

I used a phrase from *la Mort d'Orphée*, which you have there, for the *chant de bonheur*, and for the *Derniers Soupirs de la harpe*, the little movement for orchestra that finishes that scene just after the bacchanalia. Consequently I am asking you to send me that page, just the adagio that follows the bacchanalia, there where the violins take their mutes and do tremolo accompaniments to the distant song of the clarinet and several fragmentary chords for harp. I can't remember it well enough by heart and I mustn't change anything. As you see, *la Mort d'Orphée* is sacrificed. I took from it what I liked, and I could never get the *Bacchanale* played. So when I get back to Paris I will burn the score, and the one you have, if you preserve it, will be the sole surviving copy. It would be better to destroy it when I have sent you a copy of the symphony and melologue, but this is a matter of at least six hundred francs worth of copying! No matter: when I get back to Paris, one way or the other, you will have to have one.

So it's arranged: you are going to make a tiny copy of this little piece for me, and I'll wait for it in the mountains of Subiaco, where I am going to spend some time. Send it to Rome anyway.

To Ferdinand Hiller (Rome, 3 December 1831):

Veuillez aller trouver M. Réty au Conservatoire et lui demander de prendre dans ma musique la Cantate la Mort d'Orphée. *Je la lui avais demandée, mais Prévost, qui devait l'apporter, paraît ne pas devoir venir. Vous la prendez donc et vous me ferez copier sur* papier à lettre *la* dernière *page de la partition, l'adagio con tremolandi, qui succède à la Bacchanale; puis vous les mettrez sous enveloppe à la poste. J'en ai besoin absolument* (BerCG 250).

Please go find M. Réty at the Conservatoire and ask him to find in my music the cantata called *la Mort d'Orphée*. I had already asked him for it, but Prévost, who was supposed to bring it, seems not to be coming. You will take it, then, and have copied on letter paper the last page of the score, the *adagio con tremolandi* which follows the bacchanalia; then you will put it in an envelope and into the mail. I am greatly in need of it.

Berlioz's frank treatment of the borrowing from *Orphée* is all the more interesting in view of certain events of the preceding year: Ferrand seems never to have known that the *Marche au supplice* had originally been intended for his opera, *Les Francs-Juges.*

After assembling all the material in an orchestra score, Berlioz then began to copy the parts for a planned performance in Paris. Among those parts recently unearthed at the Conservatoire, it will be recalled, is the set to which Berlioz refers in the following letter:

To Ferdinand Hiller (La Côte-Saint-André, 7 August 1832):

Je copie toute la journée les parties de mon Mélologue; depuis deux mois je ne fais pas autre chose, et j'en ai encore pour soixante-deux jours; vous voyez que j'ai de la patience (**BerCG** 284).

I copy the parts for my *Mélologue* all day long. For two months I haven't done anything else, and I still have two more months to go. You see that I'm patient.

In this case, as in others, one can follow the composition of the work practically from its inception as Berlioz went walking one afternoon through various attempts to have the page from *La Mort d'Orphée* delivered through, finally, the copying of parts without the help of a copyist. These particular letters answer two questions about the manuscripts. At the point where the borrowing from *Orphée* occurs in the full score of the *Mélologue*, there was originally only a blank page with a note in the composer's hand: "*Le N⁰ 5 ('Derniers soupirs de la harpe. Souvenirs') est à la fin de ma cantate de la mort d'Orphée. C'est le petit morceau d'orchestre*, Largo, *qui suit la Bacchanale*" ("No. 5. . . . is at the end of my cantata on *la mort d'Orphée*. It is the little orchestra piece, *Largo*, that follows the bacchanalia.") Eventually, Berlioz covered the note with a pasted-in copy of the movement. It is obvious from the letters what the problem was: the composer needed the original to copy because he could not remember the piece well enough. Moreover, the correspondence indicates that Ferrand must have had the mysterious manuscript of *Orphée* all along.

Other letters offer glimpses of the composer at his desk, sometimes merely copying parts,[40] at others considering substantive issues ("For the verses I wasn't interested in chasing after rhymes; I wrote cadenced and measured prose, occasionally rhymed. That is all that music requires").[41] A letter to Ferrand of 26 March 1832 (**BerCG** 267) becomes a polemic in favor of unrhymed verse. Ferrand had evidently complained about Berlioz's preferences in poetry and the composer took insult: "Never will I love the ugly, so calm yourself. . . . Remember that three-quarters of Shakespeare is in blank verse . . . All of this is the effect of habit;

rhymed Latin verse from the Middle Ages seems barbarian to the same people who are shocked by unrhymed French verse."[42]

The autograph manuscripts of the letters (as well as some portions of the *Mémoires*) are indirectly related to the study of musical manuscripts in that they, too, show the composer's pronounced editorial and correctional vigor as he carefully shapes ideas and searches for the best phrase or word. A sentence from one letter of Berlioz to his mother, contrasting vividly with the remark he made about the beauty of his finished autographs (quoted above, p. 7), perhaps hints at the appearance of his first efforts as well: "P.S.—Don't pay attention to the sloppiness of my letter; I can't write without cross-hatching horribly. You have no idea what the manuscripts of my articles look like—it's frightful" (BerCG 535: 18 January 1838).[43]

The *Mémoires* of Berlioz also provide evidence essential to the present study. While it is true that there are modest factual dilemmas—the possibly fictitious "pinch of snuff" incident, for example, and the demonstrably inaccurate statement that all his early songs were in minor keys—the *Mémoires* nevertheless tell how Berlioz composed a number of his works. Chapter LIV, for example, describes stages in the composition of *La Damnation de Faust*, and other evidence tends to support the description. Berlioz's statements about inspiration and conditions that motivated certain compositions are especially interesting. The resemblance between certain passages in the *Mémoires* and accounts in letters of many years earlier has suggested to more than one scholar that Berlioz compiled the autobiography directly from a journal. The chronology in the chapters on his earlier years, for example, is reasonably accurate, and the description in Chapter IV of his sextet matches his letters concerning the *potpourri concertant* written forty years earlier (BerCG 3, 4).

4. Catalogue of Berlioz's Works, c. 1818-1840

Table I[44] lists the compositions of Berlioz through 1840 and their autograph sources. In cases where the work has been lost, a reference to its existence (usually by Berlioz himself), is cited. Included in the table are all works for which it is reasonably certain that some music was written. Fleeting plans mentioned once in letters and abandoned before composition began (e.g. *Robin-Hood, Atala*, various songs) are not included, and albumleaves are not cited as autograph sources. Entries for certain works conclude with remarks intended to clarify or amplify the information given above; Chapters II through IV proceed from conclusions established here.

Works are arranged chronologically in order of the date of their completion, if known, or alternatively of their first performance.

TABLE I

WORKS OF HECTOR BERLIOZ
AND THEIR AUTOGRAPH SOURCES

1. **Potpourri concertant sur des thèmes italiens pour flûte, cor, deux violons, alto et basse.**

   Date (of composition): c. 1818 (ded)[45]

   Source:[46] LOST.

   Refs.: **BerCG** 3: La Côte-Saint-André, 25 March 1819, to the publishers Janet et Cotelle; **BerCG** 4: La Côte-Saint-André, 6 April 1819, to the publisher Pleyel; **BerMém**, Chap. IV.

   The *Mémoires* indicate that the horn player for the *potpourri* was the music teacher's son, Imbert *fils*. The absence of a horn part from the quintets (nos. 2 and 3) would suggest that they were written after Imbert *fils* committed suicide (apparently in the summer of 1818) and, consequently, that the *potpourri* was Berlioz's first serious composition.

2, 3. **Two Quintets for Flute and String Quartet**

   Date: c. late 1818–early 1819

   Source: LOST (destroyed, according to Berlioz, though mm. 119-50 of the *Grande Ouverture des Francs-Juges* quote a phrase from the second quintet).

   Ref.: BerMém, Chap. IV.

   Berlioz remarks that he wrote and played the quintets when he was 12-1/2 years of age, i.e. in 1816; he also remarks that his teacher was in the group that played them. Presumably he refers to his first teacher, Imbert, whose contract with the town of La Côte-Saint-André carries the date 20 May 1817. Thus it is reasonable to guess that the three early chamber works (nos. 1-3) were actually written after Berlioz had taken his first music lessons, c. late 1818 or early 1819.

4. Romances avec accompagnement de piano

   Date: c. late 1818–early 1819

   Source: LOST.

   Ref.: **BerCG** 3: La Côte-Saint-André, 25 March 1819, to Janet et Cotelle.

   Possibly included *L'Arabe jaloux* and *L'Invocation à l'Amitié* (see nos. 10 and 15, below).

5. **Accompaniment to "Fleuve du Tage"**
   (music by Pollet, text by J. H. Demeun)

   Date: c. late 1819 (ded)

   Source:
   Manuscript copy (by Dorant), **F-CSA**, with ascription of accompaniment to Berlioz.

   The manuscript seems to be in the hand of the music teacher Dorant, who arrived in La Côte-Saint-André in July 1819 and began giving Berlioz guitar lessons shortly thereafter.

6. *Je vais donc quitter pour jamais /*
   Mon doux pays, ma douce amie
   (song from Florian's *Estelle*)

   Date: c. 1819 (ded)

   Source: LOST (destroyed, according to Berlioz). Reused in *Symphonie fantastique*, movt. I, mm. 3-16)

   Ref.: **BerMém**, Chap. IV.

7. **Le Dépit de la bergère**
   Romance
   (text anonymous)

   Date: c. 1819 (ded)

   Source: PUB. Paris: Auguste le Duc, c. 1819.

   This romance is probably Berlioz's first publication. It may well be the subject of a recently found letter of 14 August 1819 (**BerCG** 5: to an unknown publisher of music), first published by David Cairns (**BerMemCairns**, pp. 574-75).

8. Recueil de romances avec accompagnement de guitare
    [guitar accompaniments by Berlioz]

    Date: c. 1821-22 (see note)

    Source:
    Autograph score, **F-CSA**, 22 numbered pages, autograph fair copy.

    Contents (orthography after Berlioz):
    1. *La Trompette Appelle aux Allarmes / Paroles de Florian / Musique de Lintan*, p. 21 [the songs numbered 1 and 2 are actually the last two in the book];
    2. *Romance de Florian / Mise en Musique / Par / V. Martini* (inc. *"Vous qui loin d'une amante"*), p. 22;
    3. *Romance de Florian / Musique de M^r xxx* (inc. *"A Toulouse il fut une belle"*), pp. 1-2;
    4. *Air De Philippe et Georgette / Musique de D'Aleyrac / Paroles de xxx* (inc. *"O ma Georgette, toi seule embellis ce séjour"*), pp. 2-3;
    5. *Fleuve du Tage / musique de Pollet*, pp. 3-4;
    6. *Romance de Florian / Musique de xxx* (inc. *"Amour on doit bénir tes chaînes"*), p. 4;
    7. *La Simpathie / Romance de l'opéra de Félicie / Musique de Catrufo* (inc. *"La Simpathie est le lien des âmes"*), p. 5;
    8. *Romance de Gulnare ou l'esclave Persanne / Musique de D'Aleyrac*[47] (inc. *"Rien, tendre amour, ne résiste à tes armes"*), p. 6;
    9. *Romance de xxx / Musique de Bédart* (inc. *"Fais mon bonheur, tranquille indifférence"*), p. 6-7;
    10. *Romance de l'opéra / du Chaperon Rouge / Musique d'A. Boieldieu* (inc. *"Le noble éclat du diadème ici n'a point séduit mon coeur"*), pp. 7-8;
    11. *Romance de l'Opéra Comique / Musique de Dominico Dellamaria / Paroles de M^r De Ségur* (inc. *"Ah pour l'amant le plus discret"*), pp. 8-9;
    12. *Du même* (inc. *"Que d'établissements nouveaux"*), pp. 9-10;
    13. *Objet charmant / Romance Musique de xxx* (inc. *"Objet charmant, toi que mon coeur adore"*), p. 10;
    14. *Romance de Plantade / Paroles de M^r xxx* (inc. *"Bocage que l'aurore embellit de ses pleurs"*), fols. pp. 10-11;
    15. *Romance Musique de xxx* (inc. *"Depuis une heure je l'attends, conçoit-il mon impatience"*), pp. 11-12;

16. *Couplets de l'opéra / de la Romance / Musique de H. Berton / Paroles de Loreaux 3me* (inc. *"Mon coeur s'ouvrait au sentiment de ses vers"*), p. 12;

17. *Romance Du Même* (inc. *"Du tendre amour je chérissais l'empire"*), p. 13;

18. *Air du petit Jokei / Musique de Solié* (inc. *"Il faut quitter ce que j'adore"*), pp. 13-14;

19. *Romance de l'opéra / des Blaise et Babet* (inc. *"Lise chantait dans la prairie"*), pp. 14-15;

20. *Romance de Naderman / Je pense à vous,* p. 15;

21. *Faut l'oublier / Romance de xxx,* p. 16;

22. *Romance Favorite de Henri quatre / mise en musique par Lélu* (inc. *"Viens, aurore, je t'implore, je suis gai quand je te vois"*), p. 17;

23. *Le Rivage de Vaucluse / Romance d'A. Boieldieu* (inc. *"Du rivage de Vaucluse t'aimant de Laure en ces mots"*), p. 18;

24. *Le Sentiment D'amour / Romance de Messonnier* (inc. *"N'avoir sans y songer qu'une seule pensée"*), p. 19;

25. *Minverne au tombeau de Ryno / Paroles de Chénier, Musique de xxx* (inc. *"En vain la mort a fermé la paupière"*), p. 20.

The general appearance of the manuscript, the hard binding with table of contents on the cover, and a number of other details suggest that Berlioz prepared the collection for possible publication. Tiersot (in **TierB'ana** [1904], 12) recounts a story whereby Berlioz supposedly presented the manuscript to a childhood friend named Joseph Favre, but only after erasing his own name from the cover.

The collection seems never to have been published.

9. Pleure, pauvre Colette
Romance à deux voix egales
(text by Bourgerie)

Date: before March 1822 (pub)

Source: PUB. Paris: Mme Cuchet, March 1822.

10. Le Maure jaloux
Romance
(text by Florian)

Date: c. 1819-April 1822 (ded)

Source:

Autograph score, F-CSA, titled *L'Arabe Jaloux—Paroles de Florian / Musique de Mr Hector Berlioz,* 2 pp., autograph fair copy.

PUB. Paris: Mme Cuchet, April 1822.

The autograph in La Côte-Saint-André is probably from the period before Berlioz came to Paris in late 1821; the two versions differ slightly.[48]

11. Le Cheval arabe
Cantate à grand orchestre
(text by Millevoye)

Date: Autumn 1822 (ded)

Source: LOST

Ref.: **BerMém,** Chap. VI.

Berlioz began serious study with Lesueur in early 1823, and the cantata and 3-voice canon were, according to the *Mémoires,* shown to Lesueur at their first meeting. Millevoye's poem as published in his *OEuvres complètes* (Paris, 1822), is titled "L'Arabe au tombeau de son Coursier."

12. Canon à Trois Voix

Date: Autumn 1822 (ded)

Source: LOST

Ref.: **BerMém,** Chap VI.

See remark above, no. 11.

13. Canon libre à la quinte
(text by Bourgerie)

Date: before December 1822 (pub)

Source: PUB. Paris: Boieldieu jeune, December 1822.

Publication announced in *Le Réveil; Journal des sciences, de la littérature, des moeurs, théâtres, beaux-arts* of 16 December 1822:

> *Un canon nouveau vient de paraître; mais celui-là ne fera ni baisser les rentes, ni crier les journaux. C'est un canon pour rire; on ne le tire pas, on le chante. Nous engageons donc les musiciens et les musiciennes à prendre chez Mad. Dorval, rue de la Paix, n°. 9, le Canon de M. Bourgerie et Hector Berlioz, pour juger s'il résonne bien à l'oreille.*

The four songs published by Boieldieu jeune (nos. 13-16) include after the composer's name on the title page the indication *"élève de Mr Lesueur."*

14. Le Montagnard exilé
Chant élégiaque
(text by Albert Du Boys)

Date: before February 1823 (pub)

Source: PUB. Paris: Boieldieu jeune, February 1823.

15. Amitié, reprends ton empire
Romance
(text by Florian)

Date: c. 1819-February 1823

Source:
   Autograph score, **F-CSA**, titled *Invocation A l'Amitié / Paroles de Florian; Nouvellement / Mises en musique avec Acc^{ent} de Piano / Par Mr Hector Berlioz*, 2 pp., autograph fair copy.

PUB.   Paris: Boieldieu jeune, February 1823.

The autograph in La Côte-Saint-André is probably from the period before Berlioz came to Paris in late 1821; the two versions differ slightly.

16. Toi qui l'aimas, verse des pleurs
Romance
(text by Albert Du Boys)

Date: before February 1823 (pub)

Source: PUB. Paris: Boieldieu jeune, February 1823.

17. Estelle et Némorin
Opera
(text by Gerono, after Florian)

Date: mid-1823 (ded)

Source: LOST (destroyed, according to Berlioz).

Ref.: **BerMém**, Chaps. VII-VIII.

Berlioz's association with Gerono dates from the autumn of 1822. Possibly this work included in some way the song from *Estelle* that Berlioz says he had already set, *Je vais donc quitter pour jamais* (no. 6).

Concerning Gerono, see Holoman, "Berlioz au Conservatoire: Notes biographiques," *Revue de Musicologie* 62 (1976), 289-92.

18. Le Passage de la mer rouge
Oratorio with Latin text
(text from the Vulgate Bible [?])

Date: Winter 1823-24.

Source: LOST (destroyed, according to Berlioz).

Refs.: **BerCG** 26: La Côte-Saint-André, July 1824, to Lesueur; **BerMém**, Chap. VIII.

19. Beverley, ou le Joueur
Dramatic Scene
(text by Bernard Saurin)

Date: c. late 1823-early 1824

Source: LOST (destroyed, according to Berlioz).

Ref.: **BerMém**, Chaps. VII-VIII.

Berlioz describes the piece (**BerMém**, Chap. VII) as *"une scène fort sombre,... [un] fragment de musique violente écrit pour voix de basse avec orchestre."*

There is considerable confusion in the literature as to the date of its composition. The Odéon presented *Beverley*, an adaptation of an English play (Edward Moore's *The Gamester*, London, 1753), in February 1823. Berlioz apparently hoped that a certain benefit for Talma would include his piece performed by Henri-Etienne Dérivis. Boschot (**BosHB** I, 113 and 575-76) connected this event with a benefit of 1 May 1823 for the singer Lays, where Talma played the high priest in a version of Racine's *Athalie* which included choruses of Gossec. But as Cairns observes (**BerMemCairns**, p. 577), Berlioz was in the region of La Côte-Saint-André in April and May of 1823. Cairns concludes, partly on the basis of Berlioz's statement that he began work on the *Messe solennelle* shortly after finishing *Beverley*, that the work is from Spring 1824. There was in fact a benefit for Talma at the Théâtre-Français on 1 April 1824, where an orchestra was present. The balance of the evidence, then, suggests a date of late 1823 or early 1824.

20. **Messe solennelle (Messe en grande symphonie)**
    (traditional Latin text)

   20A. COMPLETE WORK: *Messe solennelle*
       Kyrie
       Gloria
       Credo
       Crucifixus
       Et Resurrexit [VERSION I]
       Domine Salvum
       Salutaris
       Sanctus
       Agnus Dei

Date: Spring–December 1824 (fp scheduled; rehearsed 27 December)

Source: LOST (destroyed, according to Berlioz, except for the *Resurrexit* [q.v., below]).

Refs.: **BerMém**, Chaps. VII-VIII; letters (1824-25); published reviews of the performances (10 July 1825 and 22 November 1827, both versions probably retouched).

   A performance was planned for 28 December 1824 at St.-Roch, and a letter of invitation was printed and mailed (published in **BerCG** 36, N.B. p. 72, fn. 1). It did not take place because of practical difficulties encountered at the rehearsal (see **BerMém**, Chap. VII and **BerCG** 41), and the first public performance did not occur until 10 July 1825. Boschot (and later Barzun) erroneously believed that the rehearsal Berlioz mentions in the *Mémoires* occurred on Innocents' Day (27 December) 1823; he constructed an elaborate theory whereby it was the oratorio *Le Passage de la mer rouge* that was actually rehearsed, since it is clear from Berlioz's letter to Lesueur of July 1824 (**BerCG** 26) that the Mass had not then been finished. This error resulted from Boschot's too-literal interpretation of a remark by Berlioz in Chapter VII, where he says he wrote the Mass shortly after (*un peu plus tard*) completing *Beverley*. Since Boschot assumed that *Beverley* was written just after the Parisian performance of the play in March 1823, he could find no reason for dating the *Messe solennelle* as late as 1824. The printed invitation to the first performance of the Mass had not then been discovered.

Berlioz names the movements of his work in **BerCG** 26 (La Côte-Saint-André, July 1824, to Lesueur; though Cairns emphasizes that the composer probably refers to the text, not a musical draft, of the *Kyrie* and *Credo*) and **BerCG** 48 (Paris, 20 July 1825, to Du Boys). Later, in *Les Grotesques de la musique* (1859), he mentions an *O Salutaris* from the Mass. The article is an obituary of the singer Madame Lebrun, and Berlioz remarks:

> *Je ne me rappelle pas sans attendrissement le compliment qu'elle m'adressa dans l'église de Saint-Roch, le jour de l'exécution de ma première messe solennelle. Après un* O Salutaris *très simple sous tous les rapports Mme Lebrun vint me serrer la main et me dit avec un accent pénétré:* "F[outaise], *mon cher enfant, voilà un* O Salutaris *qui n'est point piqué des vers, et je défie tous ces petits* b[âtards] *des classes de contrepoint du Conservatoire d'écrire un morceau aussi bien ficelé et aussi cranement religieux*" (article "Madame Lebrun").

20B. *Resurrexit*, VERSION II: revised

Date: May 1828 (fp)

Sources:

Manuscript scores: **F-G** Rés R 90665, 86 numbered pp. (1 title, 86 blank), scribal copy with autograph annotations and an inscription to Ferrand; **F-Pc** ms 1510, 70 numbered pp. (1 title, 70 blank), scribal copy (from Rome) with autograph title.

The autograph annotations in the Grenoble copy seem for the purpose of converting the *Resurrexit* into *Le Jugement dernier*, a version performed on 1 November 1829; thus the original layer of the manuscript probably records the 1828 version. Berlioz sent the same work as an *envoi* from Rome, **F-Pc** ms 1510. Although the manuscript is inscribed *"Rome: 1831"* and is in the hand of an Italian copyist, the music is that of the 1828 version. The Paris copy served as the source for the OBE.

21. **Scène héroïque à grands choeurs et à grand orchestre (La Révolution grecque)**
(text by Humbert Ferrand)

21A. VERSION I: for Chorus and Full Orchestra
    I.   *[Introduction,] Récitative et Air* (un chef grec);
    II. *Choeur de guerriers*;
    III. *Prière* (choeur de femmes);
    IV. *Final* (choeur général)

Date: Winter 1825-26 (pub)

Sources:
Published libretto, one copy bound with manuscript orchestra score, privately printed by Berlioz and Ferrand (Paris, March 1826).

Manuscript score, F-Pc D 944, 88 numbered folios, scribal copy with autograph words at one point (fols. 26^v-28^v), autograph addition of two measures (fol. 60^r), and an autograph quotation from Thomas Moore on the original title page, now covered by a copyist's title.

Contents:
    I.   *Introduction*, fols. 3^v-5^v; *Récitative*, fols. 5^v-8^v; *Air* (Lento), fols. 8^v-13^r (1^r title, 1^v-2^r blank, 2^v engraving of Greek warriors [Paris, 1828], 3^r second title);
    II. *Choeur de guerriers* (All^o assai animato), fols. 13^v-49^r;
    III. *Prière* (Larghetto), fols. 49^v-60^r;
    IV. *Final* (All^o non troppo; Mouvement double plus vite), fols. 60^v-88^v.

The published libretto was first cited in the *Bibliographie de la France* of 29 March 1826; the work had probably been completed the preceding winter. Berlioz had hoped to have the work performed during Holy Week of 1826 at Kreutzer's *Concerts spirituels*. Kreutzer, however, received the request badly (January 1826; see **BerMém**, Chap. XI), even though Berlioz had tried to pave his way by negotiating with the *administration des Beaux-Arts* (Du Boys, Le Normant, and Vicomte de la Rochefoucauld; see **BerCG** 53: Paris, 15 January 1826, to Le Normant). Additionally, Boschot (**BosHB** II, 641), cites a letter of 11 January 1826, without further reference or quotation, that led him to the conclusion that the work was performed in 1826 under the title *Le Triomphe de la Croix*. (This letter was not found by Citron.) Boschot, in this belief, overlooked the evidence of the *Mémoires*. A letter first published much later confirms that the scheme was dropped entirely (**BerCG** 61: 15 July 1826, to Edouard Rocher). The work was finally performed on 26

May 1828 and was a failure (**BerCG** 93: 6 June 1828, to Ferrand; and **BerMém** Chap. XIX), and again in an abbreviated version in 1833 (q.v., below).

Berlioz, in documents from the period, seems to have preferred the title *Scène héroïque* to *La Révolution grecque*, the title he uses in the *Memoires*.

The manuscript was probably prepared for Humbert Ferrand. Although there is no formal dedication, it resembles the manuscript of *La Mort d'Orphée* (q.v.), which was presented to Ferrand. Both are in the hand of the same copyist, and both belonged after Ferrand's death to the Martin collection in Marseille. The score has three separate title pages, two of which carry the notation: *"Exécutée pour la première fois à l'Ecole R^{le}. de Musique, le 22 Juillet 1828"* (cf. the inscription of *La Mort d'Orphée*). It was bound together with three lithographed illustrations (one dated 1828), and a copy of the printed libretto.

The scribal copy must thus have been made in late 1828 (or later), and it may, then, represent a revision of the original version of 1826. The text in the score corresponds, with minor exceptions, to that of the printed libretto as far as the *Finale* (of the libretto: inc. *"Aux armes!... Le ciel résonne"*). The published libretto, however, includes a verse of epilogue sung by a chorus of priests (inc. *"Europe, lève-toi!... regarde-les mourir..."*) not found in the score.

The words of the last chorus (*"Des sommets de l'Olympe"*) appear virtually unchanged as the last chorus of *Le Cri de Guerre du Brisgaw* (no. 23C).

21B. Version II: for Chorus and Military Band
Also called *La Triomphe de Napoléon*

   I.   *Prière de femmes*
   II. *Choeur général*

Date: July 1833 (fp)

Source:
   Manuscript parts, F-Pc L 17239 (*fonds du roi* A-J), 336 parts (10 boxes), fair scribal copy.

This version was heard only at its general rehearsals, one of which took place on 22 July 1833. An announcement of the concert planned for the Place Vendôme appeared in *L'Europe littéraire* of 24 July 1833, p. 256. Neither the concert of 28 July nor a second performance planned for 9 August 1833 actually took place. See **BerCG** 341 (Paris, 1 August 1833, to Ferrand) and **BosHB** II, 189-93.

22. Fugue for 1826 Prix de Rome *concours d'essai*

Date: July 1826

Source:
   Autograph score, F-Pn W 33 (10), 8 unnumbered pp., autograph
fair copy.
   Fugues no. 2 (Gilbert), 10 (Berlioz), 11 (Bienaimé), 12 (Guiraud),
and 13 (Paris) in the miscellany F-Pn W 33 all have the same subject.
Paris won the competition in 1826, and Guiraud and Bienaimé were
awarded second prizes; hence Berlioz's manuscript comes unquestion-
ably from 1826.
   The manuscript was stolen from the Bibliothèque Nationale in
the early 1950s, sold, and in February 1952 reinstated through the
mediation of Jacques Barzun.
   It is clear that Berlioz entered the Prix de Rome *concours* five
times, beginning in 1826. (In addition to his remark in BerMém
Chap. X that he entered and failed the preliminary test [in 1826], he
also writes at the beginning of Chap. XXIX that he entered for the
fifth time in 1830.) In 1826, then, he was eliminated in the *concours
d'essai*, i.e. his fugue was not accepted.
   The printed programs for the award ceremonies of 1827 through
1830 are preserved, and each lists other requirements of the
contestants, including contrapuntal exercises at the octave and at the
twelfth.   Apparently, however, the fugue was the only exercise
actually set. Berlioz's *feuilleton* for *L'Europe littéraire* of 12 June 1833
(pp. 182-83, abridged in BerMém Chap. XXII) reads in part:

> *Quand l'époque du concours a été fixée, les candidats viennent s'inscrire*
> *au sécrétariat de l'Institut. Ils subissent ensuite un examen préparatoire*
> *qu'on appelle le concours préliminaire, qui a pour but apparent de choisir*
> *parmi les aspirans les quatre ou cinq ou six ou sept ou huit plus avancés,*
> *car le nombre des élus varie chaque année suivant le caprice de ces*
> *messieurs. Admirable règlement élastique.   Comme le sujet du grand*
> *concours est une scène lyrique sérieuse, pour une ou deux voix et*
> *orchestre, les candidats sont tenus de prouver qu'ils possèdent le sentiment*
> *de la mélodie, la science de l'harmonie, l'art de l'instrumentation et les*
> *autres qualités indispensables pour un semblable ouvrage, en écrivant... une*
> *fugue vocale.*

23. Les Francs-Juges
    Opera
    (text by Humbert Ferrand)

   23A. Fragments of the opera (see no. 23D for information
        concerning the overture as a concert work)

Ouverture

ACTE I
1. *Choeur du peuple* (inc. *"Arnold, entends nos fers"*);
2. *Duo* (inc. *"Conrad s'arma pour nous"*);
3. *Récitative et Air* (inc. *"Va! je t'abhorre"*... *"Noble amitié"*);
4. *Elégie* (inc. *"La nuit voilant pour nous"*);
5. *Quartet* (inc. *"Frais vallons où dorment nos pères"*);

ACTE II
6. *Choeur de bergers* (inc. *"L'ombre descend dans la vallée"*);
7. *Trio pastoral* (inc. *"Vois-tu le soleil s'enfuir"*);
8. *Duo* (inc. *"N'espère plus, Lenor"*);
9. *Marche* [*Marche des gardes*];
10. *Finale* (inc. *"Malheur au parjure"*);

ACTE III
11. *Récitative et Invocation* (inc. *"Voici l'endroit fatal"* ... *"Descends et viens"*);
12. *Hymne des Francs-Juges* (inc. *"Des célestes décrets, invisibles vengeurs"*);
13. *Mélodrame*; reprise of hymn;
14. *Choeur du peuple* (inc. *"Fier Germain, reprends ces vallons"*).
[N.B. Contents reconstructed; see below.]

Date: May-October 1826 (let), revised 1829

Sources:

Autograph miscellany, **F-Pn** Rés Vm^2 177, 80 numbered fols. plus remnants. Contains fragments of orchestral score, one movement reduced for voices and piano accompaniment, and a draft libretto for a later revision.

Contents:
I. *Nocturne à trois voix concertantes avec choeur* [reduction for voices with piano accompaniment of trio from Act I]; 1 bifolio (4 unnumbered pp.; 2^v blank), autograph fair copy, 1828;
II. *Le Cri de guerre du Brisgaw* [libretto of dramatic intermezzo salvaging sections from the opera]; 20 numbered pp. (five bifolios, the middle four of which are

stacked and numbered by Berlioz 1-4; the fifth is a wrapper), autograph working copy, 1833;

III. [*Les Francs-Juges*], fragments and remnants of the opera; fols. 1^r-80bis^s [the remnants are numbered by assigning the indication *bis* and a letter, here given in superscript, to the number of the complete page before the remnants begin]: 1. *Choeur de Soldats auquel / se joint ensuite celui du peuple*, fols. 3^r-18^r (18^v blank); 2. *Duo*, fols. 20^r-55^r (19^r title, 19^v, 55^v blank); 6. *Choeur de Bergers*, fols, 57^r-66^v (56^r title, 56^v, 67 blank); 11. [*Invocation*], fols. 67bis^{a-y}; [no number. *Hymne des Francs-Juges*], fols. 68^r-73^r; [*hymne* reprise], fols, 73^r-80^v; [remnant of preceding movt.], fols. 80bis^{a-b}; [no number. *Final*], fols. 80bis^{c-s}; autograph fair copy with some revision, 1826 and later. Facsimile of two remnants from the *Invocation* in **NBE** 19, 100.

Manuscript libretto, **F-Pc** papiers divers de Berlioz, no. 45, 53 numbered pp., fair scribal copy, with autograph annotations and revisions, of the 1829 version: *Lenor, ou les derniers Francs-Juges*.

The various versions of *Les Francs-Juges* are considered in detail in the first section of Chapter IV (pp. 215-36). The libretti of *Les Francs-Juges* and *Le Cri de guerre du Brisgaw* are transcribed, respectively, in Appendix II and Appendix III.

Boschot (**BosHB** I, 236), describes another libretto that was then in the archives of the Opéra; it now seems to be lost, along with a second libretto by Ferrand that Boschot saw there, *Les Noces d'or d'Obéron et Titania*.

23B. *Nocturne à trois voix concertantes avec choeur (Mélodie pastorale)*

VERSION II: for Voices and Piano

Date: May 1828 (fp)

Source:
    Autograph score, **F-Pn** Rés Vm^2 177, item 1 (unique preserved version; see no. 23A, above).

23C. *Le Cri de Guerre du Brisgaw*

Incomplete intermezzo based on *Les Francs-Juges*

Date: November 1833-January 1834 (let)

Source:

Autograph libretto, **F-Pn** Rés Vm² 177, item 2 (see no. 23A, above).

Seven letters from 1833 and 1834 to Thomas Gounet deal with the libretto, for which Gounet was providing additional text (**BerCG** 356, 359, 368, 369, 371, 374 and 375). The libretto also includes the words of Berlioz's *Le Paysan breton* (see no. 65), composed in December 1833. The letters to Gounet also suggest that the two were collaborating on another drama, to be called *Les Brigands: "je voudrais bien avoir le* Cri de Guerre *avant l'autre; si vous pouviez le finir je m'y mettrais"* (**BerCG** 359).

23D. *Grande Ouverture des Francs-Juges*

Date: September-October 1826 (let)

Source: PUB. Paris: Richault, 1836. An autograph part for *Cornets à pistons en A*, **F-Pc** ms 17666, 1 fol.^{r&v}, may be from the original set of orchestra parts. (Later ms. sources: ms. oboe part, **F-Pc** ms 17666; ms. parts in German hands from three different sets, **GB-TWmacnutt**; ms. part for bass drum copied in Germany, **F-Pc** Rés F 1040; ms. parts, **D-DT** Mus. n 355.

24. Fugue for 1827 Prix de Rome *concours d'essai*

Date: July 1827

Source: LOST.

Ref.: **BerCG** 76: Paris, 28 July 1927, to Nanci.

The composer's letter to his sister is a succinct summary of the preliminary competition:

Le concours préliminaire a eu lieu avant-hier, pour savoir quels seraient ceux des candidats qui devaient être admis au grand concours. On nous avait donné à faire une fugue en style sévère, sorte de problème musical fort peu utile et très difficile à résoudre. Nous n'étions que quatre et sur ce nombre je suis le seul qui ait fait correctement ce qu'on nomme la réponse et qui est l'objet principal de la fugue.

See also above, no. 22.

25. La Mort D'Orphée
Cantata for 1827 Prix de Rome Competition
(text by Berton)

  I.   *Introduction*
  II.   *Larghetto*
  III. *Bacchanale*
  IV.   *Tableau musical*

Date: July 1827

Source:

  Manuscript copy of orchestral score, **F-Pn** Rés Vma ms 1,
82 numbered pp., scribal copy with autograph additions. Contents:

  Introduction, pp. 2-17 (1 title);
  Réci[ative & Air], pp. 18-34;
  Récitative, pp. 35-38;
  Bacchanale, pp. 39-80;
  Tableau musical, pp. 81-82 (83-84 blank).

An autograph note on the title page of this manuscript reads:

  Ouvrage déclaré inexécutable *par la Section de musique de l'institut et*
  exécuté *à l'école royale de musique le 22 juillet 1828. L'auteur à son
  ami Ferrand* (cf. **BerMém** Chap. XIX).

  The date *22 Juillet 1828* for a performance of the work, given
in the composer's hand, is incorrect. The same date appears on two
other manuscripts that Berlioz presented to Ferrand, the *Scène
héroïque* and the Grenoble copy of the *Resurrexit*. These copies, as
well as a copy of the *Mélodie pastorale* from *Les Francs-Juges*, were
all given to Ferrand between 1828 and 1831, and the error in dates
was thus probably the result of faulty memory.

26. Grande Ouverture de Waverley

Date: between October 1826 and February 1828 (ded).

Source:

  Autograph score, **F-Pc** ms 1507, 36 numbered fols., autograph
fair copy with a few revisions for publication. 1828, rev. 1839.

  Both *Waverley* and the *Grande Ouverture des Francs-Juges* may
have been intended for a concert of December 1827.

27. Marche religieuse des Mages
(text anonymous)

Date: before May 1828 (fp)

Source: LOST.

Ref.: **BerCG** 93: Paris, 6 June 1828, to Ferrand.

    Probably revised as *Quartetto e coro dei maggi* (1832, q.v. below, no. 59).

28. Fugue for 1828 Prix de Rome *concours d'essai*

Date: July 1828

Source: LOST

29. Herminie
Scène lyrique
Cantata for 1828 Prix de Rome competition
(text by Vieillard)

       I.   [*Introduction &*] *Air*
      II. *Air*
     III. *Air*
     IV. *Prière*

Date: July 1828

Source:
    Autograph score, **F-Pc** ms 1185, 110 numbered pp., autograph fair copy.

Contents:
    Introduction, pp. 3-14 (1 title, 2 blank);
    Air N° 1, pp. 15-20;
    Récit[*ative et*] *Air N° 2*, pp. 21-52;
    Récit[*ative et*] *Air N° 3*, pp. 53-73;
    Prière, pp. 74-107 (108-10 blank).

    Manuscript part, **F-Pc** ms 1514, partbook for soprano soloist, 18 numbered folios (1ʳ title, 1ᵛ, 18ᵛ blank), scribal copy titled by Berlioz.

30. **Là ci darem la mano**
    Variations for guitar on the theme of Mozart

    Date: c. 1828

    Source: LOST.

    Ref.: Whistling's *Handbuch der Musikliteratur 1828*, p. 387, which contains the following entry:

    > *Berlioz, Var. (Là ci darem.) Paris, Aulagnier 3 Fr.*

    Nothing more is known of this composition, though it may be related in some way to a guitar tutor published by Aulagnier which apparently contained exercises by Berlioz. Philip James Bone, in *The Guitar and Mandolin: Biographies of Celebrated Players and Composers* (London, 1914), p. 35, remarks: "Berlioz composed studies and variations for guitar alone, which were published by Aulagnier, Paris."

31. **Nocturne à 2 voix**
    Song with guitar accompaniment[49]
    (inc. *Je veux dans l'inconstance passer mes premiers ans*)
    (text anonymous)

    Date: c. 1828

    Source:
    Autograph score, US-NYcu Berlioz collection, 1 fol. (verso blank), autograph fair copy.

    The calligraphy of the autograph suggests a date before c. 1830; the work is placed here, adjacent to the variations on *Là ci darem la mano*, for convenience.

32. **Salutaris**

    Date: Winter 1828-29

    Source: LOST.

    Refs.: **BerCG** 106: Paris, end of 1828, to Ferrand; **BerCG** 121: Paris, 9 April 1829, to Ferrand.

    BerCG 106 mentions an oratorio for solo voice with organ accompaniment, of which Berlioz says he has already done half. **BerCG** 121 says that the composer has written a *Salutaris* for three voices with organ or piano accompaniment. The two titles probably represent differing versions of the same project.

33. Huit Scènes de Faust
(text from Nerval's translation of Goethe)

    I. *Chants de la fête de Pâques*;
    II. *Paysans sous les tilleuls. Danse et chant*;
    III. *Concert de sylphes. Sextuor*;
    IV. *Ecot de joyeux compagnons* (*Histoire d'un rat*);
    V. *Chanson de Méphistophélès* (*Histoire d'une puce*);
    VI. *Le Roi de Thulé. Chanson gothique*;
    VII. *Romance de Marguerite; Choeur de soldats*;
    VIII. *Sérénade de Méphistophélès.*

Date: September 1828-January 1929 (let, pub)

Sources:

Autograph score of no. VI, for voice (Sopr.) and piano, US–NYpm, 1 biofolio, autograph fair copy.

The version preserved in this manuscript probably predates the complete *Huit Scènes de Faust*, since it has only a single measure of introduction (cf. *Huit Scènes*, no. VI, mm. 1-7); thus it may well the manuscript prepared on about 14 September 1828 (see **BerCG** 99).

Autograph and manuscript parts: **F-Pc** ms 17466, 5 complete autograph parts and fragments of a 6th: clarinets I–II (no. V), bassoons I–II (nos. IV-V), bassoons III-IV (no. IV), fragment of horns I–II (no. III), horns I–II (no. V), ophicléide (no. V); 2 complete manuscript parts and fragment of a 3rd, all for no. III: violas (fragmentary), contrabasses (2); 7 complete manuscript parts for nos. IV-V: violins I, violins II (2) violas, cellos and contrabasses, contrabasses.

Published proof corrected by the composer, **F-Pn** Rés Vm² 172.

Published scores with autograph notation (see Julian Rushton, **NBE** 5, 103):
CH-Gc R 4 (aut.: *No. 39; l'auteur à Mr Bloc*), **GB-En** H. B. 1/1 (aut.: *offert à Monsieur Miel par l'auteur, H. Berlioz*) **GB-Ob** Mus. 1 c 309 (6), **GB-TWmacnutt** (1) (aut.: *Mme Lesueur*); several copies of a second issue with manuscript notation: **F-Pc** Abo 35, **GB-Lbl** Hirsch IV 703, **GB-Lcm** I K 14 (aut. inscription obliterated), **US-NH** z Mus. B44 (1).

A facsimile of the fragmentary horn part is given in Rushton's edition, **NBE** 5, 107.

The relation of this work to a ballet of *Faust* with a libretto by Victor Bohain, commissioned from Berlioz and later withdrawn, is unclear. The correspondence of the era (**BerCG** 103, 107, 111) shows that the libretto was accepted at the Opéra, then turned down after a successful *Faust* was staged elsewhere in Paris. In a review of Gounod's *Faust (Journal des Débats*, 26 March 1859; repr. as "A Propos d'un ballet de Faust" in *A Travers Champs*, pp. 361-62), Berlioz ridicules the very idea of a *Faust* ballet.

Berlioz sent a copy of the published *Huit Scènes de Faust* to Goethe on 10 April 1829 (see **BerCG** 122).

A performance of no. VII was planned for the concert of 3 February 1844 (Paris: Salle Herz), but was cancelled because of the singer's illness.

34. Chanson des pirates
(text by Hugo, from *Orientales*)

Date: early 1829 (let)

Source: LOST

Ref.: **BerCG** 113: Paris, 2 February 1829, to Ferrand.

Reused in revised form (to words by Berlioz) as the *Chanson des brigands* in the *Mélologue* (q.v. below, no. 55A).

35. Fugue à trois sujets
Fugue for 1829 Prix de Rome *concours d'essai*

Date: July 1829

Source:
Autograph score, **F-Pc** ms 1506 (bound with *Cléopâtre*, ms 1505), 4 pp. (1 bifolio) labelled A-D, autograph fair copy.

36. Cléopâtre
Scène lyrique
Cantata for 1829 Prix de Rome competition
(text by Vieillard)

   I. *[Introduction &]* *Récitative*
   II. *[Air & Récitative]*
   III. *Méditation*

Date: July 1829

Source:
  Autograph score, F-Pc ms 1505, 45 numbered fols., autograph fair copy.

Contents:
  [Introduction], fols. 2^r-6^v (1^r title, 1^v blank); *Récitative*, fols. 7^r-8^v; *[Air]*, fols. 9^r-21^r;
  [Récitative], fols. 21^v-22^v; *Méditation*, fols. 23^r-45^r (45^v blank).

37. Le Ballet des ombres
Ronde nocturne
(text by Albert Du Boys, after Herder)

Date: between April and December 1829 (let)

Source: PUB. Paris: Schlesinger, [1829].

Refs.: **BerCG** 124: Paris, 24 April [1829], to Du Boys; **BerCG** 146: Paris: 4 December 1829, to Ferrand; **BerCG** 147: Paris, 27 December 1829, to Ferrand.

  Having destroyed all the copies of the *Ballet des ombres*, Berlioz reassigned the *oeuvre* number 2 to the *Neuf Mélodies irlandaises* (no. 38). Hopkinson suggests that the *Ballet des ombres* was never put on sale.
  Both the autograph (formerly the property of Raoul Pugno) and the only surviving copy of the publication (formerly in the library of the Vicomte Spoelberch de Lovenjoul) have been lost.
  Facsimile of the title page of the print in **JullHB**, p. [41].

38-47: NEUF MELODIES IRLANDAISES.
  Specific information on the constituent works appears in nos. 39-47.

38. Neuf Melodies irlandaises
   (later called *Irlande*)
   (text by Thomas Moore, trans. Thomas Gounet)

38A. Original publication, 1830.

> I. *Le Coucher du soleil. Rêverie* (= no. 39);
> II. *Hélène. Ballade à 2 voix* (= no. 40);
> III. *Chant guerrier* (= no. 41);
> IV. *La Belle Voyageuse. Ballade* (= no. 42);
> V. *Chanson à boire* (= no. 43).
> VI. *Chant sacré* (= no. 44);
> VII. *L'Origine de la harpe. Ballade* (= no. 45);
> VIII. *Adieu Bessy. Romance anglaise & française* (= no. 46);
> IX. *Elégie en prose* (= no. 47).

Date: June-December 1829 (let)

Source: PUB. Paris: M. Schlesinger, February 1830.

Refs.: **BerCG** 126: Paris: 3 June 1829, to Ferrand; **BerCG** 134: Paris, 21 August 1829, to Ferrand; **BerCG** 145: Paris, 3 December 1829; **BerCG** 146: Paris: 4 December 1829, to Ferrand; **BerCG** 147: Paris, 27 December 1829, to Ferrand; **BerCG** 148: Paris, 28 December 1829, to Nanci; etc.

[38B. *Irlande*, a new edition of the *Mélodies* in a different format, c. November 1849.]

39. Le Coucher du soleil
   Rêverie

Date: June-December 1829 (let)

Source: PUB. (see no. 38A).

The work was performed on 18 February 1830 at the Athénée musical.

40. Hélène
   Ballade à 2 voix

40A. VERSION I: for two Voices and Piano

Date: June-December 1829 (let)

Source: PUB. (see no. 38A).

[40B.   VERSION II: for male Quartet and Orchestra, January 1844.]

41. Chant guerrier

Date: June-December 1829 (let)

Sources: PUB. (see no. 38A).

Offprints of score with autograph revisions in the text: **F-Pc** L 17277 (*fonds du roi*), 38 copies drawn from Schlesinger's edition (for the concert of 5 December 1830) marked *Tenor* or *Basse*; in 8 of the bass parts, Berlioz has revised the poetry in the fourth stanza.

42. La Belle voyageuse
Ballade

42A. VERSION I: for Voice and Piano

Date: June-December 1829 (let)

Source: PUB. (see no. 38A).

42B. VERSION II: for male Quartet and Orchestra

Date: November 1834 (fp)

Source: LOST.

Ref.: Press announcement for the concert of 9 November 1834: *Gazette musicale* I/44, 2 November 1834, p. 356.

[42C. VERSION III: for Mezzo-Soprano and Orchestra, December 1842.]

[42D. VERSION IV: for female Chorus and Orchestra, March 1851.]

43. Chanson à boire

Date: June-December 1829 (let)

Source: PUB. (see no. 38A).

44. Chant Sacré

44A. VERSION I: for Soloist, Chorus, and Piano

Date: June-December 1829 (let)

Source: PUB. (see no. 38A).

The work was performed on 18 February 1830 at the Athénée musical.

[44B. VERSION II: for Chorus and Orchestra, November 1843.]

[44C. VERSION III: for six wind instruments and Orchestra, February 1844.]

45. L'Origine de la harpe
Ballade

Date: June-December 1829 (let)

Source: PUB. (see no. 38A).

46. Adieu Bessy
Romance anglaise & française

46A. VERSION I: in A♭ major

Date: June-December 1829 (let)

Source: PUB. (see no. 38A).

[46A. VERSION II: in G major, c. November 1849.]

47. Elégie en prose

Date: c. December 1829 (let)

Source: PUB. (see no. 38A).

48. Episode de la vie d'un artiste
Symphonie fantastique en cinq parties

  I. *Rêveries, Passions;*
  II. *Un bal;*
  III. *Scène aux champs;*
  IV. *Marche au supplice;*
  V. *Songe d'une nuit du sabbat.*

Date: January–April 1830 (let)

Sources:
 Autograph score, **F-Pc** ms 1188, 5 separate fascicles, autograph working copy.

Contents:

I.   *Episode de la vie d'un Artiste / Simphonie Fantastique en A̸ 5 parties / N° 1 / Partition B̸y̸ Par / Hector Berlioz,* 63 numbered pp. (64 blank), autograph working score with various stages of revision, including collettes and addition of new papers resulting in changes in fascicle structure;

II. *N° 2   un Bal,* 46 numbered pp., autograph fair copy, some later revisions, including an added cornet part;

III. *Simphonie* [sic] *fantastique / N° 3 / Scène aux champs,* 50 numbered pp. (erroneously assembled; the page numbered 50 is a collette for p. 27, which has been deleted), autograph fair copy;

IV. *Simphonie fantastique / en A̸ 5 parties / Première partie / de la Vision / Marche du* [sic] *Supplice / N° ʒ̸ 4 / Partition / By / Hector Berlioz,* 36 numbered pp., autograph fair copy with two sketches and some alteration to original fascicle structure (the result of the adaptation of the manuscript, originally a fair copy of the *Marche des gardes* intended for *Les Francs-Juges,* as part of the score to the symphony; the original title page, as is now well known, gives the title of the march);

V.   *Simphonie fantastique / N° 5 / Seconde partie de la vision / Songe d'une Nuit / du Sabbat / Partition / By / H. Berlioz,* 83 numbered pp. (84 blank), autograph working copy. Facsimiles of titles for movts. I and IV in **NBE 16,** 182-84.

Fragment of autograph score, **F-Pmeyer,** list of instructions to conductors for the performance of the *Symphonie fantastique,* including list of instrumentalists required, 1 fol., writing on recto only. Facsimiles in **CatMeyer,** planche 3, and **NBE 16,** 185.

Autograph manuscript of program, **F-Pc** papiers divers de Berlioz no. 37, 1 bifolio (4 pp.). Facsimiles of pp. 1-2 in **NBE 16,** 186-87.

Sketches, as per Table III, below.   See also Facsimiles III. 7 and IV. 6.

Manuscript parts: a harp part, possibly early, in **F-Pc** Rés F 1040.

Published score with autograph corrections (see Nicholas Temperley, in **NBE 16,** 171–75): Autograph corrections to "advance

edition" of Schlesinger's edition (Paris, late 1844-45), **F-Pc** Rés.
F 1029.

Published parts with autograph corrections, **F-Psoc** and **F-Pn**
Rés Vma 216 (Paris: Schlesinger, c. 1845; pl. no. M.S. 4052), 74
parts at **F-Pn**, an undetermined number at **F-Psoc**, autograph titles,
notes, and minor corrections (especially to those copies that are
proofs), and the revised version of mm. 129-56 of movt. II, generally
added by autograph collette; published part for oboe in movement
III (*"derrière la scène"*), with 1 ms. correction, probably autograph,
F-Pc L 517. Facsimile of published cello and contrabass part with
autograph notation in **NBE** 16, 188.

Liszt's transcription for piano, published in 1834 (Paris:
Schlesinger; copy in **F-Pn** Ac e^{10} 888), conforms to the autograph
score in most respects.

Julien Tiersot, on p. 80 of *La musique aux temps romantiques*
(Paris, 1930), published a facsimile of mm. 3-6 of movt. I which
shows the string parts (only) in score. This document is cited in
NBE (16, 175) as an autograph source. Actually it is only a
photographic montage of portions of the autograph orchestra score,
the seams visible upon careful examination.

49. Fugue for 1830 Prix de Rome *concours d'essai*

Date: July 1830.

Source: LOST.

50. Sardanapale
Cantata for 1830 Prix de Rome competition
(text by Gail)

Date: July 1830

Source:
    Fragments of autograph score, **F-Pn** Rés Vm^2 178 (*La Nonne
sanglante*), fols. 83^r-96^v, autograph fair copy, some revisions.

51. Hymne des Marseillais
[La Marseillaise]
(arrangement; music and text by Rouget de Lisle)

51A. VERSION I: for double Chorus and Orchestra

Date: c. July–August 1830 (pub)

Source: PUB. Paris: Schlesinger, [c. December 1830].

Hopkinson (**HopBib** 11, pp. 21-22) deduces this date from the plate number of Schlesinger's publication (M.S. 1046). Berlioz transcribes a letter from Rouget de Lisle of 20 December 1830 in his *Mémoires* (Chap. XXIX) and specifies that it is in response to his arrangement of the song for choruses and large orchestra, but neither that letter nor Berlioz's reply of 29 December (**BerCG** 198) specifically mentions the work.

[51B. VERSION II: for Chorus and Piano, March 1848.]

52. Fantaisie dramatique sur La Tempête, drame de Shakespeare
(text by Berlioz [?])
Incorporated into *Le Retour à la vie* (1831; no. 55)

Date: August–October 1830 (let)

Sources:
Autograph score, **F–Pc** ms 1192, 134 numbered pp., autograph fair copy.

Fragment of autograph score, abandoned draft of mm. 21-24 as collette–verso in *Symphonie fantastique* score, movt. I, p. 22*cv*.

Manuscript parts, some autograph, bound with parts for *Mélologue*, q.v. below, no. 55. **F–Pc** D 16474 consists of 7 ms. parts for chorus used in the first performance. First performed 7 November 1830, then used as no. VI of *Mélologue*. A manuscript fragment of the score in **F–Pc** Rés F 1040 was prepared as an example for the *Traité d'instrumentation* (1843).[50]

53. Grande Ouverture du Roi Lear

Date: April-May 1831 (aut)

Source:
Autograph score, **F–Pbuffetaud**, 83 pp., autograph fair copy with some revisions.

Facsimile of a page of the score in Léon Constantin, *Berlioz* (Paris, 1934), opp. p. 166.

54. Intrata di Rob-Roy MacGregor

Date: May–July 1831 (aut: *Roma 1832*)

Source:
   Manuscript score, F-Pc ms 1512, numbered pp. 72-167 (71 title, 168-70 blank), scribal copy with autograph title.

   F-Pc mss. 1511-1512bis are bound together and paginated consecutively.

   Berlioz reports having finished *Rob-Roy* in a letter to Ferdinand Hiller of 1 January 1832 (**BerCG** 256), though it may have been revised at a later time.

55. Le Retour à la Vie
Mélologue en Six Parties
Later called *Lélio*
(text by Berlioz)

Forming a sequel to the *Symphonie fantastique*, no. 48.
N.B.:   See also *Fantaisie dramatique sur La Tempête, drame de Shakespeare* (1830; no. 52).

Introduction
   I.   *Le Pêcheur. Ballade imitée de Goethe*;
   II. *Choeur d' ombres irritées;*
   III. *Scène de brigands;*
   IV. *Chant de bonheur;*
   V.   *Les Derniers Soupirs de la harpe. Souvenirs;*
   VI. *Fantaisie dramatique sur La Tempête, drame de Shakespeare;*
Plus spoken dialogue.

55A. VERSION I.

Date: May-July 1831 (let)

Sources:
   Autograph score, F-Pc ms 1511, 70 numbered pp., autograph fair copy with some revision.

Contents:
      Introduction (piano solo), p. 1;
      Le Pêcheur, Ballade imitée de Goethe, pp. 1–6;
      N° 2 / Choeur d'ombres irritées, pp. 9–20 (7 title, 8 blank);
      N° 3 / Scène de Brigands, pp. 23–54 (21 title, 22 blank);

Chant de bonheur N° 4, pp. 55–66;

N° 5 / Les derniers Soupirs de la Harpe... / Souvenirs... ; /
pp. 67–69 (70 blank).

Manuscript parts, some autograph; F–Pc ms 17464, partially
autograph part for piano 4-hands, 21 numbered pp., pp. 1–11
autograph, the rest by a copyist; F–Pc ms 17465, 31 orchestra parts,
autograph, with later revisions entered by Rocquemont and others.
The music for *La Tempête* in each part is generally in the hand of a
copyist; these are the original parts (November 1830), on greyish
paper, whereas the other fascicles are on white paper. Berlioz,
however, copied three of the new parts; violin I.2, violin I.2*bis*, and
violin II.4 also F–Pc D 16474, 6 ms. parts for chorus of *La Tempête*
(original parts, used in 1830); F–Pc D 16475, 4 ms. parts for the
soloists; *Chant de bonheur... Harpe et chant*, titled and revised by
Berlioz; *Le chef des Brigands*, titled by Berlioz; two identical copies,
one marked *Horatio*, the other marked *Piano* for *Le Pêcheur*. In
Horatio's part the German words from m. 21 on are
filled by Berlioz.

Published libretto, F–Pc Rés 1924 (Paris: Schlesinger, 1832); a
libretto preceded by the program of the *Symphonie fantastique*.

Published excerpts, Paris: M. Schlesinger, [1833]. Three
excerpts, all arranged for piano and voice: *Le Pêcheur* (pl. no.
M.S.1389), *Chant de bonheur* (pl. no. M.S.1390), *Scène de brigands*
(pl. no. M.S.1392).

All of the important decisions involved in the composition of
the *Mélologue* had been made by July 1831 (see **BerCG** 233, 234),
that is, the composer had drafted the words and decided to reuse old
music. He still had not received the page from *La Mort d'Orphée*
necessary for the completion of the autograph score on 3 December
1831 (**BerCG** 250), so he could not have drafted the complete
definitive version until after that time. The published libretto
includes the note: *"Montagnes d'Italie—Juin 1831."*

[55B. VERSION II: *Lélio*, January 1855.]

56. Méditation religieuse
Paroles d'après Thomas Moore
(text by Thomas Moore, transl. Louise Sw. Belloc)

56A. VERSION I: for Voice and Winds

Date: August 1831 (aut)

Source: LOST

Refs.: dated autograph, **F–Pc** ms 1187 [1848]; **BerCG** 256: Rome, 1 January 1832, to Ferdinand Hiller.

The autograph of the version used for *Tristia*, **F–Pc** ms 1187, carries the date 4 August 1831. Such a precise dating on so late a manuscript implies that the composer was working from an original copy, and thus that date has been adopted for the date of composition.

The letter to Ferdinand Hiller mentions an accompaniment of seven wind instruments.

[56B. VERSION II: for Chorus and Orchestra, late 1848.]

57. Choeur
(text by Berlioz)

Date: Late September 1831

Source: LOST.

Ref.: **BerCG** 256: 1 January 1832, to Ferdinand Hiller.

In his letter to Hiller, Berlioz describes the work as *"un choeur de toutes les voix, improvisé (comme on improvise) au milieu des brouillards, en allant à Naples, sur quatre vers que je fis pour prier le soleil de se montrer."*

58. Choeur d'anges
(text anonymous)

Date: Late 1831 (let)

Source: LOST.

Ref.: **BerCG** 256: 1 January 1832, to Ferdinand Hiller.

In his letter to Hiller, Berlioz describes the work as *"un* choeur d'anges *pour les fêtes de Noël."*

59. Quartetto e Coro dei Maggi
(text anonymous)

Date: early 1832 (aut)

Source:
   Manuscript score, **F-Pc** ms 1512*bis*, pages numbered 172-89 (171 title, 190 blank), scribal copy with autograph title. Pagination consecutive with mss. 1511 and 1512.

60. La Captive
Orientale
(text by Hugo, from *Orientales*)

60A. VERSION I: for Voice and Piano

Date: February 1832 (aut, let)

Sources:
   Autograph scores: **F-Pc** ms 1173, 1 fol. (verso blank and unlined), autograph fair copy; **US-NYcu** Berlioz collection, 1 fol. (verso blank), autograph fair copy; **US-NYkallir**, 1 bifolio (1^r blank, 2^v blank).

60B. VERSION II: for Voice and Piano

Date: c. 1832 (ded)

Source:
   Autograph score: **F-G** Rés R 10759, fols. 62^v-64^r of a miscellany, part printed, part manuscript of guitar songs.

   The same miscellany includes on fols. 64^v-65^v another autograph, this one a song with guitar titled *Restons ici, Nocturne à deux voix*. It may conceivably be a composition of Berlioz, but the general style suggests that it is merely a copy of an anonymous composition.

60C. VERSION III: for Voice, Cello, and Piano

Date: December 1832 (fp)

Source: PUB. Paris: Schlesinger, 1833.

   La Captive, with a cello part written by Berlioz for his friend Desmarest, was first performed at a concert of 30 December 1832, with Mme Kunze-Boulanger as soloist. Her husband sang the same work at a concert of 6 June 1833. Berlioz wrote Albert Du Boys as early as 5 January 1833 that the work was about to be published

(BerCG 307), and he says the same thing in his letter to Adèle of 23 January (BerCG 312).

60D. VERSION IV: for Soprano and Orchestra

Date: November 1834 (fp)

Source: LOST.

Ref.: Press announcement for the concert of 23 November 1834, *Gazette musicale* I/46 (16 November 1834), p. 371.

[60E. VERSION V: for Voice and Orchestra, in E Major, June 1848.]

[60F. VERSION VI: for Voice and Orchestra, in D Major, October 1848.]

61. **Le Dernier Jour du monde**
   Oratorio
   Incomplete
   (text to have been by Ferrand)

Date: April 1831–August 1832 (let)

Source: LOST

Refs.: **BerCG** 234:   Rome, 3 July 1831, to Ferrand; **BerCG** 257: Rome, 8 January 1832, to Ferrand. A later manuscript relating to this project was advertised in the *Catalogue Charavay* no. 697 (June 1957), lot 26,325, item 2.

Although it is fairly certain no new music was ever finished for this work, the plans took definite shape (since complete summaries are included in both letters to Ferrand), and Berlioz reports that he wrote some of the words.

62. **Sketchbook of c. 1832-36**

Sketches for *Dans l'alcôve sombre,* text by Hugo

Sketches for *Le Retour de l'armée d'Italie:*

   Symphonie en 2 parties

      Adieux du haut des Alpes aux braves tombés dans les champs d'Italie

      Entrée triomphale des vainqueurs à Paris.

Date: c. 1832-36

Source: LOST.

Ref.: Tiersot's description of the autograph sketchbook, oblong with 45 leaves.

The sketchbook is described in **TierB'ana** (1906), pp. 351-52, 361-62, 367-68, and 375-76. It seems once to have belonged to the Chapot collection, but is now lost. It begins as a record of various expenditures by the composer during his return journey from Rome to Paris and ends, c. 1836, with drafts of portions of *Benvenuto Cellini*. The sketch of *Dans l'alcôve sombre* (no. XX of Hugo's *Feuilles d'automne:* Paris, November 1831) occurs in physical and thus chronological proximity to entries from 1832. A leaf containing the first 3½ mm. of the third stanza *("Songe qui l'enchante")* and dedicated to Nanci Pal (**F–G** N 3298) is probably a forgery.

Contents:
From front cover:
1. Notes on travels, expenses, and impressions;
2. Verses by Hugo accompanied by some musical notation;
3. Sketch of *Dans l'alcôve sombre*;
4. Transcription of Italian peasant song;
5. Prose-plan and sketches for *Symphonie en 2 parties*, 2 pp. of title and description, 8 pp. of music.
6. Poem on Napoleon's death (inc. *"Inclinez-vous, brillants faisceaux"*);
7. Paris addresses, c. 1833;
8. Page of unidentified musical notation;
9. Sketches for *Benvenuto Cellini*, 12 pp. (2 in pencil, 10 in ink); fugal exposition of first scene (in D instead of C; 2 pp.); Teresa's first aria (2 pp.), tavern scene and chorus of master sculptors (8 pp.); transcription of text *"A Boire!,"* etc., without music.

From back cover:
10. Notes on travels;
11. Page of musical notation;
12. Margin of page removed from album;
13. Sketches for (? *"un développement de"*) *La Captive*, 3 pp.;
14. Sketches for *Marche de pèlerins* (from *Harold en Italie*);

15. Sketch for *Orgie de brigands* (from *Harold*);
16. Sketches for *Je crois en vous* [no. 70] 3 pp.;
17. 8 mm. of "an old French march";
18. Sketches for *Benvenuto Cellini*, Act I, no. 1 (Balducci and Teresa);
19. Appointments (*"Aller chez Liszt;–chez Schlesinger prendre de l'argent,"* etc. Probably c. 1836, since Berlioz has an appointment with Louise Bertin);
20. Accounts for a concert of 4 December 1836;
21. Notes on a performance of a *messe en musique*.

63. La Chasse de Lützow
Marche favorite des hussards de la Mort
(arrangement: text by Karl Theodor Körner, music by Weber)

Date: before June 1833 (fp)

Source: LOST.

Refs.: **BerCG** 342:   Paris, 30 August 1838, to Ferrand; **BerMém** Chap. XLV

The work, for 10 male voices in four parts, string quintet, and piano, was performed 6 June 1833 at a concert sponsored by *L'Europe littéraire* and again on 24 November 1833 at the Théâtre-Italien.

64. Sur les Alpes, Quel Délice!
(Le Chasseur de Chamois, Chant Suisse)
Partsong for male voices
(text anonymous)

Date: June 1833 (fp)

Source:
Autograph fragments, including a vocal score, as collette-versos in the autograph of the *Symphonie fantastique*, movt. I: score, p. 35*cv*, autograph fair copy; part for bass, titled *Mr. Klein*, p. 36*cv*, autograph fair copy.

Berlioz heard the melody in Italy, notated it, and sent it to Mme Lesueur on 2 July 1831 (**BerCG** 233), calling it at that time *le chasseur de chamois*. It was arranged in three parts for ten male singers (with an orchestral accompaniment now missing?) specifically for the concert of 6 June 1833, an announcement of which was printed in *L'Europe littéraire* of 3 June 1833. The arrangement is transcribed below in Appendix I.

A manuscript copy of the song arranged for voice and guitar is found among Berlioz's papers, **F-Preboul.**

65. Le Jeune Pâtre breton
(Le Paysan breton)
(text by Auguste Brizeux)

65A. VERSION I: for Voice and Piano (*Le Paysan breton*)

Date: before December 1833 (fp)

Sources:
Autograph scores: F-Pc ms 1175, 1 folio (verso blank), autograph fair copy; **GB-En** H. B. 5/4, 1 yellow bifolio plus a pink scrap containing the words of the third stanza, autograph fair copy for Thomas Gounet's album.

65B. VERSION II: for Soprano and Orchestra (*Le Jeune Paysan breton*)

Date: November 1834 (fp)

Source: LOST.

Ref.: **BerCG** 416: Paris, 30 November 1834, to Ferrand.

It seems likely that the orchestrated version eventually published was not heard until 22 November 1835, where it was first titled *Le Jeune Pâtre breton*. For the concerts of 23 November 1834 and 4 June 1835, the version performed probably conformed more nearly to the piano-vocal version, possibly with a solo French horn.

65C. VERSION III: for Voice, Piano, and Horn (*Le Jeune Pâtre breton*)

Date: late 1834 (ded)

Source: PUB. Paris: M. Schlesinger, February 1835.

Tiersot, in **TierB'ana** (1905), 37, mistakenly attributes the publication to 1834. Hopkinson, in **HopBib** 17, pp. 30-31, corrects the error, noting that the work was first advertised in both the *Gazette musicale* and the *Bibliographie de la France* in February 1835. The arrangement must have been prepared, then, in late 1834.

65D. VERSION IV: for Voice and Orchestra

Date: November 1835 (fp)

Source: PUB. Paris: Ad. Catelin, [c. 1839].

Hopkinson determines the date of Catelin's publication from the plate number and the publisher's address as given on the title page (**HopBib** 17, p. 31).

66. **Romance de Marie Tudor**
(text by Hugo)

Date: December 1833 (fp)

Source: LOST.

Ref.: **BerCG** 367: Paris, 21 December 1833, to Hugo; announcements of concert; program, **GB–TWmacnutt.**

67. **Les Champs**
Romance
(text by Béranger)

67A. VERSION I: for Voice and Piano

Date: April 1834 (pub)

Source: PUB. Published in *La Romance* of 12 April 1834.

[67B. VERSION II: for Tenor and Piano, September 1850.]

68. **Harold en Italie**
Symphonie en 4 parties avec un alto principal

     I.   *Harold aux montagnes. Scènes de mélancolie, de bonheur, et de joie;*
    II.   *Marche de pèlerins chantant la prière du soir;*
   III. *Sérénade d'un montagnard des Abruzzes à sa maîtresse;*
    IV. *Orgie de brigands. Souvenirs des scènes précédentes.*

Date: January–June 1834 (let)

Source:
Autograph score, **F–Pc** ms 1189, 268 numbered pages, autograph working copy, with numerous collettes, revisions, and alterations to manuscript structure.

Contents:

[I.   *Harold aux montagnes* (no title)], pp. 1-105 (106 blank);
II.   *Marche de pèlerins (N° 2) / chantant la prière / du soir,* pp. 109-43 (107 title, 108, 144 blank);
III. *Sérénade (N°3) / d'un montagnard des Abruzzes / à sa maîtresse,* pp. 147-72 (145 title; 146 blank);
IV.   *Orgie (N° 4 / final) / De Brigands,* pp. 175-267 (173 title, 174, 268 blank).

(See Facsimiles I. 1 and III .9.)

Sketches, as per Table III, below.

Published scores with autograph notations: **F-Pn** Rés Vm^7 521, proof of published edition (Paris: Brandus, 1848), corrected and slightly annotated by composer.

Published parts with autograph notation: **F-Pc** Rés F 1562, part for 1st violins, corrected by composer, **F-Pn** Rés. Vma 230 several miscellaneous parts: violin I *("dans la coulisse"),* viola, cello, harp, *cornets à pistons,*   trumpet, and triangle; **F-Pc** ms 17664, autograph oboe part *("dans le cas où on n'aurait pas de Cor anglais");* **F-Psoc.**

A fair copy of the *Marche de pèlerins* at the Conservatoire in Brussels (W 55,833) was prepared by a copyist and titled by the composer for presentation to Leopold I of Belgium; facsimile of title page in *Bulletin de la Classe des Beaux-Arts; Académie Royale de Belgique* LI, nos. 3-5 (1969), betw. pp. 42-43.

Berlioz had originally intended to write a work for solo viola and orchestra depicting *Les Dernier Instants de Marie-Stuart.*   The *Gazette musicale* of 26 January 1834 (vol. I. no. 4), p. 34, carried the following announcement of the plan:

> *Paganini, dont la santé améliore de jour en jour, vient de demander à M. Berlioz une nouvelle composition dans le genre de la* Symphonie fantastique *que le célèbre virtuose compte donner à son retour en Angleterre.*
> *Cet ouvrage serait intitulé:* Les derniers instants de Marie-Stuart, *fantaisie dramatique pour orchestre, choeurs, et alto principal. Paganini remplira pour la première fois en public la partie d'alto.*

69. Sara la baigneuse
   (text by Hugo, from *Orientales)*

   69A. VERSION I: for male Quartet and Orchestra

   Date: Summer 1834 (let)

   Source: LOST.

   Refs.: **BerCG** 408:   Paris, 31 August 1834, to Ferrand; press
   announcements for the concert of 9 November 1834, e.g. in the
   Gazette musicale, 2 November 1834, p. 356.

   Some of the manuscript orchestra parts in the group **F-Pc D**
   16468 (for Version III, no. 69C) may have been used for the first
   performance.   The version with quartet probably resembled the
   published one, with the part for first chorus sung by soloist and no
   part for a second or third chorus.

   69B. VERSION II: for Quartet, Chorus, and Orchestra

   Date: Before March 1838 (fp)

   Source: LOST.

   Refs.: **BerCG** 549: Paris, 31 March 1838, to Ludwig Rellstab; press
   announcement for the concert in *Revue et Gazette musicale* VII/72
   (13 December 1840), p. 611; printed program for the concert (13
   December 1840), **F-CSA.**

   The soloists for the quartet were Mlle. Elian, MM. Boulanger,
   Prévôt, and Alizard. The quartet part was probably the same as the
   one performed in 1834, though for the former occasion a fourth male
   voice took the top part. The reviewer, A. Specht, remarked:

   > *J'ignore si l'*Orientale *de Victor Hugo est bien orientale, mais je sais
   > que la musique faite sur ces vers par M. Berlioz peut vous donner à
   > cet égard les hallucinations les plus charmantes, et faire
   > voluptueusement rêver aux félicités les plus musulmanes. Un quatuor
   > mystérieux y dialogue d'une façon très remarquable tour à tour avec
   > le choeur et avec l'orchestre, et de ces trois éléments résultent de
   > séduisantes combinaisons dont le travail ne saurait être analysé ici
   > surtout après une seule audition (Revue et Gazette musicale VII/73
   > [17 December 1840], p. 617).*

   [69C. VERSION III: for three Choruses and Orchestra, October 1850.]

70. Je crois en vous
Romance
(text by Léon Guérin)

Date: before September 1834 (pub)

Source: PUB.   Published in *Le Protée* of 1 September 1834;
facsimile in **JullHB**, p. 97.

71. Le Chant des bretons
(text by Auguste Brizeux)

71A. VERSION I: for male Chorus (or Tenor solo) and Piano

Date: c. April 1835 (pub)

Source: PUB. Paris: M. Schlesinger, [c. April 1835].

[71B. VERSION II: for male Chorus and Piano, November 1850.]

72. Fête musicale funèbre
Incomplete

Date: Summer 1835, intended for the concert of 22 November 1835
(let)

Source: LOST.

Refs.: **BerC** 429: 15 April 1835, to Ferrand; **BerCG** 435: 6 May
1835, to his father; **BerCG** 439: 2 August 1835, to Adèle; **BerCG**
440: Paris, c. 23 August 1835, to Ferrand.

The work was to have had seven movements, of which Berlioz
says he composed two (**BerCG** 440):

> *J'ai commencé un immense ouvrage intitulé:* Fête musicale funèbre
> à la mémoire des hommes illustres de la France; *j'ai fait deux*
> *morceaux, il y en aura sept.   Tout serait fini depuis longtemps si*
> *j'avais eu seulement un mois pour y travailler exclusivement.... Ma*
> fête musicale *ne sera pas terminée* [in time for the November
> concert], *et, d'ailleurs, elle est pour sept cent musiciens.*

In a manuscript plan for the concert (**F-Pn** papiers divers de Berlioz,
no. 10), Berlioz outlines the composition of the orchestra: in
addition to the regular forces, 8 trumpets, 2 cornets, 8 trombones, 2
ophicléides, and 10 timpanists.

His idea for a *fête musicale funèbre* may have been an
outgrowth of his ruminations concerning *Le Dernier Jour du monde*
(no. 61) and perhaps *Le Retour de l'armée d'Italie* (in no. 62).

73. Chansonette de M. Léon de Wailly
(text by de Wailly)

Date: August 1835 (aut)

Source:
   Autograph albumleaf, S–Smf collection Rudolf Nydahl, 2 loose folios (l^r blank) from the autograph book of H. Bachimont.

   F–Pc D 1172 is a manuscript transcription of the work which seems to have belonged to Charles Malherbe; the copy includes a brief description Bachimont's album.

   The chansonette, later reworked for the *De profundis* in sc. i of *Benvenuto Cellini,* is published below in Appendix I.

74. Le Cinq Mai
Chant sur la mort de l'Empereur Napoléon
(text by Béranger)

Date: c. 1830–November 1835 (fp)

Sources:
   Manuscript parts, F–Psoc, 73 parts for chorus in different formats, used for the first and later performances;

PUB. Paris: S. Richault, [1844].

75. Grande Messe des Morts
(Requiem)
(traditional Latin text)

I.	*Requiem et Kirie. Introit;*
II.	*Dies irae. Prosa;*
III.	*Quid sum miser;*
IV.	*Rex tremendae;*
V.	*Quaerens me;*
VI.	*Lacrymosa;*
VII.	*Offertoire;*
VIII.	*Hostias;*
IX.	*Sanctus;*
X.	*Agnus Dei.*

Date: late March-June 1837 (aut)

Sources:

Autograph score, **F–Pc** ms 1509, 217 numbered pp., autograph fair copy with some revisions, collettes, and passages in the hand of the copyist Rocquemont.

Contents:

Requiem et Kirie N° 1, pp. 3-19 (1 title, 2, 20-22 blank);

N° 2 Dies irae / et Tuba mirum, pp. 25-70 (23 title, 24, 70*bis* [a-b] blank);

Quid sum miser N° 3, pp. 71-73 (70*bis*[c] title, 70*bis*[d] blank);

Rex tremendae N° 4, pp. 73-90;

Quaerens me N° 5, pp. 91-94 (94*bis*[a-b] blank):

Lacrymosa N° 6, pp. 95-133 (133*bis* blank);

Offertoire / (Domine) et (Hostias) / N°s 7 et 8, pp. 135-51 (134 title, 134*bis* blank; *Hostias* begins 149);

Sanctus N° 9, pp. 153-87 (152 title, 152*bis*, 188 blank);

Agnus N° 10, pp. 189-217 (218 blank).

Facsimile of a page from the *Dies irae* in *Berlioz,* the catalogue of an exhibition at the Bibliothèque Nationale (Paris, 1969) [CatBN], p. 116; see also Facsimiles I.2 and I.3 in the present study.

Autograph part, **F-Pc** ms 1509 (bound with autograph score), for *Bombardon* [ou] *Ophicléide en Fa.*

Autograph variant (vocal part), **F-Pmeyer,** of the *Sanctus* , mm. 1-45 for tenor and soprano solo, 3 pp. (1 bifolio; last page blank), autograph fair copy prepared for the concert of 6 April 1844. Facsimile of first page in **CatMeyer,** planche 4.

Manuscript vocal score, **F-Pc** L 10485, 268 numbered pp., scribal copy with a few notations by Berlioz. Titled *Requiem.* Matches a second vocal score without autograph notation, **F-Pc** L 91.

Manuscript orchestra parts, **F-Pc** L 17235 (*fonds du roi*); 99 parts (8 boxes) prepared by copyists. Three parts (*viola 6, 1res timbales, 2èmes timbales*) contain minor annotations by Berlioz. A sketch, possibly autograph, is found on the back of the last part in the set (*8e timbales*). The parts are signed and dated by the performers (1843, 1848). Another box, **F-Pc** L 17238, contains some miscellaneous parts prepared by German copyists (probably for the performance in Berlin described by Berlioz in **BerMém**, *"Premier voyage en Allemagne, 9ᵉ lettre"*).

Lithographed chorus parts, **F-Pc** L 17236 (*fonds du roi*), 229 lithographed parts (26 boxes; Paris: Boboeuf, 1837) prepared from manuscript masters. A proof copy of a tenor part (box J, first movement only) carries Berlioz's permission to run the edition: *"Il faut tirer 100 Soprani, 100 Basses, 100 Tenors; Bon à tirer, H. Berlioz."* A bass part (box O), corrected before the first performance, includes the autograph note: *"A corriger toutes les autres d'après celle-ci. H. B."* Finally, one copy of each part was revised by Berlioz to serve as the engraver's copy when the parts were published by Brandus in 1852 (soprano: box I; tenor: box S; bass: box Q).

Published sources for later editions (Brandus, 1852; Ricordi, 1853; and Ricordi 1867): chorus parts, **F-Pn** Vm¹ 2276 (deposition copy, 1852); revised chorus parts, **F-Pc** (*fonds du roi*) L 17237; copy of Schlesinger's edition (Paris: 1838) with manuscript and autograph revisions, **F-Pn** Rés Vm¹ 243; several published copies of the work with manuscript revisions: **F-Pc** D 937 and **F-Pc** L 11038, copies of Ricordi's edition with manuscript collettes bringing it into agreement with Ricordi's revised edition; **F-Pc** D 936, a copy of Schlesinger's edition brought into agreement with Ricordi's second edition; **F-Pn** Vm¹ 23, a copy of Ricordi's revised edition. The examples in Berlioz's *Traité d'instrumentation* are from the first version of the work.

76. Benvenuto Cellini
Opéra en deux actes et quatre tableaux
(text by Léon de Wailly and Auguste Barbier, assisted by
Alfred de Vigny)

76A. Complete opera

VERSION I: Two acts and four tableaux

Résumé of the first version:

> *Ouverture*
> *Acte I, Premier Tableau. Lundi gras:*
>
>   sc. i: *Introduction* (Balducci: *"Teresa! Mais où peut-elle être?"*... Choeur: *"Tra-la-la"*); sc. ii: *Récit. & Romance (Cavatine)* (Teresa: *"Les belles fleurs"*..."*Entre l'amour et le devoir"*); sc. iii: *Récit. & Trio* (Teresa: *"J'entends quelqu'un monter"*... Cellini: *"O Teresa, vous que j'aime plus que ma*

vie!"); sc. iv: (enter Fieramosca: *"Ce n'est pas en forçant les grilles"*); sc. v: (enter Balducci: *"Eh quoi! ma fille encor dans la salle à cette heure!"*); sc. vi: (enter Fieramosca; Balducci: *"Ah, brigand! je te tiens"*), beginning of *Final* (Choeur de vieilles femmes: *"On s'assomme chez le voisin"*); sc. vii: (enter chorus: *"Ah! maître drôle, ah! libertin!"*)

Acte I, Deuxième Tableau. Mardi gras:

sc. viii: *Récit. & Romance* (Cellini: *"Une heure encore"..."La gloire était ma seule idole"*) [added after publication of libretto, i.e. late summer 1838], *Scène et choeur* (Choeur d'ouvriers ciseleurs: *"A boire!"*); sc. ix: (enter Le Cabaretier: *"Que voulez-vous? la cave est vide"*); sc. x: (enter Ascanio: *"Un instant, un instant"*), *Air* (Ascanio: *"Cette somme t'est due par le pape Clément"*); sc. xi: (enter Fieramosca: reprise of *"Honneur aux maîtres ciseleurs"*); sc. xii: (Fieramosca, Pompeo; *"C'est trop fort!"..."Eh bien frère qu'as-tu donc?"*) *Air* (Fieramosca: *"Ah! qui pourrait me résister?"*); sc. xiii: (Balducci: *"Vous voyez, j'espère, que je suis bon père"*) *Final: Le Carnaval.*

Acte II, Troisième tableau, Mercredi des Cendres:

Entr'acte

sc. i: *Scène et choeur* (Teresa: *"Ah! qu'est-il devenu?"*... Choeur de moines: *"Vas spirituale, Maria, sancta mater, ora pro nobis"*), *Prière à deux voix et choeur* (Teresa and Ascanio: *"Sainte Vierge Marie, étoile du matin"*); sc. iii: (enter Cellini: *"Teresa! ... Ma dague en main, protégé par la nuit"*); *Duo* (Teresa and Cellini: *"Quand des hauteurs* [sic] *de la montagne"*); sc. iv: (enter Ascanio: *"Ah! maître... mon cher maître"*); sc. v: *Scène et sextuor* (enter Fieramosca and Balducci; *"Ah! je te trouve enfin"*); sc. vi: (enter Cardinal [originally, Pape]: *"A tous péchés pleine indulgence"*);

Acte II, Quatrième Tableau:

sc. vii: *Air* (Ascanio: *"Tra-la-la-la-la,... Mais qu'ai-je donc?"*); sc. viii: *Récit. & Air* (Cellini: *"Seul pour lutter"... "Sur les monts"*); sc. ix: *Choeur* (*"Bienheureux les matelots"*); [scenes x-xix deleted from 3-Act version; music removed from full score and rehearsal score to *Final*]; sc. x: (Cellini: *"Que veut ce sot avec ses fier-à-bras?"*); sc. xi: (Cellini: *"Quel contretemps que ce duel-là!"*); sc. xii: (Cellini: *"Teresa! Dieu du ciel"*); sc. xiii:

(Ascanio: *"Voici ton épée"*); sc. xiv: (Teresa: *"Quoi, ma prière est en vaine?"*); sc. xv: (Choeur: *"Peuple ouvrier, que l'atelier vite se ferme"*); sc. xvi: (enter Fieramosca; Teresa: *"O Ciel! il est mort!"*); sc. xvii: (Cellini: *"Holà! qu'est ceci?"*); sc. xviii: (Teresa: *"Ah! le calme renaît dans mon âme inquiète"*); sc. xix: (all: *"Le Cardinal!"*); sc. xx: *Final* (Fieramosca: *"Du métal, du métal, il leur faut du métal!"*).

Three-act numeration:

Act I:

Ouverture
1. *Introduction* (Balducci: *"Teresa! Mais où peut-elle être?"*);
2. *Air* (Teresa: *"Les belles fleurs"*... *"Entre l'amour"*);
3. *Duo et Trio* (Teresa: *"Cellini!"*... Cellini: *"O Teresa, vous que j'aime plus que ma vie"*);
4. *Final* (Balducci: *"A nous, voisins"*);

Act II:

Entr'acte
5. *Romance* (Cellini: *"Une heure encore"*... *"La gloire était ma seule idole"*);
6. *Scène et choeur* (Choeur: *"A boire!"*);
7. *Air* (Fieramosca: *"Ah, qui pourrait me résister?"*);
8. *Final: Le Carnaval* (Balducci: *"Vous voyez, j'espère, que je suis bon père"*);

Act III:
9. *Entr'acte et choeur* (Choeur: *"A l'atelier rentrons"*);
10. *Scène* (Teresa: *"Il n'a pas reparu"*... Choeur: *"Bienheureux les matelots"*);
11. *Air* (Ascanio: *"Tra-la-la-la-la"*);
12. *Scène et choeur* (Teresa: *"Ah! qu'est-il devenu?"*);
13. *Duo* (Teresa, Cellini: *"Quand des sommets de la montagne"*);
14. *Scène et sextuor* (Balducci: *"Ah, je te trouve enfin"*);
15. *Air* (Cellini: *"Seul pour lutter"*... *"Sur les monts les plus sauvages"*);
16. *Final: La Fonte* (Un Officier: *"Son Eminence attend"*).

Date: May 1843-September 1838 (let, fp)

Sources:

Autograph score, **F-Pc** ms 1508, 3 volumes: vol. I: 161 numbered pp., vol. II: 312 numbered pp., vol. III: 271 numbered pp., working copy revised by copyists for three-act performance and publication.

Contents (numeration matches traditional version);

Volume I:
> *1. Introduction,* pp. 1-21 (22 blank);
> *2. Récit[ative] et Air de Teresa,* pp. 23-41 (42 blank);
> *N° 3. Duo et Trio,* pp. 43-118 (old pagination; pp. 75*bis*-84 inserted erroneously; they are part of Ascanio's air in Act II);
> *Récit. A.,* pp. 120-28 (renumbered 130-39, original pp. 129-30 lack);
> *N° 4. Final,* pp. 131-53, renumbered 139-61 (162 blank);

Volume II:
> *N° 5. Romance,* pp. 1-9 (10 blank);
> *N° 6. Scène et choeur,* pp. 11-73 (new pagination);
> *Air* (Ascanio), pp. 73-113 (114 blank);
> *Récit. B.,* pp 115-18;
> *N° 7. Air* (Fieramosca), pp. 119-44 (new pagination);
> *Récit. C.,* pp. 145-46;
> *Le Carnaval* [N° 8], pp. 147-312 (313-14 blank, new pagination), of which: *Pantomime,* pp. 223-33; *Ariette d'Arlequin,* pp. 234-38; *Cavatine de Pasquarello,* pp. 240-47;

Volume III:
> *N° 9. Entr'acte et Choeur,* pp. 1-22, new pagination;
> *N° 10. Scène,* pp. 22-44;
> *N° 11. Air,* pp. 45-64;
> *N° 12. Scène et choeur,* pp. 64-111;
> *N° 13. Duo,* pp. 111-34;
> *N° 14. Scène et sextuor,* pp. 135-207;
> *N° 15. Air,* pp. 208-18;
> *La Fonte* [N° 16], pp. 219-71 (272 blank).

Manuscript libretto, **F-Pan** AJ^xiii 203, item 574, libretto submitted to Opéra; 60 fols., scribal copy with two notations by Berlioz.

Fragments of autograph score: **F-Pc** ms 1516, 6 pp. cut from the end of Fieramosca's Air in Act I (N° 7: *"... une, deux, trois"*);

fragment (marked by Berlioz *"fragment ou plutôt débris"*) in collection of Oliver W. Neighbour, London, of a scene deleted from the first version (inc.: *"Quel contretemps fâcheux"*), facsimile in *The Score* (December 1954), front cover (the modulation to D major, the 6/8 metric signature, and soprano clef show that it is a recitative preceding Ascanio's aria, now in Act III; inc. *"Tra-la-la-la-la"*).

Sketches: F-Pc ms 1177, 1 folio (verso blank); F-Pc ms 1178, 1 scrap (verso blank); other sketches as per Table III, below. In the chorus *Bienheureux les matelots,* Berlioz used a phrase he had quoted in an earlier article; see "Voyage musical" in *Italie pittoresque* (Paris, 1834-36); the passage is transcribed in example 3.19, below.

Manuscript full score of first version, F–Po A 521a, vols. I-V: includes most of the first version, but the music for Act II, sc. x-xviii is missing. There is no autograph notation.

Manuscript parts: F–Po matériel, 86 volumes of parts prepared by copyists. Several are annotated by Berlioz: violin I.1 (vols. I-II), violin II.1 (vols. I–II; the last page of vol. I carries the note: *"Corrigé HB"*), Alto I.1 (vol. I and possibly II), clarinets (vols. I–II), bassoons I (vols. I–II), and possibly others. The four volumes of music for principal violin, i.e., the leader's score, are copied by Berlioz and others. The composer copied the second violin line, many cues for the vocal parts, and occasionally some of the cello line. A set of lithographed bass parts for members of the chorus (37 parts) and a lithographed vocal score (*"M' J. Cohen / Répétiteur des Choeurs"*) are without autograph notations.

Published vocal score with autograph notation, F–Pc Rés A 521c, corrected proof of piano-vocal score (Paris: Choudens, c. 1863); see **HopBib** 67, p. 157.

[*Manuscript sources for three-act version (1852-53):* Fragment of a manuscript draft of the revised libretto, **GB–TWmacnutt**: sketch for Cardinal's new passage in Act III (no. 14; inc. *"Ah, ça démon"*) bound with Berlioz's copy of *L'Enfance du Christ* (partly ms., partly published; F–Pn Rés Vm¹ 241; cf. edn. Choudens, pp. 419-20); draft of same section F–Pn W 1 item 3 (cf. edn. Choudens, pp. 420-22);[51] fragment of a dialogue between the Cardinal and Fieramosca, Dortmund Stadt- und Landesbibliothek; exchange of correspondence with Liszt (1852-53) containing autograph notation, Weimar, Goethe-Schiller Archiv (published in **BerMC**); production notes for the last finale (London version), F–Pn papier divers de Berlioz, no 31; vocal score of three-act version, Acts I, II; **F–CSA**: Act III: **US–NYcu**

Berlioz collection; draft list of characters and scenes in three-act version, sold at Sotheby's, 11 October 1954, lot 35; lithographed chorus part for English version (Italian words),[52] F–Pc D 16487; other lithographed chorus parts, F–Preboul, titled *Le Maître Ciseleur* and containing Italian and French words; ms. performance material for excerpts, F–Pn Vma ms 808, F–Pn Vma ms 870, F–Psoc; fragment of ms. piano-vocal score, F–Pmeyer, 1 bifolio, end of Act III entr'acte (no. 9) and beginning of no. 10.[53] A second orchestra score of the three-act version was mentioned in the catalogue published with Berlioz's *Les Grotesques de la musique* (Paris, 1859):

> La grande partition inédite ne se trouve qu'à Paris, chez l'auteur, et au théâtre de Weimar. Celle qui existe à l'Opéra de Paris est dans le désordre le plus complet et ne contient point les modifications importantes que l'auteur a faites à cet ouvrage avant de le faire représenter à Weimar (p. 319).

Although this score has been lost from the opera house in Weimar, the ms. score circulated in the nineteenth century by Breitkopf's rental library may have been copied from it.

Benvenuto Cellini was virtually finished in 1837: *"j'ai fini,"* Berlioz remarks to Adèle on 22 December 1836 **(BerCG 485)**, *"il me reste seulement à écrire la scène du dénouement et à instrumenter une grande partie de la partition."* The overture was not composed until the beginning of 1838, however, and there were surely revisions after the work went into rehearsal.

The original text is found in the published libretto (Paris: Jonas, 1838).

A piano-vocal edition of nine excerpts was published in 1839 (Paris: Schlesinger); see **HopBib** 67, pp. 154-58. Berlioz's friend Auguste Morel prepared the piano reduction.

In a letter to Ferrand of 22 September 1839 **(BerCG 665)**, Berlioz mentions having copied *Bienheureux les matelots* as a gift to Ferrand's brother, but such a manuscript has never been found. The same letter includes a passage of 18 measures from the first version of the chorus of master sculptors.

Choudens' publication of the full score did not appear until after the composer's death; Hopkinson deduces a date of 1886 from the plate number (A.C. 6870). The corrected proof is in the Bibliothèque Nationale, but the corrections are not (obviously) by Berlioz, as was erroneously stated in **CatBN**, item 114, pp. 58-59.

76B. GRANDE OUVERTURE DE BENVENUTO CELLINI

Date: February 1838 (let)

Source: PUB. Paris: M. Schlesinger, May-June 1839.

77. **Erigone**
   Intermède antique
   Incomplete
   (text after Ballanche)

Date: 1835-39 (ded, see note)

Source:

Autograph fragments, **F-Pc** ms 1186, an incomplete score (ms. 1186^b), 22 numbered fols., autograph fair copy (incomplete vocal lines only); and an incomplete manuscript libretto (ms. 1186^a), 1 bifolio (4 pp.) and 1 p. text with autograph notations.

Berlioz wrote to Liszt on 8 February 1838:

> Il y a longtemps d'ailleurs que je cherche à écrire quelque chose sur l'*Erigone* de Ballanche (admirable poète!). C'est là ce que je voudrais présenter à Madame d'A.; si j'en viens à bout, ou si je trouve le temps d'y travailler, tu auras de mes nouvelles (**BerCG** 538).

The autograph and manuscript libretto annotated by the composer give practically no hint as to date, but they are on the same paper (watermark: *HP*) as a number of other works from the period, and the pages are embossed with an emblem that appeared in the late 1830s.

78. **Aubade**
   (Text by Musset)

78A. VERSION I: for Voice and 2 Horns

Date: May 1839 (aut)

Source:

Autograph albumleaf, **GB-TWmacnutt**, 1 fol. (verso blank), as an albumleaf for Monsieur de Beauchesne, dated 24 May 1839.

[78B. VERSION II: for Voice and Brasses, c. 1852]

79. Roméo et Juliette
Symphonie Dramatique
(text by Emile Deschamps)

> I. *Introduction. Combats—Tumulte—Intervention du Prince;*
> *Prologue;*
> *Récitatif choral: "D'anciennes haines endormies";*
> *Strophes: "Premiers transports"*
> *Récitatif et Scherzetto: "Bientôt de Roméo la pâle rêverie",*
> II. *Roméo seul—Tristesse—Bruits lointains de concert et de bal—Grande fête chez Capulet;*
> III. *Nuit sereine—Le Jardin de Capulet, Silencieux et désert—Les jeunes Capulets, sortant de la fête, passent en chantant des réminiscences de la musique du bal—Scène d'amour;*
> IV. *La Reine Mab ou la Fée des Songes (Scherzo);*
> V. *Convoi funèbre de Juliette:* "Jetez des Fleurs pour la vierge expirée";
> VI. *Roméo au tombeau des Capulets; Invocation—Réveil de Juliette—Joie délirante—Désespoir—Dernières angoisses et mort des deux amants;*
> VII. *Final: La foule accourt au Cimetière—Rixe des Capulets et des Montagus—Récitatif et Air du Père Laurence—Serment de Réconciliation;*
> *Choeurs et Récitatif du Père Laurence;*
> *Air:* "Pauvres enfants que je pleure";
> *Serment:* "Jurez donc par l'auguste symbole".

Date: January–September 1839 (aut)

Sources:
Autograph score, F-Pc ms 1165, 464 numbered pp. plus title page and dedication, autograph working copy with many revisions and collettes.

Contents:
> *N° 1. Introduction instrumentale. / Combats. Tumulte. Intervention du prince*, pp. 1-63 (64 blank): *Prologue / en Récitatif harmonique*, p. 27; *Strophes*, p. 46; *Moderato*, p. 51; *Scherzino vocal*, p. 52; *Andante*, p. 62;
> *N° 2. Tristesse. Concert et Bal. / Grande Fête chez Capulet / orchestre seul*, pp. 65-140;

N° 3. / *Le Jardin de Capulet,* / *silencieux et désert.* / *Les jeunes Capulets sortant de la fête* / *passent en chantant des réminiscences de la musique du bal.* / *(choeur et orchestre)* / *Juliette sur le balcon et Roméo dans l'ombre* / *Scène d'amour.* / *Orchestre seule,* pp. 143-200 (141 title, 142, 201-202 blank);

N° 4. / *La reine Mab* / *ou* / *La Fée des songes* / *Scherzo* / *orchestre seule,* pp. 205-83 (203 title, 204, 284 blank);

[*N° 5*] *Convoie funèbre de Juliette* / *choeur et Orchestre,* pp. 285-99 (300-300*bis*ᵛ blank);

N° 6. *Roméo au tombeau des Capulets.* / *Invocation,* / *Réveil de Juliette.* / *Joie délirante, Désespoir,* / *Dernières angoisses et mort des deux amants.* / *Orchestre seul,* pp. 303-44 (301 title, 302 blank);

[*N° 7*] *Final,* pp. 345-76; *Air,* pp. 377-422; *Serment,* pp. 423-62 (463 note on the composition of the work, 464 blank).

Sketches: in orchestra score, as per Table III, below, and **D-Bds** mus. ms. autogr. H. Berlioz 2, autograph draft of *Convoi funèbre* presented to Bottée de Toulmon, dated 25 June 1839 and identified by Berlioz as a *"brouillon de la scène funèbre de ma dernière symphonie"*; see Facsimiles III. 4, .5, .6, .8, and .10, below.

Autograph part, **GB-TWmacnutt,** for *Cornets à Pistons ou Ventil-Trompettes,* 2 folios; facsimile of first p. in Louise Pohl, *Hector Berlioz' Leben und Werke* (Leipzig, 1900), opp. p. 282.

Manuscript vocal score, **US-NYcu** Berlioz collection, scribal copy with a few autograph notations, titled by Berlioz.

Manuscript parts, some with autograph titles and notation: **F–Pc** D 16476, chorus parts for *Serment* (original version), 10 parts (4 for chorus of Capulets, 6 for Montagues); **F–Pc** D 16477, chorus parts for *Serment* (original version), 3 parts for *"Petit Choeur–Prologues"*; **F–Pc** D 16478, parts for *"petit choeur"* in *Premiers transports,* 3 original parts copies by Rocquemont, 2 parts copied in Germany; **F–Pc** D 16479, part for *Tenor Solo* (*"M. Dupont"*), numerous autograph notations (preserves first versions of recitatives and not subsequent version; thus served for first performances only); **F–Preboul,** parts for soloists: *Contralto, Père Laurence, Ténor solo.*

Lithographed chorus parts, **F-Pc** D 16480 (Paris: Boboeuf, 1839) prepared from manuscript masters, German words added, later revisions entered; no autograph notation.

Published score with autograph notation, **F-Pn** Rés Vm^7 522, corrected proof.

Published parts with autograph notation, **F-Pn** Rés Vma 215 (Paris: Brandus, 1847; pl. no.: B. et Cie 4598), 60 printed orchestra parts, roughly half of which were proofs, corrected by Berlioz.

Miscellaneous manuscripts: manuscript score of *Fête chez Capulet,* **F-CSA**, titled by Berlioz and presented to the King of Prussia, 25 April 1843 (mentioned in **BerMém,** *"Premier voyage en Allemagne, 9e lettre")*; performance parts for chorus, **D–DT** mus. ms. 1483; parts for chorus and soloists in a German hand, **F-Psoc**; portions of manuscript libretto in French and German, **F-Pn** papiers divers de Berlioz, no. 7.

The original text is found in the published libretto (Paris; Vinchon, 1839).

The *Strophes (Premiers transports)* were published in 1839 (Paris: Catelin) in a reduction for contralto, piano (or harp), cello, and *chorus ad libitum.* There was no recomposition, however; the appropriate parts were simply extracted from the full score. Berlioz sent an early print to Ferrand with his letter of 31 January 1840 (from London: **BerCG** 700): *"Je vous envoie le livret d'Emile Deschamps et les couplets du prologue, le seul morceau que j'aie voulu publier."*

80. Grande Symphonie funèbre et triomphale

80A. VERSION I: *Symphonie militaire,* for military band alone

    I. *Marche funèbre*
    II. *Hymne d'adieu*
    III. *Apothéose*

Date: June-July 1840 (let)

Source:

Manuscript score, partly autograph, **F-Pc** ms 1164; pp. 1-6 are autograph, followed by a signature at the end of p. 6; the rest is in the hand of the copyist Rocquemont, with numerous autograph revisions and the following exceptions: p. 71 (first page of *Apothéose*) almost entirely autograph; mm. 228-33 of movt. III autograph except for strings (pp. 106-107); and all parts for chorus, timpani, and bass trombone in movt. III autograph. Fair copy of the second version (with chorus; earlier version lost), c. 1842.

Contents:
Marche funèbre, pp. 1-52 (title p.$^{r\&v}$ unnumbered);
Oraison funèbre, pp. 54-70 (53 blank);
Apothéose, pp. 71-108.

Facsimile of title page and p. 1 in NBE 19, 97-98.

[*Sources for later versions:* Manuscript vocal score, autograph notations, F-Pc ms 17463 (English words and revisons by Berlioz); manuscript vocal parts used in Germany, F-Pc D 16489, Apothéose only; printed parts titled by Berlioz, F-Psoc (Paris: Schlesinger, October 1843, though one set was drawn from the plates somewhat earlier); autograph correction to published horn III-IV part, GB-En H. B. 219 (2-3); proofs for choral parts corrected by Berlioz, cited by Tiersot, TierB'ana (1905), p. 292.]

Optional parts for strings were added for a concert of early February 1842, and a chorus part, to a text by Antoni Deschamps, was added by 26 September 1842 (fp). For a concert in August 1844, the original words were replaced with words to celebrate the Festival de l'Industrie (*"Gloire et triomphe à l'Art vainqueur! /... Venez, héros de l'Industrie"*; cited by Tiersot in TierB'ana [1905], p. 292, transcribed by Macdonald in NBE 19, 110). A piano-vocal score published in London in 1848 contained still a third text (also transcribed in NBE 19). A newly-recovered manuscript vocal score used in London for two performances in February 1848 contains the English version of the words in Berlioz's hand.

[80B.　VERSION II: for Band, with Orchestra and Chorus *ad libitum*, February and September 1842.]

[80C. APOTHEOSE, Version III: for solo Voice, Chorus, and Piano, March 1848.]

[81-87: LES NUITS D'ETE.　Specific information on the constituent works appears in nos. 82-87.]

81. Les Nuits D'été

Collections of six songs, issued as *Oeuvre 7*
(texts by Théophile Gautier)

     I.   *Villanelle* (= no. 82);
    II.   *Le Spectre de la rose* (= no. 83);
   III. *Sur les lagunes; Lamento* (= no. 84);
   IV. *Absence* (= no. 85);
    V. *Au Cimetière; Clair de lune* (= no. 86);
   VI. *L'Ile inconnue* (= no. 87).

Date: March–late 1840 (ded)

Sources:
   Autograph scores, see below, nos. 82-87.

There is no documentation to support the commonly-held
notion that the *Nuits d'été* were begun in 1834 (see, for example
BerCG II, p. 677). *Absence* and *Le Spectre de la rose* were probably
written first, for a planned performance of 8 November 1840 (see
Revue et Gazette musicale VII/61 [4 November 1840], p. 519); the
others surely followed shortly thereafter.

    The ordering of the songs was apparently changed just before
publication; the order specified in the autographs is: *Villanelle,
Absence, Le Spectre de la rose, L'Ile inconnue,* [*Sur les Lagunes*], and
Au Cimetière.
The first edition was published by Ad. Catelin et Cie. in 1841.

[81B. VERSION II: for various Voices and Orchestra, February and
March, 1856.]

82. Villanelle

82A. VERSION I: for Voice (Mezzo-Soprano or Tenor) and Piano

Date: March 1840 (ded)

Sources:
   Autograph scores, F-P ms 1179, 1 bifolio (2[v] blank), autograph
fair copy; D-DS mus ms 978, 6 numbered pp., autograph fair copy.

    The Darmstadt manuscript was used for a facsimile that
appeared in the *Allgemeine Musikalische Zeitung* 42/46 Beilage 8 (16
November 1842). Tiersot, after Prod'homme, cites the wrong date for
the periodical; **TierB'ana** (1905), pp. 355-56.

[82B. VERSION II: for Voice and Orchestra, March 1856]

83. Le Spectre de la rose

83A. VERSION I: for Voice (Mezzo-Soprano or Tenor) and Piano

Date: mid-1840 (ded)

Source:
   Autograph score, **F-Pc** ms 1181, 1 bifolio, autograph fair copy, some revisons.

[83B. VERSION II: for Voice and Orchestra, late 1855-January 1856.]

84. Sur les Lagunes
Lamento

84A. VERSION I: for Voice (Mezzo-Soprano or Tenor) and Piano

Date: mid-1840 (ded)

Source:
   Autograph score, sold at Sotheby's, 17 June 1947. Ex collection Arthur F. Hill. Present location unknown.

[84B. VERSION II: for Voice and Orchestra, February-March 1856.]

85. Absence

85A. VERSION I: for Voice (Mezzo-Soprano or Tenor) and Piano

Date: mid-1840 (ded)

Source:
   Autograph score, **F-Pc** ms 1180, 1 bifolio (1^r title), autograph fair copy.

[85B. VERSION II: for Voice and Orchestra, February 1843.]

86. Au Cimetière
Clair de lune

86A. VERSION I: for Voice (Mezzo-Soprano or Tenor) and Piano

Date: mid-1840 (ded)

Source:
   Autograph score, **F-Pc** ms 1183, 1 bifolio, autograph fair copy.

[86B. VERSION II: for Voice and Orchestra, February-March 1856.]

87. L'Ile inconnue

87A. VERSION I: for Voice (Mezzo-Soprano or Tenor) and Piano

Date: mid-1840 (ded)

Source:

Autograph score, **F-Pc** ms 1182, 1 bifolio and 1 folio, autograph fair copy.

[87B. VERSION II: for Voice and Orchestra, March 1856.]

Chapter Two

Practical Matters

A musical manuscript is most useful as a historical document when it has been properly identified: when its date and purpose have been accurately determined, and whether or not its original structure has been altered by revisions or deletions. Although these conclusions are directly related to the music itself, they are not usually the result of musical analysis, but rather of analysis of a manuscript's physical characteristics. Calligraphic, diplomatic, and chronological criteria—the practical considerations of manuscript study—establish a proper and comprehensive identification.

1. Berlioz's handwriting

Distinguishing Berlioz's autograph from all the other hands that appear in the manuscript sources for his music should be easy enough. In fact, erroneous attribution of manuscript to the composer has been a severe problem in Berlioz research. For one thing he worked closely with his copyists, occasionally leaving portions of an autograph score to be completed by his librarian. The handwritings of Berlioz and his chief copyist, Rocquemont, are remarkably similar. Identifying the composer's handwriting is, then, not as simple as it might first seem, particularly in view of the appearance of forged documents on the open market.

The most notable characteristic of Berlioz's handwriting is its consistency; every author who has studied the hand has noticed how little it changed over the years. Julien Tiersot, describing an early autograph, remarks:

> This handwriting is Berlioz's own; it did not change from the time he wrote out these first songs (surely before his eighteenth birthday and possibly even earlier) through the day he wrote the last note of *Béatrice et Bénédict*.[1]

In his moving chapter on Berlioz's last days, Boschot reaches the same conclusions:

> His handwriting is painful to see. An admirable hand, until now, artistic and elegant, forthright, one that had not changed for fifty years. From his first autograph (1819) to those of 1868, his hand had a constant steadiness, and it recorded on the paper, without the slightest lapse, the reflexive and spontaneous

proof of a prodigiously brazen personality. . . . One trembles, one weeps before these autographs from early 1868, where the hand that had written so many masterpieces begins to vacillate like a baby's.[2]

Establishing terminal dates for documents according to characters that evolve as the composer ages is thus difficult indeed. But it is too easy to decide, as Tiersot went on to do, that a detailed analysis of Berlioz's handwriting would not be worth the trouble, and to abandon all hope of establishing datable criteria.

Berlioz's musical notation is that of a working musician; it is proper and legible but entails little superfluous decoration. Characters are small and elegantly formed, and though it is not a calligraphic hand, the overall impression is one of extraordinary neatness combined with practicality.

The earlier G-clefs take slightly more than an entire staff and are looped at the top (Facsimile II.1). Later clefs, especially the ones in the narrow staves of full orchestra scores, are smaller and more angular without the loop at the top (Facs. II.2). This pointed G-clef is one of the distinctive characters of Berlioz's penmanship. Bass clefs open into the margin and seldom go outside the upper- and lowermost lines of the staff. They tend to be well-rounded, and invariably include the two dots around the F-line (Facs. II.3 and II.4).

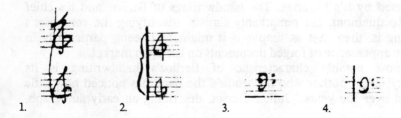

1.   2.   3.   4.

Facsimile II: 1) *Symphonie fantastique*, aut. movt. I, p. 1, violin staves; 2) *Requiem*, aut. p. 3, violin staves; 3) *Symphonie fantastique*, aut. movt. I, p. 1, bassoon staff; 4) *Requiem*, aut. p. 3, bassoon staff.

There are three different C-clefs. Berlioz most often uses the simple clef
of Facsimile II.5, but the more angular clef of Facsimile II.6 sometimes
appears and, later, the stylized clef of Facsimile II.7. Some dates for
these clefs are established later in the chapter.

5.   6.   7.

Facsimile II: 5) *Les Francs-Juges*, aut. fol. 73^V, alto and tenor lines; 6) *Symphonie
fantastique*, aut. movt. I, p. 1, viola staff; 7) *Les Troyens* aut. (F-Pc ms 1162:   *Les
Troyens à Carthage*), aut. p. 1, viola staff.

Berlioz often superposes the sharps and flats (but not naturals) in key
signatures (Facs. II.8-.10); this trait is slightly less common in
manuscripts after 1845 or so. The upper portion of the C and ₵ used in
metric signatures is usually concave (Facs. II.11-.12). Other metric
signatures occur from the earlier manuscripts on with a slash between the
two numbers, as though a fraction (Facs. II.13-.14). The signature—clef,
sharps or flats, and including the metric indication—is the hallmark of an
authentic manuscript.

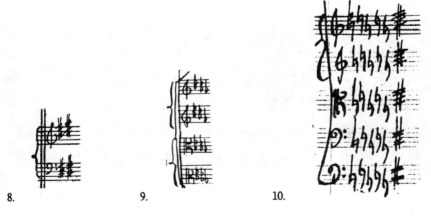

8.   9.   10.

Facsimile II. 8) *Harold en Italie*, aut. p. 112, harp staves; 9) *Requiem*, aut. p. 112 (first
page of *Sanctus*), violin and viola staves; 10) *L'Invitation à la valse*, aut. (F-Pn Vm^7 Rés
664), fol. 16^V, strings staves.

11.   12.   13.   14.

Facsimile II. 11) *Requiem*, aut. p. 112, cello and contrabass staves; 12) *Symphonie fantastique*, aut. movt. I, p. 1, violin staves; 13) *Les Francs-Juges*, aut. fol. 57^r (first page of *Choeur de bergers*), violin and viola staves; 14) *Le Spectre de la rose*, aut. p. 1, piano part.

Noteheads are neatly formed, with two distinctive strokes for white notes. Practically all noteheads in the period under consideration are carefully rounded, although one of the tendencies in Berlioz's later manuscripts may be toward flat noteheads written with a single stroke (e.g. in a fragment from *L'Enfance du Christ* given in facsimile in **JullHB** p. 233). He tends to beam groups of eighth-notes slightly before the end of the stems, leaving ragged beams. All stems and flags are to the right of the notehead (Facs. II.15).

Facsimile II. 15) *Symphonie fantastique*, aut. movt. I, p. 35c.

Berlioz's music script is, in short, simple and easy to read. Perhaps its most striking general characteristic is its strict vertical orientation (see, for example, Facs. I.2). The overall appearance of a manuscript, when the musical symbols are posed on horizontal staff-lines, is strongly perpendicular, lending the elegance that so impressed Tiersot and Boschot.

The composer's letters are more highly stylized than his musical symbols. The letter *d*, for example, has no vertical stroke; instead there is a loop that generally begins well to the left of the lower part of the character. Instead of retracing the loop, he always broke his stroke before beginning the next letter (Facs. II.16-.18). The upper case letters are equally distinctive, particularly *P*, *S* and *T* (Facs. II.19-.25). The perpetrator of the recent forgeries recognized this characteristic of Berlioz's hand and used these upper case letters as often as he could.

16.

17.

18.

Facsimile II. 16) *Symphonie fantastique*, aut., movt. IV, title page (beneath *collette*); 17) Ibid.; 18) *Les Troyens à Carthage*, title page.

Prologue

19.

Partition

20.

Premiere partie

21.

Marche du Supplice

22.

23.

Facsimile II. 19:   *Les Troyens à Carthage*; title page;   20) *Symphonie fantastique*, movt.
IV, title page (*collette*); 21) Ibid.; 22)   Ibid.; 23) *Symphonie funèbre et triomphale*, title
page.

24.

25.

Facsimile II. 24) *Les Francs-Juges*, aut. fol. 73^V; 25) *Benvenuto Cellini*, aut. title page.

Most highly stylized of all are the three prominent letters of the composer's signature, *H, B,* and *z.* The *H* is formed with loops in the lower left and upper right portions of the letter, often with a third loop in the center beam. The *B* becomes progressively more pointed at the top and looped at the bottom until the symbol eventually resembles a *W* in script. The *z* invariably ends with a flourish, either to the right and up, or down and to the left. Facsimiles II.26-.28 reproduce typical signatures from the 1830s and 40s with, in II.28, exemplary *B*'s in both the signature and the word "*Benvenuto.*"

Facsimile II. 26) *Symphonie funèbre et triomphale*, title page.

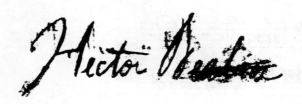

27.

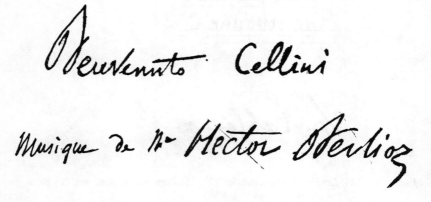

28.

Facsimile II. 27) *Waverley*, title page (signature to dedication); 28) *Benvenuto Cellini*, title page.

Berlioz had both an ordinary signature and an ornamental one that he often put on title pages; two examples of the latter appear in Facsimiles II.29 and II.30 (see also the title pages of the autograph score of *La Damnation de Faust* and *Le Roi Lear*). Facsimiles II.31-.33 show some typically encountered variations in the composer's signature.

Berlioz's handwriting can usually be distinguished from contemporaneous scripts. His clefs and upper case letters, for example, are not so similar to those of his contemporaries that they should be confused. His corrections and additions to copyists' manuscripts are slightly less decorative than the scribes' own work and were, of course, always added with a different pen. In the case of a manuscript copy of *Le Spectre de la rose* (**GB-En** H. B. 5/6) where Berlioz filled in the piano part after the copyist had prepared the rest of the manuscript, the difference in the two hands is one of angle and the very slightly less neat aspect of the composer's writing.

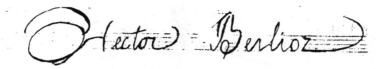

Facsimile II. 29) *Waverley*, title page (ornamental signature).

30.

31.

Facsimile II. 30) *Symphonie fantastique*, movt. IV, title page (beneath *collette*); 31) *Resurrexit*, aut. title page.

It is comparatively simple to identify Berlioz's additions to a scribal copy; detecting a forgery is much more difficult. The forger may have begun to work as early as the mid-1960s; not until 1967-68 were the first forgeries discovered. The identity of the forger is known; he had direct access to one of the important private collections of Berlioziana and filled it with forgeries, stealing at the same time some authentic manuscripts and offering them for sale. It seems possible that shortly before his arrest he hired a second, more skillful criminal to produce fake documents of stunningly high quality, complete with postmarks. The unfortunate effect of the better forgeries has been to cast doubt on the value of many manuscript sources that for one reason or another had not been rigorously authenticated before the fakes appeared.

32.

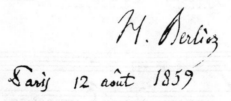

33.

Facsimile II. 32) *Symphonie fantastique*, aut. movt. IV, title page (*collette*); 33) *Les Troyens*, autograph libretto (**F-Po** Rés 589), title page.

Facsimiles of two forgeries were unintentionally published by Cecil Hopkinson, in "Two Important Berlioz Discoveries" (*Fontes Artis Musicae* XV [1968], betw. pp. 16 and 17). Here the forger has made a good imitation of Berlioz's *P*'s, a less successful one—for it is much too small—of the signature, and a shoddy attempt at the musical notation. Both documents, as long as they were considered authentic, implied false conclusions. The fragment of *Le Spectre de la rose* seemed to show that the long introduction had been written in 1834, well before the song itself was probably composed and nearly two decades before the introduction (originally written for the orchestral version) was first published in piano transcription. The other suggested that Berlioz had copiously annotated a copy of the *Mélologue* in 1860 but incorporated the annotations in none of the later issues of his work. The inscription of the leaf for *Le Spectre de la rose* should have aroused suspicion from the first, for it provides information (*"au jour de naissance de notre fils, Louis ... 15 août 1834"* / "for the birthday of our son, Louis, 15 August 1834") a good deal more likely to impress an autograph collector than to have interested Harriet. It stands to commercial reason that nearly all the forged documents include a prominent signature.

Two tiny sketchbooks (one at **F-G** N 3276; the other in a private collection) containing bits from *Béatrice et Bénédict* are much too small (approx. 12 x 10 cm.) to have actually been used for composition. The one in Grenoble has only six entries, three of them fragments of music designed to look like sketches of important motives (Ex. 2.1):

Example 2:1 Musical entries in *forged* sketchbook, **F-G** N 3276.

More amusing is the address scrawled at the end of the book:[3]

> *Estelle*
> *chez Monsieur Fornier*
> *Notaire*
> *St. Symphorien d'Ozon*

A third notebook, containing a draft of *La Mort d'Ophélie* (**F-G** N 3299) is wrongly dated 1848—the autograph, **A-Wg** A 170, comes from May 1842—and the forger's concept of a sketchbook is impractical: he has ruled two staves across the width of each oblong page, then filled the book with musical notation. Berlioz would never have sketched in a physical situation that did not allow him to see what he had just written.

A fourth forged sketchbook once existed and was purchased by Columbia University; it was subsequently returned to the vendor and presumably destroyed. One albumleaf, with the unlikely dedication, *"A Nanci Pal, ma soeur, souvenir de notre cher pays, de notre enfance; La Côte St. André, Sept. 1848,"* contains a phrase copied either from Tiersot's transcription of Berlioz's 1832-36 sketchbook or directly from the book. The page is typical of the many forged albumleaves in circulation.

Forged albumleaves, however, are relatively harmless. The forgeries of sketchbooks, fragments of musical works, and biographically significant letters are a more serious matter.[4] (Most serious of all was the theft of authentic manuscript sources. The forger seems to have been responsible for the loss of Berlioz's only authentic sketchbook and may have been involved with the theft of one of his competition fugues from the Bibliothèque Nationale. Jacques Barzun, asked to authenticate the fugue, recognized it as the property of the Bibliothèque Nationale and arranged its return.) The sad result of the scandal is that any autograph which surfaced during the last decade must be held suspect if there is the slightest irregularity in its appearance. No full autograph score, however, seems to have been affected by forged additions, and none of the important public collections, with the exception of the library at Grenoble, has acquired and kept forged documents.

In short, a document should be considered false when suspicious details combine with an unlikely overall appearance to jeopardize its usefulness. A dubious signature is one such suspicious detail, as is any inscription that contains information of greater interest to a potential collector than to the presumed dedicatee. Any new document that has extraordinary biographical implications (as did the fragment of *Le Spectre de la rose*) must be reconsidered. The authenticator must continually rely on a broad and precise knowledge of what is normal in Berlioz's authentic script, the subtle changes that occur in his characters over the years, and so on.

2. Copyists

Berlioz habitually relegated most copying of individual orchestra parts to professional copyists, having learned as early as the first rehearsal of his *Messe solennelle* (27 December 1824) not to rely on amateurs.[5] Later (25 April 1825; **BerCG** 46), he reports to his father that he has spent part of his allowance on copying and paper, presumably for the revised version of the Mass. There are numerous other references in the early correspondence to expenditures for copy. He had parts professionally copied for portions of *Les Franc-Juges* (**BerCG** 70) and at about the same time promised Ferrand he would order a copy of the revised *Resurrexit* (1828).[6]   Two thousand three hundred copied pages of performance material were required for the first performance of the *Symphonie fantastique*, at a cost to the already bankrupt young composer of 400 francs (**BerCG** 162).   In Rome, he engaged two or possibly three different Italian copyists to prepare the scores required by the Conservatoire as *envois*.[7]

Until his return from Rome, however, professional copying was an expensive luxury that he avoided whenever possible by preparing his own parts.   He seems to have copied the master parts for several movements of *Huit Scènes de Faust* (see **BerCG** 128) as well as nearly all the parts for his *Mélologue* (see **BerMém** Chap. XLIV, and **BerCG** 256 and 284). Autograph parts from both sets survive.

Back in Paris, writing for ever larger numbers of performers, Berlioz required large quantities of legible copy quickly produced.   By the mid-1830s, he had little to do with the preparation of parts, having engaged Rocquemont as his chief copyist.   Rocquemont eventually became Berlioz's librarian, stage manager, and trouble shooter.   By the late 1830s, the composer had become dependent on him to take care of all the practical problems of organizing concerts. He was even asked at times to supervise rehearsals: in a letter of 14 February 1850 (**BerCG** 1304), Berlioz asks Rocquement to make sure the *Ronde des paysans* from *La Damnation de Faust* is properly rehearsed despite the composer's absence.

Several letters and notes from Berlioz to Rocquemont are preserved, among them a lengthy list of instructions concerning the 1850 performance of the *Requiem*. It deals exclusively with practical arrangements for the concert:

Vendredi, 26 avril [1850]	Friday, 26 April [1850]
Mon cher Roquemont [sic],	My dear Rocquemont,
Veuillez aller trouver Mr Leroy à la bibliothèque du Conservatoire et le prier de ma part de vous prêter toute la musique de mon Requiem dont vous ferez apporter les parties de Soprani chez Sax. La répétition des Tenors et des Basses ayant lieu Lundi prochain à 9 h. dans la grande salle du Conservatoire, vous pourrez laisser ces parties chez le concierge du Conservatoire. Celles de Soprani devront être chez Sax car la répétition des femmes et enfants aura lieu	Be so kind as to go and find Mr. Leroy at the library of the Conservatoire and ask him on my behalf to lend you all the music for my Requiem, of which you can have the soprano parts taken to Sax's. Since the rehearsal is taking place next Monday at 9:00 in the hall at the Conservatoire, you can leave these parts with the concierge at the Conservatoire. The soprano parts will have to be at Sax's, for the rehearsal of women and children will be on Monday at

chez lui Lundi à la même heure que les hommes. Vous [les] *ferez porter rue de Boursault 19. Veuillez vous charger de faire porter un piano et une partition de chant chez Sax pour ce* jour-là.* *Un autre piano et une autre partition de chant* à la grande Salle dite *du Conservatoire dont M* G. Delavigne, Conservateur du garde meuble national, m'a donné la disposition pour ce jour-là. De plus veuillez aller demander de ma part à M* Defitte à la salle Ste. Cécile, s'il veut bien nous prêter tous ses pupitres pour la répétition et l'exécution de mon Requiem qui auront lieu à St.-Eustache*

Le Jeudi à 2 h;
et Le Vendredi à 10 h.

D'autre part veuillez voir M de Bèze, cour d'Orléans, rue St.-Lazare, et lui demander s'il veut bien nous prêter ses pupitres qui doivent être chez Sax. Il nous faudra en tout 100 pupitres plus 3 pour les chefs* Total *103.*

Si l'ensemble des pupitres de M Defitte et de M* de Bèze ne suffisait pas à fournir ce total, vous auriez recours au tapissier de la rue de la Tour d'Auvergne qui nous louerait l'excédent. Il demeure presqu'au coin de cette rue et de la rue des Martyrs.*

Veuillez informer ainsi M Moncotel (14 rue Croix des Petits Champs) du jour et de l'heure de la répétition générale qui aura lieu à St.-Eustache le Jeudi à 2 heures et pour laquelle il aura à faire porter à l'Eglise:*
        20 contrebasses
        21 violoncelles
62   *22 altos*
[sic] *22 violons*
        8 paires de Timbales avec leurs
          baguettes à tête d'éponge
        2 grosses caisses
        3 paires de cymbales
        2 tamtams.

*Pour les pianos, il faut voir de ma part Mlle Laquianthe au magasin d'Erard, rue du Mail 13.

the same time as the men. You can get them taken to rue de Boursault 19. Please arrange to have a piano and a vocal score delivered to Sax's for *that day.** Another piano and another vocal score in what they call the hall of the Conservatoire, which M. G. Delavigne, the supervisor of the state furniture warehouse, gave me the use of for that day. Also go ask M. Defitte at the salle Ste.-Cécile, on my behalf, if he will lend us all his stands for the rehearsals and performances of my Requiem, which will take place at St.-Eustache

Thursday at 2:00
and Friday at 10:00.

Also go and see M. de Bèze, cour d'Orléans, rue St.-Lazare, and ask him to lend us his stands, which should be at Sax's. Altogether we need 100 stands plus three for the conductors, making a total of 103.

If the stands belonging to M. Defitte and M. de Bèze are not enough to make the total, you can resort to the upholsterer on the rue de la Tour d'Auvergne, who will rent us the rest. He lives almost at the corner of that street and the rue des Martyrs.

Please tell M. Moncotel (14 rue Croix des Petits Champs) of the date and time of the dress rehearsal, which will be at St.-Eustache on Thursday at 2:00; for this he will have to have carried to the church:
        20 contrabasses
        21 cellos
62   22 violas
        22 violins
        8 pairs of timpani with sponge-
          headed sticks
        2 bass drums
        3 pairs of cymbals
        2 tamtams

*For the pianos, you have to see on my behalf Mlle Laquianthe at Erard's salesroom, rue du Mail 13.

Je vous prie, mon cher Roquemont, de vous charger de ces détails, assuré que je suis que vous n'oublierez rien et que tout sera en ordre.	I hope, dear Rocquemont, that you will take care of these details, since I am convinced you won't forget anything and that all will be in order.

Tout à vous
H. Berlioz

Best wishes
H. Berlioz

(F-G N 2920; published in 1978 as **BerCG** 1321)

The peremptory tone of this letter suggests that the two enjoyed a closer professional than personal relationship, yet in the *Mémoires* Berlioz refers to Rocquemont with genuine affection:

Je consulte de l'oeil mon bibliothécaire, M. Rocquemont, homme d'une rare intelligence, d'une activité infatigable, et dont l'amitié pour moi aussi réelle que la mienne pour lui, l'a fait, en maintes circonstances analogues, me rendre de ces services qu'on n'oublie jamais (Chap. LIII).	I glanced inquiringly at my librarian, M. Rocquemont (a man of uncommon intelligence and a tireless worker who out of regard for me—as sincere as mine for him—has rendered me unforgettable services on many occasions) (BerMemCairns).[8]

Biographical data concerning Rocquemont are sparse. He never listed himself in a Bottin or other directory, not even in the list of copyists in a musician's directory with which Berlioz was associated.[9]   His family relationship to a more famous calligrapher of the same surname, the F. Rocquemont who wrote a *Méthode complète & infaillible pour arriver promptement à la perfection des écritures commerciales et administratives* (Paris, 18th edn., 1863) is unclear, but they were almost surely different people.[10] The music copyist may have sung in performances of the *Scène héroïque* (1833) and the *Requiem*, for his signature appears on top of tenor parts that seem unrelated to his scribal duties.

Rocquemont first copied for Berlioz when he prepared some of the parts for the *Scène héroïque*. Shortly afterward, when Berlioz decided to rewrite the part for viola solo in the first movement of *Harold en Italie*, he had Rocquemont attach and clef the necessary collettes in the autograph score. By 1840, the scribe had become Berlioz's chief copyist, directing the copying of all the performance parts and adding occasional passages in the autograph scores. He became indispensable when Berlioz began to travel outside France. Although he never accompanied Berlioz, he carefully organized and labelled every part the composer took with him. Before each trip he would bring the parts up to date by adding revisions entered in the score since the previous performance; few of the preserved orchestra parts are without some annotations in Rocquemont's hand. (In one published score of the *Requiem*, undoubtedly used for conducting by Berlioz himself, Rocquemont had attached to the front cover a list of personnel for the four brass choirs.) While Berlioz was away from Paris, Rocquemont acted as his Parisian contact when emergency parts were needed or when an errand had to be run. A letter to Amédée Méreaux of 29 July 1854 (**BerMC**, p. 223) shows that one went directly to Rocquemont for access to the composer's manuscripts: "M. Rocquemont controls everything pertaining to my musical library."[11] His script occasionally appears in scores and parts of works by other composers, notably in a few passages of the score of Louise Bertin's *Esmeralda* (1836).[12]

Rocquemont was also affiliated with the copying service at the Opéra; his job with Berlioz, of course, occupied only a part of his time. The general account book, or *Grand Livre*, of the Opéra for 1839-41, includes the entry (p. 121; November 1839):

Rocquemont, copie de morceaux de musique p[ou]r le Festival de la Toussaint . . . . 247 [*fr*].

In a letter to Urbain of c. April 1845 [**BerCG** 951], Berlioz mentions that Rocquemont can be found at the *bureau de copie de l'Opéra*. (Payment records to individual copyists were not ordinarily kept at the Opéra, however; each month a sum of money was allotted to the head copyist, Leborne, who distributed it to individual scribes according to the number of pages each had copied that month.)

In the 1840s, Rocquemont began to use a rubber stamp to identify parts he had copied or corrected (Facsimile II.34).

Facsimile II. 34: Rocquemont's rubber stamp.

There were actually two stamps: on parts and score for the *Symphonie funèbre et triomphale*, Berlioz's orchestration of *L'Invitation à la valse*, and *La Damnation de Faust*, the address is *rue des Martyrs, 52*. On the parts for *L'Enfance du Christ*, the address has become *38* on the same street, and Berlioz cites the same address in his letter to Méreaux of 29 July 1854. From 1854 on, Rocquemont's parts, including the large set for *L'Impériale* (1855) bear the later address. Parts copied before 1840 have no stamped address, unless they were later overhauled, but Berlioz directs a letter of 28 October 1839 (**BerCG** 672) to:

> *Monsieur Rocquemont*
> *N° 6 petite rue Royale*
> *(près de la barrière Pigalle)*
> *à Montmartre*

Distinctive characters of Rocquemont's hand are the narrow, thin-lined G-clefs, the vertical sharps and stems, and the fine, unslanted italic script. The quarter rests most often lie horizontally in the third space, and the vertical C-clef, with cross beams of unequal length, is easily recognized (see Facs. I.3, staves 1-9, 28-30).[13] Rocquemont's script is distinct from that of other Parisian copyists who worked for Berlioz, but it is similar enough to the composer's fair handwriting to cause some confusion. The two men may even have competed to see who could produce handsomer manuscript. In a letter cited above (p. 7), Berlioz remarks of his score of *Les Troyens*: "I dare my copyist to do anything like it!"

Rocquemont did not have a school of young copyists, but rather subcontracted the work he could not handle himself. The scribes he hired were professionals; their calligraphy is skilled and stylized, and they do not attempt to imitate Rocquemont's hand. Sub-contracting of copying assignments was a typical arrangement in nineteenth-century Paris; each performing group or institution had a librarian whose responsibility was to see that his organization always had proper parts. The librarian would present a bill for each extraordinary copying job based on the total number of pages copied, and he would distribute the funds to his assistants accordingly. The account books at the Opéra, for example, show that Amboise-Simon Leborne (1797-1866), the *chef de copie* at the Opéra from 1829 until his death, received payment for practically all the copying of scores and parts. His distinctive hand, however, occurs no more often than the hands of a dozen other copyists, including Rocquemont, so he must have hired assistants. The same system was used at the Conservatoire, where Leborne and a certain Fernière directed most of the copying assignments.[14, 15]

In a note on the back of an ophicléide part for the *Requiem*, Berlioz specifically requires Leborne's services:

Aller à la copie de l'Opéra pour faire copier	Go to the copying department at the Opéra
par Leborne ce qui manque pour Wartel et F.	to have Leborne copy the missing parts for
Prévost et pour les 4 1^r Tenors dans le choeur	Wartel and F. Prévost and for the four first
de vieilles femmes.	tenors in the chorus of old women.

The note refers to parts for *Benvenuto Cellini*, for which the office of copy at the Opéra was of course responsible.

Some two dozen different hands can be identified in the manuscript parts for Berlioz's music. Rocquemont, familiar with Berlioz's demanding requirements for cues and rehearsal letters, generally prepared the master parts. For the *Requiem* and many later works he copied most of the wind parts as well. He would then distribute the masters for duplication in the required number. Rocquemont usually hired the same copyists to assist him; several hands occur repeatedly in the Berlioz parts, from the *Scène héroïque* through *L'Impériale* and *L'Enfance du Christ*. Additionally, Rocquemont supervised the preparation of lithographed choral parts of the *Requiem, Roméo et Juliette, Benvenuto Cellini* (printed in Paris for the London production 1852-53), and the *Te Deum*.

Berlioz was careful to maintain amicable relations with his copyists, convinced of their importance in assuring a smooth sequence of rehearsals for a new work. Rehearsals cost too much to have them ruined, as they often must have been in the nineteenth century, by errors in the parts. Berlioz carefully estimated the cost of professionally prepared copy into the projected list of expenses for each concert.[16] One of his greatest concerns when the government cancelled the first performance of the *Requiem* was that the copyists had not been paid (see for example **BerCG** 512). The system he developed, in which the copying was always supervised by the same, well-trained chief copyist, resulted in clear, easy-to-use parts, copiously annotated with rehearsal letters and orchestra cues.[17] Berlioz's insistence on carefully prepared performance material is not the least of his many contributions to the technique of producing concerts.[18]

There are two reasons why familiarity with Berlioz's copying establishment is indispensable to a study of sources for his works. The first is that parts prepared by copyists are valuable in reconstructing how certain works changed over the years. Since they were used almost exclusively for performances supervised or conducted by Berlioz, every annotation and change may reflect a decision of the composer himself. A vocal score of *Roméo et Juliette* prepared by Rocquemont from the original full score, for example, was revised by cross-hatching the deleted passages. The corresponding pages of the full score were cut from the manuscript and thrown away. Rocquemont's manuscript preserves, then, a number of passages from the original version that otherwise would be lost. Similarly, the performance material for *Benvenuto Cellini* permits a reconstruction of the Paris version, whereas the autograph full score was radically altered for the familiar Weimar version and for the subsequent publication. Moreover, revisions in the manuscript and lithographed performance material are often easier to spot than they are in the full scores. In short the manuscript parts, at least the ones prepared in Paris by Rocquemont and his assistants, are primary sources of the greatest importance in determining how Berlioz's works evolved.

The first-hand association of Berlioz with performances of his works is to some extent the cause of erroneous identifications of manuscript sources as autographs. An awareness of the system he had set up for the preparation of manuscript parts can usually prevent these false attributions. Berlioz himself did not copy many parts after the *Mélologue*, and, though he annotated a large number of scribal parts, he did not proofread them all himself. Changes added to manuscript parts by a second hand are more often than not in the hand of Rocquemont. In a manuscript of the *Traité d'instrumentation* at the Bibliothèque Nationale, for example, there is no autograph music or text, though the musical examples have been thought to be in the composer's hand.

3. Papers and Watermarks

From the moment a composer puts musical symbols on a piece of paper, a relationship is established such that changes in the musical text are reflected in the physical makeup of the document. Irregularities in a manuscript's structure—fascicles with uneven numbers of pages, new watermarks, remnants of pages—usually signal a change in the music as well, most often a revision entered by the composer himself.

Berlioz bought small quantities of staff paper as necessity demanded, seldom buying more paper than he could use in a few weeks. With few exceptions his works appear on staff paper well-suited to the genre: no songs occur on thirty-two-staff paper nor symphonies on twelve-staff paper. Occasionally he filled every staff on the original page and then went back to add an instrument, for which he then had to add a staff in the lower margin (e.g., the fourth movement of the *Symphonie fantastique*, where he added an ophicléide part). At times he seems determined to fill up the paper, and he obviously took pleasure in the appearance of a large piece of paper with notes on every staff. In Chapter IV of the *Mémoires* he remarks:

Un jour, une feuille de papier réglée à vingt-
quatre portées me tomba sous la main. En
apercevant cette grande quantité de lignes, je
compris aussitôt à quelle multitude de
combinaisons instrumentales et vocales leur
emploi ingénieux pouvait donner lieu, et je
m'écriai: "Quel orchestre on doit pouvoir
écrire là-dessus!"

One day I came across a piece of paper with
twenty-four staves ruled on it. When I saw
that great array of lines I suddenly became
aware of the multitude of instrumental and
vocal combinations that lay open to an
ingenious hand, and I exclaimed: "What an
orchestra one could write down on that!"
(BerMemCairns).

The fact that Berlioz remembered (or invented) this incident from his childhood may indicate that he was tempted from the first to write for large performing groups but only gradually discovered the techniques for doing so.

Staff paper was manufactured by individual retailers in Paris, who printed or templated the lines on varying grades of paper. The inexpensive paper was green or blue (colors which disguised its inferior quality); practically all the manuscript performance parts from nineteenth-century Paris are on greenish-blue paper. Berlioz also used French white papers of medium quality for his less important scores. The fine papers were generally English or Dutch. Most of the orchestra scores from *Harold en Italie* on are made up of imported paper.

Many of Berlioz's papers from 1832 on are embossed with the name of a stationer he frequented, Dantier fils. The emblem is an oblong octagon bearing the name in the center and the address around the outside: *DANTIER FILS, rue du Temple 106*. It appears in upper left corners of pages, most pronounced (obviously) at the beginning of a gathering than anywhere else.[19] Two other embossings occasionally appear: *Lard-Esnault, 25, rue Feydeau*; and *Charnez, rue du Temple, 106*. Dantier succeeded Charnez as owner of the establishment on the rue du Temple in 1838 or so.[20] The embossed seal found on many of the parts for *La Fuite en Egypte* no longer includes *succ. de Charnez*; an occasional manuscript is embossed *Boul. du Temple, 35*; and in the *Bottin* of 1859 the address is given as *Boul. du Temple, 33 & 35*.[21]

Most of the staff paper Berlioz used was watermarked. The variety of watermarks and formats supports the contention that he generally bought small quantities of paper to use for specific tasks. The scores from the period are generally on upright quarto paper (prepared from sheets four times as large as the pages are). Thus a sheet watermarked as follows:

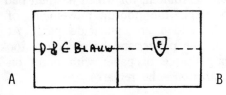

A   B will, when folded, cut, and gathered into upright fascicles, yield the following array of individual pages:

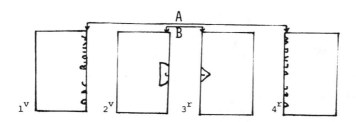

A considerable number of Berlioz's manuscripts were split and trimmed for binding, with hinges attached to the individual leaves. On those pages only the vestiges of a watermark can be distinguished:

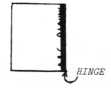

One of the manuscript papers Berlioz often used, however, was prepared from sheets of a smaller format, so the watermark (the letters *HP* on one side and a bell containing the same letters on the other) appears in the center of the page.

Table II is a list, with tracings, of the watermarks in Berlioz's autograph scores from the period under consideration.

TABLE II

WATERMARKS IN BERLIOZ'S ORCHESTRAL SCORES
(and other selected mss.)

Manuscript (call no.; date)	Watermark
Les Francs-Juges (**F-Pn** Rés Vm² 177; 1828) *Fugue* (**F-Pn** W 33, item 10; 1828)	B + bunch of grapes

La Mort d'Orphée (**F-Pn** Rés Vma ms 1; September 1828?) B + lion
Scène héroïque (**F-Pc** D 944; 1828?)

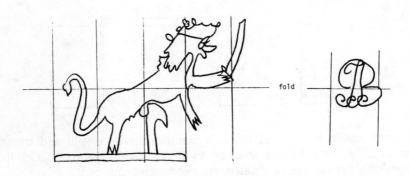

Scène héroïque, fols. 4^{r-v} and 5^{r-v}.

Similar marks in *Waverley* (**F-Pc** ms 1507; May 1828), pp. 30*bis*, 31, 32, 35, and 36 (other fascicles unmarked); and *Herminie* (**F-Pc** ms 1185; July 1828), pp. 95-110 (other fascicles marked as cited below).

Herminie (**F-Pc** ms 1185; July 1828) *Farge senerol* [?] + cross

Herminie, pp. 5-6, 41-42.

Huit Scènes de Faust, manuscript parts   *M* + bunch of grapes
      (**F-Pc** ms 17466)

Le roi de Thulé (**US-NY**pm)

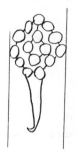

Huit Scènes de Faust, violon II.2.

Autograph parts have no watermark.

Cléopâtre (**F-Pc** ms 1505; July 1829)   Illegible name in script +
                                              globe, cross, and letter *F*

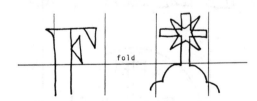

Cléopâtre, fol. 14^{r-v}.

Symphonie fantastique (**F-Pc** ms 1188; mid-1830)

> Movement I, original fascicles   *C WISE 1828*
> Movement V, original fascicles

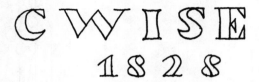

Symphonie fantastique, movt. I, pp. 39*o*-40.

Watermark distinctive on pp. 6-7, 9-10 of movt. V.

> Movement II: Roman paper described below
> Movement III: No visible watermark
> Movement IV: *BLAGONS* + shield with cross

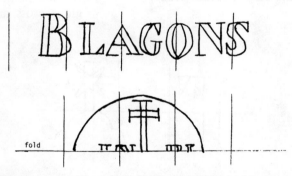

Symphonie fantastique, movt. IV, pp. 29-30 (monogram), 19-20 (emblem).

Similar watermark on orchestral parts for *Mélologue*, **F-Pc** ms 17465. Various collettes in the manuscript of the *Symphonie fantastique* watermarked with *LALIGANT* and *HP* monograms described below.

Fantaisie dramatique sur La Tempête   *LALIGANT &C AMARESQUEL 1829*
(**F-Pc** ms 1192; October-November 1830)

La Tempête, pp. 115-16, 121-22.

A few pages in the manuscript—pp. 9-10, 13-14, 23-24, 35-36, 99-100, and 111-112—are watermarked with the lion and saber (facsimile below). Page 22c^{r-v} of movement I of the *Symphonie fantastique*, a page taken from the score of *La Tempête*, is watermarked with the *LALIGANT* monogram.

La Tempête, pp. 9-10, 23-24.

Le Roi Lear (**F-Pbuffetaud**) 1831; fascicle added c. 1840).

Added fascicle watermarked *HP* + bell, described below; no watermark apparent in other fascicles.

Mélologue (**F-Pc** ms 1511; 1831)   *AL PARADISO* + shield

Rob-Roy (**F-Pc** ms 1512; 1831-32)

Quartetto e Coro dei Maggi (**F-Pc** ms 1513; 1832)

Resurrexit (**F-Pc** ms 1510; c. 1832)

Symphonie fantastique, movt. II, and certain collettes in movt. I

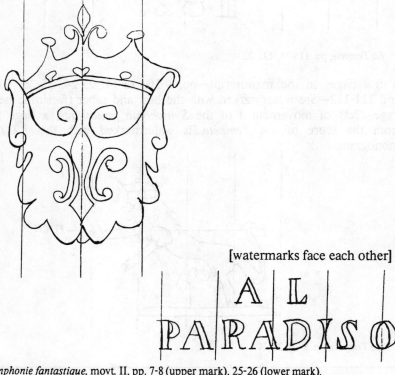

[watermarks face each other]

Symphonie fantastique, movt. II, pp. 7-8 (upper mark), 25-26 (lower mark).

Harold en Italie (F-Pc ms 1189; 1834)   *HP* + bell

Le Paysan breton (F-Pc ms 1175; 1833-34)

Roméo et Juliette (F-Pc ms 1165; 1839), 24-staff papers in aut.

Les Nuits d'été (F-Pc mss 1179-83; 1839-40)

Erigone (F-Pc ms 1186^b; c. 1840)

Symphonie fantastique, movt. I, pp. 63-64; also page of instructions to conductors (F-Pmeyer)

Barcarolle, from *Les Nuits d'été* (F-Pc ms 1182).

Same or similar watermark in later works: *La Belle Isabeau* (F-Pc ms 1515), *Invitation à la valse* (F-Pn Rés Vm^7 664), fragment of *La Tempête* copied by Rocquemont for *Traité d'Instrumentation* (F-Pc Rés F 1040), *Hélène* (VERSION II: F-Pc ms 1172).

Benvenuto Cellini (F-Pc ms 1508; 1838),   *D & C BLAUW* + shield
    original fascicles only   [facsimile on following page]

Roméo et Juliette, 30-staff paper in aut.

Requiem ophicléide part (bound with F-Pc ms 1509; 1837)

Benvenuto Cellini, orchestra parts (F-Po; 1838)

Scène héroïque, orchestra parts (F-Pc L 17239; 1833)

[watermarks on opposite pages]

Requiem, ophicléide part

The autograph of the *Requiem* is probably made up of paper manufactured by Blauw, but no watermark is apparent.

Similar watermark in ms. parts for *Sara la baigneuse* (VERSION III: **F–Pc** D 16468), and *Sérénade agreste à la Madone* (**F·Pc** ms 1166).

The two watermarks that occur repeatedly after Berlioz's return from Rome are the initials *HP* and the name *D. & C. BLAUW*. (The shield accompanying Blauw's monogram varies with the grade and size of the paper.) Dirk and Cornelius Blauw owned one of the most famous Dutch paper mills. In 1822 the name of the firm became De Erven Dirk Blauw (the heirs of Dirk Blauw), though the famous monogram persisted through the mid-nineteenth century. Only gradually did the latter name appear in watermarks.[22] Use of fine paper made by Blauw was widespread in Paris, particularly for ledgers and legal papers.[23]

Berlioz most frequently used the paper marked with a bell and the letters *HP*. These initials were associated in the seventeenth century with the merchant H. Pannkoek, whose firm still existed in the nineteenth century. It was the practice of Dutch paper makers to manufacture paper in lots specifically for sale to an important buyer, and in those cases the paper was often watermarked not with the maker's monogram, but that of the merchant. It may be that the *HP* paper was also manufactured by Blauw; two manuscripts from Berlioz's time carry both the Blauw shield and the letters *HP* (but not the bell).[24]

In the 1840s Berlioz began to buy more and more papers with English watermarks, many of which include precise dates. Pages added to the autograph of *Benvenuto Cellini*, for example, are watermarked *WHATMAN 1853*, and the manuscript of *Tristia* is marked *S. EVANS.1843*. A set of orchestra parts for *La Captive* (E-major version, F-Psoc) is marked *LET° 1847*, showing that the manuscripts cannot have been for the original performance of the song in the late 1830s. One group of revisions for *Roméo et Juliette* can be dated with confidence: the name and address of the maker appear in the margin of one page of the small green paper used for revisions: *"bei Joh. Hoffman in Prag."* Berlioz presented a series of concerts in Prague in 1846 and is known to have made substantial changes in *Roméo et Juliette* there.

Because few of the watermarks before 1843 include dates, they are not as valuable for precise dating as they are for proving that the fascicle structure of the manuscript has been altered. The most striking such case before 1840 occurs with the manuscript of the *Symphonie fantastique*, where the evidence of the watermarks leads to the only satisfactory explanation of certain stages of composition. Similarly, the watermark of a fascicle added to the autograph of *Le Roi Lear* allows those pages to be identified as revisions for the publication of 1840.

The watermark and dealer's embossed seal are not the only distinctive characteristics of a paper. Its color and texture, format, or size may also distinguish it from others. The length of the system of staves, from the top line of the first staff to the bottom lines of the last, seldom varies. (The width of the system may, however, vary or be uneven, while the size of the page itself was generally altered in the process of binding. Mechanically-drawn staves often have uneven side margins with dribbles of ink at the ends of lines.) Changes within a manuscript of any of these dimensions may signal an alteration of the musical text.

4. Dating

The ultimate goal of analyses of handwritings and papers is to increase the number of known facts about a manuscript. What is being sought, relative to other documents as well as in an absolute chronological sense, is simply an improved date for the manuscript. These dates, correctly interpreted, often make it easier to determine how any given page relates to the chronology of a musical work. It is appropriate, then, to review those characteristics of Berlioz's manuscripts that can effectively be used to date them.

First, the format of Berlioz's orchestral scores changes, most strikingly in the late 1820s. An early vocal score has upper strings on the top, then woodwinds and brass, then vocal parts, and finally cello and contrabass (e.g. *Les Francs-Juges, Sardanapale, La Tempête*). The scribal copy of the *Scène héroïque*, surely copied from an autograph source, is also in the earlier format. Moreover, the early scores are on coarse French paper of small size, and there is a general trend for the composer to use larger, finer papers as his prestige and financial condition improved. The scores of *Herminie, Cléopâtre*, and the *Symphonie fantastique*, Berlioz's earliest works in modern format, are still on papers of distinctly inferior quality to those used later on. Indeed, the appearance of a fascicle of *Les Francs-Juges* with violins at the foot of the page leads to far-reaching speculation concerning the development of the opera (see below, Chapter IV, pp. 235-36).

The names by which Berlioz identifies instruments and voice parts undergo subtle change over the years. In the early manuscript and published works, he typically refers to the chorus parts by the French names rapidly becoming obsolete: *dessus, haute-contre, taille*, and *bassus* or *basse-taille* (e.g. *Les Francs-Juges, Scène héroïque*, the early songs). These terms rarely appear in manuscript sources after the 1833 performance of the *Scène héroïque*, though certain copyists persist in using them. In the years surrounding the Italian sojourn Berlioz often uses Italian nomenclature for the orchestral instruments; in these manuscripts almost any combination of names and languages can appear. Eventually (c. 1837-39) Berlioz settles down to the standard repertoire of modern French terms: *Petite flûte, Hautbois, Clarinette, Basson, Violon, Alto, V'elle* (for *Violoncelle*), and *C. Basses* or merely *C. B.;* see Facs. III.10, below.

Changes in Berlioz's handwriting, though difficult to date within a single year, are occasionally useful in determining the general era of a questionable page. As the *B* of Berlioz's signature becomes more and more idiosyncratic, so, too, do the *B*'s in *Basson*, and *Basses* (see, for example, the array of *B*'s in Facs. III.10 below; it is typical of Berlioz's manuscripts that the *B* in *Contre-Basses* on the lowest line of score most resembles his signature initial). There is, as noted above, a tendency for

Berlioz to use a broader pen-stub beginning in the mid-1850s, producing flatter noteheads.

Berlioz used three different types of C-clefs during his life (see Facs. II.5-.7, above). Relatively precise dates can be established for each. The most common of the clefs is, by far, the simple clef with the curved arms, to be called hereafter *Type I* (Facs. II.5). This clef appears in autographs from *Les Francs-Juges* through, with very few exceptions, *La Damnation de Faust*. The squarer clef hereafter called *Type II* (Facs. II.6) is most common in manuscripts of the early 1840s. Finally, the clef with a curved lower beam, *Type III* (Facs. II.7) begins to appear regularly in the mid-1840s and is the clef commonly used in the autographs of the 1850s and 60s (see, for example, the sketches for *Faust:* Facs. III.2 and .3, below). A fourth clef, possibly in imitation of a copied source, appears in Berlioz's earliest datable manuscript, the Gluck score owned by Richard Macnutt (facs. in **CatV&A**, p. 2).

The composer's use of the Type II clef is puzzling. It seems to be at a midpoint, calligraphically, between the two other types. It first appears, however, on p. 1 of the first movement of the *Symphonie fantastique*, where it is seen only in the viola part, and is used consistently in the *Marche au supplice*. (While the clef on p. 1 of the first movement could conceivably be a later addition, those in the *Marche* cannot be from any time but 1829-30.) Berlioz used the same type of clef in the *Grande Ouverture de Waverley* (1828).

The clef does not occur again until it appears in the album *Souvenirs-Bêtises-Improvisations*, prepared in Belgium and Germany in 1842-43, and in the first correction layer of *Le Corsaire* (1844, rev. 1851). (The revisions of *Le Corsaire* are particularly interesting in this regard: the original layer employs the Type I clef; the first level of correction, Type II; and the last, Type III.) The Type II clef is seen on one page of the score of *Roméo et Juliette*, in conjunction with revisions demonstrably entered in the mid-1840s. Berlioz's standard clef through the period covered in this study is Type I.

Other datable characteristics of watermarks, embossings, and scribes often suggest reasonably sound criteria for the dating of manuscript leaves. For example, Berlioz does not seem to have begun to purchase paper from Dantier and Lard-Esnault before he returned from Italy in 1832. Papers watermarked *D. & C. BLAUW* or *HP* are generally from the mid- and late-1830s (or later); papers with late or unusual watermarks are demonstrably later additions to the fascicles. Rocquemont's affiliation with Berlioz began in about 1832, although he does not seem to have been chief copyist until about 1837-38. The address given by Rocquemont's rubber stamp changes from *rue des Martyrs, 52* to *38* on the same street in about 1854.

External information, most of it provided in contemporaneous periodicals or by the composer's letters, will occasionally clarify the date of a work. The original autographs of most of Berlioz's songs have been lost; for the period 1832-40, the only hint as to the date of composition of songs comes from references in press announcements for concerts. So established are dates for the song *Le Chasseur des chamois,* the versions for solo and orchestra of *La Captive* and *Le Jeune Pâtre breton,* and the arrangements for male quartet and orchestra of *Sara la baigneuse* and *La Belle Voyageuse* (see Table I, above). The correspondence is the clue to determining the dates of such mysterious manuscripts as the scribal copies of *La Mort d'Orphée* and the *Scène héroïque.*

The dangers of the various techniques described here must also be mentioned. Title pages are often poor evidence, since they were frequently altered. In other cases, the titles and dedications are signed and dated by the composer considerably after the completion of the manuscript itself (e.g. *Le Roi Lear, Waverley*).[25] An early date (the date of composition) was sometimes added by the composer to late copies (e.g. *Tristia, La Captive*). Modern bindings have destroyed the original fascicle structure in many cases; papers can change several times in a single manuscript, and there are even some fascicles originally made up of two or three different papers. Watermarks from the nineteenth century have not received the same attention from specialists that earlier ones have; as noted above, the mechanization of paper manufacturing and European political instability (causing the dates of some watermarks to have little meaning) make it virtually impossible to use the watermarks themselves for unambiguous dating.

On the whole there are few manuscripts of Berlioz whose provenance and general date remain completely obscure. In many cases, however, relevant data concerning the physical characteristics of manuscripts and parts of manuscripts have been overlooked. The evidence of handwriting, watermarks, and similar criteria will be cited frequently in the following pages in support of new interpretations of autograph documents.

Chapter Three

Methods of Work

Berlioz's autographs are most significant for the evidence they offer of his methods of musical composition.[1] Virtually every autograph change in musical text reflects a decision that can be properly termed compositional in nature. As a group these manuscript indications represent a complex but often predictable series of choices that culminates in the finished work. Separately they show a vast range of musical problems encountered and solved. Considered along with Berlioz's own statements about how he composed, the manuscript evidence yields a well-documented view of the genesis and execution of certain musical ideas. This chapter examines that evidence: sketches, drafts, alterations, deletions, and in general any autograph indication that illuminates his methods.

This sort of source-critical analysis is based on the assumption—or, according to Lewis Lockwood, the truism—that "in musical masterpieces the means of organization of content and the means of expressing that organization in graphic form are bound up with one another in the closest possible way."[2] Truism or not, Boschot found it hard to believe that an autograph of Berlioz showed much about how his thoughts developed. In reference to *La Damnation de Faust* he wrote:

> These pages are neither draft nor sketch. They show neither the first nor the second state of a thought which is searched for, corrected, and brought to precision little by little, which by retouching attains its definitive form. One cannot stumble here upon the secret and intimate genesis of a work that is going to be born. This manuscript shows only a work already born, completely formed and even scrupulously corrected over a period of eight years during the source of successive hearings. . . . The manuscript of the *Damnation* gives the *last form*, the result of this effort at perfection. It is *polished*, a *fair copy* used by the engraver: thus it differs hardly at all from the definitive edited text.[3]

There are two fundamental mistakes in Boschot's analysis: he did not understand the implication of the rather remarkable structure of the manuscript (which he described in some detail), and he did not realize that the "scrupulous corrections" are for Berlioz an integral part of "secret and intimate genesis."

Boschot may actually have been bothered by a different but closely related problem. Because the sources for Berlioz's works are only randomly preserved they simply do not permit analysis of any single work in every stage of its development from first sketched idea to finished publication. More importantly, Berlioz (like Mozart) may have first notated much of his music as neat, finished score, without recourse to sketches, drafts, or extensive revisions in the manuscript. Statements about his process of musical composition must therefore be developed from a limited amount of specific evidence, and too often it seems that half the pieces are missing from an already difficult puzzle.

The evidence suggests that most of Berlioz's musical works resulted from a chain of thoughts and operations that can be grouped as follows:

    I.   First steps

        A. Inspiration; development of a descriptive intent
        B. Choice of libretto or text
        C. Early decisions on musical organization
            1. Nature of movements, i.e. form, tempo, earliest melodic ideas
            2. Performing force
            3. Use of pre-existing music

    II.   Sketches and drafts

        A. Initial sketches
        B. Advanced sketches
        C. Sketches for revision
        D. Drafts

    III.   Revisions in the autograph score

        A. Large-scale revisions
        B. Revision of details
        C. Practical considerations

    IV.   Publication[4]

        A. Correction of proof
        B. Subsequent changes to published text
        C. Reprinting of work

There is significant compositional activity generally concurrent with each of four developments in the chronology of a work: its inspiration, completion in draft, first performances, and publication.

No composer has a single compositional process. His techniques vary from piece to piece, and they undergo substantial change during the course of a lifetime. Still, a number of Berlioz's attitudes toward composition remained constant throughout his life; many specific procedures were evidently habits. He considered as active, significant creation every step from the choice of a dramatic goal for a work to the revisions, usually years later, for publication. The conscientiousness with which he approached even the dreary tasks of editing and proofreading is remarkable. A study of his methods of work must thus investigate a multitude of topics, ranging from the composer's reading matter to the color of his editor's pencil.

I. First Steps

Few Frenchmen of the Romantic era questioned the premise that a work of art was the result of an inspiration; the *Mémoires* indicate that Berlioz never really questioned it. But inspiration is a nebulous matter at best, outside the realm of pencil and paper; understanding someone's inspiration often depends solely on the accuracy of his recollections. The documentary evidence of Berlioz's first ideas and earliest plans for a work is slight. On the one hand, smaller pieces and occasional compositions were written too quickly for prior thoughts, if there were any substantive ones, to have been mentioned in writing. For each of the larger works, on the other hand, fundamental ideas were considered for years[5] and become inextricably mixed with fleeting or eventually abandoned plans for other works. The few substantive hints as to what Berlioz actually thought about his works occur mostly in prose accounts, references in letters, some written plans, and retrospective (and occasionally inaccurate[6]) passages in the *Mémoires*. Inasmuch as they record initial, motivating thoughts about a piece, they permit some investigation of germinal ideas and early plans.

Berlioz occasionally mentioned ideas for new compositions in letters, particularly those to Humbert Ferrand. He refers in three letters, for example, to plans eventually laid aside:

J'ai dans la tête depuis longtemps une symphonie descriptive de Faust qui fermente; quand je lui donnerai la liberté, je veux qu'elle épouvante le monde musical (**BerCG** 113 2 February 1829; to Ferrand).

I've had a descriptive symphony on *Faust* fermenting in my head for a long time; when I let it out, I want it to frighten the musical world.

Il s'agissait d'un oratorio colossal pour être exécuté à une fête musicale *donnée à Paris, à Opéra ou au Panthéon, [ou] dans la cour du Louvre. Il serait intitulé* le Dernier Jour du Monde. *J'en avais écrit le plan à*

It had to do with a colossal oratorio to be performed at a musical celebration in Paris at the Opéra or the Panthéon, or in the court of the Louvre. It would be called *Le Dernier Jour du monde*. I wrote the plans

Florence et une partie des paroles il y a trois mois (BerCG 234: Rome, 3 July 1831; to Ferrand).

for it in Florence, and some of the words three months ago.

A propos, je vais faire un opéra italien fort gai, sur la comédie de Shakspeare (Beaucoup de bruit pour rien) (BerCG 311: Paris, 19 January 1833, to Joseph d'Ortigue).

By the way, I'm going to do a very gay Italian opera on Shakespeare's comedy (*Much Ado About Nothing*).

Like other references to new compositions in letters, these indicate that the composer has begun to think in general terms (*colossal, descriptive, fort gai*) about the music itself. The first excerpt also describes a period of creative ferment to which Berlioz frequently alludes.

He mentions the same sort of compositional rumination in several letters from early 1830, as the plans for the *Symphonie fantastique* begin to take definitive shape:

J'ai à faire une immense composition instrumentale pour mon concert de l'année prochaine, auquel il faudra bien que vous assistiez (BerCG 149: Paris, 2 January 1830; to Ferrand).

I have an immense instrumental composition to do for my concert next year, to which you absolutely must come.

Pour accomplir mon dessein, je prépare beaucoup de musique nouvelle; entre autres une immense composition instrumentale d'un genre nouveau, au moyen de laquelle je tâcherai d'impressioner mon auditoire. Malheureusement, c'est très considérable, et je crains de ne pouvoir être prêt pour le 23 mai, jour de l'Ascension; d'un autre côté, ce travail de feu me fatigue excessivement; quoique depuis longtemps j'ai le squelette de mon ouvrage dans la tête, il faut beaucoup de patience pour en lier les parties et bien ordonner le tout (BerCG 151: Paris, 30 January 1830; to Nanci).

In order to achieve my goal, I am preparing a great deal of new music, among other things an immense instrumental composition in a new genre, by which I mean to impress my audience strongly. Unhappily it is a major undertaking, and I'm afraid I won't be able to finish it before the 23rd of May, Ascension Day. Besides this furious work tires me excessively. Even though I've had the skeleton of my work in my head for a long time, it takes a lot of patience to tie the parts together and to straighten it all out.

J'étais sur le point de commencer ma grande symphonie (Episode de la vie d'un artiste),[7] où le développement de mon infernale passion doit être peint; je l'ai toute dans la tête, mais je ne puis rien écrire.... Attendons (BerCG 152: Paris, 6 February 1830: to Ferrand).

I was just about to begin my grand symphony (*Episode de la vie d'un artiste*), where I am going to portray my infernal passion. It's all in my head, but I can't write anything. We'll wait.

His mental struggles were severe: on 19 February 1830 (BerCG 155) Berlioz complains to his father that he is in great pain, physically with a toothache and artistically with his new composition; he says he cannot distinguish between the two.   The next letter to Ferrand (BerCG 158: 16 April 1830) contains the earliest known draft of the program, in which it is clear that the symphony has been completed.[8]   Altogether he must have been considering various possibilities for the work for months before he began to write.

He came very close to outlining his *Roméo et Juliette* as early as 1832. In his "Lettre d'un enthousiaste sur l'état actuel de la musique en Italie," he reviews a production at La Scala of Bellini's *I Montecchi ed i Capuletti*.   (A revised version of the same essay is included in the *Mémoires*, Chap. XXXV.)   He would have written the music differently, he says emphasizing:

... le bal éblouissant dans la maison de Capulet;... puis ces combats furieux,... cette inexprimable scène de nuit sur le balcon de Juliette, où les deux amants murmurent un concert d' amour,... et enfin le serment solennel (Revue européenne, Vol. III [March-May 1832], p. 48).	. . . the dazzling ball at the house of Capulet, . . . then those furious swordfights, . . . that indescribable night scene on Juliet's balcony, where the two lovers murmur a concert of love, . . . and finally the solemn oath.

Berlioz had evidently decided to set *Romeo and Juliet* as a dramatic symphony just after Harriet Smithson's performance of 1827.   In the preface of his translations of *Romeo and Juliet* and *Macbeth* (Paris, 1844), Emile Deschamps remarks that he began to collaborate with Berlioz ten years before the symphony finally appeared.[9]   After the Smithson performance, Berlioz supposedly declared: "This woman is going to be my wife, and on this play I shall write my grandest symphony."[10] Though he denies the remark in the *Mémoires* (Chap. XVIII), attributing it to the fancy of an English critic, it was actually reported in Jules Janin's review of the first performance of Berlioz's symphony (*Journal des Débats*, 29 November 1839), to which the composer did not take exception at the time.   Consciously or not, Berlioz must have been considering music for each of the sections he describes in his "Lettre d'un enthousiaste" for close to a decade before he actually began to write.

Two letters, when viewed along with known historical facts, cast light on a more precipitous kind of inspiration.   In each Berlioz describes setting a poem shortly after he had read it for the first time:

J'ai fait avant-hier, en voiture, la ballade du	Day before yesterday, in a carriage, I wrote
Roi de Thulé en style gothique (**BerCG** 99:	the ballad of the King of Thule in gothic
Grenoble, 16 September 1828; to Ferrand).	style.

Berlioz must have read Nerval's translation of *Faust* shortly before; it was advertised in November 1827, and in general circulation by mid-1828.[11]

Avez-vous lu les Orientales *de Victor Hugo?*	Have you read the *Orientales* by Victor
Il y a des milliers de sublimités. J'ai fait sa	Hugo? It is inestimably sublime. I did his
chanson des pirates avec accompagnement de	pirates' song with accompaniment by a
tempête (**BerCG** 113: Paris, 2 February	tempest.
1829; to Ferrand).	

The *Orientales* were published in January of the same year. Both *Faust* and the *Orientales* obviously struck the composer from first reading as suitable for setting to music.

He refers to a similar case of inspiration in Chapter XVIII of the *Mémoires*, describing how he noticed a copy of Moore's *Mélodies irlandaises* open to the *Elégie en prose* and was moved to sit down and write the song at once.[12] "It was the only time," he remarks, "that I happened to be able to portray such a sentiment while still under its active and immediate influence."[13] Whatever Berlioz really means by the phrase "active and immediate influence," he recounts precisely the same set of circumstances regarding the composition of *La Captive* (**BerMém** Chap. XXXIX). Perhaps he is merely reflecting the widely held Romantic belief that creation was impossible during the first flush of inspiration, but in each case he clearly recalls having been strongly moved by the first reading of the poem.

Among the composer's autographs are early plans in prose for three works, none of which were finished. In his Italian sketchbook, he entered the following summary:[14]

Le Retour de l' armée d'Italie

Simphonie [*sic*] *militaire en 2 parties*

1°- Adieu du haut des Alpes aux braves tombés
dans les champs d' Italie.

2°- Entrée triomphale des vainqueurs à Paris

L'idée de Simphonie en 2 parties m'est venue à Turin le 25 mai 1832 en revoyant les Alpes, le coeur plein des souvenirs Napoléoniens que le pays que je venais de parcourir avait réveillés.

Several musical sketches follow the description (q.v. below, pp. 140-41).[15]

In one of his several efforts to salvage *Les Francs-Juges*, Berlioz set out a plan for a dramatic intermezzo that included ideas for newly composed passages: *"une valse en style Suisse avec la 4me note du ton diézée,"*... *"Chant... pendant une froide nuit d'hiver accompagnée des gémissements du vent du nord et interrompue souvent par la plainte de l'Enfant —'Ah, père, j'ai froid.' Le père répondra toujours à cette plainte en récitant le De Profundis.... Arrivée d'une confrérie de moines."*[16] Another movement of the same scene was to be reconstructed from sections of the opera in progressively faster tempi: *"Ce serait ainsi un andante, suivi d'un allegro développé et de plus en plus énergique."*

The most detailed scenario in prose is also for a work that was never written, a "colossal oratorio" to be called *Le Dernier Jour du Monde*. Berlioz outlined his project in a letter 3 July 1831 to the proposed librettist, Ferrand:

J'avais un grand projet que j'aurais voulu accomplir avec vous; il s'agissait d'un oratorio colossal pour être exécuté à une fête musicale *donnée à Paris, à l'Opéra [ou] au Panthéon, ou dans la cour du Louvre. Il serait intitulé* Le Dernier Jour du monde. *J'en avais écrit le plan à Florence et une partie des paroles il y a trois mois. Il faudrait trois ou quatre acteurs* solos, *des choeurs, un orchestre de soixante musiciens devant le théâtre, et un autre de trois cents ou deux cents instruments au fond de la scène étagés en amphithéâtre.*

Les hommes, parvenus au dernier degré de corruption, se livreraient à toutes les infamies; une espèce d'Antéchrist les gouvernerait despotiquement... Un petit nombre de justes, dirigés par un prophète trancherait au beau milieu de cette dépravation générale. Le despote les tourmenterait, enlèverait leurs vierges, insulterait à leurs croyances, ferait déchirer leurs livres saints au milieu d'une orgie. Le prophète viendrait lui reprocher ses crimes, annoncerait la fin du monde et le dernier jugement. Le despote irrité le ferait jeter en prison, et, se livrant de nouveau aux voluptés impies, serait surpris au milieu d'une fête par les trompettes terribles de la résurrection; les morts sortant du tombeau, les vivants éperdus poussant des cris d'épouvante, les mondes

I had a great project that I wanted to realize with you; it had to do with a colossal oratorio to be performed at a musical celebration in Paris at the Opéra or the Panthéon or in the court of the Louvre. It would be called *Le Dernier Jour du monde*. I wrote the plans for it in Florence, and some of the words three months ago. It would take three or four solo actors, choruses, an orchestra of sixty musicians in front of the theater, and another of two or three hundred instruments at the rear of the stage, stacked in amphitheater fashion.

The men, having arrived at the last stage of corruption, indulge in every sin; a sort of Antichrist governs them despotically. A few worthy people, led by a prophet, cut off in the midst of this general depravity. The despot torments them, kidnaps their virgins, insults their beliefs, and has their holy books destroyed during an orgy. The prophet comes to reproach him for his crimes and announces the end of the world and the Last Judgment. The enraged despot has him thrown into prison, and while indulging again in impious sensual pleasure is surprised in the middle of a feast by the terrible trumpets of the Resurrection. The dead leaping from the tomb, the damned crying frightfully, the

fracassés, les anges tonnant dans les nuées, formeraient le final de ce drame musical. Il faut, comme vous pensez bien, employer des moyens entièrement nouveaux. Outre les deux orchestres, il y aurait quatre groupes d'instruments de cuivre placés aux quatre points cardinaux du lieu de l'exécution. Les combinaisons seraient toutes nouvelles et mille propositions impracticables avec les moyens ordinaires surgiraient étincelantes de cette masse d'harmonie.

Voyez si vous avez le temps de faire ce poème, qui vous va parfaitement, et dans lequel je suis sûr que vous serez magnifique. Très peu de récitatifs... peu d'airs seuls... Evitez les scènes à grand fracas et celles qui nécessiteraient du cuivre; je ne veux en faire entendre qu'à la fin. Des oppositions... des choeurs religieux mêlés à des choeurs de danses; des scènes pastorales, nuptiales, bachiques, mais détournées de la voie commune; enfin, vous comprenez... (BerCG 234: Rome, 3 July 1831; to Ferrand).

shattering world, the thunder of heavenly hosts make up the *finale* of this musical drama. As you can see, it is necessary to use entirely new forces. Besides the two orchestras, there are four groups of brass instruments placed in the four main corners of the place of performance. The combination is completely new, and ideas not practical with the ordinary forces will emerge sparkling from this mass of winds.

See if you have time to do the poem, which suits you perfectly and in which I am sure you will be magnificent. Few recitatives, few solo airs. Avoid scenes of consternation and those that will require brass; I don't want them heard until the end. Some contrasts—religious choirs mixed with dance choruses; pastoral, nuptial, and bacchic scenes, but out of the ordinary; well, you understand.

Ferrand never received (or never answered) the letter from Rome, so Berlioz presented him with the same general proposition in a letter written six months later. The plan had been revised in several details by that time, notably with the addition of a sequence in which the tyrant stages a mockery of the Last Judgment.

Puisque vous n'avez pas reçu ma première lettre, où je vous parlais d'un certain plan d'oratorio, je vous renvoie le même plan pour un opéra en trois actes. Vous le musclerez; en voici la carcasse:

Since you didn't get my first letter, where I spoke to you about a certain plan for an oratorio, I send you the same plan for an opera in three acts. You will put muscles on it; here is its carcass:

LE DERNIER JOUR DU MONDE

LE DERNIER JOUR DU MONDE

Un tyran tout-puissant sur la terre; la civilisation et la corruption au dernier degré; une cour impie; un atome de peuple religieux, auquel le mépris du souverain conserve l'existence et laisse la liberté. Guerre et victoire, combats d'esclaves dans un cirque; femmes esclaves qui résistent aux désirs du vainqueur; atrocités.

Le chef du petit peuple religieux, espèce de Daniel gourmandant Balthazar, reproche ses crimes au despote, annonce que les

A tyrant powerful over all the earth; civilization corrupted to the ultimate degree; an impious court; a cell of religious people, preserved and left free by the sovereign's scorn. War and victory, combat between slaves in the arena, slave women who resist the desire of the conquerors; atrocities.

The leader of the tiny group of religious people, a sort of Daniel chiding Balthazar,

prophéties vont s'accomplir et que la fin du monde est proche. Le tyran, à peine courroucé par la hardiesse du prophète, le fait assister de force, dans son palais, à une orgie épouvantable, à la suite de laquelle il s'écrie ironiquement qu'on va voir la fin du monde. A l'aide de ses femmes et de ses femmes et de ses eunuques, il représente la vallée de Josaphat; une troupe d'enfants ailés sonne de petites trompettes, de faux morts sortent du tombeau; le tyran représente Jésus-Christ et s'apprête à juger les hommes, quand la terre tremble; de véritables et terribles anges font entendre les trompettes foudroyantes; le vrai Christ approche, et le vrai jugement dernier commence (BerCG 257: Rome, 8 January 1832; to Ferrand).

reproaches the despot for his crimes, announces that the prophecies are going to be accomplished, and that the end of the world is near. The tyrant, hardly provoked by the audacity of the prophet, forces him to attend a shocking orgy in the palace, during which he cries ironically that they are going to see the end of the world. With the help of his wives and his eunuchs, he shows the valley of Josaphat, a group of winged children plays on little trumpets, imitation corpses emerge from the tombs; the tyrant plays Jesus Christ and gets ready to judge mankind, *when the earth quakes;* real and terrifying angels sound blasts of trumpets; the true Christ approaches, and the *true Last Judgment begins.*

The project was not immediately abandoned. A spirited argument ensued between the collaborators over the merits of rhymed verse. In **BerCG 267** (26 March 1832), Berlioz was referring to the plan when he remarked: *"Vous acceptez donc mon sujet."* Six months later (**BerCG 288:** 10 October 1832), he was still urging Ferrand to finish the libretto. Eventually he gave up on Ferrand and recruited Emile Deschamps and Jules de Saint-Félix to finish it, and by August, 1833, the proposal had been rejected at the Opéra (**BerCG 342:** 30 August 1833).[17]

In all of these cases, Berlioz has begun work on a composition by first choosing a dramatic subject and then making some basic decisions about the music itself. In practically every case where he indicates what he is going to write, it is a musical work *about* something; *Faust*, for example, or Italian souvenirs, or *Romeo and Juliet*. Even the first musical sketches for his work seem to have been written with a dramatic idea in mind. Only the *Rêverie et Caprice*, some pieces for harmonium, and perhaps the trio from *L'Enfance du Christ* are without programmatic background.

Berlioz read widely and often drew his subject matter from boc's he had just finished. Occasionally the first reading of a new poem would generate such euphoria that he would set the words to music at once, as in the three cases cited above. The plans for a *Symphonie fantastique* did not begin to take definitive shape until after Berlioz had read Hoffmann's *Contes fantastiques* (**BerCG** 148, 149; December 1829-January 1830); that title marked a new and popular use in French of the term *fantastique* (i.e. implying *grotesque, surnaturel*) in the sense Berlioz was to apply it.[18] Berlioz asks Ferrand if he has read the *Contes fantastiques* in the very letter where he mentions the immense composition he has to do (q.v. above, p. 114), and the two ideas were joined shortly thereafter with the *Symphonie fantastique*. Plans for other compositions, including those after Goethe, Shakespeare, and Virgil, developed over decades of the composer's life.

Once he actually began to compose, however, Berlioz focused his attention on musical structure and content, not on the details of the chosen situation. Music conceived for one context was easily transferred to another: the first movement of *Harold en Italie*, for example, was originally intended to depict *Les Derniers Instants de Marie-Stuart* and had already been borrowed from the *Intrata de Rob-Roy MacGregor*. The dramatic plan served to motivate the music, but the music once written exists more or less independently of its dramatic context.

Early planning for some compositions also included the choice of a text. Since the directors of the Opéra accepted or declined new works solely by reading the proposed libretto, the search for suitable texts was a matter of considerable concern for a young composer.[19] Berlioz often asked friends and acquaintances for texts, generally without success. As early as 1823, the *Mémoires* indicate, he applied directly to the librettist François Andrieux for an operatic poem, and the amused author personally carried his regrets to the composer's apartment (**BerMém** Chap. VII). His correspondence refers to a dozen libretti that for one reason or another failed to materialize.[20] Even in those projects that did work out, his relationship with librettists was never quite satisfactory; from *La Damnation de Faust* on, he preferred to write his own words (see **BerMém** Chap. LIV). Berlioz, like Wagner, came to regard the words and music as so closely allied that only the composer himself could provide a suitable libretto.

There seems to have been no substantive correspondence with the more important librettists (Léon de Wailly, Auguste Barbier, and the brothers Deschamps);[21] they lived in Paris, where negotiations could be conducted in person. The letters to both Ferrand and Léon Compaignon, on the other hand, shed some light on the composer's ideals for musical texts.

The letters to Léon Compaignon deal almost exclusively with revisions of his libretto called *Richard en Palestine*, drawn from Scott's *The Talisman*.[22] They reveal Berlioz's well-developed—indeed, practically dogmatic—convictions about poetry and music as well as an instinct for theatrically effective situations. Berlioz continually cautions Compaignon that certain scenes or lines do not fit the dramatic context. He warns the writer (**BerCG** 55: 30 May 1826) that a verse form with three masculine rhymes in a row (*bouclier, imposant,* and *voyant,* in an *a b b, a c c,* etc., pattern) is almost impossible to set. The argument that evidently ensued gave Berlioz an opportunity to state once again that masculine rhymes are often too severe to be set to music. The abandonment of the project is not surprising; Berlioz's notions about proper poetry were too firmly established for the amateur Compaignon to be able to please him.

Berlioz and Ferrand enjoyed a much closer relationship. They worked well together, even though the librettist was habitually lethargic with projects that Berlioz considered urgent. Ferrand's 1829 revision of the libretto for *Les Francs-Juges*, which contains some clever poetry, struck Berlioz as excellent. Nevertheless, the two disagreed more and more as Berlioz began to advocate unrhymed verse for musical setting. Ferrand evidently found that notion too iconoclastic to support, and the two never actually collaborated again after *Les Francs-Juges* was declined at the Opéra.

Berlioz had by that time refined his ideas of the role of text in music. He wanted to avoid verse forms like ballades and romances, and developed a special dislike for rhymed verse. "I wasn't interested in running after rhymes," he remarks in reference to the *Mélologue* (**BerCG** 231), and he vigorously defends unrhymed verse in the letter to Ferrand of 26 March 1832 (**BerCG** 267). This vehemence subsides after the composition of the *Mélologue*, in which he seems to have satisfied his desire to write poetic prose. In *Benvenuto Cellini*, the *Requiem*, and *Les Nuits d'été*, Berlioz had little difficulty dealing with rhymed, metric text.

Almost nothing can be ascertained about how he chose poetry for songs, although it has been shown here that certain poems seemed to have an immediate appeal as suitable for musical setting. Other songs were written because a *partie vocale* was required for most concerts, still others, primarily to keep the composer in the public eye.[23] Two little pieces, the *Chansonette* of 1835 and *Nessun maggior piacere* (**OBE** XVII, 211), were evidently written as albumleaves. Though two manuscript copies of poems are among the composer's papers,[24] neither contains notation for musical setting.

Even though the letters and written plans do not usually include musical notation, they at times imply that certain decisions on musical organization have been reached. The plan for the two-part symphony suggests for the second part a triumphal march, an idea later achieved in both the *Symphonie funèbre et triomphale* and the *Te Deum*. From the *Francs-Juges* fragment, there is the plan that includes tempo indications and the tonal scheme of a waltz. (This waltz in Swiss fashion is an idea derived for a *Walze au chalet* attributed by Pixis to Weber: Berlioz explains in a letter to his sister of 1 November 1828 [**BerCG** 100] how the modal scale colors the piece, and that it is the result of the sharp eleventh partial emphasized by alphorns. He had himself already used the idea in the sixth scene from *Faust, Le Roi de Thulé*, based on the following theme [Ex. 3.1]:)

Example 3.1: *Le Roi de Thulé*, mm. 7-15, vocal part.

Explicit in a number of plans and implied in others are decisions on performing force to be deployed. The *Symphonie fantastique* was conceived from the beginning as a work for extremely large orchestra, full of new effects (**BerCG** 149, 151). The title and subject of the military symphony suggest that Berlioz might have been considering at that point the military band that he later used in the *Symphonie funèbre* (1840). The overture *La Tempête* was conceived as a work for piano and choir with orchestra (see **BerCG** 173, 175; the part for harmonica seems to have been added as an afterthought, and it was eventually removed). The letters concerning the *Messe solennelle* and *Le Dernier Jour du monde* indicate that the idea of individual brass choirs placed around the concert hall and announcing the Day of Judgment matured from a first effort in the *Resurrexit* of the Mass through several rewritings and a planned reuse in *Le Dernier Jour*.[25] Berlioz's outline of the oratorio makes it clear that the focus of the work will be the earthquake (to be portrayed, one might guess, by a large number of percussion instruments)[26] followed by the *clangor tubarum* of the Last Judgment. One of the composer's first firm ideas about *Roméo et Juliette* was apparently to employ a choir that would chant narrative passages (see below, p. 186). Finally, an early idea for *Benvenuto Cellini* implies the use of a large male chorus to sing the song of master sculptors.[27]

Several further musical details are included in the description of *Le Dernier Jour du monde*. From the beginning the composer has a relatively firm idea of the orchestral force he plans to use: three or four solo actors, choirs, several orchestras, and the four small brass choirs. There will be few recitatives and arias, and the brasses will be saved for the end. Emphasis is on the theatrical. There will be dances, pastoral scenes, and a combat of slaves. And although the plans are eventually abandoned, several of the ideas (a ballet of slaves, the *tuba mirum*, an orgy) reappear in completed works.

At some preliminary stage in composing the masterpieces, Berlioz checked through his manuscripts and notes to find previously written material suitable for the new context. The practice is obvious enough from a cursory glance through his works: there is significant borrowing of passages from *Herminie* in the *Symphonie fantastique*, from *Cléopâtre* in *Benvenuto Cellini*, and from the *Resurrexit* in both *Cellini* and the *Requiem*. Little doubt now exists that the *Marche au supplice* from the *Symphonie fantastique* comes from a version of *Les Francs-Juges*. Additionally, there is the composer's own testimony on self-borrowings in the *Mémoires* (e.g. in Chaps. IV, XI, LIV)[28] and a piquant remark scribbled into the manuscript of *La Nonne sanglante*: *"Fragment... à consulter et à brûler après ma mort"* (aut. p. 41).

In his definitive study of this stage of the creative process,[29] Hugh Macdonald concludes that one of the composer's initial impulses, particularly when he was pressed for time and money, was to reuse good music from an otherwise forgotten piece. He tried to destroy sources or self-borrowings when the reworked version achieved success; it will be recalled that the scores of *Rob-Roy*, the *Resurrexit*, and *La Mort d'Orphée*, all sources of major borrowings, were preserved only in second copies that had already been given away when the borrowing occurred. Certain early works may have been completely destroyed for the same reason. There are almost surely other borrowings from the revised version of *Les Francs-Juges*, and possibly from the lost portions of *Orphée*, *Sardanapale*, and the *Messe solennelle*.

Berlioz's habit of borrowing from himself is both clever and thrifty. He did not ordinarily use sketchbooks to scribble themes and ideas for later use, and he generally finished works begun, leaving, all in all, very few incomplete pieces. Several unsuccessful pieces, however, contained good music not likely to be heard again. His systematic reuse of these passages is simply a matter of good sense. What is important about the procedure is the composer's unyielding belief in the strength of his early ideas and his ability to rework them viably into later compositions.

There are two kinds of borrowings. The large-scale removal of movements from one piece to another resulted from a calculated plan. These sections were surely copied intact, with the source manuscript at hand. (Berlioz steadfastly refused, over a period of several months, to recompose the *"derniers souvenirs"* section of *Orphée* that he wanted to use again in the *Mélologue*. Instead, he waited for the score to be sent

from Paris, leaving in the meantime an explanatory note in his
autograph.) But subtler borrowing occurs throughout Berlioz's music, as
in these falling fifths, first used in the *Ballet des ombres* (Ex. 3.2):

Example 3.2: *Ballet des ombres*, mm. 71-77.

then in a passage eventually deleted from *Benvenuto Cellini* (Ex. 3.3):

Example 3.3: *Benvenuto Cellini*, Act II, no. 8 (after Macdonald in **MacSelf**, p. 33).

and finally in *La Reine Mab* (Ex. 3.4):

Example 3.4: *Roméo et Juliette*, movt. IV, mm. 655-61.

A decision to reuse such short phrases and motives may well occur in
relatively advanced stages of composition and thus be unrelated to the
process of planning. Ideas may simply be remembered out of context
and borrowed inadvertently. The reuse of motives like the falling fifths
may be no more the result of conscious intent than is a habitual cadence

formula. "At the smaller end of the scale, selfborrowing merges with the normal stylistic fingerprints to be found in the work of any composer."[30]

II. Sketches and Drafts

A composer's sketches, like a painter's cartoons and studies, are merely left-overs from his workshop, private documents never meant for investigation and public display. As concrete indications of the creative process in action, however, they are invaluable sources. Sketches show variables tested, choices made, unsuitable material discarded, and diverse musical ideas made to relate to a coherent whole. The best sketches hint at priorities and purpose; all lay certain stages of the creative process open to scrutiny.

Since so few sketches and drafts of Berlioz have been preserved, it has generally been assumed that for most pieces there is no detailed evidence of his compositional efforts prior to the orchestral score. Only the sketches for *Les Troyens* have been preserved intact. Boschot describes a sketch for the overture to *Béatrice et Bénédict* and one for the *Invocation à la nature* from *Faust*; both are now apparently lost.[31] For the period under consideration the only commonly known sources are the lost sketchbook, a few pages of drafts for *Benvenuto Cellini*, and a two-page fragment of a draft of *Roméo et Juliette*. Except for some laconic references in the *Mémoires*, there has been very little evidence that Berlioz, at least in the early years, sketched at all.

During the course of this study, evidence of more systematic sketching has gradually mounted. Now it is clear that, while he never sketched with Beethoven's intensity, Berlioz often worked out his ideas with pen and paper before drafting the orchestra score. By the time he wrote the *Requiem* (1837), he had formed the habit of drafting his entire work in pencil before preparing a copy in ink.

The new sketches and drafts are an integral part of the most familiar sources: several dozen individual sketches are preserved by virtue of the composer's editorial technique in the autograph sources themselves. Berlioz added revised readings to his scores with *collettes* (pasted-on revisions).[32] Since the dots of paste which affixed the revision to the original page of score have dried and become brittle, the collettes have loosened and can be examined with ease. In many cases the composer wrote a revised reading for pasting-over on the blank side of sheets he had previously used for sketching. The *verso* surfaces of collettes may thus be covered with musical notation. In addition to the sketches so preserved, there is even an otherwise unknown arrangement by Berlioz found on *collette-verso* surfaces, the three-part setting of a song called

Sur les Alpes, quel délice![33] Malherbe removed most of the collettes in Berlioz's scores to examine original readings, but he evidently failed to grasp the significance of the musical notation on many of the *verso* surfaces.

Other sketches occur in margins of the autograph scores, on otherwise blank front and back covers, and on blank pages of manuscript orchestra parts. Pencil sketches in autograph scores were usually erased before the manuscript was sent to the engraver, but they can sometimes be deciphered from the indentations left in the paper.

Although the sketches for *Les Troyens* were prepared considerably later than the period covered by this study, there is some likelihood that they show typical techniques of written composition prior to the orchestra score. A brief description of this corpus of documents provides an effective point of departure for the study of earlier sketches.[34]

Altogether there are seventy-odd pages of plans for *Les Troyens*. (The exact total depends on whether the count includes some peripheral documents possibly unrelated to the opera.) Half the sketches, mostly those for Acts I, III, and IV, are in the collection of André Meyer.[35] Sketches for Acts II, III, and V are collected in a miscellany at the Bibliothèque Municipale in Grenoble (F-G Rés R 9028). One sketch, for the love duet *Nuit d'ivresse* (Act IV, no. 37), is in the Musée Hector Berlioz, though it belongs with other pages of the same sketch in Meyer's collection. One leaf at the Columbia University Library containing notes on modal scales and cannon fire has been separated from an item in Grenoble (F-G N 3264). The sketches seem to preserve much of the work prior to the autograph for twelve numbers (out of forty-five) as well as plans for a scene ultimately deleted. They are on single leaves and bifolios which were simply stacked in piles before modern binding; there are no pin holes or stitches. At least six different papers were used, with the sheets occasionally torn into small fragments. The paper was selected at random, and there is no correlation of papers with levels of sketching.

Berlioz generally considers one or two specific points on each leaf or bifolio: declamation and phrasing, for example, or harmonic structure, or intricate transition. There is extensive sketching in short score with accompaniment reduced to one or two staves below the vocal line. Occasionally notations for instrumentation are added above the staves of accompaniment. A few of the sketches are for the purpose of establishing the musical continuity of a long passage. Virtually all are accompanied by written reminders of formal decisions reached, for example: *"Allez à B. Non, allez encore en Sol ♭ à A"* (**F-Pmeyer**, re *Nuit d'extase*) and

"Pédale sur ut.   2de fois en re mineur" (**F-G** Rés R 9028, fol. 12ʳ, re *Marche troyenne*). In one place, Berlioz notes his progress on the work:

> *Il me reste 28 pp. à faire ce Dimanche 21 Juin. J'emploierai 3 jours au feuilleton, 22-23 et 24; en 6 jours en faisant 4 pages par jour, je ferai 24 pp. Donc au plus tard le 4 Juillet je devrai avoir fini* (**F-G** Rés R 9028, fol. 8ᵛ).[36]

Perhaps the most unusual sketches in the group are the composer's experiments with scales and chord progressions. One page (**US-NYcu**) shows a modal scale followed by a brief tune based on it (Ex. 3.5):

Example 3.5: Experimental scale and incipit of song (from sketches for *Les Troyens*), **US-NYcu**: cf. transcription of entire song, Appendix I.

A page in Meyer's collection is devoted to other experiments with modal scales (Ex. 3.6):

Example 3.6: Sketches for *Les Troyens* [?] (**F-Pmeyer**).

There are two series of chords drawn up to harmonize a single note, obviously for use in recitative-like passages where the singer always has the same pitch. One is for the scene in Act V (no. 42) where the ghosts appear to Aeneas, always chanting the pitch *D* (Ex. 3.7):

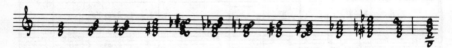

Example 3.7: Ibid., re Act V, no. 42 (**F-G** Rés. R 9028, fol. 8[v]; cf. **NBE** 2b, 639-44).

Berlioz does not use the entire sequence in order; it is rather a collection of possibilities. A very similar sketch occurs in the Meyer collection. Here the pitch *F* is harmonized in fifteen chords followed by a cadence in A minor. The scene for which the sketches were intended is not clear (Ex. 3.8):

Example 3.8: Ibid. (**F-Pmeyer**).

Over the sketches for the lament of the Trojan women (Act II, no. 15), Berlioz has notated his experimental scale at the beginning of every page (Ex. 3.9):

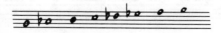

Example 3.9: Ibid., re Act II, no. 15 (**F-G** Rés R 9028, fols. 3[v], 4[v]).

A few simple melodies are notated, one along with a schedule of things to do (Ex. 3.10):

Vendredi à 1 hr. chez Mr. de Mirécourt
Chez Mr. Varcolier et Mr. Damercy
Chez Mr. Kamininsky
Mr Thuilleux
91 rue Blanche

Midi 1/2 et 5 min

Example 3.10: Ibid. (F-Pmeyer).

There is also a set of overtone tables for transposition of cornet and trumpet parts in E♭ (Ex. 3.11):

Example 3.11: Ibid., transposition tables for brass (F-G Rés. R 9028, fol. 20ʳ).

There are no sketches in full score, and very few indications of how passages are to be orchestrated.

Several conclusions about Berlioz's methods of work for *Les Troyens* can be drawn from this material. There are three levels of sketching, each with a different purpose: early sketches for organization, detailed sketches for experimentation, and drafts of lengthier passages to achieve the continuity and plan how the accompaniment will fit with the chosen vocal part. Berlioz's chief concern in the sketches, as Macdonald observes, is with the vocal line, particularly as it relates to phrase structure. Even for sections that seem to have been constructed around the interplay of motivic ideas in the orchestra (e.g. in Act I, no. 1, the C-major section in 2/4, mm. 139ff), the non-motivic vocal part was the one first worked out on paper.[37] The sketches testify to a marked facility in the composition of some movements and to a much more labored genesis of others. For many movements, no sketches exist at all. "There is no apparent correlation between the climaxes of musical interest and the ease of composition."[38]

It is difficult to establish whether or not there were sketches for earlier works like those for *Les Troyens*. Berlioz was convinced that the opera would be his last work, and he may have planned it in greater detail than any of his other compositions.[39] Yet it does not seem likely that he could have written his larger works without considerable sketching. It is still a mystery why the sketches for *Les Troyens* are preserved intact while the rest have virtually disappeared. For the present the question of how representative these sketches are must be left unanswered, but it will be taken up again in the course of this study.

The early sketches are, in a very general sense, similar to the material for *Les Troyens* in that the bits and pieces can be grouped into three general categories:

A. *Initial sketches*: First notation of ideas and immediate experimentation and elaboration. Before the orchestra score.

B. *Advanced sketches*: Detailed work on specific passages and problems. Before or contemporaneous with the score.

C. *Sketches for revision*: Solution of problems, changes in overall structure or details. Contemporaneous with score or later.

In addition to sketches, there were also:

D. *Pencil drafts of the full score.*

Table III lists the sketches, c. 1818-1840, and where they are found.

TABLE III

BERLIOZ'S SKETCHES

Movement	Page or folio in autograph[40]	Ink or pencil	Passage sketched[41]	Approximate location of sketch[42]	Nature[43]	Facs. or Trans.[44]
LES FRANCS-JUGES, aut.						
2	51^r-54^r bottom	ink	voice parts, accompaniment	same (below score)	rev./ exp.	4.6

Movement	Page or folio in autograph	Ink or pencil	Passage sketched	Approximate location of sketch	Nature	Facs. or Trans.
SYMPHONIE FANTASTIQUE, aut.						
I	22o	ink	mm. 198-239; violins	mm. 190-200	rev./ cont.	4.42
I	35o top	ink	m. 279; flute	passage deleted from movement	rev.	
I	35o bottom partially cut off	ink	mm. 289-303, strings (two-line sketch?)	same	rev./ cont.	4.43
I	42o-43o	ink	mm. 344-53, violins	same	rev./ cont./ exp.	4.44-.46
	44c-51o	both	mm. 358-405, oboe, harmonic progression	same	exp./ rev.	4.47
I	62o	ink	abandoned idea for ending	mm. 483-87	rev.	4.48
IV	35o	pencil	mm. 164-68, clarinet	same	rev.	III.7 3.36-.39
SYMPHONIE FANTASTIQUE, collette-versos in published parts, F·Pn Rés Vma 216						
II	violin I part	ink	mm. 120-38, short score	same	exp.	IV. 6
II	violin II part	ink	mm. 139-56, short score, cont.	same	exp.	IV.6
II	viola part	ink	deleted	same	exp.	
II	cello part	ink	deleted	same	exp.	
II	cello part	ink	deleted	same	exp.	

Movement	Page or folio in autograph	Ink or pencil	Passage sketched	Approximate location of sketch	Nature	Facs. or Trans.
SARDANAPALE, aut. fragment (**F·Pn** Rés Vm^2 178, fols. 83^r-96^v)						
	96^v (back cover)	pencil	verbal note and sketch from Beethoven's *Christus am Ölberge*	back cover	exp.	3.17
DANS L'ALCOVE SOMBRE, sketchbook of 1832-36						
		both	1st, 3rd, and 4th stanzas, with direction: *"5e mineur comme le 1er"*		exp.	3.12-.13
MELOLOGUE, cello part (**F·Pc** ms 17465: *"1er violoncelle"*)						
	back cover	ink	unfinished song (inc. *"Il est beau"*)		exp.	3.15
SYMPHONIE EN 2 PARTIES (LE RETOUR DE L'ARMEE D'ITALIE), sketchbook of 1832-36						
	both[45]		prose plan with three musical sketches		exp.	3.14
LA CAPTIVE, sketchbook of 1832-36[46]						
		(ink)	3 pp. of musical sketches		?	

Movement	Page or folio in autograph	Ink or pencil	Passage sketched	Approximate location of sketch	Nature	Facs. or Trans.
HAROLD EN ITALIE, sketchbook of 1832-36						
I		(ink)	8 mm. of movt. II		exp.	
IV		pencil	motive in G minor at beginning of movt.		exp.	
IV		both	motive originally intended for *Symphonie en 2 parties* and eventually used in *Harold*, movt. IV, mm. 176ff.		exp.	
HAROLD EN ITALIE, aut.						
I	7(o)	ink	mm. 32-36, flute, oboe, clar., harp, viola	same	cont.	III.9
I	13cv	ink	mm. 7-12	mm. 61-64	cont.	3.33
I	16-25 top[47]	pencil	mm. 73-92	same	cont.	
I	29 top	pencil	mm. 106-09, cello	same	cont.	
I	39 top	pencil	mm. 156-57; viola solo	same	cont.	
I	54cv	pencil	rubric: *"Trompette en fa Trompette en — Trompette en Si♭"*	mm. 204-205	rev.	
II	117 bottom	pencil (erased)	mm. 90-97	same	rev.	

Movement	Page or folio in autograph	Ink or pencil	Passage sketched	Approximate location of sketch	Nature	Facs. or Trans.
II	122-24*o* bottom	pencil, then ink	mm. 144-61, viola solo	same	rev.	
II	124*cv*	ink	the two themes of movt. II	mm. 155-65	exp.(?)	3.34
III	156*cv*	ink (some pencil)	*Invocation à la nature* (no. XVI of *La Damnation de Faust*)[48]	mm. 70-76	exp.	III.3 3.21
III	158*cv*	ink	*Invocation* from *Faust*	mm. 84-90	exp.	III.2 3.20
III	158*o*	both	mm. 84-90, flute, oboe, Eng. hn., clar., hn. I	same	rev.	
III	160-61 bottom	pencil (erased)	abandoned idea?	mm. 99-110	rev.	
III	163 bottom	pencil (erased)	m. 122	same	rev.	
IV	187*cv*	ink	mm. 45-46 winds	mm. 77-78	cont.(?)	3.30
IV	197*cv*	both	mm. 54-56, strings	mm. 133-38	cont.(?)	3.29
IV	248*o*-49*o*	pencil	mm. 441-48, strings	same	cont.	
IV	248*cv*	ink	mm. 473-82; solo strings offstage	mm. 441-46	cont.	3.44
(IV)	(249*cv*)	(ink)	(Schedule of appointments)	(mm. 447-50)		
IV	255-57	pencil	mm. 483-505, viola	same	rev./ cont.	
IV	265	pencil	mm. 561-63 brasses	same	rev.	

Movement	Page or folio in autograph	Ink or pencil	Passage sketched	Approximate location of sketch	Nature	Facs. or Trans.

JE CROIS EN VOUS, sketchbook of 1832-36

| | | (ink) | sketch | | exp. | |

REQUIEM, *ophicléide monstre* part (bound with full score, F-Pc 1509)

| | back cover | ink | passage from *Benvenuto Cellini* Act III, no. 13, mm. 374-75, cornet and trumpet | | exp. | 3.35 |

REQUIEM, 8th timpani part (F-Pc L 17235)

| | back cover | ink | autograph sketch (or merely a cue?) of an unidentified passage | | ? | 3.18 |

BENVENUTO CELLINI, sketchbook of 1832-36

Act I, no.1		pencil[49]	first entries in sc. i (in D major; 2 pp.)		exp.	
Act I, no. 2		ink	Teresa's aria, including passages later deleted (2 pp.)		exp.	
Act II, no. 6		ink	*"Les maîtres ciseleurs"* (inc. *"A boire!"*; 8 pp.)		exp.	

Movement	Page or folio in autograph	Ink or pencil	Passage sketched	Approximate location of sketch	Nature	Facs. or Trans.
BENVENUTO CELLINI, sketch (**F·Pc** ms 1178)						
Act III, no. 14		ink	passage deleted from movement (inc. *Cardinal: "à la justice de par dieu je livrerai ta tête"*)		cont.	3.23
[BENVENUTO CELLINI, sketch (**F·Pn** Rés Vm^1 241; NB: c. 1852)]						
Act III, no. 14		ink	passage deleted from movement (inc. *Cardinal: "Ah–ça démon, pour te calmer que faut-il donc?"*)		cont.	
BENVENUTO CELLINI, sketch (**F·Pc** ms 1177)						
Act III, no. 15		ink	passage deleted from movement (inc. *Cellini: "pasteur; mais non, non, je suis Cellini"*)		cont.	3.24
BENVENUTO CELLINI, aut. (**F·Pc** ms 1508)						
Act I, no. 3	52*o*	pencil	mm. 47-48; viola, cello	same	rev.	
Act I, no. 3	128*cv* (misnumbered; actually 138*cv*)	pencil	*Te Deum,* movt. VIII[50]	recit. A, at end of No. 3	exp.	3.32

Movement	Page or folio in autograph	Ink or pencil	Passage sketched	Approximate location of sketch	Nature	Facs. or Trans.
ROMEO ET JULIETTE, ms leaf (**D-Bds** mus. ms H. Berlioz 2)						
V		ink	early draft of mm. 1-41 of the *Convoi funèbre*, presented to Bottée de Toulmon		(cont.)	III.4
ROMEO ET JULIETTE, aut.						
I	58 (*o*)	pencil	choral recit. following scherzetto (deleted)[51]	same	rev.	III.10
I	63*cv*	ink	mm. 36-55 of *Prologue*, "*flauti, etc.*"	mm. 138-42	cont.	III.5
III	184 (*o*)	pencil then ink	mm. 317-20 strings	same	rev.	
III	194 (*o*)	pencil	mm. 358-60, flute	deleted; fair copy of same passage follows	cont./ rev.	
VI	309*o*	ink	m. 48, viola, cello	same	rev.	
VI	310*o*	pencil	mm. 49-52, strings	same	cont.	
VI	342	pencil (erased)	mm. 193-210, violin I	mm. 195-203	cont.	
VII	396	ink	mm. 785-93, violins, for IV (*La Reine Mab*)	collette-verso marked "*N° 5 / 2me Prologue*" opp. mm. 103-07 of III.3	exp.	III.6 3.42

Movement	Page or folio in autograph	Ink or pencil	Passage sketched	Approximate location of sketch	Nature	Facs. or Trans.
VII	396	ink	early version of mm. 6-8, brass in *"fa, re, la, ut"* and trombones	collette-verso marked *"N° 5 / 2ᵐᵉ Prologue"* opp. mm. 103-07 of III.3	exp.	III.6
VII	383 (*o*)	ink	mm. 37-39 violin I	same (original reading)	rev.	
VII	397	pencil then ink	mm. 238-40	same	rev./ exp.	III.8 3.41

ERIGONE, aut. (fragmentary, F-Pc ms 1186ᵃ)

| | 22ᵛ | pencil | ?, three unidentified passages | | exp. | III.1; 3.16 |

A. Initial sketches.

The principal source for these sketches is a notebook Berlioz kept between May 1832 and December 1836, most comprehensively described by Tiersot in *Berlioziana*.[52] It is one of only two bound albums Berlioz is known to have used for sketching. (A sketchbook for *Le Roi Lear* caused Berlioz to be questioned by agents in Nice, who suspected he was a spy taking notes; see BerMém Chap. XXXIV. He must have destroyed it later, for it has never been described by anyone else.)[53] He began using the later book as he left Rome to return to France; his accounts of expenditures and observations on Italian villages seen *en route* (Narni, Spoleto, Foligno) permit a detailed reconstruction of his homeward itinerary. Now and then he records ideas for new compositions, two of which Tiersot transcribes. In Paris, Berlioz made frequent use of his book, notating ideas for *Harold en Italie* and *Je crois en vous* and extensive passages from *Benvenuto Cellini*.

The first important sketch is for a setting of *Dans l'alcôve sombre*, the twentieth poem in Hugo's *Feuilles d'automne* (pub. November 1831). Berlioz has copied six of the nine stanzas with the text running along

under the staves. He set the first stanza in C minor with one indication
of an accompanying figure (mm. 10-11) (Ex. 3.12):

Example 3.12: *Dans l'alcôve sombre*, stanza 1, in sketchbook 1832-36.

No music was written over the words for the second, but the third and
fourth stanzas were set in G major (Ex. 3.13):[54]

Example 3.13: Ibid., stanzas 3-4.

After that the only notation Berlioz entered was *"5e mineur comme le 1er."* He planned to have, then, the first two stanzas in C minor, the middle two in G major, and the last two back in the minor key.

There is a similar sketch for *Je crois en vous* (1834). Here, according to Tiersot, Berlioz set the strophe several different times, only to return to his first idea.

Three melodic sketches accompany the plans for the *Symphonie en 2 parties.* The third eventually appears in the last movement of *Harold en Italie* (movt. IV, mm. 177ff). The first, intended for the triumphal march, is related in its triplet scalar patterns to the third movement of the *Symphonie funèbre et triomphale* (Ex. 3.14):

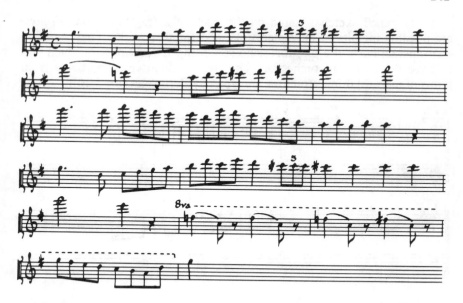

Example 3.14: Sketches for *Symphonie en 2 parties (Le Retour de l'armée d'Italie)* (sketchbook of 1832-36), after **TierB'ana.**

Another melodic sketch[?], possibly for a song, is scrawled on the back of a cello part for the *Mélologue;* the words have not been identified (Ex. 3.15):

Example 3.15: Sketch, cello part for *Mélologue.*

Three pencil sketches found on the back of a fragment from *Erigone* are possibly incipits of movements planned for that work. There are two instrumental cues, the one for piano surprising if for *Erigone*, which was to have been for full orchestra. The figures themselves, particularly in terms of their rhythmic structure, are typically Berliozian (Ex. 3.16):

Example 3.16: Sketches from fragment of *Erigone*, fol. 22^V. See Facsimile III.1.

On the back of the fragment of *Sardanapale* occurs a pencilled note: *"une grande fanfare de cuivre avec* vivat *à la fin de la dernière ritournelle,"* followed by an unrelated quotation from the last movement of Beethoven's *Christus am Ölberge* (Ex. 3.17):[55]

Facsimile III.1: Sketches from fragment of *Erigone*, fol. 22^V.

Example 3.17: Sketch from *Christus am Ölberge*, fragment of *Sardanapale*, fol. 96^V.

One autograph notation[56] may either be an experimental sketch of some sort or merely an orchestral cue. It is found on the back of the 8th timpani part for the *Requiem*, but is not related to the work (Ex. 3.18):

Example 3.18: Sketch[?], timpani part for *Requiem*.

Another peripheral item can be considered a sketch. Berlioz wrote two articles about his Italian sojourn for *Italie pittoresque* (Paris, 1834-36), a serialized encyclopedia of articles about that country. In *"Voyage musical"* he transcribes the following song of the *pifferari* (Ex. 3.19):

Example 3.19: Musical example for *Italie pittoresque, "Voyage musical,"* p. 10.

Its basic structure (accompaniment in thirds and sixths and ornamented scalar melody) resembles that of the serenade in *Harold en Italie* (movt. II, mm. 4ff, 33ff), in which Berlioz was clearly imitating the style. Moreover, he quotes the whole passage in a chorus of *Benvenuto Cellini*, *"Bienheureux les matelots"* (Act III, no. 10, edn. Choudens, pp. 323ff).

Compensating somewhat for this paucity of early sketches are two collette-versos in the score of *Harold en Italie* used to plan a movement from *La Damnation de Faust*, the *Invocation à la nature* (scene XVI, OBE XI-XII, pp. 360-70). They constitute the only evidence before the material for *Les Troyens* of detailed experimental sketching, yet they have never been described in published source studies. Berlioz indicates in the *Mémoires* (Chap. LIV) that he wrote the words to the *Invocation* during his travels in Germany in 1845-46. He must have sketched the movement shortly thereafter, since the finished autograph score of *Faust* bears the autograph date 19 October 1846. Ultimately the blank sides of these two pages from the corpus of *Faust* sketches were filled with final revisions for movement III of *Harold* and added to the orchestral score sometime before its publication in 1848.

Page 158*cv* is basically a two-line sketch, with the vocal part in one line and chordal accompaniment in the other. It is a sketch of the entire movement, though a small portion was cut off at the bottom when the collette was prepared. Page 156*cv* is a three-line sketch (soloist plus accompaniment in treble and bass clefs) of roughly the first third of the movement, another page or two having been lost. This sketch, much closer to the final version than the other, is clearly the later one (hereafter, the second sketch; thus p. 158*cv* is the first sketch) (Facsimiles III.2 and III.3, pp. 146-47):

In the first sketch, Berlioz planned the basic shape of the movement, the melodic character of its vocal part, the declamation, and the accompaniment. He has set up the score with a line each in treble, tenor, and bass clef, intending to put chords in the top staff, bass figuration in the bottom, and the vocal line in the middle. He soon discarded that format in favor of a two-staff system with the bass line temporarily abandoned.

The first measures testify to numerous changes in concept undergone during the early moments of sketching. Berlioz had, to judge from these first two measures, certain characteristics of the movement firmly in mind: it would have chordal accompaniment, scalar figures in the bass, and a beginning dynamic of *pianissimo*. He had made few other decisions. The "C" metric indication became 9/8 as soon as he began to set the first words. The ambiguous tonal framework of the first measure (B minor?) did not firmly evolve to C# minor until the second sketch.

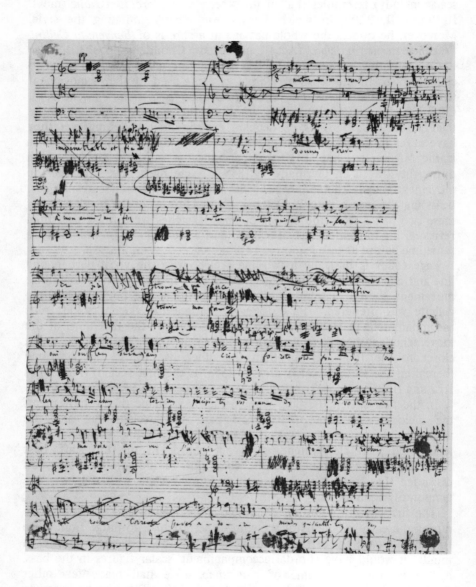

Facsimile III.2: Sketch for the *Invocation à la nature*, found in *Harold en Italie*, aut. p. 158cv.

Facsimile III.3: Ibid., p. 156*cv*.

Berlioz discarded his first setting of the vocal part (staff 2, mm. 3-5) and adopted a subtler version (staff 1, m. 6). Then he began a series of experiments with the harmonic progression for those measures, not to be definitively settled until well into the later sketch (version 1: staff 3, mm. 4-6 and staves 4-5, mm. 7-8; version 2: staves 1-2, mm. 3-6; version 3: staff 6, m. 9a-d, circled). The circled progression has the strongest bass motion of the three as well as a perfect cadence; it was eventually adopted with modifications.

Having settled on basic formulations of meter and declamation, Berlioz proceeded to sketch the rest with greater ease. He set out the basic harmonic structure on the first or second try. The declamation was seldom changed, nor was the poetry ever altered. Most of the changes affect the melodic shape of certain phrases. Berlioz subjected the line *"je retrouve ma force et je crois vivre enfin"* to several revisions (Exs. 3.20a&b):

Example 3.20a: Sketch: *"je retrouve ma force"* (p. 158cv), first versions.

Example 3:20b: Ibid., later version.

Twice he decided to begin a descending passage with an upbeat from above rather than below (mm. 25, 29). His original setting of *"forêts, rochers, torrents, je vous adore"* (mm. 41-43) was discarded in favor of a revised melodic structure (mm. 37-40). He never adopted a key signature, using accidentals throughout.

The second sketch has the key signature for C♯ minor and an established meter of 9/8. It opens with the chordal introduction in C♯ minor eventually adopted without change. Berlioz began in what is now m. 11 to harmonize the words *"impénétrable et fière"* with the sequence of chords circled in his previous sketch. He went on to try two other alternatives, attempting to avoid the leap from A♭ to C♮ in what he obviously hoped would be a rising scale. Then he came back to his original idea, marking it *"bon"*. (He solved the problem by adding the

C♮ as a second voice in the first violin part; the effect is thus one of rising intensity, as intended). In the space to the left of these experiments, he sketched in pencil the figure that became an important melodic motive (Exs. 3.21-.22):

Example 3:21: Pencil sketch (p. 156cv), mm. A-B.

Example 3.22: *Invocation à la nature*, final version, mm. 11-12.

Thereafter, this sketch closely resembles in format and purpose the continuity drafts for *Les Troyens*, although the accompaniment occupies two staves instead of the more typical single staff. Berlioz's second sketch matches his final version in most respects. He next prepared an orchestral draft in pencil on the pages that would be used for the orchestral score in ink (cf. aut. IV, 41-55, where the woodwind and bass lines are drafted in pencil).

The aspect of these sketches most interesting to the present study[57] is their concision. As the obvious effort of a composer beginning written work on a movement, page 158cv must be the earliest sketch. Page 156cv is no doubt the last; nothing more could have been accomplished in a further sketch. (The scalar figuration and orchestration were added in the pencil draft). The second sketch must immediately succeed the first, for the experiments in m. 11 of the second begin from a progression reached in m. 9 of the first. This evidence, like that of the *Troyens* sketches, shows Berlioz's sketching to be a highly concentrated process.

Like the *Troyens* sketches, these two are as interesting for what they do not contain as for what they do. There is only the single sketch of the scalar passage that seems in performance to be a primary organizing factor. Berlioz leaves no written indication of a preconceived harmonic or formal structure; in fact, he seems rather to be led on by his music in the early measures, not to be following a careful plan. There is nothing to suggest that he had begun to formulate plans for the orchestration; the scoring and ornamentation are from a later stage of composition. At the same time, a considerable evolution takes place in the course of sketching: the first sketch begins as a tentative first step in composition, while the latter half of the second has every characteristic of a continuity draft.

B. Advanced sketches.

Another group of sketches comes from a more advanced stage of composition. The planned work has begun to assume its definitive shape, and the composer prepares sketches to work out its details. The sketches thus represent solutions to passing and often minor difficulties of composition: intricacies of counterpoint, transposition, and modulation. They are for the most part contemporaneous with the draft of the full score, thus separate sheets of paper used by Berlioz when he encountered problems. Decisions on orchestration, contrapuntal detail, and nuances of phrasing and dynamics are reached therein.

Two sketches, both from *Benvenuto Cellini*, are fragments of a transitional stage of planning, where the composer attempts to chart the continuous musical direction of a passage. Berlioz has already established his musical text, notating it without hesitation or change. Yet he makes no more advanced decisions about the nature of the movement; his purpose is merely to set the passage down in writing. Since both are sketches of passages added to the original version, c. 1838,[58] they may well have been loose leaves added to a short score of at least portions of the work. They are now preserved independently, having been found among the composer's papers.

One of the two is for a continuation of the Cardinal's ultimatum to Cellini: *"Si Persée enfin n'est fondu / Dès ce soir tu seras pendu"* (Act III, no. 14; edn. Choudens, pp. 424-25). Berlioz sketched only the vocal line in each system, so he must have added the accompaniment directly into his full score. *"Ah, maintenant"* at the end is a cue for another paragraph of the Cardinal's text deleted from the three-act version (Ex. 3.23):

à la jus-ti- ce de par dieu je li-vre-rai ta tê- te

Example 3.23: Sketch for *Benvenuto Cellini* (F-Pc ms 1178).

This passage was performed in the version of 1838; it is found in the manuscript conductor's score (F-Po A 521a, IV, 429-33).

In a similar sketch Berlioz works out the transition between Cellini's air *"Sur les monts"* (Act III, no. 15) and the chorus *"Bienheureux les matelots."* In the original version the two movements occurred in succession at the beginning of the fourth tableau, during the day of grace granted by the Cardinal in the preceding scene. Cellini's cadenza (*"Ah! que ne suis-je un pauvre pasteur,"* edn. Choudens, p. 437) precedes the sketch, which begins with the cue *"pasteur."* It goes on with the vow of Cellini to Teresa: *"je vais sauver ma gloire."* The last cue, *"Choeur dans la coulisse, guitares"* is for the G-major introduction of *"Bienheureux les matelots"* (cf. edn. Choudens, p. 323) (Ex. 3.24, pp. 152-53). Berlioz probably added this segment at the same time he added Cellini's cavatina (*"La gloire était ma seule idole"*) to the first act, since both deal with the concept *gloire*; the vow to Teresa, however, seems not to have been performed.

A folio in Berlin (**D-Bds** mus. ms H. Berlioz 2) is among the most interesting of Berlioz's pre-score autographs, a fragment of a continuity draft for the *Convoi funèbre de Juliette* (see Facsimile III.4, pp. 154-55).

Example 3.24: Sketch for *Benvenuto Cellini* (F-Pc ms 1177).

Example 3.24 (continued)

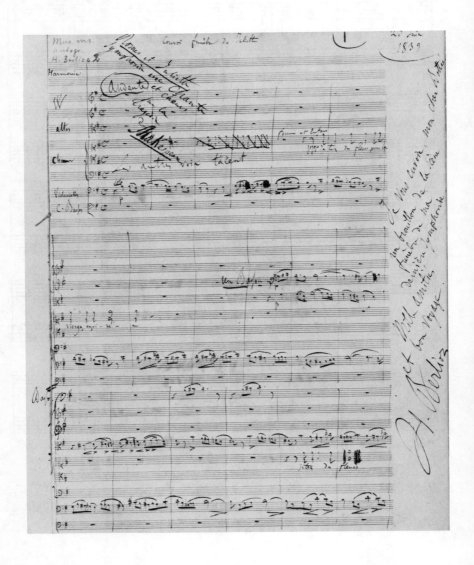

Facsimile III.4: *Roméo et Juliette*, draft (**D·Bds** mus. ms H. Berlioz 2), pp. 1-2.

Facsimile III.4 (continued)

It cannot be a page removed from the finished full score, since the calligraphy is not careful enough and the wind parts are reduced in two staves marked *"harmonie."* Moreover, Berlioz signed the dedication on 28 June 1839. He did not finish the symphony until 8 September, according to a note at the end of the full score. *"Cette symphonie commencée le 24 janvier 1839 a été terminée le 8 septembre de la même année"* ("This symphony, begun on the 24th of January, was finished the 8th of September of the same year"). (Two notes in the body of the score confirm those dates. Berlioz marked *"commencé le 24"* at the beginning of the *Fête chez Capulet* [aut. p. 65] and *"[fini] Sept 8"* at the end of the section *Roméo au tombeau de Juliette* [aut. p. 344]). Thus the leaf was presented to Bottée de Toulmon, a librarian at the Conservatoire, considerably before the work was complete. At least the *Convoi funèbre* must have been in score, however, or Berlioz would never have given the leaf away. The composer himself identifies it as a *brouillon*, or draft.

There are several musical variants between the draft and the version in the autograph score. The only chorus Berlioz first envisioned was for women and children (m. 5). Many of the doublings for winds are not in the draft, so they were added during preparation of a fair score. A number of dynamics were also added at a later time, but in general the fragmentary draft is itself carefully prepared with regard to phrasing and dynamics. Hairpin crescendo indications and Berlioz's idiosyncratic accents are common. Some of the nuances are more carefully noted—or at least are more complex—than in the autograph. In mm. 23-24, for example, Berlioz has marked for the second violin (Ex. 3.25):

Example 3.25: Draft for *Convoi funèbre*, mm. 23-24, violin II.

This direction is the same as the one accompanying the first statement by the cello, but in the full score the two indications no longer agree.

The untidiness in the second system of the verso page is the result of an error in copying. In the first version of mm. 29-30, Berlioz repeated the figure in m. 28, then went ahead in m. 30 with the figure actually planned for m. 29 (Ex. 3.26):

Example 3.26: Ibid., mm. 29-30, original reading.

The violin line had already been written, so the passage as originally set must have been a clerical error. The first version noted for the contrabass was also a measure off (Ex. 3.27):

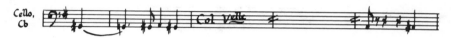

Example 3:27: Ibid., first version of contrabass line.

At mm. 38-39 Berlioz either left out a planned measure while copying the violin line, or, more likely, decided to extend the phrase by a measure before reaching the cadence. The original barline comes just between present mm. 38 and 40; the planned reading was as follows (Ex. 3.28):

Example 3.28: Ibid., mm. 38-40, violin.

He decided to make the change before writing any of the other parts, for in all the other instrumental parts, three measures have been wedged into the space originally planned for two. The vocal line, however, had already been drafted, for the whole rest first intended for the single measure has been crossed out and replaced by two whole rests. The melodic and vocal lines were thus noted first, after which Berlioz went back to fill in the cello line, inner strings, and finally the woodwinds.

It is clearly possible that these two pages are removed from a complete draft of *Roméo et Juliette* in short score. But Berlioz may have had some specific difficulty in composing this particular movement that kept him from being able to go directly from sketches to a full score. The counterpoint is relatively complex, and the choral interjections irregularly spaced. The question cannot be answered on the basis of the document, which is the only one of its kind among Berlioz's manuscripts.

Two tiny remnants of sketches for the fourth movement of *Harold en Italie* may have come from a larger group, since they seem to be sketches for continuity cut from a sheet covered with musical notation. One shows a fragment of the E-minor statement of the main theme (mm. 54ff, **OBE** p. 111/9) (Ex. 3.29):

Example 3.29: Sketch for *Harold en Italie*, aut. p. 197 *cv*.

The other collette has on its verso four notes from a slightly earlier passage (m. 45, **OBE** p. 111/6) (Ex. 3.30):

Example 3.30: Ibid., p. 187 *cv*.

The implication is strong that the sketch was for the purpose of outlining the transitional section, mm. 44-59.

A revision added to the score of *Roméo et Juliette* shows on the collette-verso a draft of the orchestral interlude between the first and second choral recitatives (movt. II, mm. 36-55, **OBE** pp. 20-21; see Facsimile III.5). Several details of this sketch are characteristic of sketches contemporaneous with the orchestral score, including the instrumental cues and markings of dynamics and phrases. Like both the drafts for *Benvenuto Cellini*, it effects a modulatory transition. The melodic material was eventually scored only for winds; the violins do not enter with melody until m. 52 (sketch m. 20).

Another type of sketch frequently encountered merely sets up the proper transposition for brass instruments.[59] There is a chart for transposing ophicléide parts on the last page of the *Requiem* score (Ex. 3.31):

Example 3.31: Transposition table for ophicléides, *Requiem,* aut. fol. A^r (after p. 217).

Facsimile III.5: Sketch for orchestral interlude in movt. II of *Roméo et Juliette* (mm. 36-55; OBE III, 20-21, aut. p. 63*cv*).

In a sketch for the finale of *Roméo et Juliette*, Berlioz transposes a modulatory passage for horns in F, D, C, and A, trumpet in E, and three trombones (see Facsimile III.6; cf. movt. VII mm. 6-8, OBE pp. 182-83). Similarly, in a pencil sketch found in *Benvenuto Cellini*, Berlioz notates an idea in C before transposing it for saxhorns and trumpets (Ex. 3.32; facsimile in Holoman, "The Present State of Berlioz Research," *Acta Musicologica* 47 [1975] opp. p. 40).

Example 3.32: Sketch, *Benvenuto Cellini*, aut. I, 128*cv*.

This is a sketch for the last movement of Berlioz's *Te Deum* (completed 1849, revised and first performed 1855),[60] the *Marche pour la présentation des drapeaux*. Despite the deletion of this passage from the autograph score (in the Saltykov-Shchedrin State Public Library, Leningrad), it can easily be identified, since the page of score on which it appears calls for *saxhorn suraigu en Bb*. Berlioz calls for that instrument only in this movement and in a few passages of *Les Troyens*.[61] Vestiges of a title are barely legible at the top of the page: *"Marche pour la présentation des drapeaux."*

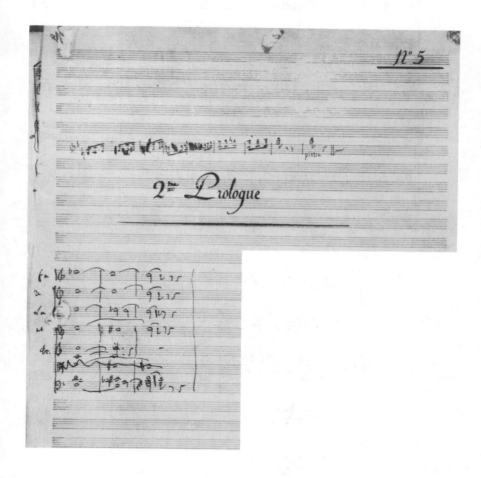

Facsimile III.6: Sketches for *Roméo et Juliette*, aut. p. 396: coda of *La Reine Mab* and transposition table for movt. VII.

Another situation in which Berlioz relied heavily on sketching was the composition of intricate contrapuntal passages. In a sketch for the fugal opening of *Harold en Italie* (movt. I, mm. 7-12, **OBE** p. 2), he enters the parts for strings in score and adds the woodwind solos to a single staff at the top (Ex. 3.33):

Example 3.33: Sketch, *Harold en Italie*, aut. p. 13*cv*.

He makes a few changes, deleting a contrapuntal passage first notated in the flute line (m. 3), rewriting the bass and cello line at m. 5, and altering the musical text in minor ways. The figured bass indication "*6*" (m. 3) is the first of several that will be encountered. The remarkable aspect of the fragment, however, is how little actually is changed; here he has notated a version quite close to the one actually adopted.

Counterpoint seems to be at issue in another sketch from *Harold en Italie*. Although incomplete, it can be identified as part of an attempt to fit the *idée fixe* back into the texture of the *Marche de pèlerins* (cf. the finished version, movt. II, mm. 64ff, **OBE** pp. 60ff). Berlioz sketched two versions: first, the *idée fixe* as a phrase of the march, then in its usual configuration in the viola. Here again Berlioz had not settled for certain on the idea of identifying the sustained *idée fixe* with the solo viola (Ex. 3.34):

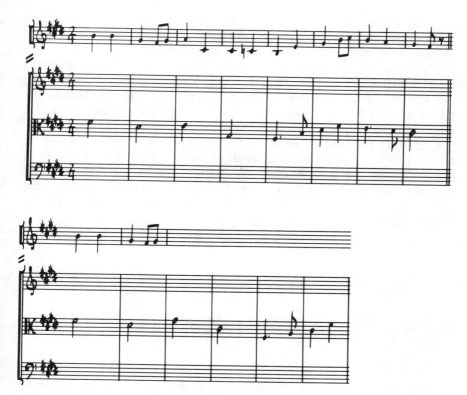

Example 3.34: Sketch, *Harold en Italie*, aut. p. 124cv (facs. in Holoman, "The Present State of Berlioz Research," *Acta Musicologica* 47 [1975], opp. p. 40).

On the back of a part for ophicléide monstre bound with the score to the *Requiem* is a sketch of a passage for trumpet and cornet (Ex. 3.35):

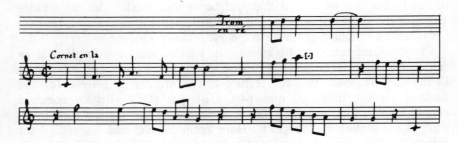

Example 3.35: Sketch, *Requiem*, ophicléide monstre part.

In this sketch, Berlioz worked out details of a trumpet call that accompanies the duet of Teresa and Cellini, *"Quand des sommets de la montagne / L'aigle entend la voix de sa compagne"* (Act III, no. 13). For this particular passage (mm. 66-75, edn. Choudens, pp. 374-75) the cornet doubles first Cellini's part, then Teresa's, with the trumpet (eventually, the second cornet) entering in the third measure. In the sketch, the cornet doubles Teresa's part as far as the end of the phrase. This idea was eventually dropped.

One other item should be mentioned as a sketch whose purpose is to solve a problem encountered in drafting. At the end of the autograph of the *Symphonie fantastique*, movt. IV, Berlioz can be seen adapting the excerpt from *Les Francs-Juges* to become an integral part of the symphony. The sketch evolves through three different stages,[62] first in eighth notes for the first measure (Ex. 3.36):

Example 3.36: Sketch for the *Marche au supplice* from the *Symphonie fantastique*, aut. movt. IV, p. 35o, first version. See Facsimile III.7.

then in quarter notes, with the same second measure (Ex. 3.37):

Example 3.37: Ibid., second version.

and finally, in the staff above, in the final form (Ex. 3.38):

Example 3.38: Ibid., third version.

The whole complex has the following appearance, caused by the conflation of the two separate plans (Ex. 3.39):

Example 3.39: Ibid., entire sketch.

In this sketch (as well as in other advanced sketches) the marks for phrasing and articulation are an integral part of the musical idea.

C. Sketches for revision.

A consideration of sketches for revision might logically follow rather than precede the section about drafting. The sketches treated in the following pages have indeed been somewhat arbitrarily selected, and similar sketches are noted in conjunction with certain revisions mentioned

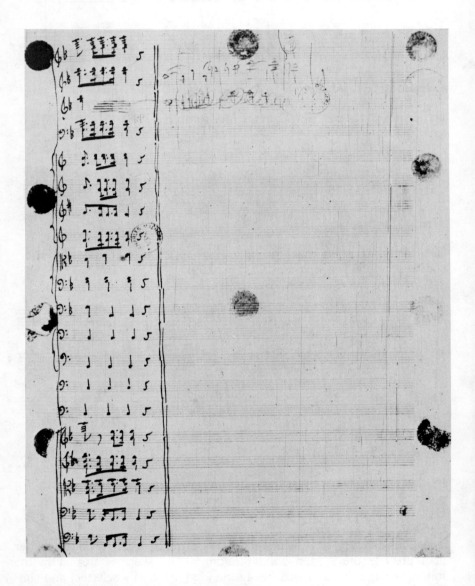

Facsimile III.7: *Symphonie fantastique*, aut., movt. IV, p. 35o.

later in the chapter. But all sketches are alike in that they are plans for musical passages, and thus each of these has characteristics that relate it to the ones previously considered: most are still found on collette-verso surfaces, and each deals with plans for composition.

One sketched revision concerns a point of transition in Friar Lawrence's air from *Roméo et Juliette* (movt. VII). Originally, the strophe ended at m. 102 (**OBE** p. 207/6), and the dialogue of Montagues followed, based on the opening motive from the symphony (Ex. 3.40):

Example 3.40: *Roméo et Juliette,* finale (movt. VII), mm. 105-07 (**OBE** p. 208/3-5).

Berlioz perhaps felt that the transition was too abrupt and that the words *"Mais notre sang rougit leur glaive"* would be lost in the furious dialogue that followed. He decided to add a straightforward declamation of the line at the beginning of the passage. He has taken the extraordinary step of sketching these two simple measures in three stages: a first trying-out in pencil of the figure, a further pencil sketch with the words added, and a definitive version in ink (Exs. 3.41a-c):

a.

b.

c.

Example 3.41a: Sketch, *Roméo et Juliette*, aut. p. 397, first version. See Facsimile III.8.

Example 3.41b: Ibid., second version.

Example 3.41c: Ibid., final version.

The new passage accomplishes its purpose: the listener can hardly fail to understand the words.

Berlioz was often dissatisfied with the endings of his pieces (see, concerning *La Reine Mab*, BerMém Chap. XLIX [transcribed below, p. 181]). A typical revision was the addition of a coda. Sketches for three such added codas are preserved. One collette-verso in *Roméo et Juliette* contains a one-line sketch for the last measures of *La Reine Mab* (Ex. 3.42), obviously the revision to which Berlioz refers in Chapter XLIX:

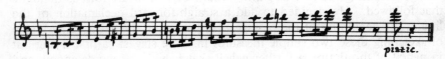

Example 3.42: Sketch, Ibid., p. 396. See Facsimile III.6, upper sketch.

Similarly, the coda to the *Menuet des follets* from *La Damnation de Faust* is sketched in pencil and bound into the autograph score. It is one of the most complete sketches of a lengthy section that exists, with phrase markings, dynamics, tempi, and instrumentation all specified (Ex. 3.43):

Facsimile III.8: Sketch for revision in *Roméo et Juliette*, movt. VII, mm. 238-40 (OBE III, 208), aut. p. 397; sketch in staves 23-26.

Example 3.43: Sketch, *Menuet des follets*, from *La Damnation de Faust*, aut. III, 199.

Example 3.43 (continued)

Berlioz still had difficulty bringing the section to an end, and he has drafted the final measures three times before deciding on the proper phrase length. (In the definitive version, he extends the coda again, adding the clever twelve measures now at the very end.)

The last reminiscence of the *Marche de pelèrins* in movement IV of *Harold en Italie* is also an addition. A fragment of the sketch for it is preserved as collette-verso in the autograph (Ex. 3.44):

Example 3.44: Sketch, *Harold en Italie*, aut. p. 248*cv*.

Revisions of more minute details accompanied by sketching are too numerous to mention individually. Berlioz habitually reviewed his scores with a pencil in hand, noting new versions in the margin before adopting them in the more definitive medium of ink. As the details involved become more and more minute, it becomes progressively more difficult to define the difference between a sketch for a revision and the revision itself.

D. Drafting.

Upon completing the preliminary sketching, Berlioz drafted the movement or work he was considering. Like Beethoven's composing scores,[63] Berlioz's drafts must have been full of major revisions and changes of every kind of musical detail. Yet in no case is there an autograph of Berlioz that looks like one of Beethoven's composing scores. Even in the most complex autographs the first layer, before it was revised, was entered firmly with few revisions, in a neat if not especially elegant hand. The autographs of the *Symphonie fantastique,* movement I, and *Harold en Italie,* for example, are full of both major and minor revisions, but Berlioz obviously drafted them in a fair hand and only then went back to do the revisions. His handwriting is as sure at the bottom layer of a heavily edited work as in the fairest copy.

A link is surely missing between the latest sketches, where only the basic melodic and harmonic structure have been determined, and the autograph draft in ink, where the composition is more or less complete. Moreover, Berlioz's own remarks in several letters suggest that a stage is missing:

J'ai presque terminé l'ouverture du Roi Lear; *je n'ai plus que l'instrumentation à achever* (BerCG 223: 6 May 1831; to Gounet et al.).

I have almost finished the overture *Le Roi Lear;* I have only the orchestration left to do.

Vous voulez savoir ce que j'ai fait depuis mon arrivée en Italie;... 2° ouverture de Rob-Roy MacGregor *(esquissée à Nice, et que j'ai eu la bêtise de montrer à Mendelssohn, à mon corps défendant, avant qu'il y en eût la dixième partie de fixée). Je l'ai finie et instrumentée aux montagnes de Subiaco* (BerCG 256: Rome, 1 January 1832; to Ferdinand Hiller).

You want to know what I have done since my arrival in Italy; . . . 2) an overture called *Rob-Roy MacGregor* (sketched in Nice, and which I was stupid enough to show to Mendelssohn, against my will, before it was a tenth corrected). I finished and orchestrated it in the mountains around Subiaco.

Enfin aujourd'hui, n'ayant ni partition à instrumenter, ni vérification du travail de mon copiste à faire...(BerCG 409: Paris, 23 September 1834; to Adèle).

Finally today, having neither scores to orchestrate, nor proofreading of my copyist's work to do . . .

These are among Berlioz's most striking references to his own composition, since they imply that the orchestration of a work occurred subsequent to what the composer believed was its completion. Such a conclusion is all the more unexpected as it comes from a composer who contributed so much to the techniques of orchestration; one might expect the instrumentation of a work to be part of its initial conception. But there is little reason to doubt Berlioz's honesty here. How, then, did he accomplish his orchestration?

The answer lies in a hitherto unrecognized—or, if recognized, then undervalued—characteristic of the autograph scores. In many of his autographs there is an underlying pencil draft where Berlioz did exactly the sort of work he describes. The Requiem is the earliest piece where the pencil draft is consistently visible, though there are traces of it in passages of the *Symphonie fantastique, Harold en Italie,* and *Benvenuto Cellini.* In portions of *Roméo et Juliette* the underlying draft can be spotted in every measure. The manuscript of *La Nonne sanglante* provides conclusive proof of this procedure, for Berlioz abandoned the work before erasing his pencil marks. Some passages in that score are substantially complete in ink, with others carefully worked out in pencil. The pencilings include copious marginal notes (*"changer à cause de La Juive,"* fol. 37r) and schedules of things to do or sections to complete (*"25 juillet, 27 juillet,"* fol. 55r). Similarly, in *Roméo et Juliette* a fragment is preserved (p. 310o) which shows the typical appearance of a pencil draft. Berlioz becomes more and more dependent on this form of drafting, and he tends to erase it less and less. It is haphazardly erased in *Roméo et Juliette* and plainly visible in much of *Faust.*

Table IV lists the places where drafting may be seen on a relatively large scale.

TABLE IV

PENCIL DRAFTS IN BERLIOZ'S AUTOGRAPH SCORES

Movement	Page	Approximate measure numbers	Parts drafted[64]
SYMPHONIE FANTASTIQUE, aut.			
I	29-32	249-75	flute
I	44c-50	360-402	flute, oboe, accpt.
I	51cv	403-07	violin cue staff
V	43-46	277-96	oboe, violin I, cello
HAROLD EN ITALIE, aut.[65]			
III	161-64	111-28	viola line
IV	191-92	87-90, 97	cello, contrabass
IV	204-05	179-84	cello, contrabass
IV	206-07	192-98	contrabass
IV	208	200-01, 203-04	brass parts, reduced to one staff
IV	211-13	215-16, 219-20, 223-33	brass parts
IV	248	442-49	violin (abandoned version)
IV	260-61	527-41	ophicléide, brass
REQUIEM, aut. throughout			

Movement	Page	Approximate measure numbers	Parts drafted

BENVENUTO CELLINI, aut.: throughout, on the pages of the original version (e.g. I, 52-53o, 54-56).

ROMEO ET JULIETTE, aut.

Movement	Page	Approximate measure numbers	Parts drafted
I	3-13	14-86	bassoons, clarinet, brass
I	19-22	127-61	strings
I	47-50	Entire movement: *Premiers transports*	cello[66]
I	52-57	Entire movement: *Scherzetto: Mab*	general
III[67]	143-74, 191-94, 199-200	Entire portion on original paper: *Scène d'amour*	general
IV	205-72, 275-80, 283	Entire movement: *La Reine Mab*	general
VI	285-99	Entire movement: *Convoi funèbre de Juliette*	general
VI	303-10o, 311-14, 317-44	Entire portion on original paper: *Roméo au tombeau des Capulets*	general
VII[68]	345-60, 371-80, 383-94, 397-448, 451-60	Entire portion on original paper: *Finale*	general

Unerased drafts in later works, e.g.:

Le Corsaire, aut. (**F-Pc** ms 1159)
La Damnation de Faust, aut. (**F-Pc** ms 1190, 4 volumes)
La Nonne sanglante, aut. (**F-Pn** Vm^2 Rés 178; see in particular pp. 56^v, 57^r-64^r).

For the manuscripts now covered with ink draft, it is often impossible to tell exactly what was accomplished in pencil. The pencil marks in *Harold en Italie* seem to be reminders of music already planned. A pencilled line that runs through the staves for cello and bass in the fourth movement (visible on pp. 208, 210, 248 and 249) outlines the musical continuity. It includes cues for the brass chords in mm. 363 (**OBE** fig. 51) and 366 (Ex. 3.45):

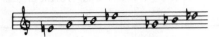

Example 3.45: *Harold en Italie*, aut. p. 208.

as well as in mm. 378ff (**OBE** p. 150) (Ex. 3.46):

Example 3.46: Ibid., p. 211.

The pencil marks in the score of the *Requiem*, to be discussed in detail below, seem at times to outline the harmonic framework on a single staff and at others to set out all the details of orchestration. But it is clear that Berlioz determined the specifics of his orchestration at this level. Verbal notes on instrumentation are quite common. One can be seen through the erasures in *Harold* (aut. p. 82): *"La V^{elle} solo avec les Bassons."* And in *Roméo et Juliette* (aut. p. 416, concerning movt. VII, mm. 100ff, **OBE**, p. 220) he writes: *"l'intervalle des cors deviendra du double plus fréquente en approchant à la Fin."*

Perhaps the most interesting pencil marks of all occur on a blank page of the *Requiem* (aut. p. 21). Berlioz has noted there a schedule for the completion of the work, now erased and only barely legible:

à instrumenter:	Dies irae et Tuba mirum	3 j[ours]
	Rex tremendae	3 id
	Sanctus	4 id
	Lacrymosa	4 id
	Agnus	4 id
	Offertoire	3 id
	Le requiem et introit	
ainsi que	le Quid sum miser	
	et le Quaerens me	
	il faut faire [recopier? - illegible]	8 j
	Total un mois pour tout cela (Juin)	

The *Requiem* must have been substantially complete by the time Berlioz entered this note in his score. He had announced its completion on 22 May 1837, in a letter to Liszt (BerCG 498). Three movements had been drafted already. The note thus clarifies the definition of *"instrumenter"* as used by Berlioz in the schedule and in the letters cited above: it means "working out all the details of instrumentation."

Only one page shows much detailed evidence of the final drafting procedure. Page 7 of the autograph of *Harold en Italie* is a collette-verso on which there is an ink draft eventually abandoned by Berlioz (Facsimile III.9). Notable are the vigor with which the parts for violins and cello have been copied, the sketched viola part, tentative sketches of the harp part, and the hesitantly scratched revisions in the lines for winds. He must have been unsure of the entry of the harp and winds, and the contrapuntal passage for viola must have been a second (or third) idea. Probably he worked the problem out on another piece of paper, removed the page from his fair copy (only to replace it later as a collette), and began again.

It has been possible to cite here some hitherto unrecognized examples of Berlioz's methods of written work prior to the orchestra score. The new evidence answers some old and stubborn questions. A missing link in the compositional process, the pencil draft, is the stage where Berlioz's brilliant orchestral effects originated. It is now clear that he also had sketch paper on hand during most stages of composition. Considered together, the sketches and drafts suggest a typical procedure: sketching of ideas and plans, working-out of sections, drafting in short score, drafting in pencil in full score, and copying of the draft in ink. This new evidence consists of a limited number of bits and pieces gleaned from what may have been a much larger body of manuscript sources. As such it poses two questions central to a consideration of the composer's methods: Do these sketches represent procedures and techniques typical of Berlioz's composition? On the basis of what is preserved, can other sketches be assumed to have existed?

Berlioz must often have solved simple mechanical problems on paper. Transposition tables, for example, are common in his manuscripts. He seems habitually to have noted his ideas for revisions and improvements either in the orchestral scores or on separate sheets; in these cases the composer required only one or two tries to arrive at the proper solution of a musical problem. It can be inferred from the documents for *Benvenuto Cellini, Les Troyens,* and *Harold en Italie* (cited above, pp. 150-53, 126-30, and 158, respectively) that there are sketches in which sections or possibly entire movements were set out in short score with the

Facsimile III.9: Abandoned draft of *Harold en Italie*, movt. I, mm. 32-36, aut. p. 7.

accompaniment reduced to one or two staves. Possibly this type of sketch existed for every work.

For earlier stages of sketching, very little can be deduced. The material for *Les Troyens* and the lost sketchbook contain simple melodies, few of them actually used. In every case they are related to a formerly conceived dramatic idea, as in the one-line sketches for the ballets in Act IV of *Les Troyens* and the triumphal march for the military symphony. At least for *Les Troyens*, there were some attempts to plan the harmonic structure of certain movements in writing, but this practice seems more an exception than a rule. Berlioz began the *Invocation* from *Faust* with no firm plan of how it would work out and developed its basic structure at a single sitting.

There must have been other sketches. The same considerations that caused Berlioz to resort to sketching the preserved items must in similar situations have led to other sketches. He may simply have destroyed them in the conflagration of 1867.[69] Obviously he thought little of obsolete sketches, since he used the blank surfaces for collettes. The fragments in *Harold en Italie*, for example, were cut from a more extensive set of sketches, reflecting the composer's lack of interest in them once they were no longer needed for reference.

It appears, however, that for a great deal of Berlioz's music, sketching with pencil and paper was a secondary, mechanical procedure. The organization and structure of a work, as well as many specific details, seem to have been well in mind before he first picked up his pen. There is no indication that for many pieces (including the majority of movements in *Les Troyens*) he did any sketching at all. Berlioz recalls extraordinary facility in setting certain works (e.g. the *Marche au supplice* and the *Marche hongroise*; see **BerMém** Chap. XXVI and *"Deuxième voyage en Allemagne, troisième lettre"*). *"Je l'ai toute dans la tête,"* he tells Ferrand of the *Symphonie fantastique* ("I have it all in my head").[70] For songs, shorter movements, and possibly vast stretches of the major works, no sketch may ever have existed. We can never know how much of his own material Berlioz destroyed, but the preserved sources suggest that sketches were by no means necessary for every work.

3. Revisions in the autograph

After beginning serious written work on a composition, Berlioz ordinarily went ahead to complete a satisfactory version in short order. Even the larger works seldom required more than a few months of sustained work; smaller ones were finished in a matter of days. He seldom began a new piece while at work on another, and he would drop as many other engagements and responsibilities as he could in order to finish. Each new composition became an obsession. From the first announcement of its idea to its first rehearsal, the *Symphonie fantastique* took a little over three months (February-May 1830). *Le Roi Lear* took about two (April-May 1831), and the *Mélologue*, with music adapted from previously-written material, took only a few weeks in June 1831. Most of the work on his colossal composition *La Damnation de Faust* was accomplished in a single summer (1846).[71]

But he did not leave the first version of a major work alone for long. It would undergo a long, complicated process of revision, beginning immediately and lasting until the definitive publication. Berlioz reviewed every detail of his work in the course of its performances, usually noting in his own score the changes he wanted to make in the musical text. Several important stages of revision are found in a typical autograph, interrelated in complex ways. A movement's basic structure may be completely changed (e.g. movts. I, II, and III of the *Symphonie fantastique*). More frequently a minor detail will never quite satisfy the composer, and he will revise it again and again (e.g. the "dissonant" bells in movt. II of *Harold en Italie*). "Retouching," as Berlioz called it, was a significant step in his compositional technique.

He frequently notes having revised a work, occasionally explaining the nature and purpose of the alterations:

Je me suis mis à retoucher cet oratorio du Passage de la mer Rouge *que je vous ai montré il y a sept ou huit mois et que je trouve à présent terriblement barbouillé dans certains endroits* (**BerCG** 26: July 1824; to Lesueur).	I have begun to retouch that oratorio, *Le Passage de la mer Rouge,* that I showed to you seven or eight months ago and that I now find awfully sloppy in certain places.
Ma Messe a été exécutée le jour de la Sainte-Cécile avec un succès double de la première fois; les petites corrections que j'y avais faites l'ont sensiblement améliorée (**BerCG** 77: 29 November 1827; to Ferrand).	My mass was played on St. Cecilia's Day, twice as successfully as the first time; the little corrections that I made noticeably improved it.
... Mais quand est venu le Resurrexit *de ma Messe, que vous n'avez jamais entendu depuis que je l'ai retouché...* (**BerCG** 93: 6 June 1828; to Ferrand).	. . . But when the *Resurrexit* of my Mass came up—which you haven't heard since I retouched it—. . .
Je la retoucherai encore dans quelques menus détails.... (concerning *Harold en Italie*; **BerCG** 425: 10 January 1835; to Ferrand).	I will touch it up again in several minor details.

*Malgré la complexité de son tissu har-
monique, je mis aussi peu de temps à
composer cette symphonie que j'en ai mis en
général à écrire mes autres ouvrages;
j'employai aussi un temps considérable à la
retoucher. Dans la* Marche des Pèlerins
*même, que j'avais improvisée en deux heures
en rêvant un soir au coin de mon feu, j'ai
pendant plus de six ans introduit des
modifications de détail qui, je le crois, l'ont
beaucoup améliorée* (concerning *Harold en
Italie;* BerMém Chap. XLV).

Despite its complex harmonic organization,
the symphony took me as little time to
compose as my other works have usually
done; but once again I spent a considerable
time revising it. The Pilgrims' March
itself—which I sketched in a couple of
hours one evening, musing by the
fire—underwent many changes of detail
during the next six years or more which I
think greatly improved it (BerMemCairns).

The most complete and eloquent statement on the motives and values
that lie behind his revisions is in the *Mémoires*, in reference to changes
in *Roméo et Juliette:*

*M. Frankoski (le secrétaire d'Ernst) m'ayant
signalé à Vienne la mauvaise et trop brusque
terminaison du scherzo de la fée Mab,
j'écrivis pour ce morceau la* coda *qui existe
maintenant et détruisis la première. D'après
l'avis de M. d'Ortigue, je crois, une
importante coupure fut pratiquée dans le
récit du père Laurence, refroidi par des
longueurs où le trop grand nombre de vers
fournis par le poète m'avaient entraîné.
Toutes les autres modifications, additions,
suppressions, je les ai faites de mon propre
mouvement, en l'entendant à Paris, à Berlin,
à Vienne, à Prague. Si je n'ai pas trouvé
d'autres tâches à y effacer, j'ai mis au moins
toute la bonne foi possible à les chercher et ce
que je possède de sagacité à les découvrir.*

*Après cela que peut un auteur, sinon
s'avouer franchement qu'il ne saurait faire
mieux, et se résigner aux imperfections de
son oeuvre? Quand j'en arrivai là, mais
seulement alors, la symphonie de* Roméo et
Juliette *fut publiée* (BerMém Chap.
XLIX).[72]

M. Frankoski, Ernst's secretary, drew my
attention in Vienna to the weak and much
too abrupt ending of the Queen Mab
scherzo, and I wrote the present coda in its
place. On the advice of (I think) M.
d'Ortigue, a cut was contrived in Friar
Lawrence's narration which greatly
improved it; I had made it too long, led
astray by the excessive number of lines
furnished by the librettist. All the other
modifications, additions and suppressions
I made on my own initiative, by dint of
observing the effect of the work as a whole
and in detail when I heard it in Paris,
Berlin, Vienna and Prague. If there are
other blemishes that I have missed, at least
I have tried sincerely and with what
judgment I possess to detect them.

After which, what can a composer do
but admit candidly that he has done his
best, and resign himself to the work's
imperfections? When I had reached that
point, and only then, the *Romeo and Juliet*
symphony was published (BerMemCairns).

Autographs of Berlioz typically show multiple stages of critical re-
evaluation that are best visualized as layers of work. They are easily
distinguished, since writing implements change from layer to layer.
Berlioz generally made several early sweeps through the score, noting in
pencil revisions to be entered later in ink. Other levels may be in brown
and black inks of slightly differing shades. Corrections in red ink, like

the ones in *Harold en Italie* and *Le Roi Lear*, were usually entered just before publication, and notations in red chalk are almost always associated with the last steps before publication. The revisions can be grouped by categories in descending order of their importance to the music itself:

A.   Large-scale revisions

B.   Revisions of details

C.   Practical problems

A. Large-scale revisions.

Among those revisions generally affecting more than a few measures at a time are addition, deletion, and reornamentation of sections.

By far the most common revision encountered in Berlioz's autographs is the deletion of a passage. Significant deletion occurs in every major work. Cuts made in the first movement of the *Symphonie fantastique* radically altered its structure: several measures at the beginning of the first movement were deleted[73] along with at least two sections of development (OBE I, xxvi-xxix). An introduction for solo piano was removed from the *Mélologue* before publication (OBE XIII, v). There are two major deletions from the first movement of *Harold en Italie* (OBE II, viii, xvii-xix). Scenes x-xx were removed from the original Act II of *Benvenuto Cellini*. Two important cuts were made in the *Requiem* well after it had first been published; Berlioz made these deletions by removing pages from the autograph and destroying them. For those deletions signaled by the initial and final measures of a passage remaining in the score (because the rest of the music on those two pages was still good), it is reasonable to conclude, as does the OBE, that a self-contained section of some length has been deleted. Altogether the number of deletions evident from the sources is remarkably large.

Berlioz's willingness to cast out large sections of his works was, to judge from his remarks about *Benvenuto Cellini* and *Roméo et Juliette*, rooted in a desire for popular success. The *Mémoires* indicate that he paid close attention to reactions of his audiences, attempting to correct *longueurs* by deleting them altogether. Moreover, as he grew older he became progressively more aware of the limitations inherent in the looser musical forms he had used as a younger composer. He seems to have developed in the late 1830s a more refined sense of musical concision, removing extraneous ideas from a number of works—*Le Roi Lear*, the *Symphonie fantastique*, and the *Requiem*, for example—as they were prepared for publication.

The deletion of an episode from *Harold en Italie*, movement I (aut. pp. 41-43, **OBE** fig. 7; trans. of deleted passage in **OBE** II, xvii-xviii) is typical. It tightens the developmental treatment of the second figure in the Allegro (Ex. 3.47):

Example 3.47: *Harold en Italie*, movt. I, mm. 166-69.

by deleting the motive (Ex. 3.48):

Example 3.48: Ibid., aut. p. 41.

and adding the canonic dialogue of mm. 173-79.

The insertion of a new fascicle in the same movement (aut. pp. 53 [c]–68) replaces a passage of unknown length. Berlioz introduced the inflection (Ex. 3.49):

Example 3.49: Ibid., m. 200 (**OBE** p. 30/3).

as a still later afterthought, since it is itself on a collette replacing an unrelated motive (Ex. 3.50):

Example 3.50: Ibid., aut. p. 54o.

The discarded section must have introduced the rising scalar motive (Ex. 3.51):

Example 3.51: Ibid., aut. p. 69.

as well as the motive (Ex. 3.52):

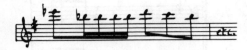

Example 3.52: Ibid.

because the two measures left over on p. 69 of the autograph contain them both. The original version and the replacement have identical conclusions, and it can be guessed that the new version is not a radical change but a shortening or simplification.

Among the most extensively revised works, as suggested by the *Mémoires*, is *Roméo et Juliette*. Berlioz's principal revision was to delete many of the chant-like passages for chorus, including a 34-line prologue to the third part (not mentioned by **OBE**). Fragments of the original version are found in the autograph score and more completely in a copyist's vocal score, now in the Columbia University Library, that was unknown to Malherbe and Weingartner; the text is complete in the printed libretto. In addition to the second prologue, the earlier version had more extensive description of the dramatic situation, for example:

> *Poussé par un désir que nul péril n'arrête,*
> *Roméo, sous le masque, ose entrer dans la fête,*
> *Parler à Juliette... et voilà que du bal*
> *Ils savourent tous deux l'enivrement fatal.*
> *Tybalt, l'ardent neveu de Capulet, s'apprête*
> *A frapper Roméo que tant d'amour trahit,*
> *Quand le vieillard, touché de la grâce et de l'âge*
> *Du jeune Montagu, s'oppose à cet outrage*
> *Et désarme Tybalt, qui, farouche, obéit,*
> *Et sort, en frémissant de rage,*
> *Le front plus sombre que la nuit.*[74]

It also presented an editorial comment from the composer:

> *Tels sont d'abord, tels sont les tableaux et les scènes*
> *Que devant vous, cherchant des routes incertaines,*
> *L'orchestre va tenter de traduire en accords,*
> *Puisse votre intérêt soutenir nos efforts!*[75]

These lines are something of an improvement on the version found in the autograph score (aut. p. 58*o*), where the words are:

> *Tels sont les images*
> *Et les premiers tableaux*
> *Que pour nouveaux hommages*
> *L'orchestre va traduire en accords.*
> *Puisse votre intérêt soutenir nos efforts.*[76]

Berlioz entered the revision on a collette after sketching it at the bottom of aut. p. 58*o* (Ex. 3.53):

Example 3.53: Sketch, *Roméo et Juliette*, aut. p. 58o. See Facsimile III.10.

He had been thinking of this type of narration for some time, for in 1835,[77] he added a note to the program of the *Symphonie fantastique* that included this remark:

Si les quelques lignes de ce programme eussent été de nature à pouvoir être récitées ou chantées entre chacun des morceaux de la symphonie, comme les choeurs des tragédies antiques, sans doute on ne se fût pas mépris de la sorte sur le sens qu'elles contiennent.[78]

If the few lines of this program had been the sort that could be recited or sung between each of the movements of the symphony, like the choruses of the tragedies of antiquity, their meaning would not have been misunderstood.

In *Roméo et Juliette* he endeavored to use exactly that plan, but found it unwieldy. Unwilling at first to begin the symphonic movements without indicating the precise background to the audience, he moved in the revisions toward a more abstract setting. Upon reflection and experience (since the recitatives were removed after the first performance), he decided that the choral recitative was tedious and had either to be made more interesting or deleted. Accordingly he removed three such scenes entirely and reorchestrated a passage of recitative in the first movement (mm. 69-77, **OBE** fig. 7), adding a motive from the *Scène d'amour*.

There were other major deletions, notably from the originally tedious *dénouement* (movt. VII). Berlioz removed some 91 mm. from Friar Lawrence's *Air* in part III (trans. **OBE** III, xxiff), a passage of unknown length from the love scene (**OBE** xv-xvi), and a long passage just before the end of the work (**OBE** xxiii-xxiv). He replaced and probably shortened the transition to the *Larghetto espressivo* (m. 81) of the long movement at the beginning of the second part (*Roméo seul*, etc.), though a bit of the earlier version can be seen in the score (trans. **OBE** pp. xii-xiii).

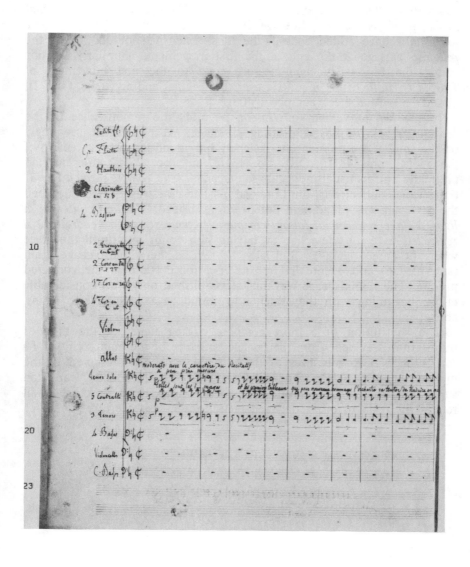

Facsimile III.10: Sketch for revision in *Roméo et Juliette*, originally at the end of movt. I (cf. OBE III, xxxiii-xxxiv), aut. p. 58*o*; the sketch is in staff 23.

Other changes involved the addition of a musical passage, generally as closing material. As has been noted, Berlioz had a critical eye for the endings of his pieces, and codas were frequently added. The sketched codas to *La Reine Mab* and the *Menuet des follets* have been transcribed in the previous section. Four of the five movements of the *Symphonie fantastique* have added codas,[79] the most extensive addition being the *religioso* passage at the end of the first movement. Similarly, Berlioz added the furious nineteen-measure coda to the first movement of *Harold en Italie*, using a collette over the original ending (trans. OBE II, x) and a new final sheet (aut. pp. 105-06).

In the last movement of *Harold*, he adds the reminiscence of the *Marche de pèlerins* played by strings off-stage. At a later time, seemingly on the spur of the moment, he sketched and added the final statement of the viola (mm. 483ff, OBE pp. 161ff, aut. pp. 255ff), for he had originally put his usual indication for *tacet*: *"L'alto compte jusqu'à la fin"* ("the viola counts [rests] until the end"). The note was crossed out when the new part was added, and Berlioz wrote instead: *"Il faut conserver sa ligne à l'alto solo en lui faisant compter des pauses jusqu'à l'endroit où il rentre"* ("leave the viola line in, having him count rests until the place where he enters again"). Still later, he revised the whole passage again (aut. p. 256) and eventually rewrote it a fourth time in the corrected proofs. The reminiscence was thus accomplished only with considerable effort, beginning with the sketch now found as a collette-verso (trans. above, pp. 171-72).

The subsitution of a more complex closing figure at the time of publication is evident from the fascicle structure of the manuscript of *Le Roi Lear*.[80] Two measures of the original coda are preserved in the manuscript. (Ex. 3.54). The new passage, with its added Neapolitan suggestion, represents a subtle refinement in the tonal structure, as it relates the coda to other flattened inflections in the overture.[81]

Example 3.54: *Le roi Lear*, aut. p. 25.

Another substitution occurs in the *Scène d'amour* (movt. III) from *Roméo et Juliette*. At measure 317 (aut. p. 184, **OBE** p. 114/7), the beginning of a different passage can be seen in the autograph (trans. **OBE** III, xv). A pencil sketch, completed in ink, sets out the transition and beginning of the new section (Ex. 3.55):

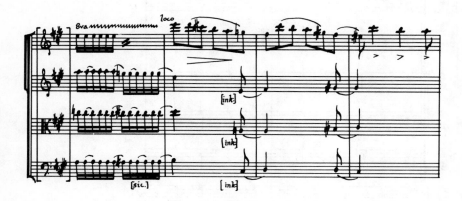

Example 3.55: *Roméo et Juliette*, aut. p. 184.

Then the whole page was covered by a fair copy of the new version (aut. p. 186), which includes some refinements in the wind parts (m. 317).

In the same movement, the composer replaced a passage with another, possibly shorter, one (aut. p. 194; trans. **OBE** xvi). Again, the first few bars of the original version are still in the autograph. Berlioz has sketched the new version in pencil (Ex. 3.56):

Example 3.56: Ibid., p. 194.

Reornamentation is a term conveniently applied to a number of operations designed to improve musical elegance: emendations in orchestration, part-writing, melodic shape, and accompanying figures. Large-scale reornamentation is not always easily detected in Berlioz's works. He seldom went back to rewrite a counterpoint, alter a melody, or recast a section directly in the autograph, preferring instead to remove whole sections and put new ones in their place. For original versions found under collettes, however, and especially in those cases where an instrumental part is removed or rewritten through the entire piece, some comparison is possible.

In *Benvenuto Cellini*, on an original autograph surface under a copyist's collette is found the following passage (Ex. 3.57):

Example 3.57: *Benvenuto Cellini*, aut. I, 52o (cf. edn. Choudens p. 35/15-36/1).

On empty lines above the staff, Berlioz entered a pencil sketch headed by the comment: *"il faut mettre la phrase à l'orchestre seul"* (Ex. 3.58):

Example 3.58: Ibid., sketch, aut. I, 52o.

In this revision (part of a longer set of sketched revisions in that movement), the composer delayed Fieramosca's vocal entry, substituting an orchestral statement of his motive.

A section of *Sardanapale*, part of the *incendie*, has been carefully revised in pencil. Here Berlioz improves the part-writing in piccolo, viola, and contrabass (Ex. 3.59):

Example 3.59: *Sardanapale*, aut. fol. 94[r].

One of the most significant revisions of *Harold en Italie* is the complete rewriting of the viola and harp parts in the first movement, for which Berlioz went to the length of having a copyist attach and clef the collettes for the revised version. The overall effect of this change was to remove the harp from all except the introductory statement of Harold's song (mm. 35-92, **OBE** pp. 5-17), and to so simplify the figuration of the viola part that it becomes almost solely concerned with the *idée fixe*.

This change reveals a remarkable fact: the idea of unifying the whole symphony with Harold's theme as stated by the viola developed well after the drafting of the first movement was underway. The second statement (mm. 73ff) of the theme is, in the final version, a canon arrangement between harp, brass, and celli followed by viola solo and winds. But the original idea is the one given by **OBE** (II, vii), visible underneath the collettes in the manuscript, where the orchestra had the song, and the harp and viola part accompanied with virtuoso figuration instead of the present simpler (and stronger) device. Perhaps the more complex part was intended to please Paganini and was removed after the violinist had lost interest in the work. In any event Berlioz went back through the viola part, simplified it to the point where Harold's song became identified with the viola itself—i.e. the viola began to assume the role of Harold—and liked the idea so much that he went on to use it in the other movements.[82]

The rewriting of the viola part was preceded by a suggested reading scrawled in pencil at the top of each page, a cue-line for the new version. But it is marked *"V^elle solo"* and was originally in the bass clef (thus very similar to the version in *Rob-Roy* from which it is borrowed). An early plan had been to have the cello state the theme; here is still another indication that the idea of unifying the whole symphony with the *idée fixe* simply stated by the viola had not yet occurred to the composer. Similar revisions remove or simplify the viola and harp parts in the rest of the movement. In mm. 259ff (**OBE** p. 37/8), the viola figuration has been changed from a version visible under collettes (trans. **OBE** ix) and worked into dialogue with the first violins. Virtually all these steps were accompanied with pencilled notations. **OBE** remarks that the final version of the viola and harp parts is the third stage of development of this passage; actually it is the fourth, for there is still another line of erased sketch visible underneath the cue-line.

Berlioz completely revised the orchestration of the *Fantaisie dramatique sur La Tempête* when he adopted it for the last movement of his *Mélologue*. The basic change was to substitute second violins *soli* for the harmonica part. At the same time, he took the opportunity to rewrite the *secondo* part for the piano four-hands, substituting sextuplets for groups of 32nds throughout (first version trans. **OBE** xxiv-xxxii). Later he went back and simplified the part for the four second violins (trans. **OBE** xxvii). These larger revisions were accompanied by changes of smaller details, to be noted.

Among the many intricate accompanying figures found throughout Berlioz's music are several that, as is obvious from the autographs, were only reached after other versions had been tried and rejected. The purpose of a number of these revisions seems to be to arrive at a perfect balance of melodic line with an accompaniment active enough to draw attention but not too busy or dense. At m. 48 in the *Invocation* of *Roméo et Juliette* (movt. VII, mm. 48ff, **OBE** p. 170) begins one of these passages where the accompaniment was extensively revised. Berlioz had originally left a detailed sketch in pencil of how the section was to go (Ex. 3.60):

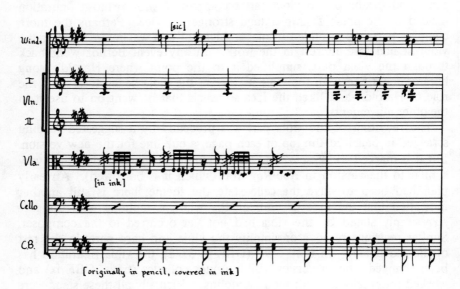

Example 3.60: *Roméo et Juliette*, aut. p. 310o.

He immediately covered the bottom line in ink. After a measure or so of filling in an extremely complicated figure (Ex. 3.61):

Example 3.61: Ibid., aut. p. 309o.

he decided to adopt a simpler version, which he sketched at the bottom of p. 309 (Ex. 3.62):

Example   3.62:   Ibid.

He incorporated the new version by adding a new page (p. 310[c]), no doubt having decided that the first accompaniment would be too complex, too buzzy.

Berlioz also revised the figure that accompanies the statement of the *idée fixe* at the beginning of the *Symphonie fantastique* (mm. 72-111). The original version was accompanied by a static eighth-note pattern (Ex. 3.63):

Example 3.63: *Symphonie fantastique*, aut. pp. 11-14 (entire passage trans. in **OBE** I, xxv-xxvi).

It was replaced with a solo statement, the *tutti* strings entering in m. 78 with detached eighths (Ex. 3.64):

Example 3.64: Ibid., mm. 72-79.

There is one significant category of revisions not technically covered by a study of autograph documents, those the composer made in passages borrowed from earlier works. No doubt the best known of these are the borrowing of a phrase from the competition cantata *Herminie* for the *idée fixe* in the *Symphonie fantastique* and of the *Huit Scènes de Faust* entire in *La Damnation de Faust* nearly twenty years later. The latter borrowing has been the subject of a number of published accounts, all of which agree that the versions found in the later *Faust* are more sophisticated, subtle, dramatic, and better set than in the *Huit Scènes*.[83]

An example from each of these cases bears directly on the present consideration. In the *Chant de la Fête de Pâques* occur the following measures (Ex. 3.65):

Example 3.65: *Chant de la Fête de Pâques*, from *Huit Scènes de Faust*, mm. 48-49.

When incorporated into the later *Faust*, the same passage had the following appearance (Ex. 3.66):

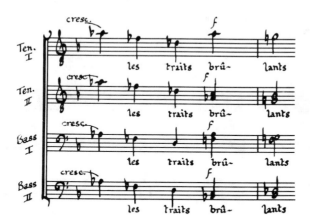

Example 3.66: Ibid., from *La Damnation de Faust*, scene iv, mm. 46-47 (of the *Chant de la Fête de Pâques*) (**OBE XI-XII**, 85).

This is one of only two cases encountered where Berlioz "corrected" what would traditionally be considered a grammatical error, the parallel fifths in the outer parts. The passage in the autograph of *La Damnation de Faust*, however, is fairly copied; there is no written indication that Berlioz actually regarded the change as a correction.

The setting of the *idée fixe* passage in *Herminie* is significant in that it is the first version of an idea revised and reset twice more. In 1828, Berlioz wrote the following accompaniment (Ex. 3.67):

Example 3.67: *Herminie*, mm. 1-7 (cf. exs. 3.63-.64, above).

As in other cases noted above, the composer has moved here from a comparatively complex statement, the version in *Herminie*, to a simpler one where the power of the bizarre melody is not lost in a dense accompaniment. The first version tried (and rehearsed) for the *Symphonie fantastique* erred by substituting a mundane ostinato accompaniment in eighths. The final version, of course, is best of all: the artist's song, basically unaccompanied, is interrupted by eighths that were probably intended to depict the anxiety of the passionate artist.

B. Revisions of details.

Berlioz is often at his most musical when revising minor details. While they may be of little importance to the overall line, these revisions are usually subtle, clever improvements of orchestral effects, of details consistently missed in performance, or of cumbersome or trivial passages. A typical revision is the simple step of delaying a clarinet entry in movement I of *Harold en Italie* from mm. 38ff to mm. 46ff (aut. p. 10o [original], 11 [revised], **OBE** II, 5, 6). The phrase is strengthened merely by establishing an antecedent-consequent relationship, where the second phrase is developed by the introduction of the new part. Another minor change makes a measure of the viola solo part noticeably more elegant. Here the composer extends the pedal-note *D* of the double-stopped figure from the third and fourth beats to the first and second (Exs. 3.68–.69):

Example 3.68: *Harold en Italie*, movt. I, aut. p. 15, first version.

Example 3.69: Ibid., m. 72, revised version.

Berlioz has consistently rewritten the figure introduced in the second measure of *Waverley*, adding a passing note (Ex. 3.70-.71):

Example 3.70: *Grande Ouverture de Waverley*, mm. 2-3, aut. p. 2^r, original version.

Example 3.71: Ibid., second version (sketched in pencil, then added).

To the *Grande Ouverture des Francs-Juges*, Berlioz added in 1829 the solo for bass drum (mm. 288-341, **OBE** V, 57-59), presumably so as to have a solo for himself at the concert of November 1829 (**BerCG** 140: Paris, 30 October 1829; to Ferrand).

A scribal copy of the *Resurrexit* at the Bibliothèque Municipale in Grenoble includes a number of interesting revisions in the hands of both Berlioz and Ferrand. The musical text is, with few variants, the same as in the version Berlioz later sent from Rome as an *envoi* to the Conservatoire. (The latter copy provided the source for the edition published by the **OBE**; the editors were unaware that the other manuscript existed.)   In the copy presented to Ferrand, the composer entered descriptive comments that bring to mind the version presented at the concert of 1 November 1829. Berlioz called that version *Le Jugement dernier* in letters to his father and to Ferrand (**BerCG** 140, 141), and it was advertised in the journal *Le Corsaire* (28 October 1829) as *"Grand choeur final de M. Berlioz (Resurrexit, annonce du Jugement dernier, les* *chanteurs debouts),"* later, *"choeur d'effroy du peuple de la terre, avec une expression de terreur toujours croissante."* Ferrand himself added over the last measures *"Et d'ailes et de faulx dépouillé désormais, sur les mondes détruits le tems dort immobile,"* and below, *"Anéantissement des mondes."*[84]

In addition to the descriptive remarks, Berlioz added an *arpeggio* for harp in the last measure (Ex. 3.72):

Example 3.72: *Resurrexit*, aut. revision in Grenoble copy (F-G Rés R 90665), fol. 43[r].

Underneath Ferrand writes *"La voix des élus et des choeurs d'anges monte et se perd dans le ciel."*[85] Berlioz has also made several revisions in the timpani part, calling for covered and uncovered drums (*"timballes* [sic] *découvertes,"* fol. 14[v]; *"timballes couvertes éponges,"* fol. 38[r]) and various types of sticks (*"baguette en bois sans éponges,"* fol. 42[r]). These changes mark the beginning of Berlioz's keen interest in percussion instruments (the concert of 1 November 1829 also featured the bass-drum solo in the overture to *Les Francs-Juges* and a recitative for the *Resurrexit* accompanied by four pairs of timpani).

If the hypothesis (p. 38, above) that Berlioz presented this copy of the *Resurrexit* to Ferrand in 1828 is correct, then these are additions made by Berlioz during a later visit, since they clearly reflect the recasting of the work with emphasis on the Last Judgment. Berlioz visited Ferrand in January 1831 (see BerCG 205), probably making the revisions then. In any event, the marginal annotations strikingly foreshadow the idea for *Le Dernier Jour du monde*, developed in July 1831.

The manuscript of *Le Roi Lear* has been carefully edited by Berlioz. The opening passage, for example, has been rephrased for the published edition (Exs. 3.73-.74):

Example 3.73: *Le Roi Lear*, mm. 1-4, aut., first version.

Example 3.74: Ibid., second version.

In m. 83, for no apparent reason other than to add variety of tone color, a phrase is taken from the first clarinet and given to the first oboe (Exs. 3.75-.76):

Example 3.75: *Le Roi Lear*, m. 82, aut., first version.

Example 3.76: Ibid., second version.

In m. 84, the timpani part was originally a simple repeat of the previous measure. When Berlioz altered it to a more complex version (Ex. 3.77):

Example 3.77: Ibid., m. 84.

he was constrained to add a note to his copyist: *"il faut copier la partie des timballes à toutes les parties pour ces 2 mesures"* ("You must copy [cue] the timpani part for these two measures in all the parts").

As the composer related in his *Mémoires* (Chap. XLV), certain details of *Harold en Italie* underwent careful revision. A figure in the third movement is consistently rewritten from the first version below to the second (Exs. 3.78-.79):

Example 3.78: *Harold en Italie*, movt. III, mm. 42-45 (and similar passages).

Example 3.79: Ibid., revised version (except for the first statement, m. 37, where Berlioz forgot to make the change).

The latter reading, implying 3/4 instead of 6/8, must have seemed for some reason indicative of the desired phrasing. It seemed a pointless change to Malherbe and Weingartner (**OBE** II, xii), who changed back to the original reading for publication.

The *Marche de pèlerins* from *Harold* was revised several times because the composer was dissatisfied with the effect made by the convent bells as imitated by the harp and horn.[86] He may have been reacting to the sharp public criticism of the dissonant notes, for the passage at the end of the movement (mm. 278ff, **OBE** p. 81/11ff) has been revised three times.   The duration of dissonance is reduced with each successive version (Exs. 3.80-.82):

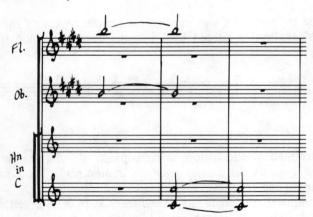

Example 3.80: *Harold en Italie*, movt. II, mm. 278-80, first version: aut. p. 139(*o*).

Example 3.81: Ibid., second version; aut. p. 137(*c*).

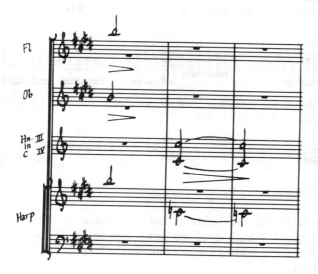

Example 3.82: Ibid., third version: aut. p. 137 (*c*, revised).

C. Practical problems.

Since he conducted or was present at nearly all the performances of his own works during his lifetime, Berlioz enjoyed the opportunity to study their every detail as executed in rehearsals and performances. A number of the revisions previously cited may well have followed live renditions, and one group of alterations is almost surely the simple result of the inadequacy of players or the impracticality of the passage itself. On a large scale, practical considerations often dictated changes in instrumentation. The parts for *cor anglais* in *Harold en Italie*, the *Symphonie fantastique*, and the *Carnaval romain* overture were regularly replaced in Germany by clarinet and oboe, and the many harp parts by piano. For one performance of the *Symphonie fantastique*, a virtuoso cornet part was added to the second movement.[87] The *Sanctus* of the *Requiem*, one of Berlioz's own favorite movements, had occasionally to be cut from a program for lack of a qualified tenor. Parts for valved brass instruments were substituted for a number of parts for natural horns.

Smaller revisions reflect similar considerations for places that did not sound in performance as imagined. The only logical explanation of a revision in the bassoon line of the *Symphonie fantastique*, movement V (mm. 47ff) is that players could not play it (Exs. 3.83-.84):

Example 3.83: *Symphonie fantastique*, movt. V, mm. 47ff, aut. pp. 14-16o, first version (entire passage trans. NBE 16, 215, ex. 13).

Example 3.84: Ibid., aut. pp. 14-16c, second version.

Berlioz also removed the lightning-fast chromatic scale in 16ths from strings in measures 4 and 15 of the same movement (NBE 16, 215, exs. 11-12), and a section with difficult runs for celli (aut. pp. 2, 6; NBE 16, 209/5 and 210/4).

In *La Tempête* (m. 22) Berlioz covered a too-ambitious tenor part with a collette containing the homophonic setting adopted for those measures (Exs. 3.85-.86):

Example 3.85: *La Tempête*, mm. 22-23, aut. p. 9 (OBE p. 71/1-2), first version.

Example 3.86: Ibid., revised version.

In the following measure he simplified the part for second violins as well (Exs. 3.87-.88):

Example 3.87: Ibid., mm. 24-25, first version.

Example 3.88: Ibid., second version.

For the version revised in Rome, Berlioz planned to repeat mm. 14-24, but ultimately struck out the repeat and first ending. The first version of measure 24 can be seen in the score (trans. **OBE** xiv), and the ten extra measures are deleted from the orchestra parts (c. 1832). A version of the very page of score in question, probably intended to cover these several changes with a clean copy, was abandoned and eventually appears as a collette-verso in the *Symphonie fantastique*, movt. I (aut. p. 22*cv*).

Passages from various works that were at first heavily scored in the lower octaves sounded too dense in performance and were removed. The eight measures of timpani choir that originally closed the *Requiem* were surely deleted because they sounded too muddy to provide a clear ending for the work. In *Waverley*, Berlioz removed two voices from the descending passages for bassoons and celli at the end of the introduction (mm. 77-80) in order to clarify the passage (Exs. 3.89-.90):

Example 3.89: *Grande Ouverture de Waverley*, mm. 77-80, aut. p. 7, first version.

Example 3.90: Ibid., second version (**OBE** p. 8).

Other cases of simplification were noted in the section on revisions, above.

The most interesting revision along these lines is in the third movement of *Harold en Italie* (mm. 72ff, aut. pp. 156-60, **OBE** fig. 33). Each of these pages carries an indication in red editor's pencil in the top margin: *"à changer tout,"* *"idem,"* and *"à changer presque tout."* The pages have already been revised twice, once with collettes on 24-staff paper (watermarked *HP*) and again on the collettes with the sketches from the *Invocation* of *Faust* on the verso. The first version has been covered with numerous attempts to revise, both in pencil and ink. Moreover, there is on every page of this section a remnant of a collette that was later removed; probably it carried instructions to the copyist or engraver.[88]

The problem here was no doubt one of orchestral texture; Berlioz was dissatisfied with the balance. The *idée fixe* was lost in the rumble of the accompanying figures. Originally the dialogue was accompanied by a buzzing figure in the cello and bass (**OBE** II, xx-xxiv) and *tremoli* in the other strings, with Harold's song in solo viola and bassoon. Finding this texture too heavy, he removed the sixteenths from all the instruments but the cello, replacing them with quarter-notes *pizzicato*, and he raised the accompanying figure in the bassoons by an octave. Still fearing the melody would be covered, he then doubled Harold's song in all the strings.

After this last change, Berlioz added the dialogue that now occurs in the winds (mm. 55ff, **OBE** p. 91). This addition required considerable further effort. The new idea was first sketched (aut. p. 158o) in both pencil and ink, and the words *"cl. & petit flut"* [sic] were entered over the sketch in m. 88 of the clarinet line. At this point, he decided to cover the whole section, which had become messy, with the collettes over pages 158-59.

4. Publication

A great deal of confusion exists concerning certain published volumes of Berlioz's music that supposedly contain significant changes in the composer's hand. Possibly two dozen published volumes are thought to contain autograph revisions, but most are merely presentation copies with an autograph dedication and a correction or two in the first few bars representing no genuine compositional change. Of all the copies mentioned by Hopkinson or noted in the catalogue at the Bibliothèque Nationale as having autograph notations, only a small fraction actually show alteration of the music itself, and only three or four are important sources. He seldom entered substantive changes in his own copies of the published versions.[89]

There are a number of proofs,[90] however, that preserve evidence of a stage of composition between the last version seen in the autograph and the published version for general circulation. The vast majority of changes entered by the composer at this point are merely proof-reader's corrections: changes in accidentals, phrasings, or sometimes errors in pitch content. (By and large, the work of Berlioz's engravers is impressively accurate.) Of, for example, over seventy-five autograph notations in the proof of the piano-vocal edition of *Benvenuto Cellini* (F–Po Rés A 521c), none represents significant compositional change.

Berlioz's primary concern with proofs, then, was their appearance and accuracy. He was extremely careful with certain aspects of the physical layout: *"mal en rapport,"* he often comments when notes of similar rhythmic position are not aligned, or *"ôtez ce 2me ♯ à l'ut; il est inutile."* Small dots of paste on heavily-edited pages suggest that the revisions or corrections were accompanied with verbal instructions written on separate sheets pasted into the score. A typical correction sheet for instrumental parts is bound with the proof of *Roméo et Juliette*:

Parties Séparées de Roméo et Juliet[t]e

Cornets à Pistons
Planche 3—ligne 10—mesure 9
il faut mettre un ♭ au mi—
corriger à la main les parties imprimées
corriger la planche 22 des seconds violons
ôter les chiffres [pencil:] *aussi au Conservatoire*
[ink:] *Altos*
Planche 11 2ème mesure des
deux dernières lignes
mettez un ♯ au ré qui est
dessous la fa ♯
Planche 14—2me ligne
Mesure 7me mettez sol au lieu
de fa
corriger le sol ♭ de la
planche 185 de la partition dans l'alto
Contrebasses [pencil:] *aussi au conservatoire*
et voir q. la planche 21
de l'alto est corrigée.
[ink:] *1re page*
Mesure 12 (après les pauses)
corriger ainsi:

> [pencil:] *faire exporter la planche 2*
> *des contrebasses pour la corriger et*
> *ôter les chiffres*
> *Corriger aussi les Hautbois de*
> *la page 186 de la partition*
> *dans les parties séparées*

In the same proof (p. 119) Berlioz notices a system with all the whole rests missing: *"6 pauses qui manquent et qui ont échappé aux dernières corrections. 28 mars 1854 (Hanôvre)"* ("Six rests are missing that were overlooked in the last series of corrections").

There are, however, a few striking last-minute changes of mind evident in the proofs of each of the major works. Some reflect continuing improvements in instruments and notation: Berlioz has, for example, added chromatic trumpet parts for B♭ piston trumpet to both *Harold en Italie* and *Roméo et Juliette.* He has consistently renoted the harmonics in the harp part of the proof for *Harold en Italie,* moving the notes down an octave and adding a small circle over the note (a procedure recommended in the *Traité d'instrumentation*).

Berlioz made one major change between the so-called "advance edition"[91] of the *Symphonie fantastique* and the definitive publication in 1845. In the second movement, measures 129-56, he replaced the accompaniment of the *idée fixe* with an entirely different passage (trans. OBE I, 34-35). Perhaps the engraver failed to catch a revision intended all along, or perhaps the idea of combining the *idée fixe* with the waltz motive occurred at the last minute; this matter will be considered in more detail in Chapter IV. (Combining the two themes of a movement had by 1845 become a favorite device, used in the fifth movement of the *Symphonie fantastique,* the third of *Harold en Italie,* and the *Fête chez Capulet* from *Roméo et Juliette.*) At any rate, the revision is one of those that heightens the movement by making the section a more integral part of the waltz.

Some minor changes were made in *Roméo et Juliette.* In the *Fête chez Capulet* (movt. II, mm. 278ff, **OBE** p. 274), Berlioz reorchestrated the bassoon part for the first and assistant-first players, probably as the result of poor performances by players of the second part. Several measures later (mm. 298ff, **OBE** fig. 27ff), he revised the harp parts from the first version below to the second (Exs. 3.91-.92). Berlioz was probably correcting an oversight here, for the second version is clearly the correct realization of the idea. At the same time, he added slurs to the triplets in the violin parts, mm. 332ff (**OBE** fig. 29ff), perhaps also the result of inadequate performances of the original version.

Example 3.91: *Roméo et Juliette*, movt. II, m. 298, first version: aut. p. 121(ff).

Example 3.92: Ibid., second version, proof of printed edition.

He altered the statement of the *Marche de pèlerins* at the end of movement IV of *Harold* one last time, from the revised version in the autograph to its present form. This is the third revision of the phrase. (Ex. 3.93):

Example 3.93: *Harold en Italie*, movt. IV, mm. 473-80, aut. p. 253-54.

These alterations are insignificant when compared with the other stages in the complex task of composing, but they do show that works were not considered finished until the very last opportunity for revision. These precise changes after so many years are ample indication of Berlioz's continued interest in improvements. By contrast, he considered the work finished when published, and for both his performances and his private use regarded the publications as the standard texts for his music.

Chapter Four

Three Examples

The theory that a composer's typical habits or methods can be determined from his autographs is tenable only insofar as the manuscripts are generally similar. In fact a composer himself is not often concerned with methods as such; his actions are simply responses to specific musical situations encountered. Sketches, drafts, and revisions thus are less related to each other than to the compositions of which they are parts. Complementing an overall view of Berlioz's methods of work should be a consideration of representative works as entities, to determine how they were planned, written, and first performed.

The autograph sources for three compositions—an opera, an "architectural" work,[1] and a symphony—have been selected for closer examination. *Les Francs-Juges* exists only in fragmentary condition, but Berlioz neither forgot his opera nor destroyed it beyond recognition. The *Requiem* was published in three different versions; comparing them shows some of the musical criteria behind the changes. Finally, the autograph of the *Symphonie fantastique* is reviewed for traces left by the composer at work. Two newly-identified autograph fragments are evidence of hitherto unknown aspects of the history of the work as it evolved between 1830 and 1845.

1. *Les Francs-Juges* (1826)

Les Francs-Juges is the earliest large-scale composition of Berlioz for which autograph sources have been preserved. All are now in the Bibliothèque Nationale.[2] The fragmentary orchestra score (F-Pn Rés Vm² 177) contains five complete movements and remnants of pages from several others.[3] A manuscript libretto annotated by the composer was found among his miscellaneous papers (F-Pn papiers divers de Berlioz, no. 45; transcribed in Appendix II; see Facsimile IV.1). Bound with the full score is an autograph libretto titled *Le Cri de guerre du Brisgaw* (transcribed in Appendix III; see Facsimile IV.2) in which portions of the opera are arranged to form an intermezzo of one act. Also bound with the score is an autograph manuscript of the *Mélodie pastorale* from Act II, titled *Nocturne à trois voix concertantes*, in a reduction for voices and piano (see Facsimile III.3). Additionally Boschot describes a libretto once at the library of the Opéra but now lost; certain indications in it led him to believe that it had belonged to Ferrand's family.[4]   Several sets of manuscript orchestra parts for the overture exist, but none of them comes from the period 1826-30.

The fragmentary sources for *Les Francs-Juges* are confusing in that each represents a different attempt to have it accepted for production. The proper distinction of versions has never been made, partly because of a curious lacuna in the correspondence that led later observers to misconstrue the meaning of Berlioz's other remarks about the work. Recently the gap has been filled: supporting evidence has come to light that enables each manuscript to be associated with the proper version.

Ordinarily in Berlioz study, the composer's correspondence confirms or broadens the evidence of the autograph sources. Until the publication of the *Correspondance générale*, however, exactly the opposite was true for *Les Francs-Juges*. Berlioz seemed to have first mentioned his opera in a letter to Ferrand of 28 June 1828 (**BerCG** 94): "I await with great impatience the first and third acts of *Les Francs-Juges*." No statement could seem less enigmatic: the composer was obviously waiting for the libretto, so he could not (it appeared) have begun work on the opera. Brenet and Tiersot confidently concluded that the opera was written in 1828. Their view conflicts directly with the account in the *Mémoires*, however, where the author recalls (Chap. XI) interrupting work on *Les Francs-Juges* to write the *Scène héroïque* (1826), also to a libretto by Ferrand.[5] Moreover, a concert of 26 May 1828 had included the first performance of the overture, and in the letter of 28 June Berlioz transcribed twenty-six measures of the finished version. The evidence of the *Lettres intimes* notwithstanding, Boschot reasoned that Berlioz must have written the work in Autumn 1826, when he was not occupied with other responsibilities (**BosHB** I, 242, fn. 1).

The first hint that the chronology recalled in the *Mémoires* might be approximately correct came with the publication of a collection of letters from Berlioz to Edouard Rocher (*Revue des Deux Mondes*, March 1944):[6] the composer mentions *Les Francs-Juges* in a letter of 15 July 1826 (**BerCG** 61). With the inclusion in the *Correspondance générale* of the twelve new letters to Léon Compaignon,[7] the situation became clear. *Les Francs-Juges* was actually composed in 1826, and the letter to Ferrand of June 1828 refers to a revised libretto.

Berlioz and Humbert Ferrand decided in 1825 or early 1826 to collaborate on an opera about the secret vigilante (Vehmic) courts in medieval Germany. Ferrand set to work on the libretto, modeled on a play by J.-H.-F. de Lamartelière (1761-1830) called *Les Francs-Juges, ou les tems de barbarie; Mélodrame historique*.[8] Meanwhile, Berlioz began to persuade the directors of the Odéon to accept newly-composed operas.

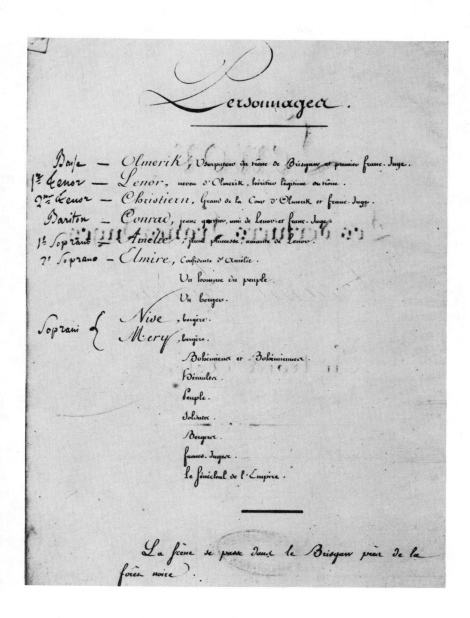

Facsimile IV.1: *Les Francs-Juges*, libretto, p. 3.

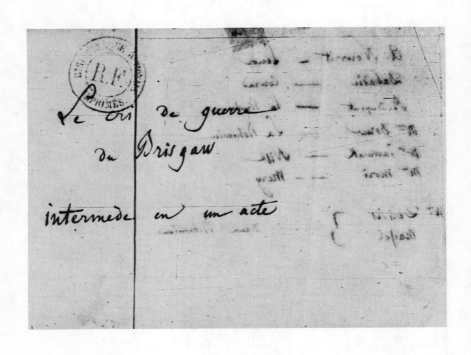

Facsimile IV.2: *Le Cri de guerre du Brisgaw,* libretto, cover.

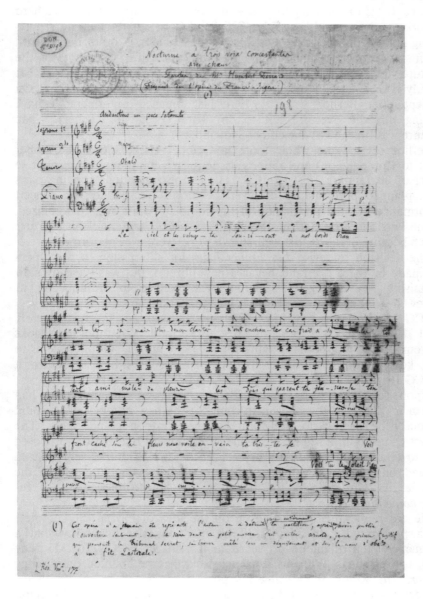

Facsimile IV.3: *Nocturne à trois voix concertantes*, p. 1.

A letter of 30 May 1826 (**BerCG** 55: to Compaignon) indicates that he had begun serious composition. By the end of June (**BerCG** 59: 29 June 1826; to Compaignon) he had finished the first act and was hard at work on the second. In July 1826 (**BerCG** 61: to Rocher) he reports having shown his music to Lesueur: "M. Lesueur is quite happy with the first two acts; I shall do my best for the third." Except for the overture, the work was finished by the end of the summer (**BerCG** 62: 24 July 1826; to Compaignon: "I'm just about to finish it"). On 10 September Berlioz writes: "I've just finished my opera; I have nothing but the overture left to do" (**BerCG** 63: to Rocher). The overture was finished by the end of September.

Berlioz revised the whole score in October (**BerCG** 67: 14 October 1826; to Compaignon) and reports its definitive completion in a letter to Nanci of 20 January 1827 (**BerCG** 71). He also mentions copying parts for a planned performance of several excerpts, but neither the concert performance nor the production of the complete work ever materialized. Of the version completed in 1826, only an aria, a trio, and the overture (which became Berlioz's first well-known work) were ever performed.

The decision to revise *Les Francs-Juges* for submission to the Opéra was made in 1828. Ferrand began a new libretto, but was typically slow to finish;[9] by Spring 1829 Berlioz was reduced to pleading for it: "Farewell—I beg you to hurry up and send me the *Francs-Juges*" (**BerCG** 113: 2 February 1829). This new libretto was finished in early April 1829 (**BerCG** 121: 9 April 1829; to Ferrand: "A thousand thanks for your opera; Gounet is copying it over right now"). Gounet seems to have kept the original draft, for Berlioz later asks him to return it (**BerCG** 161: May 1830).

Upon receipt of the libretto, Berlioz reviewed the music he had written in 1826 and then began to compose the new numbers that would obviously be needed to transform his piece into a grand opera. The project came to an abrupt halt; a jury at the Opéra rejected the proposed libretto (**BerCG** 126: 3 June 1829; to Ferrand). Within a year he had decided on possibly his first significant self-borrowing, the use of the *Marche des gardes* from the opera as the fourth movement of his *Symphonie fantastique*.

He did not immediately give up on the idea of having the complete opera performed. In May 1830 he mentions the possibility that a German version might be produced in Karlsruhe (**BerCG** 162: 13 May 1830; to Ferrand). With his usual self-assurance he counted on winning the *prix de Rome*, then using his powers of persuasion and political connections to get exemption from the Italian sojourn so that he could go directly to Germany. He did finally win the *prix de Rome*, of course, but was not granted exemption from the required year at the Villa Medici. The Karlsruhe production was forgotten; Berlioz never went to Germany as a laureate of the Conservatoire. Upon returning from Rome, however, he devised a further plan, to have *Les Francs-Juges* translated into Italian (BerCG 341 and 357, 1 August and 25 October 1833). This project, too, was abandoned.

Eventually, Berlioz became convinced that he would never see the entire opera produced and so began to dismantle it, finding new uses for the completed music. In 1833 he prepared the libretto for an intermezzo of one act, *Le Cri de guerre du Brisgaw*, salvaging several numbers from the full opera. He composed passages intermittently over a period of two years, but never finished the scene. Beginning with *Benvenuto Cellini* (comp. 1834-38) he began to incorporate appropriate musical passages from *Les Francs-Juges* in new works. A sentence in Chapter XI of the *Mémoires* specifically acknowledges the procedure:[10]

J'ai employé ça et là les meilleures idées de cet opéra, en les développant, dans mes compositions postérieures, le reste subira probablement le même sort, si l'occasion s'en présente, ou sera brûlé.

I have taken some of the best ideas in the opera and developed them in later works. What is left will probably go through the same process or else be thrown away (BerMemCairns).

Portions of the score had already been destroyed when Berlioz wrote those remarks: in a letter of 20 September 1838 (BerCG 570), he tells Ferrand of having burned several movements. He probably intended to destroy the rest before his death, as well as the score of *La Nonne sanglante*; a note pencilled on a fragment of the later opera reads: *"A consulter—à brûler après ma mort."*[11] An executor less conscious of the value of historical sources than Damcke was might well have followed the composer's instructions.

Three references in letters of 1859 to Carolyne Sayn-Wittgenstein evidently refer to a last attempt to produce a work about the Vehmic tribunals. Berlioz had been invited by Edouard Bénazet to submit a new opera for the annual music festival at Baden. On 20 June he describes the libretto:

Je vais commencer mon autre partition, l'opéra pour le théâtre de Bade, si la guerre lui permet de s'élever. Ce serait pour 1861. La pièce est d'Edouard Plouvier; il y a de belles situations. C'est un épisode de la guerre de 30 ans. Il y a Duc Bernard de Saxe-Weimar, une Bohémienne, des Francs-Juges, le Diable,... et son train (BerCSW XXVI, pp. 97-98: 20 June 1859).

I am going to begin my other score, the opera for the theatre in Baden, if they can produce it in spite of the war. This would be for 1861. The play is by Edouard Plouvier; there are some nice situations. It's an episode from the Thirty Years' War. There are Duke Bernard of Saxe-Weimar, a Bohemian girl, some Francs-Juges, Satan—and his followers.

Any passages from *Les Francs-Juges* still unused in 1859 could easily have been worked into the new dramatic situation; Lenor's music could have been reworked for Duke Bernard, Olmerik's for the devil, and so on. Berlioz mentions the plan in two other letters (**BerCSW** XXV and XXIX) but eventually abandons it:

Non, je ne ferai pas la Légende de Plouvier,	No, I will not do Plouvier's Legend; I've
je viens d'écrire à Bénazet pour le prier	just written to Bénazet asking him to release
instamment de me rendre ma parole	my from my obligation.
(**BerCSW** XXXI, p. 110).	

It was thus not until after 1859 that the ill-fated venture was given up for the last time.

The fragmentary autograph score is one of two primary sources for the opera containing musical notation. Five pieces in it are complete, and remnants of two others can be identified. The numeration is the composer's own:

1. *Choeur du peuple*, fols. 3^r-18^r;
2. *Duo:* Olmerick and Christiern, inc. *"Conrad s'arma pour nous,"* fols. 19^r-55^r;
6. *Choeur des bergers* (Act II, sc. i), fols. 56^v-66^v;
11. Remnant of invocation and dream sequence, fols. $67bis^{a-y}$;
? *Hymne des Francs-Juges*, 68^r-73^r [complete];
? Melodrama, followed by reprise of hymn, fols. 73^v-80^r [complete];
? Remnant of *Finale*, fols. $80bis^{c-s}$.

Dozens of variants between the text set in the score and that of the manuscript libretto indicate that they represent two different versions. Most obvious is the change of the hero's name, from Arnold (in the score) to Lenor (in the libretto).[12] The libretto is in fact formally titled *Lenor, ou les derniers Francs-Juges*, whereas practically every other reference to the work is simply to *Les Francs-Juges*. A chorus of heralds at the beginning of the libretto does not occur in the score. A letter from Berlioz to Ferrand of 9 April 1829 (**BerCG** 121) shows that the *finale* in Act I as included in the libretto is new:[13]

Oh! mon cher, que vous êtes poète! Le finale	Oh, dear fellow, what a poet you are! The
des Bohémiens, au premier acte, est un coup	Bohemians' finale, in the first act, is a
de maître; jamais, je crois, on n'aura présenté	master touch; never, I think, will anyone
de poème d'opéra aussi original et aussi bien	have presented such an original, well-
écrit; je vous le répète, il est magnifique.	written libretto; I repeat, it's magnificent.

The libretto requires several more musical numbers than the fifteen originally in the autograph. It is, then, Ferrand's revision of 1829, probably prepared by Gounet. The score was prepared in 1826.

Berlioz has annotated the libretto, marking passages finished and those left to do (*musique faite, musique à faire*), portions that will be spoken (*parlé*), and some notes on the music planned for a passage (*Coda, 2me choeur*, etc.). The notations *musique faite* make it a simple matter to deduce the contents of the first version:

LES FRANCS-JUGES

Probable Contents of the 1826 Version

[* = preserved, either fully or in remnant]

*Ouverture

**1.   *Choeur du Peuple*, inc. "*Arnold* [Lenor]*, entends nos fers.... Ah! voici le tyran*";

**2.   *Duo.* Olmerick and Christiern, inc. "*Conrad s'arma pour nous*";

3.   Recitative and air. Conrad, inc.: "*Va! je t'abhorre.... Noble amitié, ta voix, ta voix chérie*";

4.   *Elégie.* Amélie: "*La nuit voilant pour nous ces murs et nos montagnes*";

5.   Quartet. Lenor, Conrad, Amélie, Elmire, inc. "*Frais vallons où dorment nos pères*";

**6.   *Choeur des bergers*, inc. "*L'ombre descend dans la vallée*" ["*choeur de danse à faire*" marked in score];

**7.   *Trio pastoral.* Nise, Mery, Lenor, inc. "*Vois-tu le soleil s'enfuir?*";

8.   *Duo.* Amélie, Lenor, inc. "*N'espère plus, Lenor, effrayer mon courage*";

9.   March [?; see remarks below];

10.   *Finale.* Conrad, bergers, soldats, femmes, inc. "*Malheur au parjure*";

**11.   Recitative and invocation. Lenor, inc.: "*Voici l'endroit fatal... Descends et viens,*" and dream sequence;

**12.   Hymn of the Francs-Juges, inc. "*Des célestes décrets, invisibles vengeurs*";

**13.   Melodrama and reprise of hymn;

**14.   *Choeur du peuple*, inc. "*Fier Germain, reprends ces vallons*".

The overture, *Mélodie pastorale*, and Conrad's aria *Noble amitié* were first performed on 26 May 1828, along with the revised version of the *Resurrexit*. Conrad's aria was to be heard again on 1 November 1829 (BerCG 138; 3 October 1829), but seems not to have actually been performed. Since the composer's note in the piano-vocal copy of the *Mélodie pastorale* refers to Arnold, it is probable that Berlioz prepared it for one of the concerts in 1828. After the rejection of his libretto at the Opéra, he scheduled only the overture for concert performance.

The libretto of 1829 was considerably longer than the original had been, and Berlioz decided to add more music. In his letter to Ferrand of 3 June 1829 (**BerCG** 126), he writes:

J'ajouterai quatre ou cinq morceaux, tels que le finale du premier acte, les quintetti, l'air de Lenor, etc. etc.

I will add four or five numbers, like the finale of the first act, the *quintetti*, Lenor's aria, and so on.

The new libretto required a minimum of four or five new numbers; he might well have added a dozen sections. But the libretto confirms his intentions, since the words *"à faire"* occur six times:

LES FRANCS-JUGES

Revisions for 1829 version, marked *"à faire"* in the libretto.

Act I, sc. i: 4 heralds, inc. *"Olmerik d'Amélie est aujourd'hui l'époux"*;

Act I, sc. v; Amélie: *"Vous le savez, Conrad, il osait chaque soir / Braver pour moi de trop sûres alarmes"*;

Act I, sc. viii (finale): inc. *"Mêlons à la voix des trompettes"*;

Act II, sc. i; Ballet;

Act II, sc. iv: Lenor, *"Tu ne me verras plus, ô ma douce Amélie"*;

Act II, sc. vii: Quintet (Olmerik, Christiern, Lenor, Amélie, Elmire), inc. *"Ombres de nos aïeux, ombres de la patrie."*

Only one new movement was actually finished. The letter of 3 June 1829 also announces rejection of the libretto. Other projects soon attracted Berlioz's attention: the 1829 *prix de Rome* competition, a concert in November 1829, and the new *Symphonie fantastique*. He did not even finish the number that most impressed him, the finale of Act I; it was 1833 when he finally composed the music. The quintet, arias for Lenor and Amélie, and the ballet music were never written.

He must, however, have written the version of the *Marche des gardes* that became movement IV of his *Symphonie fantastique*. It is practically inconceivable that such a rousing piece, had it been completed, would not have been played in the concerts of 1828 and 1829[14] along with the overtures to *Les Francs-Juges* and *Waverley*. Physical characteristics of the autograph fascicle also suggest a date later than 1826. It is completely different in format and calligraphy from the fragmentary opera score; had the fascicle come from an 1826 score, the violins would have been at the top of the page. The musical style corresponds to that of the period of the *Symphonie fantastique*, and Berlioz was able to work the march into the symphony without difficulty.

Curiously, Berlioz entered neither *musique faite* nor *à faire* in the libretto by the direction that called for a march (libretto, p. 38; transcription, p. 315):

D'innombrables bataillons apparaissent tout à coup sur les hauteurs et entrent de toutes parts en scène au bruit d'une musique farouche.

Countless forces appear all at once on the ramparts, entering the stage from all sides to the accompaniment of fearsome music.

Nor did he mention a march in the letter of 3 June. The idea must have occurred to Berlioz afer he had entered his notations in the manuscript libretto. According to his own *Mémoires*, the movement was precipitously written in a single evening, possibly as an afterthought. The manuscript itself was still clear, with an original title page and a few left-over sheets of staff paper, when he began the *Symphonie fantastique*. It was perfectly logical for him merely to add the score to his new symphony, substitute a new title page on the same paper, and work the *idée fixe* in as a coda. The present version of the march must have been written in late 1829.

There may well have been a simpler march for the version of 1826. If the texts known to have been set in 1826 (because they are marked *musique faite* in the libretto) are matched with the numbers found on title pages in the score, it appears that all but one, no. 9 in the scheme above, fall naturally into place. The stage direction requiring *musique farouche* occurs after the *Duo*, no. 8, and before the *Finale* of Act I, no. 10. A tiny fragment reminiscent of the march appears in the autograph; it occurs in scene i of Act III, where Lenor falls asleep and begins to dream. The passage was first observed and described by Macdonald, who reconstructed the complete quotation as follows (Ex. 4.1):[15]

Example 4.1: Reconstruction of quotation from *Marche des gardes*, after **MacCent**, p. 41. See Facsimile IV.4.

Since the point of the music in this section is that certain quotations from earlier movements will depict Lenor's dream, it seems reasonable to conclude that what is missing from the 1826 version of Act II is an earlier, less-developed example of *musique farouche*. It may have had no

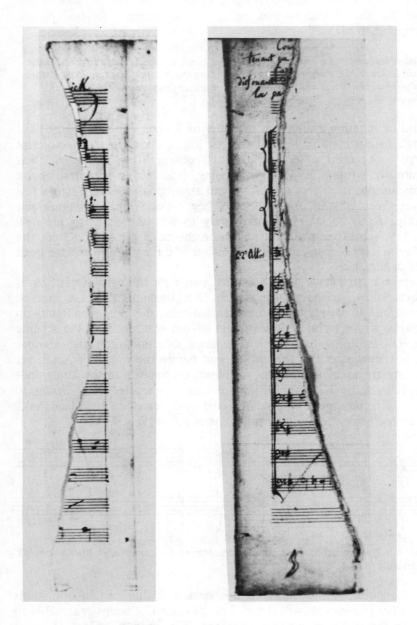

Facsimile IV.4: *Les Francs-Juges*, quotation of *Marche des gardes*, aut. fol. 67*bis*^v-u^r.

more in common with the march than the first phrase as quoted in Lenor's dream. (Berlioz discovers in this type of musical reminiscence, incidentally, a device that becomes a mark of his style.)

The intermezzo salvaged from *Les Francs-Juges* in late 1833 was titled *Le Cri de guerre du Brisgaw.*[16] Dramatically, it is a good deal stronger than the full opera. Lenor, in peasant dress, joins a rustic merry-making, confesses his true identity as heir apparent to the usurped throne of Wenceslas, and (encouraged by Conrad) organizes a popular revolt against the illegitimate rule, leading his army away as the curtain falls. The tribunal of *Francs-Juges* is never mentioned; Berlioz seems not to have wanted the intermezzo associated with his well-known overture. Otherwise the general situation is the same as in the opea, and most of the stage directions are identical. Conrad, however, becomes an entirely different character, a loyal friend of Lenor from the beginning who never considers betraying him.

Eight musical numbers were planned:

1. The Bohemians' scene, inc. *"Mêlons à la voix des trompettes,"* to which has been added the shepherd's chorus from Act II, inc. *"L'ombre descend dans la vallée"*;

2. Ballet and chorus of Bohemians: *"Aux armes! La charge sonne,"* followed by the double quartet of shepherds;

3. *Mélodie pastorale*;

4. Recitative and Air: *"Fureur et vengeance!"*;

5. Cavatina: Lenor, inc. *"Tu ne sais pas trahir le malheur qui t'implore,"* and invocation: *"Descends et viens"*;

6. *Chanson du bûcheron*;

7. Duo: Conrad and Lenor, inc. *"Noble amitié"* (autograph notation: *Andante, Allegro*);

8. Chorus and finale: *"Eh bien, qu'il nous prouve sa race."*

Five pieces (nos. 1, 2, 3, 5 and 7) are borrowed from *Les Francs-Juges*. The texts of two (nos. 4 and 8) are otherwise unknown, probably supplied expressly for the project by Thomas Gounet.[17] A third author is easily identified, Auguste Brizeux, the poet of the *Chanson du bûcheron* (no. 6), taken from his *Marie* (Paris, 1832). The song became popular in its own right as *Le Jeune Pâtre breton* (Table I, no. 65). Only the second half of the first stanza, beginning *"oh! Nenni da!"*, can be heard as the shepherd approaches the stage, but otherwise the words are unaltered.

The composer neglects to mention in his letters to Ferrand that he has added these sections by other poets.

The music for the intermezzo was nearly finished. On 25 October 1833, Berlioz writes Ferrand:

J'ai toujours sur ma table les Francs-Juges, *et je n'ai pas besoin de vous dire le serrement de coeur que j'éprouve à voir vos vers si cadencés, si musicaux, rester enfouis et inutiles. J'ai écrit la* Scène des Bohémiens *en y mêlant le choeur qui commence le second acte: "L'ombre descend." Cela fait un choeur immense et d'un rythme curieux. Je suis à peu près sûr de l'effet. Je le ferai à mon prochain concert* (BerCG 357).

I still have the *Francs-Juges* on my desk, and I don't have to tell you of the grief I feel when I see your verses, so rhythmic, so musical, still buried away, unused. I have written the Bohemians' scene, working into it the chorus which begins the second act, *"L'ombre descend,"* this done for an enormous chorus and with curious rhythms. I'm practically certain it will be a sensation. I shall have it done for my next concert.

Having finished the longest scene seems to have prompted Berlioz to find some use for it. *Le Cri de guerre du Brisgaw* is obviously constructed around the version of the *scène des Bohémiens* that he describes to Ferrand. Gounet's contribution, whatever it was, was received the following January (1834: **BerCG** 374, 375). The libretto itself shows that he had another musical change in mind, the addition of an obligato part for coloratura soprano (*"avec un accompagnement de traits brillants et légers"*) to the *Mélodie pastorale*.

As late as April 1835, Berlioz was still working on the intermezzo. He reports to Ferrand having completely rewritten *Noble amitié*, in a refined version for a single voice rather than the duet outlined in the libretto:

Je viens de refaire ou plutôt de faire la musique de votre scène des Francs-Juges: *"Noble amitié..." Je l'ai écrite de manière qu'elle pût être chantée par un ténor ou un soprano, et, quoique ce soit un rôle d'homme, j'ai eu en vue mademoiselle Falcon en l'écrivant: elle peut y produire beaucoup d'effet: je lui porterai la partition ces jours-ci* (BerCG 429).

I have just rewritten or rather written the music for your scene from *Les Francs-Juges: "Noble amitié."* I wrote it in such a fashion that it could be sung by either a tenor or a soprano, and even though it is a man's role, I had Mlle Falcon in mind when I wrote it: she could make quite an effect with it. I'll take her the score one of these days.

This letter is followed in a week by a reference to "an operatic scene for my next concerts" (**BerCG** 430: 17 April 1835; to Adèle) which, out of context, seems to refer to *Benvenuto Cellini*. But an announcement of December 1834 in the *Gazette musicale* may well refer to *Le Cri de guerre*:

M. Berlioz will give a fourth concert in the Menus-Plaisirs next Sunday. This
time we will hear his two great symphonies, the *Fantastique* and *Harold*, separated
by a charming intermezzo which the composer has not yet completed.

The chronological proximity of the scene from *Benvenuto Cellini* called
Les Ciseleurs de Florence (intended for the concert of 7 December 1834;
never performed) and the intermezzo, coupled with the loss of the music
for both, makes it impossible to tell exactly which piece Berlioz had in
mind.

One further idea for revision is preserved in autograph. Written
sideways across the botton of page 1 of the autograph score is the
following plan (see Facsimile IV.5):

*N° 1 serait le Duo terminé en choeur de
Francs-Juges et précédé par l'hymne des
Francs-Juges au tribunal secret. Ce serait
ainsi un andante, suivi d'un allegro développé
et de plus en plus énergique.*

No. 1 would be the duo, followed by the
chorus of the Francs-Juges and preceded by
their hymn at the secret tribunal. Thus it
would be an andante followed by an allegro
that becomes progressively more complex
and energetic.

*N° 2 Trio pastoral suivi sans interruption
d'une Valze en style suisse avec la 4me note
du ton dièzée.*

No. 2. The pastoral trio followed without
interruption by a waltz in the Swiss manner,
with the fourth note of the scale sharpened.

*N° 3 Chant du Meurtrier d'Olmerick, caché
avec son jeune fils dans la forêt noire
pendant une froide nuit d'hiver accompagnée
des gémissements du vent du nord et
interrompue souvent par la plainte de
l'Enfant—"Ah père, j'ai froid." Le père
répondra toujours à cette plainte en récitant
le De Profundis. Mort de l'un et de l'autre.
Arrivée d'une confrérie de moines qui
emportent les deux corps....*

No. 3. Song of Olmerick's assassin, hidden
with his son in the black forest on a cold
winter night, accompanied by the moaning
of the north wind, and frequently
interrupted by the child's plaint: "Ah
father, I am cold." The father answers this
plaint each time by chanting the *De
Profundis.* Death of both. Arrival of an
order of monks, who carry the two bodies
away . . .

*Final et Choeur du peuple finissant en
majeur avec l'explosion et les thèmes de la
coda de l'ouverture.*

Finale and chorus of the people, ending in
major with the explosion and the themes
from the coda of the overture.

Of the five different projects Berlioz devised to salvage *Les Francs-Juges*,
this one is the most difficult to account for. Unlike *Le Cri de guerre du
Brisgaw*, it includes the Francs-Juges themselves. He may have intended
to begin it with the overture. It outlines a tragedy in which the villain
Olmerik is murdered and the murderer (presumably a Lenor-like
character) and his child subsequently freeze to death, their bodies carried
away by a group of monks in solemn procession. Thus it extends the
second half of the original story, whereas the *Cri de guerre* had dealt

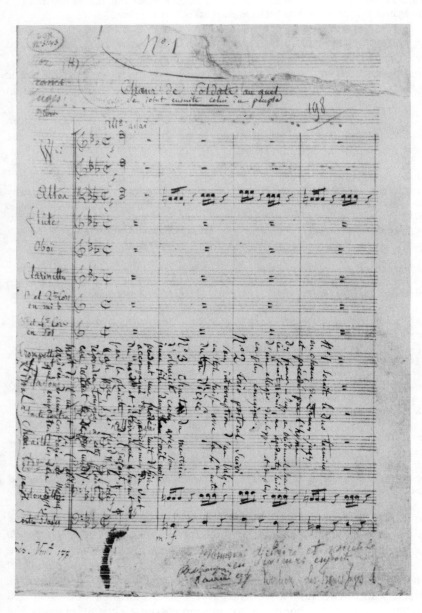

Facsimile IV.5: *Les Francs-Juges*, aut. fol. 3[r].

primarily with the first. But the two intermezzos cannot have been intended for performance in a single evening, since both reuse the *Mélodie pastorale* and Act III finale. The explosion comes from the end of the opera, where the mysterious idol of the tribunal is engulfed in flames.

Certain details of the musical setting implied in the outline suggest a date after Berlioz's trip to Italy: the procession of monks, the *De Profundis* (parodied in *Benvenuto Cellini*), and a solemn funeral procession. This last idea intrigued Berlioz for some time; he describes a funeral at some length in one of the more notorious passages from the *Mémoires* (Chap. XLIII), and he later composed marches for *Roméo et Juliette* and *Hamlet*. The best hint as to the date, however, is the phrase about a waltz in the Swiss manner. Berlioz described exacly that sort of movement in his letter to Nanci of 1 November 1828 (**BerCG** 100), referring to a *Walze au chalet* [sic] attributed in Pixis' piano arrangement to Weber. The outline probably comes, then, from just after the rejection of the full libretto in 1829; possibly it is a plan for a shorter opera to be submitted to the Théâtre–Allemand (see **BerCG** 161).

This outline was cited in Chapter III as representative of Berlioz's earlier general plans for a musical composition. In the three scenes there would have been seven separate musical sections. The duo, hymn, pastoral trio, and finale are all borrowed from movements of *Les Francs-Juges* completed in 1826. The aria by Olmerik's murderer (possibly equivalent to *"Fureur et vengeance"* in *Le Cri de guerre du Brisgaw*) is new, as is the march for monks and the waltz. The melodrama in no. 3 might well have included music from Lenor's dream later used in the *Symphonie funèbre et triomphale*. But Berlioz never refers to this plan in his correspondence, and at some point he gave it up.

The last thing he did with his score was to destroy certain passages. Macdonald's tantalizing idea (in **MacSelf**) is that he destroyed material used later in other works. The state of the orchestra score lends strong support to that view: there are no borrowings from any of the movements entirely preserved, but several are obvious in the remnants. The most notable of these is the reuse of the *Invocation* in Act III as the second movement of the *Symphonie funèbre*. One phrase from the *Hymne des Francs-Juges* becomes a motive in the Roman carnival music (Ex. 4.2):

Example 4.2a: Fragment of *Les Francs-Juges,* aut. fol. *80 bis* d^v-e^r.

Example 4.2b: *Le Carnaval* from *Benvenuto Cellini*, m. 10 (edn. Choudens, p. 203; the motive is more extensively used in the scene following Pompéo's murder, edn. Choudens, pp. 275-78).[18]

If it is true that what Berlioz destroyed was music used elsewhere, then borrowing can be expected from the following numbers: 3) Arnold: *Noble amitié*, rev. 1835; 4) *Elégie*;[19] 5) Quintet; 8) Duo; 10) Finale; 14) *Choeur du peuple*, and possibly some ballet music. Berlioz almost surely reused both *Noble amitié* and the enlarged Bohemians' scene from Act I; if he did not, it would be one of the few times in his life that he completed a movement of some length and never performed or reused it. The autographs of both fragments have disappeared completely, no doubt precisely because they were reused. Moreover, two passages in *Le Cri de guerre du Brisgaw* have been subsequently deleted in red pencil by Berlioz: the *scène des Bohémiens* (where he has crossed out the note *musique faite*) and the *Chanson du bûcheron* (entirely cross-hatched). The *Chanson du bûcheron* was published in 1834 as *Le Jeune Pâtre breton*; it was sung at several of Berlioz's concerts and must have been familiar to the composer's followers. Thus it was crossed out in the libretto (possibly as late as 1859, when he was considering the new opera for Baden) because it had become well known in another context. The same reasoning leads to the conclusion that the *Scène des bohémiens* was deleted because it, too, had become famous in another guise.

The most likely works to have absorbed these borrowings are *Benvenuto Cellini*, the *Requiem*, and *Les Troyens*. If Berlioz's other self-borrowings are any indication, phrases or sections, rather than complete movements, were adopted in the later works. The composer's description of the bizarre rhythmic nature of his Bohemians' scene and the autograph indication *scherzando* in the libretto suggest that passages may well have been worked into the Roman carnival of *Benvenuto Cellini*, known to have the other borrowings described above. The duo of Amélie and Lenor may have been used as *"Quand des sommets de la montagne"* in Act III. Admittedly these are guesses for which there can be no proof other than the discovery of new documents.[20]

There are in the score of *Les Francs-Juges* four changes of musical text subject to evaluation: three are accomplished with collettes (over fols. 59^r, 66^r, and 72^r), the fourth, a major revision in the duo of Christiern and Olmerik from Act I, is in a staff added underneath the finished score. Additionally, a pencil mark on fol. 49^v represents the end of a cut, and some revisions on one of the remnants, fol. 67*bis*$^{r\&v}$, are too fragmentary for analysis.

The collettes cover relatively minor changes in the music. One, on fol. 72^r, is merely to remove flats from a figure because they are already in the signature (Ex. 4.3):

a.

b.

Example 4.3a&b: *Hymne des Francs-Juges*: a. Before change, aut. fol. 72^r*o*; b. After change, aut. fol. 72^r*c*.

Here the composer has done a great deal of copying for a minor (and unnecessary) correction. The flats could have been removed by erasure or hidden under a tiny collette. Berlioz was doing his best to impress both his teacher and the jury at the Odéon, however, and he probably thought that with a pristine score he could more easily accomplish his purpose.

Both of the other collettes were attached in order to alter the declamation. (The first is curious in that the preceding page does not lead directly to the original layer; a small cut may also be involved.) The changes are as follows (Exs. 4.4 and 4.5):

Example 4.4a&b: *Choeur des Bergers:* a. Before revision, aut. fol. 59^{r}o; b. After, aut. fol. 59^{r}c.

Example 4.5a&b: Ibid., fols. 66^{r}o and 66^{r}c.

The purpose of the revision is to improve the poor declamation. The conjunction *et* is displaced to a weaker metric position, and *-sirs* of *plaisirs* assumes its rightfully strong place in the measure. In Example 4.5 the change of declamation improves in turn the effect of the decrescendo in the second and third full measures.

More interesting is the revision of the duo (fols. 51^{r}ff.) of Olmerik and Christiern. The revised version is found in a hand-drawn staff at the bottom of folios 51^r-54^r. At first the staff contains a reduction, with minor revisions, of the vocal line. Gradually it becomes a sketch of an entirely new version, ending with a line found in neither the libretto nor the original score (Ex. 4.6).

The musical effect of the new section is considerably stronger than in the original version. The composer has introduced a new rhythmic complexity, the triplets of mm. 16ff of the example (*"frappons-les, sans pitié ni merci"*) replacing a conventional ending with repeated statements of *"au courroux qui m'anime."* There is a net reduction in the revision of 28 measures, with a good deal of pointless repetition deleted. Most notable is the added chromaticism, with a modulation from E minor to A

Example 4.6: Duo of Olmerik and Christiern (no. 2); sketch in lowest line, fols. 51ʳ-54ʳ.

minor through F major. Such clever inflections as the D♭ in m. 17 and the chromaticism in mm. 26-28 represent a more sophisticated level of composition than occurs anywhere in the 1826 version.

Berlioz planned to use the duo in the 1829 version as well as in the short drama about Olmerik's murderer. In this second plan, the duo was to come between the hymns of Francs-Juges and chorus such that the music became faster as the movement progressed. The revisions in the autograph score were evidently made with this idea in mind, for the new version does not end, but comes to a clear-cut point of transition (mm. 32-39). The tail was probably intended to connect with an existing modulation from A minor to C minor found in the chorus of Francs-Juges (fols. 67*bis*xʳ&ᵛ). At the same time, a new fascicle was added to the manuscript score of the hymn (fols. 75-80); the violin line, when it enters, is in the standard modern position. Finally two lines added to the duet:

> *Frappons-les tous les deux sans pitié ni merci,*
> *C'est l'ordre de Dieu.*

seem deliberately similar to the sentiment in the hymn:

> *Des célestes décrets, invisibles vengeurs,*
> *Vous dont le bras fatal est redoubtable au crime,*
> *Frappez, frappez votre victime;*
> *A la pitié fermez vos coeurs.*[21]

If this is indeed the correct interpretation, then the sketch represents the only musical evidence that Berlioz actually began to work on the drama hastily outlined in his original score.

Les Francs-Juges, then, is not completely lost. Steps in its composition can be determined and the general nature of its musical content as well. Berlioz himself never seems to have had any doubt that his opera was a reputable work of high calibre, nor to have abandoned hope that the music could be put to good use. At the same time he realized its youthfulness: every plan for reuse implies organic revision of the music and the addition of newly-composed movements. The unresolved mystery is the last step: we can never know which passages from *Benvenuto Cellini*, say, or *Les Troyens* actually originated in a student work of 1826.

2. *Requiem* (1837)

The idea of mustering a large performing force to participate in a musical *clangor tubarum* announcing the Day of Judgment occurred to Berlioz in 1824, as he was planning his first Mass. It is almost certainly an outgrowth of his exposure to the religious music of Lesueur and Cherubini and of his increasing knowledge of musical instruments and their possibilities. The *Requiem* was composed thirteen years later with the same idea in mind. It was published in three different editions, first by Schlesinger in 1838, then twice more by Ricordi (1853, 1867). Substantial musical changes were made for each edition. Altogether the composer was occupied with one form or another of his idea for forty-three of the fifty years he wrote music.

The autograph and manuscript sources for each version along with related correspondence constitute a body of some five hundred items. Arranged chronologically, they are:

1. Letters describing the *Messe solennelle* of 1825 and the retouched *Resurrexit* (performed 1827-29):[22]

2. Two manuscript scores of the *Resurrexit*, **F-Pc** ms 1510 and **F-G** Rés R 90665 (see no. 20B in Table I, above);

3. Letters describing an intermediate project, *Le Dernier Jour du monde* (**BerCG** 234, 257), and a manuscript document relating to it (cited in Table I, no. 61);

4. Letters and documents describing another intermediate project, a *Fête musicale funèbre à la mémoire des hommes illustres de la France* (**BerCG** 429, 435, 439, 440, and **F-Pn** papiers divers de Berlioz, no. 10; see Table I, no. 72);

5. Letters describing the *Requiem* itself;[23]

6. The autograph score, **F-Pc** ms 1509, containing sketches, drafts, and revisions;

7. Manuscript parts prepared for the first performance: two vocal scores, **F-Pc** L 10485 and **F-Pc** L 91; manuscript orchestra parts, **F-Pc** L 17235 (*fonds du roi*);

8. Lithographed vocal parts prepared for the first performance (Paris: Boboeuf, 1837), **F-Pc** L 17236; one copy of each revised by Berlioz for the engraver of Brandus' 1852 publication of the parts;

9. Autograph draft of *Sanctus*, mm. 1-45, arranged for soprano and tenor, a vocal part for the concert of 6 April 1844, **F-Pmeyer**;

10. First published edition (Paris: Schlesinger, 1838), copy **F-Pc** D 935;

11. Copy of Schlesinger's edition with revisions entered by Berlioz and his copyist, **F-Pc** D 937 and **F-Pc** L 11038.

12. Second published edition (Milan: Ricordi, 1853); two copies include later alterations, **F-Pc** D 937 and **F-Pc** L 11038.

13. Published chorus parts (Paris: Brandus, 1852): parts in **F-Pn** (deposition copies) conform to Ricordi's first edition, **F-Pn** Vm^1 2276; parts in **F-Pc** conform to Ricordi's revised edition, **F-Pc** L 17237 (*fonds du roi*);

14. Revised second edition of score, incorporating Berlioz's revisions (Milan: Ricordi, 1867)[24], **F-Pn** Vm^1 23; edition published by Brandus (printed, not engraved) c. 1884, conforming to Ricordi's second edition, **F-Pc** D 938;[25]

15. Miscellaneous items: Quotations from the work in the *Traité d'Instrumentation*;[26] various copies of the two editions altered by Berlioz's copyist to agree with the second Ricordi edition;[27] albumleaves; and the **OBE**, which incorporates a few changes that Berlioz would probably have made but overlooked.[28]

There were three distinct versions of the *Requiem*: the reading in the autograph (to which Schlesinger's edition generally conforms), the version published by Ricordi in 1853, and Ricordi's revised edition of 1867.

Berlioz composed the *Requiem* in response to a governmental commission for a work commemorating victims of the revolution of July 1830. He must already have been considering a large work (possibly the completion of his *Fête musicale funèbre*), because one of the conditions of his contract was that he be allowed several hundred performers. Reporting to his father on the offer (**BerCG** 490: 8 March 1837), he alludes to a huge *Dies irae*. He was actively at work in early April:

Je finis aujourd'hui la Prose des morts, *commençant par le* Dies Irae *et finissant au* Lacrymosa*; c'est une poésie d'un sublime gigantesque... j'ai dominé mon sujet, et je crois à présent que ma partition sera passablement grande* (**BerCG** 493: 11 April 1837).	Today I finish the prosa for the dead, beginning with the *Dies irae* and ending at the *Lacrymosa*; it is a poem of sublime enormity. I've mastered my subject, and I now think that my score will be of considerable proportions!

The verb *finir* refers only to the poetry;[29] Berlioz does not mean he has written the music. He has understood the Latin to his satisfaction and probably made some basic decisions on musical content.

By 22 May 1837, *finir* refers to the music as well. In a letter to Liszt, he writes:

Mon Requiem *est fini, je me débats avec la matière. Ce sont les copistes, les lithographes, les charpentiers....* (**BerCG** 498).	My *Requiem* is finished; I'm struggling with practicalities. These include the copyists, the lithographers, the carpenters . . .

He can only mean that he has completed a draft, however, since the formal orchestra score is dated 29 June 1837, and it is unlikely that much material was submitted to the copyist as early as May. To have finished even a completely-sketched version in a month and a half means that he composed the piece with dispatch. He would later compose other masterpieces at the same rate, notably *La Damnation de Faust* and *Les Troyens*, but by contrast, *Roméo et Juliette* took nine months and *Benvenuto Cellini* took over a year. There is little correspondence from the month of June, when he was drafting the full score, but it is clear from the note on p. 21 of the autograph (trans. above, p. 176) that he allotted the entire month for the task.

Berlioz wrote relatively few letters describing his first ideas for the *Requiem*, but his basic approach can be inferred. His goal was to depict the Last Judgment in music, with a huge number of performers. He then made a conscientious attempt to "dominate his subject," devoting a full month (mid-March to mid-April) to study and thought.[30] From the beginning he must have planned to use one or more sections of the *Messe solennelle*.

The borrowing for the *Requiem* of a passage from the *Resurrexit* of his first Mass (mm. 76-106; **OBE** p. 8/7-p. 12/5; cf. *Requiem*, movt. II, mm. 141-71, **OBE** p. 19-p. 24/4) is among the most extensive self-quotations in Berlioz's music. (It was only for Ricordi's revised second edition that the original words *"Et iterum venturus est cum gloria judicare vivos et mortuos"* were suppressed and the correct words of the *Requiem* were substituted, *"Tuba mirum,"* etc.) Including the passage was not simply an afterthought; the *Requiem* was specifically designed to incorporate it. Berlioz described its hypnotic effect in a letter of July 1825:

*... Dans l'*Iterum venturus, *après avoir annoncé par toutes les trompettes et trombones du monde l'arrivée du jugement suprême, le choeur des humains séchant d'épouvante s'est déployé; ô Dieu! je nageais sur cette mer agitée, je humais ces flots de vibrations sinistres; je n'ai voulu charger personne du soin de mitrailler mes auditeurs, et après avoir annoncé aux méchants, par une dernière bordée de cuivres, que le moment des pleurs et des grincements des dents était venu, j'ai appliqué un si rude coup de tam-tam que tout l'église en a tremblé. Ce n'est pas de ma faute si les dames surtout ne se sont pas crues à la fin du monde* (**BerCG** 48: 20 July 1825; to Albert du Boys).

... In the *Iterum venturus*, after the announcement of the Last Judgment by all the trumpets and trombones on earth, the choir of terrified humans is deployed. Oh God, I swam in this stormy sea, I swallowed a tide of sinister vibrations. I didn't want to delegate to another soul the responsibility of gunning down my audience, and after announcing, by a last blast of brasses, that the moment for tears and gnashing of teeth had come, I threw in such a violent stroke of the tam-tam that the whole church quaked. It isn't my fault if the ladies in particular didn't think they were at the end of the world.

The composer tried repeatedly to win popular approval of his favorite excerpt from the Mass. He included a retouched version in concerts of 1827 and 1828 and attached both a recitative accompanied by timpani and a programmatic description for a concert in 1829. He deliberately led his supervisors at the Conservatoire to believe that the movement had been written in Rome, sending a score as one of his *envois*.[31] (In their formal report the judges complimented Berlioz for taking their advice to abandon the bizarre styles of his earlier works; see Boschot's transcription **BosHB** II, 117). Two abandoned projects would no doubt have made further use of the *Resurrexit*, the oratorio *Le Dernier Jour du monde* and the *Fête musicale funèbre*. Berlioz's musical style had matured by the time he finally did reuse the passage; nevertheless he adopted it with little alteration.[32]

The autograph of the *Requiem*, a large volume of 32-staff folio paper, is so elegant that it seems at first glance to be a fair copy of an earlier score.   The few revisions generally have to do with matters of declamation. Most of the changes are in the *Requiem et Kyrie* and *Dies irae*, where several revisions were made before the first performance. The strict repetitions in the *Lacrymosa* and *Agnus Dei* are in Rocquemont's hand. It does not, in short, seem to be the kind of document likely to suggest much about Berlioz's methods of work.

As a matter of fact, it is with the autograph of the *Requiem* that Berlioz first begins to rely heavily on a pencilled draft in the full score, later covered with ink.[33] The unusually neat appearance of the autograph is a direct result of this technique, for it is certain that the entire work was originally set out in pencil. Sometimes Berlioz noted only the outer lines or the melody, but often he dealt with details of orchestration and nuance as well.

Berlioz may refer to this procedure in the *Mémoires* (Chap. XLVI), when he writes of the *Requiem*:

Le plan d'un morceau n'était pas esquissé que celui d'un autre se présentait; dans l'impossibilité d'écrire assez vite j'avais adopté des signes sténographiques qui, pour le Lacrymosa *surtout, me furent d'un grand secours. Les compositeurs connaissent le supplice et le désespoir causés par la perte du souvenir de certaines idées qu'on n'a pas eu le temps d'écrire et qui vous échappent ainsi à tout jamais.*	The outline of one piece [movement] was barely sketched before the next formed itself in my mind. It was impossible to write fast enough, and I devised a sort of musical shorthand which was a great help to me, especially in the *Lacrymosa* . All composers know the agony of forgetting ideas and of finding that they have vanished forever, for want of time to set them down **(BerMemCairns)**.

The *Lacrymosa* is, in fact, one of the most carefully drafted movements. There do not seem to be any stenographic signs among the pencil marks, however; perhaps Berlioz quickly sketched the basic melodic and harmonic structure in pencil, leaving various sorts of symbols to remind him of the planned orchestration. Then, confident that the essentials of his work had been recorded, he went back to work out the details. This type of sketching virtually presupposes the use of open score, so the pencil marks visible in the autograph may be related in some way to the symbols Berlioz recalls.

Probably, though, the stenographic signs belong to an entirely different stage, a separate draft in short score now lost. Such a draft must have been prepared, at least for the choral parts, for there is no pencil under the vocal lines in the score. The version in ink was entered directly, copied from another source that may have contained the shorthand. But there is no evidence of shorthand signs in similar sketches for later works; the closest Berlioz comes to shorthand is his habitual use of curved lines and indications *Bis* to plan the phrase structure of a passage. Either the remarks about musical shorthand are in part fabricated (in which case Berlioz would have been referring merely to the pencil draft), or the use of shorthand was abandoned before the sketches for *La Damnation de Faust* and *Les Troyens.*

The pencil draft generally includes at least a bass line. In certain passages all the parts are sketched: Berlioz would occasionally stop (or come back) to orchestrate a phrase in full. He abandoned one section sketched in pencil (movt. I; cf. mm. 103-07, **OBE** p. 6/9-13) and covered it with a collette; thus underneath the collette can be seen an example of pencil draft not covered in ink. He had originally intended to continue the eighth-note motion through the next episode, settling on the following accompaniment (Ex. 4.7):

Example 4.7: Detail of pencil draft of the original version, movt. I, mm. 103–07, aut. p. 11.

He changed his mind several times while sketching the passage, such that there are several layers at this point in the autograph. The vocal parts are in ink, surrounded by notation in pencil (Ex. 4.8). He eventually decided to replace the entire passage, probably in order to add the canonic statement of *Te decet hymnus* (mm. 101-06, sopranos and altos; **OBE** p. 6/7-12), of which there is no trace in the first version.

In making this change by covering the abandoned version with a collette, Berlioz left good evidence of how his pencil drafts worked. He must usually have followed the same general procedure, first experimenting with the idea, then adopting one of the alternatives. In this case, and doubtlessly in many others, he finally decided to delete the whole passage as sketched in favor of an entirely new idea.

As for other works, the pencil drafts for the *Requiem* seem to be most directly associated with decisions on orchestration. In the last two staves of pp. 52-54 of the autograph, for example, there is a draft of the chord progression for timpani in the *Tuba Mirum* (Ex. 4.9).

Example 4.8: Ibid., complete transcription.

Example 4.9: Pencil draft of the *Dies irae*, mm. 165-76, timpani part, aut. pp. 52-54 (**OBE** p. 23/5-p. 25/3).

This complicated operation required another set of notes. In m. 169 and again in m. 174, each at the beginning of a page, Berlioz jotted down a reminder of the pitch dispersement of pairs of timpani (Ex. 4.10):

staff:

Example 4.10: Ibid., aut. pp. 53-54.

With the matrix thus set up, Berlioz orchestrated the passage for timpani with little difficulty.

The fanfare for brass choirs earlier in the same movement was to have been much shorter, to judge from the underlying draft. The entry of the chorus (equivalent to present mm. 163ff) appears in the draft on pp. 48–49 of the autograph, a page later covered by the longer brass fanfare; mm. 194ff of the *Dies irae* (**OBD** p. 21ff) now appear at that point in the score. The introduction as first planned was thus about the same length as the comparable section in the *Resurrexit*; Berlioz had considered an even more direct borrowing to begin with.

Berlioz has left pencilled reminders for orchestration throughout the autograph score. On p. 124 (*Lacrymosa*, m. 158; **OBE** 5 mm. after Fig. 57) he indicates the entry of brasses: *"Tromb:"* . . . *"Cor en ut."* At the bottom of pp. 114 and 116 of the same movement are similar instructions: under m. 102 (**OBE** Fig. 53) he writes: *"Entrée des timb. Les cuivres dialoguent toujours,"* and under m. 113 (**OBE** Fig. 54): *"Entrée des grosses caisses, tous les cuivres réunis."* On p. 183 (*Lacrymosa* m. 174, **OBE** Fig. 89), he notes: *"Tremoli commencent ici."* Occasionally, these notes are ignored; on p. 26, for example (*Dies irae*, m. 13) he wrote: *"Les flûtes seules avec les voix,"* though eventually scored it for flute, oboe, and clarinet.

One intriguing set of pencil marks, a series of figured bass symbols, occurs in the *Sanctus*. Beginning in m. 146 appear the following figures (Ex. 4.11):

Example 4.11: Figured bass in second *Hosanna* from *Sanctus* (mm. 146-66), aut. pp. 178-81; **OBE** p. 104/8-106/9. (The figures continue, somewhat less densely, through the rest of the passage.)

Despite his scorn for the stuffy teaching methods of Reicha and Lesueur, Berlioz was quite happy to make use of his training in figured bass. The figures do not represent plans for the harmonic structure, for the same *Hosanna* had already been fully drafted earlier in the movement (mm. 46-91). In the second statement, however, there is a new sustained accompaniment in strings. The figures were added as the chords were entered, primarily to check the voice-leading in the added parts. (Berlioz uses figures in a number of sketches and drafts. In *La Nonne sanglante*, for example, occurs the following passage [Ex. 4.12]):

Example 4.12: Figured bass in *La Nonne sanglante*, fol. 72ᵛ (pencil version).

There are various other indications in pencil. Some are merely instructions to Rocquemont, who filled in the musical repetitions. An estimated performance time, *"8 minutes,"* occurs at the end of the *Offertoire* (aut. p. 148). There is a late note on the cover of the *Sanctus* (aut. p. 158), the beginning of which reads *"A corriger dans la partition d'orchestre et les parties séparées:..."* (The remainder is illegible, covered by layers of dirt in the corner where the page is turned.) On p. 9 of the autograph, Berlioz reminds himself to add a collette, *"coller une bairde,"* where some changes in orchestration have resulted in a sloppy appearance.

One of Berlioz's remarks about the *Requiem* is directly contradicted by the evidence of the pencil drafts. He told Liszt that he had finished the work before the pencil draft could have existed; the letter to Liszt (cited above, p. 238) carries the date 22 May 1837, but the draft was still incomplete in June (see p. 176, above). He must have considered the piece already "written" before much of the orchestration had been done. But genuine compositional change was involved at the level of the pencil draft whenever he incorporated second thoughts and changes in the formal arrangement of the work. Moreover, it seems clear that the first composition of certain contrapuntal lines was accomplished in pencil. Not until the pencil draft did a movement become a cohesive musical unit.

While preparing the full ink draft of the first movement, Berlioz replaced two sections with more sophisticated ideas. He rejected both the original readings immediately, for they are merely cross-hatched; he went on to draft a new version in the following measure. After m. 70 (**OBE**

p. 4/13) a section of five measures was deleted and replaced with mm. 71ff (Ex. 4.13):

Example 4.13: Passage deleted after m. 70 of first movement, aut. p. 7-8.

Also deleted was a section after m. 77 (Ex. 4.14):

Example 4.14: Passage deleted after m. 77 of first movement, aut. p. 8.

Other sections in the original draft were simply deleted. Margins of four leaves cut from the *Dies irae* (between aut. pp. 34-35) and another three from the *Rex tremendae* (between aut. pp. 84-85) can be seen in the manuscript.[34] A measure between mm. 4 and 5 of the *Sanctus* was crossed out of the score. The original idea was that the violins *tutti* (mm. 1-5) would end with a half note, followed by a half-measure of rest and then the entry of solo parts (Ex. 4.15):

Example 4.15: First version of *Sanctus*, mm. 4-5 (violins), aut. p. 153.

On second thought he removed the extraneous bar and had the entry of *soli* instruments overlap the violins *tutti*. There is some confusion in the vocal score at this point (**F-Pc** L 10485), but the lithographed chorus parts and manuscript orchestra parts have only the revised reading.

Berlioz used only a few collettes in the manuscript to revise the musical text.   One reflects his penchant for adding complex accompanying figures. There is a collette over m. 16 of the *Rex tremendae* (aut. p. 75, **OBE** Fig. 32); underneath is the identical soprano part, but with no measure of rest before. The vocal part had already been drafted in ink when Berlioz decided to add the rather complicated accompanying figure (Ex. 4.16):

Example 4.16: Accompanying figure in *Rex tremendae*, mm. 16-17.

He felt that it needed a measure of introduction, so he added a collette to include the new measure, squeezing three measures into the space of two.

A series of collettes was pasted over the choral parts in the *Dies irae*, mm. 13-64. This is the first indication of a long, complex, but never entirely successful effort to improve the counterpoint and declamation of the Latin text. The first changes were as follows (Ex. 4.17):

Example 4.17: First and second versions of choral parts in *Dies irae*, mm. 13-64; OBE pp. ix-xi and 12-14.

Each is designed to improve the musical interest of the passage without altering the basic melodic and harmonic shape or the phrase lengths. The most noticeable effect in the second and third examples above is a distinct improvement in the cadence structure of the third excerpt. In the first excerpt, Berlioz merely reshapes the contrapuntal line; the net effect is a less faulty declamation of the words *solvet saeclum* and *dies illa*.

Shortly before the first performance of the *Requiem*, Berlioz had all the performance parts prepared. Most are still preserved, including a set of manuscript orchestra parts and the original lithographed chorus parts. There are also two manuscript vocal scores prepared by Rocquemont, probably for use of the chorus masters. One, F-Pc L 91, is merely a copy, but the other, F-Pc L 10485, has a few notations by Berlioz himself, as well as a hastily prepared reduction for piano in what seems to be another hand. A number of the parts have been signed and dated by the performers, showing that they were used for performance in France, Germany (Dresden, 10 and 17 February, 1843; Leipzig, 22 February; Brunswick, 9 March; Hamburg, 22 March; Berlin, 8 and 23 April), and England (7 February 1848). Though these parts have been carefully revised to agree with Schlesinger's edition, they give no evidence that the work was altered in the performances in Germany and England. Nor is there evidence that they were used for the Paris performance of 1850, though that seems likely, since published chorus parts did not appear until 1852. One copy of each part (see Table I, above) has been revised by Berlioz for publication and subsequently used by the engraver; the bass part is headed in Berlioz's hand; *"Deuxième édition / corrigée par l'auteur."* The parts conform almost perfectly to Ricordi's first edition of the full score. The manuscript orchestra parts have also been revised for the later version.

The changes in the *Dies irae* noted above had been made before the parts were prepared, that is, the "after" version is the one that appears in the lithographed and manuscript parts. But other changes in the movement were made after the parts were prepared (but before Schlesinger's score was printed). Beginning in measure 72 of the *Dies irae* (**OBE** p. 14/19ff), Berlioz has altered the note values in tenors and bassoons from the first version below to the second (Ex. 4.18):

Example 4.18: *Dies irae*, mm. 72-73, first and second versions of figure for tenors and bassoons.

Further along, the upper voice in the passage beginning at m. 106 (**OBE** p. 16/16ff) was removed from the bass part and given to the second tenors. The original version, visible in all the parts and the autograph score (but not, again, in Schlesinger's edition) was as follows (Ex. 4.19):

Example 4.19: Ibid., mm. 106-09, first and second version of melodic figure.

The revised reading was added to all the sources, presumably before the first performance.

Of somewhat greater musical significance is a change in the *Quaerens me*. To the phrase beginning *"Culpâ rubet vultus meus,"* a section ultimately removed from the movement, Berlioz added two new ideas. The first version is clear in the parts and can be detected in the score (see Facsimile I.2), where the superfluous rests have been blotted out. The first statement had been routine (Ex. 4.20):

Example 4.20: *Quaerens me*, original version of passage deleted from movement (cf. **OBE**, p. xvii).

Possibly finding that section banal, he added the overlapping motives for
tenor II and soprano II (Ex. 4.21):

Example 4.21: Ibid., revised version.

The new version was published by Schlesinger (see complete transcription, **OBE**, p. xvii) and performed until 1852-53.

Never content with the way his works ended, Berlioz revised the
closing bars of the *Agnus Dei*, which had first included four measures of
the tonic chord played by the choir of timpani (trans. **OBE**, p. xx). He
may have deleted them because he found the sound of the timpani
muddy and the static G-major chord too long. The passage is cross-
hatched in the score and covered by collettes in the affected parts.

Minor alterations of the autograph score and early parts reflect
problems encountered in the early rehearsals. The reason for virtually all
these revisions is to remove impractical passages, particularly pitches that
exceeded the upper limit of amateur singers. In the *Dies irae*, mm. 200-
203, the bass parts originally read as follows (Ex. 4.22):

Example 4.22: *Dies irae (Tuba mirum)*, mm. 200-03, original bass part (cf. **OBE** p. 28/5-29/1).

The *F♯* and *E♭* were evidently too much for the basses I to manage, so Berlioz assigned the part to tenors I and II. This change is carefully entered in the parts, a somewhat complicated operation in the case of the tenor parts, where measures of rest had at first been indicated.

In the *Rex tremendae*, m. 49 (**OBE** p. 42/4), the pitches for bass II have been added in the parts. They have been added to the score as well, but there the change has been so skillfully made that it is hardly noticed. The same is true in the *Lacrymosa*, mm. 32-37 (**OBE** p. 59/4-60/4); the lower bass part has been added to both score and parts, but the change is practically undetectable in the score.

In the *Hosanna* from the *Sanctus*, Berlioz displaces the second soprano parts by an octave for those who could not manage the octave leap originally included (mm. 50, 85: **OBE** p. 98/5, 99/17, resp.). He does not accord the sopranos a similar courtesy in the expanded second *Hosanna*. This change is visible only in the parts; it was not made in the autograph score.

At m. 150 of the Offertoire (OBE p. 92/17), Berlioz has added an *F♯* to the tenor I part and an A to the tenor II. Both changes are designed to leave the tenors on a pitch in mid-range for the final chord, pianissimo, even though the part writing suffers. Berlioz restores the proper pitches (A and D, respectively), when revising the parts for publication in 1852, but fails to make the change for Ricordi's score (1853). It is likely that he meant for the higher pitches to be restored and simply neglected to change the measure in Ricordi's proof. The example demonstrates strikingly Berlioz's willingness to let practical considerations override the finer points of musical grammar. The essence of the music lay in its effect, and the effect was produced by human beings with all too human limitations.

In 1852, Berlioz agreed to let Ricordi publish an edition of the *Requiem*. A new edition was called for; numerous performances of excerpts and three performances of the entire work since Schlesinger's edition had suggested many new ideas to the composer. The most extensive stage of musical revision probably occurred in connection with a complete performance at St.-Eustache on 22 October 1852; for this performance, published parts (Brandus, February 1852;[35] F-Pc L 17237 [*fonds du roi*]) conforming to Ricordi's edition (which had not yet appeared) were used. It is conceivable that significant revisions were made for a performance on 3 May 1850, but not likely, considering some tempestuous events that preceded the concert.[36] By February 1853, in any case, Berlioz was correcting the proofs of the new edition. In a letter to Ricordi of 22 February (BerMC, pp. 62-63), he compliments the engraver but warns that there are many changes still to be made.[37] The compliment may indicate that Berlioz was not overly concerned with actual errors in the text, but rather wanted to make some substantial last minute musical changes. In fact Berlioz asked to be sent a second proof with, in addition to the textual changes, a new title page: *"DEUXIEME EDITION revue par l'auteur, et contenant plusieurs modifications importantes"* ("SECOND EDITION, reviewed by the author, and containing numerous important changes").

One copy of Schlesinger's edition, F-Pn Rés Vm¹ 243, has been revised with manuscript notations and collettes by both Berlioz and Rocquemont. It was probably used for the concert of 22 October 1852, for Rocquemont has pasted a seating chart for the brass choirs into the front cover. A very similar copy must have been sent to Ricordi, since in most particulars his edition matches the version in the corrected Schlesinger edition. There are significant alterations in declamation, length, and part-writing for this later version, the product of the composer's fourteen years of experience with his work.

Berlioz's most striking revisions for the new publication occurred when he deleted two short passages. In the *Quaerens me*, ten measures have been removed between mm. 39-40 (trans. OBE p. xvii). Berlioz has thus deleted two variations on his thematic motives (Exs. 4.23 and .24).

Example 4.23: Melodic motive removed from *Quaerens me*, mm. 7-9 of deleted passage.

Example 4.24: Rhythmic motive removed from *Quaerens me* mm. 3-4 of deleted passage.

He was primarily interested in the rhythmic figure used for the phrase *"Culpâ rubet vultus meus,"* since it consistently resulted in a false declamation. The net result, however, is the loss of a phrase of text and the cadence in C♯ minor that originally ended the passage. He could just as easily have adopted the proper rhythmic motive, the one used through the rest of the movement (Ex. 4.25).

Example 4.25: Hypothetical declamation of *"Culpâ rubet vultus meus,"* mm. 3-6 of deleted passage.

Some seventeen measures were cut from the *Offertoire*[38] between mm. 101 and 106 (trans. **OBE**, pp. xviii-xix); Berlioz left only four of the original bars, mm. 102-105. In this movement the chorus, until the very end, sings only the pitches *A* and *B♭*, for example (Ex. 4.26):

Example 4.26: *Offertoire*, mm. 6-16.

In the original passage, beginning in m. 96, there were 27 measures of an
accompanying motive (Ex. 4.27):

Example 4.27: *Offertoire*, mm. 96-97 (violins I) and 102-103 (cellos and contrabasses).

Berlioz probably removed the seventeen measures simply to prevent the
section from becoming tedious.

The composer has revised the choral lines in several spots, carefully
distinguishing between the first and second divisions of each part. The
very first entry of the voices (movt. I; basses, m. 26; tenors, m. 28;
sopranos, m. 30) were in Schlesinger's edition intended for the full
section. Desiring a softer, more distant sound, Berlioz marked the
seconds out of the entry. He followed the same procedure for the first
section of the *Dies irae*, removing second sopranos (altos) and first (mm.
25-28) or second (mm. 29-48) tenors. In mm. 109, 110, and 112 of the
Requiem et Kyrie, he wanted the opposite effect, a forceful, supported
statement; thus he added lower octaves to the high notes in each part
(Ex. 4.28):

Example 4.28: Movement I, mm. 109-12, first and second versions.

To build the crescendo, he added the second tenors to the rising scale
just before (mm. 105-08: *"ad te omnis caro [veniet]"*).

Berlioz mentions in his orchestration treatise (p. 233) that it is often
helpful to support passages in high tessitura of a given voice with
doublings in the comfortable range of another. He quotes as his example
a passage from the first version of the *Lacrymosa*, mm. 9-13 (Ex. 4.29):

Example 4.29: *Lacrymosa*, mm. 9-13; the example is actually transcribed from Schlesinger's edition, which differs in a few details.

The version published by Ricordi carries the same idea further by continuing to support the higher voice in mm. 11-13 (Ex. 4.30):

Example 4.30: Ibid., second version.

The definitive reading is in equal measure the result, no doubt, of the composer's theoretical speculations and his practical experience.

He also rewrites the vocal parts in two passages in the *Rex tremendae*. The original version of mm. 6-8 (and mm. 90-91) read as follows (Ex. 4.31):

Example 4.31: *Rex tremendae*, mm. 6-8, first version.

For Ricordi's edition, Berlioz completely rescored the same idea (Ex. 4.32):

Example 4.32: Ibid., second version.

The high *A*'s have been removed from the first tenor part and the second sopranos given a separate line. Berlioz had tried to build a powerful climax into the broad crescendo by having the tenors enter just before the climax, but he preferred on second thought to double the rising scale with the second tenors, allowing the melodic line itself to effect the climax.

Someone, possibly Ricordi, must have alerted Berlioz to several cases of faulty declamation of Latin in his work. In addition to deleting the poor *Culpâ rubet*, the composer made two other last-minute changes of declamation. At the end of the *Rex* (mm. 85-110, **OBE** p. 48/2-p. 50), he consistently altered the words *Salva me* (Ex. 4.33):

Example 4.33: *Rex tremendae*, mm. 85ff., first and second versions.

In the phrase *"Quaerens me, sedisti lassus"*, the note value for the syllable *-ti* of *sedesti* is reduced by half; the reason must be some subtle point of declamation, perhaps to separate the words *sedesti* and *lassus* (since *-ti* and *las-* are sung to the same pitch) (Ex. 4.34):

Example 4.34: *Quaerens me*, mm. 1-4, first and second versions.

Berlioz also rephrased the florid line for tenors in the *Dies irae*, mm. 104-38 (*"Quantus tremor est futurus,"* **OBE** pp. 16-18). The musical text was not radically altered, but the prosody was improved (original version trans. **OBE** p. xii).

Each of the minor revisions effects a subtle improvement. In m. 78 of the *Dies irae* (**OBE** p. 15/4), Berlioz has provided the sopranos I who could could not leap to an *A* with an alternate pitch, *E♭*. In mm. 117ff, (**OBE** p. 17/11ff) he has written a lower part for second sopranos. An extremely slight change was made in the bass part at m. 69 of the *Rex tremendae* (Ex. 4.35):

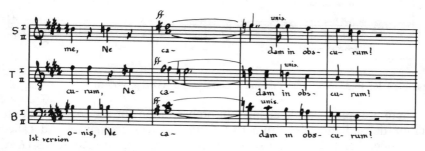

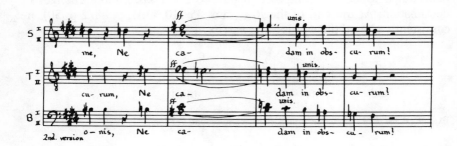

Example 4.35: *Rex tremendae*, mm. 69-71 (**OBE** p. 45/2-4), first and second versions.

One of his most inspired revisions was the addition of the ethereal C♮ to oboes, clarinets, and sopranos in mm. 97-98 of the *Rex*, where originally there had been only B♮'s (Ex. 4.36):

Example 4.36: Ibid., mm. 94-98, first and second versions (**OBE** p. 49/2-6).

There are some simple changes in orchestration for the second edition. Berlioz deleted the bass drum part from the *Rex tremendae* and called for wooden-headed timpani sticks instead of sponge headed sticks (*Rex,*

mm. 70ff, **OBE** Fig. 36).   The ophicléide monstre, finally becoming
obsolete, was abandoned in the *Tuba mirum* and *Lacrymosa*, replaced by
two tubas. A flourish of brasses in m. 171 of the *Dies irae* was rewritten
to include fifth and sixth horns and the cornet from the first orchestra;[39]
the trombones alone had not provided the volume or tone quality
desired.

Possibly as an afterthought, Berlioz added a subtitle to the *Offertoire:
Choeur des âmes de Purgatoire.* This description had first been used in
connection with a performance of 7 February 1848 in London, where the
program and advertisements mention a *Chorus of souls in Purgatory.*
Later the subtitle was removed.   After revising some details in a second
proof,[40] Berlioz released the new edition.

In 1867 Ricordi published the *Requiem* a second time,[41] incorporating
three last revisions by the composer.   In the first Berlioz alters the
declamation in the *Dies irae*, a third time.   The changes are as follows
Ex. 4.37):

Example 4.37:   Final revisions of *Dies irae*: mm. 23-25; mm. 35-37; mm. 62-64.

The point of each change is to improve the pronunciation of *in favillâ*. The proper text of the *Tuba mirum* was finally substituted; in the other edition, the words from the *Resurrexit ("Et iterum venturus est")* had appeared (See **OBE**, p. xiii).[42] The last change was also a matter of declamation (Ex. 4.38):

Example 4.38: *Hostias*, mm. 2-3, declamation of first and second versions.

The new version is noticeably better than the original, but still not entirely correct; he should have corrected the passage as follows (Ex. 4.39):

Example 4.39: Hypothetical correction of *Hostias*, mm. 2-3.

There is some support to the theory that Ricordi himself pointed out the flaws in declamation in that Berlioz corrected declamation in the second Ricordi edition as well as the first. In any event, the changes for the new edition were relatively minor. Before releasing the revised second edition, Berlioz removed the subtitle of the *Offertoire*, added as recently as 1853.

The *Requiem* is unusual in that it is Berlioz's only work to have been published in three editions each reviewed and revised by the composer. In one respect the re-editions are easy to explain: Berlioz simply liked his composition and wished to keep it before the public. He realized that it was one of his masterpieces, thus performed it often and with each performance became more and more intimately acquainted with his work. He thought the musical changes were important enough to warrant new published editions despite the confusion that would inevitably result. And in this notion he was right: with each successive revision, the work became stronger, more unified, and easier to perform with precision. The singers in 1850 may have had some reason to complain that Berlioz's music exhausted them, but in the final version the *Requiem* is no more difficult to sing than dozens of other standard works.

Certain problems remain, but by and large they are situations that for one reason or another had to be left as they had originally been written. The timpani choir, for example, is not really effective as it stands: particularly in a large church, the distinct pitches are lost by the time the sound reaches an audience. Berlioz was aware of the problem, and attempted to correct it by removing the passage at the end of the *Agnus Dei* and, to clarify the texture of the *Tuba mirum*, reducing the number of instruments required by half. But after the first performance the passage was too well known to permit extensive change.

Interestingly enough the *Tuba mirum*, the very *raison d'être* of the work, remains relatively unchanged. Berlioz worked carefully to improve the first part of the *Dies irae*, but other than that attended to other movements: the *Rex tremendae, Lacrymosa,* and *Quaerens me.* Few of his revisions are for some structural reason or are attempts to perfect an overall formal design or harmonic framework. The problems he deals with are mostly practical matters, solved in the most practical ways imaginable. Declamation and instrumentation are his primary concerns.

Revisions were not entered for each performance.[43] It seems, rather, that Ricordi's new edition was the product of a single period of careful thought by the composer about the strengths and weaknesses of his work in performance during the fourteen years between 1838 and 1852. Many of the changes must nevertheless have been motivated by recollections of specific events: performances marred because the second tenors or sopranos missed the higher notes, nuances that had always caused difficulty, and so on. Thus the changes represent the same kind of thought that lies behind specific revisions, in other works, for specific concerts, the sort of changes most notably obvious in the sources for the *Symphonie fantastique*.

One of the reasons Berlioz wrote a *Requiem* to begin with was to present a series of magnificent musical effects: the *clangor tubarum*, of course, the choir of timpani, the persistent ostinato figures in the *Lacrymosa* and *Hostias*. It was in order to experiment with these ideas that Berlioz conceived the *Requiem*, pondered it for decades, and repeatedly revised it. He says in the postscript to his *Mémoires* that of his own works, he most prefers the *Scène d'amour* from *Roméo et Juliette*, but a letter to Ferrand of 11 January 1867 (**BerLI CXXXII**) may reveal a more telling passion:

Si j'étais menacé de voir brûler mon oeuvre
entière, moins une partition, c'est pour la
Messe des morts que je demanderais grâce.[44]

If I were threatened with seeing my entire
output burned, less one score, it would be for
the *Messe des morts* that I would beg mercy.

3. *Symphonie fantastique* (1830)

The *Symphonie fantastique* is surely one of the most influential first
symphonies ever to be composed. It earned Berlioz life-long advocates
and equally tenacious critics; it attracted the attention of Liszt and
Schumann, and through them a vast European audience. A full score was
finally published in 1845 and in that form the symphony became
recognized as one of the masterpieces of Romantic art in France.

The published version, however, is strikingly different from the one
Berlioz wrote in 1830. ("It's true that it hardly resembled what it is
today," he says of the *Scène aux champs* [**BerMém** Chap. XXXI], which
was unsuccessful at the first concert.) He extensively revised the entire
symphony after its first performance and made dozens of other changes
over the years. Thus he settled on the definitive text in a leisurely way,
maintaining an active interest in improving it for the better part of two
decades.

When Tiersot and Boschot, in the first scholarly debate over a Berlioz
source, argued for months about one aspect of the manuscript score, they
had become entangled in an issue more complex than either of them
ever realized.[45]   Assessing the manuscript's physical structure and
interpreting the chronology of composition so involved is at best a
tedious matter. It is clear that the autograph preserves multiple efforts by
the composer to rewrite and revise his work, but explaining how they are
related is more difficult.

Examination of the papers and watermarks leads to conclusions that
considerably modify previous accounts of how the composition changed
between May 1830 and December 1832. In the case of the first
movement, which was rewritten but not entirely recopied, it is possible to
retrace the composer's steps in some detail.

Berlioz's plan to write a *Symphonie fantastique* developed from the
simultaneous impact of several literary works: Goethe's *Faust* (trans.
Gérard de Nerval, 1828), E. T. A. Hoffmann's *Contes fantastiques* (Paris,
1829),[46] Thomas de Quincey's *Confessions d'un anglais mangeur d'opium*
(trans. Alfred de Musset, 1829), Chateaubriand's *René* (1805), and a
poem from Hugo's *Odes et Ballades* (1826).[47]   A *Faust* ballet was
originally envisioned, and Berlioz's first reference to a large dramatic
symphony, in February 1829 (**BerCG** 133: to Ferrand), also mentions

Goethe's masterpiece: "I've had a descriptive symphony of *Faust* fermenting in my head for a long time." He worked on it through early 1830 (**BerCG** 149, 151-53: " . . . an *idée fixe* is killing me; all my muscles are trembling, like those of a dying man"), and on 16 April 1830 he transcribed his program in a letter to Ferrand (**BerCG** 158).   Berlioz says he has just written the final note, and there are enough musical details included in the letter to show that he was referring to the full score, not just a sketched version. In the *Mémoires*, he recalls the following circumstances:

Immédiatement après cette composition sur Faust [Huit Scènes de Faust], *et toujours sous l'influence du poème de Goethe, j'écrivis ma* Symphonie fantastique *avec beaucoup de peine pour certaines parties, avec une facilité incroyable pour d'autres. Ainsi* l'adagio (Scène aux champs) *qui impressione toujours si vivement le public et moi-même, me fatigua pendant plus de trois semaines; je l'abandonnai et le repris deux ou trois fois. La* Marche au supplice, *au contraire, fut écrite en une nuit. J'ai néanmoins beaucoup retouché ces deux morceaux et tous les autres du même ouvrage pendant plusieurs années* (Chap. XXVI).	Immediately after the composition of the Faust pieces, and still under the influence of Goethe's poem, I wrote my Fantastic Symphony: very slowly and laboriously in some parts, with extraordinary ease in others. The adagio (the Scene in the Country), which nearly always affects the public and myself so keenly, cost me nearly a month's arduous toil; two or three times I gave it up. On the other hand, the March to the Scaffold was written in a night. But I continued to make considerable changes to both movements, and to the rest of the work, over the course of several years (BerMemCairns).

A performance was planned for the end of May 1830, but so many problems were encountered in the rehearsals that it was cancelled (see **BerCG** 163; **BerMém** Chap. XXVI). Berlioz did hear at least two of the movements rehearsed (the *Bal* and *Marche au supplice*),[48] and certain indications in the autograph suggest that he may on that occasion have tried to conduct the first movement himself. He revised a few passages before the first performance, which finally occurred on 5 December 1830. The first three movements were then rewritten in Rome (see **BerMém** Chaps. XXVI, XXXI and XXXIX). Berlioz does not characterize the differences between the two versions, however, referring only to a coda added to the second movement.

A final set of revisions preceded publication of the score and parts in 1845. Some weeks earlier, an "advance edition" (i.e. a partially corrected version distributed to subscribers) of the score and proofs of the parts had been run. This version is almost identical with the later publications, but includes the unrevised version of a passage in movement II (mm. 129-56).

Altogether, then there are four stages of revisions to the score originally drafted in early 1830:

1.   Original version, rehearsed in May 1830;

2.   Slightly revised version, performed on 5 December 1830;

3.   Completely rewritten version from Rome (1831-32) of the first three movements,[49] first performed in Paris on 9 December 1832; (the symphony was in this form when transcribed by Liszt);

4.   Version in the "advance edition," 1844-45;

5.   Version in the general publication, 1845.

The autograph score of the *Symphonie fantastique* is similar in many ways to Berlioz's other working scores.   There are corrections and collettes, several kinds of paper, some sketches and drafts, and abundant revisions. It differs from the others in that each movement is a separate fascicle. The paper of the fifth movement and part of the first is the same, but movements II, III, IV, and another part of I are on papers each different from the others.   By determining how they relate to the revisions, it is possible, especially for the first movement, to analyze the musical criteria that motivated the changes.

The principal papers can be summarized as follows:

Movt. I: 24-staff paper (NBE's paper *b*),[50] wm.: C. WISE 1828;[51]
              20-staff paper (NBE *d*), wm.: C. WISE 1828;

Movt. II: 20-staff paper from Rome, in folio with two systems of ten staves each (NBE *i*), wm.: AL PARADISO and shield;

Movt. III: 16-staff paper (NBE *j*), no wm. evident;

Movt. IV: 20-staff paper, larger than in movt. I, and lighter in tint (NBE *a*), wm.: BLAGONS and emblem.

Movt. V: 24-staff paper, the same as in movt. I (NBE *b*).

In addition, numerous other papers were used for the collettes containing the revised readings:

Movt. I: p. 21*c*, 12-staff paper (NBE *f*), revised version of mm. 185-94,[52] wm.: INC and shield;

Movt. I: pp. 22*c*-24, 20-staff paper (NBE equates with *b*, but it is a separate paper, as shown by the watermark); revised version of mm. 197-219, wm.:   LALIGANT &C / AMARESQUEL 1829; on p. 22*cv* is an abandoned passage from *La Tempête* (fp November 1830);

Movt. I: pp. 25-26, 16 staff bleached white paper (NBE *g*); revised version of mm. 220-34; wm: top of round shield;

Movt. I: pp. 35-35c and 35cv, 36c and 36cv, 14-staff blue paper (NBE *h*); collette versos contain score and parts for Berlioz's arrangements of *Sur les Alpes*, collettes contain revised version of mm. 274-300;

Movt. I: pp. 37-39cv, 42(c)-43cv, and 51-51cv, 20-staff paper from Rome (NBE *i*), revised version of, respectively, mm. 301-22, 338-55, and 401-09 (original version);

Movt. I: pp. 63-64 (last page), 24-staff paper (NBE equates with *b*, but it is a separate paper), wm.: HP; new *religioso* ending (mm. 496-525);

Movt. IV: p. 36, 20-staff paper (NBE identifies it as a separate paper, *c*, but actually it is the same as NBE *b*), wm.: C. WISE 1828 (very faint), revised version of mm. 171-78.

Two collettes on the same 24-staff paper used in the first and fifth movements were cut from the original score of the second: on p. 62cv of the first movement is the original title of the *Bal* and on p. 18cv a tiny fragment from its original ending (not identified in NBE's list). (The title and the last page of a movement, if on recto surfaces, are the only pages of a completed score with blank versos suitable for use as collettes; Berlioz thus used both available pages from the original score of the second movement when preparing collettes for the first.) Most of the collettes were added when the work was revised in 1831-32.

The autograph of the second movement is the fair copy prepared in Rome, since the watermark is Italian and all the other works from Italy (the *Quartetto e Coro dei Maggi, Rob-Roy*, the *Mélologue*, and the copy of the *Resurrexit* now at the Bibliothèque Nationale) are on the same paper. Scrawled in the upper margin of the first page is a note from the composer, later deleted:

Je n'ai pas le temps de finir moi-même; qu'on finisse alors comme dans mon autre copie; il faut recopier toutes les parties à cause des changements.[53]

I don't have the time to finish it myself, so let somebody else finish it after the other copy. All the parts must be recopied because of the revisions.

The autograph score of the fourth movement was originally intended as a fair copy of the *Marche des gardes* from *Les Francs-Juges*. It was prepared in late 1829 or early 1830, with the *idée fixe* added when Berlioz decided to use his march as a movement of the *Symphonie fantastique*. The revised *Scène aux champs* is copied on a paper with a French watermark similar to the mark on some of the orchestral parts (copied in La Côte-Saint-André) for the *Mélologue*. It may thus not have been drafted in fair copy until Berlioz reached his home in the late Spring of 1832.

Nicholas Temperley has constructed a reasonably accurate view of how the many papers in the first movement relate to the events of 1830-32. According to his view, Berlioz drafted the entire movement on 24-staff paper. After the rehearsals of May 1830 but before the first performances, he rewrote all but the first twenty pages on the 20-staff paper. In Rome, or at least before the first performance of the revised version (December 1832), he rewrote the movement again, adding collettes and a coda, marked *religioso*. (The quotations on the title page, incidentally, must have been added in Rome or afterward; see **ConeFant**, p. 19). By 1833 the autograph looked approximately as it does today. Temperley thus postulates two sweeping revisions of the first movement.

Temperley's reconstruction, however, must be clarified in several details and one important point. The 20-staff paper is part of the original draft, and the first set of revisions was less extensive than he imagined. Both papers used for the draft of movement I have the same watermark, which indicates that they were made by the same maker in the same year, and by inference, were sold by the same vendor at roughly the same time.[54] The original text has been altered for the same kinds of musical reasons on both papers; and music on the 20-staff paper is no less revised at a later time than is that on the 24-staff paper.

There is conclusive proof that both papers belong to the same draft. A series of large black Xs runs through the entire fascicle. They occur only on the passages watermarked C. WISE 1828 and are covered by the collettes prepared in 1832 and even by a collette demonstrably from late 1830.[55] Thus the marks must have something to do with the rehearsals of May 1830. An X often appears at the beginning of an important figure or when an instrument enters after a long period of rest; each, then, is a conductor's cue. It is hard to imagine that the rehearsals in May (Berlioz mentions two; **BerCG** 163) did not include at least an attempt to read the first movement, even though he does not specifically recall it in the *Mémoires*. Perhaps he imagined conducting one of the rehearsals himself—or actually tried.

Temperley's explanation of the 20-staff paper as evidence of an extensive revision accomplished between May and December 1830 is based on the obvious premise that a page with a fragment of *La Tempête* on the verso could not have been there before composition of the overture in Autumn 1830. Believing that the paper was identical with the rest of the 20-staff paper in the first fascicle, he concluded that it was all added in late 1830 and thus was firm evidence that over half the movement had been rewritten before December. But the watermark of the collette is LALIGANT &C / AMARESQUEL 1829; it is different from every other page of 20-staff paper in the manuscript. The correct explanation is simpler: every page of the first movement having 20 or 24 staves as well as the watermark C. WISE 1828 belongs to the original draft, and the movement was not revised so extensively between May and December that it was necessary to recopy forty pages of score and, consequently, all the orchestra parts.[56]

On the other hand, the rehearsals in May were so traumatic for Berlioz that he surely took some steps to prevent a similar disaster in the future. Among the earliest revisions are those signaled in the manuscript (movements I, IV, and V, i.e., the original fascicles) by notations in red chalk. Most of these include reminders to correct the orchestra parts, a superfluous indication for the later revisions, since all the parts then had to be entirely recopied or carefully reviewed.[57] One such mark in red chalk occurs in conjunction with the collette over p. 22o, the one with a fragment from *La Tempête* on the verso, so the red marks cannot be from before Autumn 1830. Further, some of the notations in red were removed in 1832 when the first movement was overhauled; there are two notes that refer to a symbol ($\boxtimes$) no longer in the manuscript.

Revisions in red chalk, then, were made for the performances in December 1830. Berlioz has deleted for that occasion a series of technically difficult passages–some of them simply by cross-hatching in black ink–in both the first and fifth movements (the original texts transcribed in **NBE** 16: p. 200, both examples; pp. 209-10 and 211, first example; and p. 215, exs. 11-16). Additionally, he made one significant change in the structure of the development. After m. 184, a section was removed in which the half-step relations in the theme underwent further treatment (Ex. 4.40):

Example 4.40: Development in abandoned section after m. 184.

The first seven bars of this section are still in the manuscript (aut. p. 20, trans. **NBE**, p. 201, second example), crossed out in red chalk. Somewhat further along, there was a passage in which the first and second themes were stated simultaneously and then in close succession. A page of fifteen measures from that section is preserved in the autograph, pp. 21o-22o (trans. **NBE**, p. 202). The original development connected with the G-major "recapitulation" of the first theme (mm. 232ff).

Berlioz kept only seven of these measures, now mm. 191-98, in his
final version, replacing the others with two new musical ideas. At the
beginning of the section he completed his modulation to C with a strong
emphasis on the dominant, adding four measures of an unrelated ostinato
figure in strings (Ex. 4.41):

Example 4.41: Aut. p. 21c, added passage, mm. 187-90.

After two straightforward statements of the second theme, he put in a
more interesting idea, the chromatic scales in first inversion triads,
mm. 198-228. This revision was first sketched at the bottom of p. 22o
(only the last measures are included in NBE's section on sketches, p. 216,
ex. a). Berlioz specifically designed the passage to join the original
version after a general pause (Ex. 4.42):

Example 4.42: Sketch for mm. 198-239, aut. p. 22*o*.

Evidently the first development included a similar chromatic passage, but only for violins; a direction on p. 22*c* reads: *"il faut corriger les basses et altos depuis ⊗ jusqu'au même signe,"* suggesting that the violins did not require change. Berlioz's note also indicates that the scalar passages in the next section (mm. 238-69, original version trans. **NBE,** p. 213, ex. 4) were removed at the same time, since the second symbol does not appear until m. 269.   The revisions for December consisted of little more, however; the composer was occupied between May and December with other problems, political and amorous as well as musical. He could have made these revisions in the score and altered the orchestra parts accordingly in a few days.

As a result of the revisions of both 1830 and 1832, the movement must have been radically restructured.   It is impossible to tell exactly how the sections were revised, but several series of measure numbers in the composer's hand show something of the movement's original shape. Two enumerations begin at the Allegro (*Passions*, m. 64). Allowing for minor inaccuracies in the composer's count, it appears that there were roughly 620 measures in the original form of the movement, 553 in the Allegro (as far as the original ending) plus the 64 measures in the Introduction (or 67 measures, before the deletion of three measures in the section). The first measure number following the cuts evident in the manuscript is 375 (p. 35o), and the development begins, in the same numeration, at m. 103; there were thus 272 bars between them. Of these, some 82 can be seen on various original surfaces in the autograph, so about 190 measures of the original version are missing, between ten and fifteen folios.[58]

Both of Berlioz's major revisions involved the structure of the development and developed recapitulation of the first movement, the sections after the double bar, m. 167. In 1830 he revised the development by deleting a passage that may have been about 193 measures long. In 1832 he looked again at the developed recapitulation (mm. 232-439). Though the length of the passage has not been substantially altered, practically every measure has been reworked in some way. The composer was interested in improving the bland orchestral texture of the original version. (Measures 89-100 of the *Marche au supplice* were probably revised at the same time. In this revision, he replaced the original accompaniment for violas and cellos, changing sixteenths to triplets, and adding triplets in mm. 93-94 and the chromatic passage to all five strings parts in m. 95.)

After m. 274 of the first movement, a section has been rewritten, probably shortened. Berlioz sketched a portion of the new section in short score at the bottom of p. 35o, though the lower staff has since been cut off (Ex. 4.43):

Example 4.43: Sketch for mm. 289-303, aut. p. 35o.

The main reason for this change was to reintroduce the ostinato figure (mm. 297-300) that had been used in an earlier revision. Thereafter the

original and revised versions are about the same (original layer: aut.
pp. 36*o* and 39*o*; revised version, pp. 36*c* and 37-39).

Berlioz put collettes over pp. 42 and 43 of the autograph simply to
add the dialogue of first and second violins in mm. 344-53; otherwise the
original passage was exactly the same (aut. pp. 42*o*-43*o*). This idea, too,
was first sketched in the margins of the original score. The sketch is one
of Berlioz's most interesting, since it shows the genesis and development
of a relatively simple idea. He first sketched the basic idea (Ex. 4.44):

Example 4.44: Sketch for mm. 344-53, first version, aut. pp. 42*o*-43*o*.

Next, he elaborated on it, carefully joining the passage to a pre-existing
modulation (Ex. 4.45):

Example 4.45: Ibid., second version.

Finally, he decided to score the phrase as a dialogue for violins I and II
and rewrote the passage with the orchestration in mind. This version was
adopted, with some minor revisions, in the fair copy (Ex. 4.46):

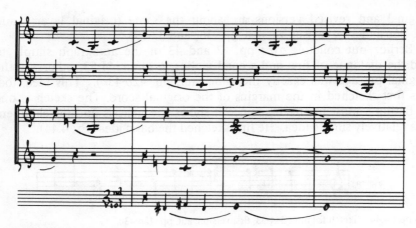

Example 4.46: Ibid., third version.

Revisions in the next section incorporate the most interesting addition to the original musical text. The passage beginning at m. 358 did not at first include the solo for oboe (flute and oboe, beginning at m. 375); there was only the development of the *idée fixe* in lower strings with accompaniment figures in the other parts. By adding the oboe melody, Berlioz hoped to increase the complexity and therefore the musical interest of an otherwise routine section. He sketched the oboe line in pencil, having little difficulty until the harmonic texture became more and more complex. Starting at m. 397 he reduced the chords on a single staff at the top of the page, and then went back to fill in a proper solo line. The following transcription of the sketch has been drawn from eight pages of orchestra score (Ex. 4.47):

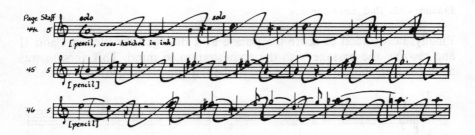

Example 4.47: Sketch of oboe solo, mm. 358-405, aut. pp. 44c-51o.

At the same time, Berlioz substituted triplet quarters in the first violin for the eighths of the original draft (trans. **NBE**, p. 213, ex. b).

The composer was typically indecisive about how the movement should end. A fragmentary draft appears on p. 62o, showing that the original idea was to have a precipitous move from the passage now at m. 482 to the short closing figure (mm. 487-91; draft trans. **NBE**, p. 216, ex. c, identified as a sketch). Before he had finished drafting the page, however, he sketched a section of eight measures to insert before the cadence (Ex. 4.48):[59]

Example 4.48: Sketch of passage to fit between mm. 482 and 487, aut. p. 62o, staff 16.

The sketched version, or something similar, was adopted and added to the score as a collette. The first collette has since been replaced with a second, but its margin can still be seen in the score, along with ten extra dots of paste on p. 62o not used to attach the present collette. While revising the symphony in Rome, Berlioz rewrote the end of the first movement again, adding the scalar figures in mm. 483-86. This new version was drafted on a second collette and added to the orchestra score. There was still no extended coda; the movement ended at m. 491 with a double bar easily distinguished in the manuscript.

Two fragments of the original draft are found when the collette over p. 44 is removed and examined; both are passages that were revised immediately after being drafted for the first time. One is the first idea drafted for the transition to the section beginning at m. 358 (trans. **NBE**, p. 216, ex. b, as a "sketch"[60]). Similarly, an early version of mm. 233-39 is found on p. 44cv (Ex. 4.49):

Example 4.49: Draft of mm. 233-39, aut. p. 44cv.

The rising fourth in first violins is the same as in the version finally adopted, but the composer has replaced the tonic implication with a dominant. The sustained horn note in m. 236 is an afterthought entered in late 1830.

There were substantial deletions from two other movements. A passage of about fifteen measures was removed from the newly-copied autograph of the *Scène aux champs*. The first three and last four measures of the section are still in the manuscript (aut. pp. 24o and 27o; trans. **NBE**, pp. 204-05). Finally a section of about forty measures[61] was deleted from the fifth movement (first described by Temperley, **NBE**,

p. 211), possibly as early as 1830; three measures of the original are left over.

The first group of revisions was, then, largely prompted by practical considerations, the result of Berlioz's determination not to repeat the fiasco of May 1830. In these cases, as elsewhere in his works, substantive musical change is the result of the composer's experience with the performance of his works. Questions of technical difficulty aside, there may also have been changes in passages that sounded in performance other than he had imagined. Other revisions reflect the composer's second thoughts about what he had written, about the length, the ending, and the accompanying figures. His addition of mm. 297-300 is a clever device to integrate the ostinato figure of mm. 187-90. From m. 344 on, Berlioz seems specifically concerned with the musical sophistication of his developmental passages. Possibly there was a larger issue behind the revision: in its present form, the movement has a striking sectional arrangement, the keystoned arch described by both Schumann and Cone (**ConeFant**, pp. 220-48 and 249-77, respectively). It could not have been quite so clear in the longer version. There would have originally been about 400 measures before the return of the *idée fixe* in G, with 225 measures or so afterward; the arch could hardly have existed at all. It is also possible that changes in the music reflect changes in the depictive and biographical aspect of the work. The rewritings show conclusively that Berlioz had by 1830 begun the serious struggle with formal organization of his free-flowing melodic ideas that occupied him for most of his life.

Between Liszt's version, which conforms in most respects to the autograph, and the publication of 1845, Berlioz revised several more passages. A notice in the *Gazette musicale* for a concert of 9 November 1834 refers to some of them: "M. Berlioz has added several new orchestral effects to his work that noticeably increase its effect." Possibly the remark refers to the *religioso* ending and the phrase *"ses consolations religieuses"* in the program. This change was in fact incorporated in Liszt's edition, but probably at the last minute.

It is extremely difficult to date the versions of the program, since the leaflets do not, as a rule, carry dates. The phrase *"ses consolations religieuses,"* an obvious reference to the new coda, seems first to have been used in the version of the program circulated with Liszt's piano transcription.[62] Em. Mathieu de Monter, in an early biography of Berlioz (*Revue et Gazette musicale*, 36 [1869]), transcribes on pp. 307-08 his copy of the program of 9 December 1832, which does not contain the phrase. (Temperley rightly considers this an unreliable source.) Temperley describes a program (**GB-Twmacnutt**) distributed at the concert of 22 December 1833 that still does not have the phrase. In that case, the phrase and the musical coda were added for the concert of 9 November 1834. Liszt therefore incorporated the change in his transcription at the last minute, or it was written specifically with the piano version in mind.

The most pronounced alteration of the first movement after Liszt's edition was the replacement of the last section before the coda (mm. 410-38) with divided parts for strings (original version trans. **NBE** p. 191, ex. 3). The announcement in the *Gazette musicale* could conceivably refer to that change as well, but this is unlikely, since the change does not occur in the autograph, while the *religioso* ending does; probably the *divisi* section was added in the later 1830s. The new version may have been added to be more depictive of the "jealous fury" referred to in the program. The orchestration is noticeably more complex than elsewhere in the movement, though Berlioz uses approximately the same device in mm. 32-39 of the fifth movement, included in the first version.   The passage had been added by 1843 at the latest; Berlioz cites it in his *Traité d'instrumentation* as a good example of writing for divided strings.

Additionally, he made numerous changes in detail. Second violins were simplified in mm. 17-18, the original version probably having been too dense to provide the desired effect. Wind parts in m. 37 were unified with other measures. Measures 121-24 were rescored in the strings with quarter-notes instead of eighths. The most effective change was that of note values for the second violin in mm. 234-36, from eighths to quarters and eighths. The composer thus provides increases of both rhythmic and harmonic intensity as he leads into the recapitulation. Berlioz may have borrowed the idea for another bit of rewriting from Liszt's transcription. In m. 290, he has rewritten the bassoon part, seemingly taking Liszt's cue for voice-leading (Ex. 4.50):

c.

Example 4.50: Three versions of bassoon line in m. 290: a) in autograph score; b) in published edition; c) in Liszt's piano transcription.

With one exception (to be cited), the *Symphonie fantastique* changed little after the proofs were prepared in late 1844 or 1845. Berlioz was reasonably conscientious with the proofs, altering nuances according to lessons learned over the years. The effect of his last-minute changes, however, has been to cause dozens of variants, particularly of phrases and dynamics (see **ConeFant**, pp. 197-219).

Two newly-identified sources provide evidence concerning the second movement. Both are found on verso surfaces of autograph collettes.

A collette added when the first movement was revised (p. 18*cv*, not transcribed in published editions) was cut from the last page of the original score of movement II, the *Bal*. The musical text is as follows (Ex. 4.51). The fragment shows enough musical details that the appearance of the page of full score from which it was cut can be reconstructed. There were two systems: the fragment contains a nearly-complete system at the bottom and a bit of the last line of the upper system. The top line is a fragment of the first version of measures 331-32, and the lower staves contain the last two measures of the movement. There must have been eight to twelve more measures in the upper system.

Berlioz specifically mentions adding a coda to the *Scène du bal* (**BerMém**, Chap. XXXIV). The fragment shows that the addition consisted of mm. 364-68, the *animez* section and transition. The original version must have gone from m. 333 to a closing figure similar to present mm. 365-68. It is significant that the version ended with the same tag used in the second, for at that point in the fair copy there are two sets of double bars, the first after m. 367. Berlioz first intended to end the revised version of the first beat of m. 367, then crossed out the double bar and added the original tag (aut. p. 46).

Example 4.51: Original ending of movt. II, aut. movt. I, p. 18*cv*.

Temperley contends that because the bar lines of the fair copy prepared in Rome are unruled after m. 318 (end of aut. p. 39), the manuscript becomes a composing score at that point. He supports his view by citing Berlioz's uncertainty at mm. 367-68. But there are no substantive changes of mind in the last section, just slips of the pen or minor second thoughts. Now it is certain that the tag existed all along. Actually Berlioz was copying (and possibly scoring) the coda from a pre-existing draft. The unruled barlines are insignificant: he started the new section on ruled paper, ran out, and did not take time to go back and rule more lines.

The fragment reveals other interesting details. First, there was no clarinet part in the first version. Second, two horn parts (in C) have been added in red ink to the original two parts (in E), showing that the first version was first scored for only two horns. The reading adopted for the final version is still different from the one of the fragment; in rewriting the movement, Berlioz rescored the four horn parts, adopting a traditional voicing in the last two measures. He alludes to both changes in his description of attempting suicide (1831), though in a context that could not be construed until identification of this fragment:

En prenant la partition de la scène du Bal *dont la* coda *n'était pas entièrement instrumentée, j'écris en tête: "Je n'ai pas le temps de finir; s'il prend fantaisie à la société des concerts de Paris d'exécuter ce morceau en l'absence de l'auteur, je prie Habeneck de doubler à l'octave basse, avec les clarinettes et les cors, le passage des flûtes placé sur la dernière rentrée du thème, et d'écrire à plein orchestre les accords qui suivent; cela suffira pour la conclusion"* (BerMém, Chap. XXXIV).	Next I took the score of the Ball Scene, and, as the coda was not completely orchestrated, wrote across it, "I have not had the time to finish this. If the Conservatoire Concert Society should happen to want to perform the work during the composer's *absence,* I beg Habeneck to double the flute passage at the last entry of the theme with clarinets and horns at the lower octave and to score the chords which follow for full orchestra. That will do for the ending" (BerMemCairns).

Although the note at the top of the first page of the revised autograph score is in fact slightly different, Berlioz obviously recollects having added the clarinet and horn parts when revising the *Bal.*

The version of mm. 129-51 of movement II eventually published by Schlesinger in 1845 differs from the one found in his advance edition (first version trans. NBE, p. 198). One set of parts, no doubt proofs for the composer to check, was drawn from the plates when they still contained the earlier reading. But Berlioz needed the parts, possibly to use in one of several concerts outside Paris in late 1844 and 1845. He did not wait for the new section to be engraved in the parts, but rather added the new version on autograph collettes. Parts in both the

Conservatoire and the Société des Concerts include these autograph collettes (see facsimile of a cello part so corrected, NBE, p. 188).

Five of them have on the verso surface fragments of a sketch for the revised section. Assembled in the proper order, the sketch is nearly complete (see Facsimile IV.6).[63] Berlioz thus cut the collettes from a slightly larger sheet originally used to superpose reminiscences of the waltz motive on the statement of the *idée fixe*. Two systems, found in the first and fifth fragments, contain the bulk of sketching (mm. 120-38, 139-56, respectively). Between them, two more systems were crossed out after the melody was set down the first time.

There are few pronounced differences between the version sketched and the one adopted. Most of the variants involve a simplification of the parts for viola, cello, and bass. The cello in mm. 129-30 was to have had a moving part in sixteenths, and in mm. 130-31 the viola[?] was to have entered with a phrase from the waltz. In m. 140, Berlioz substituted sixteenths for the eighths originally envisioned. A rhythmic figure in mm. 145-47 was rejected (Ex. 4.52):

Example 4.52: Rejected rhythmic figure.

The differences between the music sketched and that generally adopted show that Berlioz went back to relieve whatever density he had first written into the section by removing all but the essential ideas. Superposing the two motives of the movement had become by that time one of Berlioz's favorite devices, and he had little trouble working the two melodies together. He had somewhat more difficulty achieving the gossamer effect he desired, abandoning any hint of heavy accompanying figures.

Including the unrevised version in the advance edition was not, then, simply a mistake of the engraver. Berlioz could not have sketched the new passage until he was correcting proof; otherwise he would never have had that particular piece of paper still lying on his desk when he began to fashion collettes. It was a last-minute change. He then prepared a clean copy of the new version for the engraver to use in making new plates and covered the blank surface of his sketch with the new parts for pasting in.

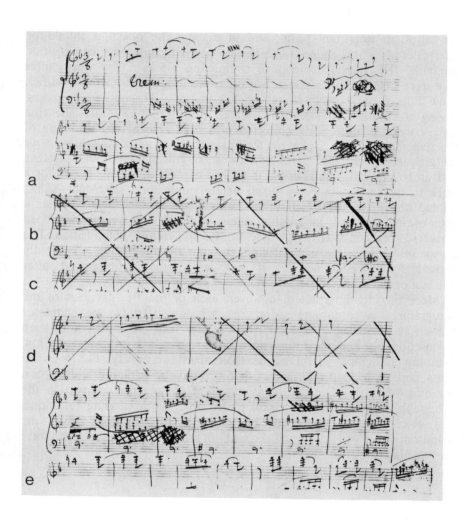

Facsimile IV.6: Sketch for revised version of *Symphonie fantastique*, movt. II. Found on collette-versos of printed parts, **F-Pn** Rés Vma 216.

Temperley remarks of the *Symphonie fantastique* autograph:

> The score underwent constant revision from the time of its conception until at
> least the end of 1832, so that it is difficult to say when composition ended and
> revision began (**NBE** 16, ix).

He raises an important point, and in closing, the question should be
reconsidered: when, indeed, did Berlioz himself consider a composition
finished?   His announcements of completing pieces a few weeks after
they were begun are forthright, but often are followed with the qualifier,
"now I have only the orchestration left to do."   His autograph scores,
among them the *Symphonie fantastique*, reflect that attitude. The first
fully-scored ink draft was completed in a single clean sweep.   None of
the five fascicles that make up the manuscript score of the *Symphonie
fantastique* is from that point of view a composing score; the sketches
and drafts are lost.   But Berlioz is no less explicit about his hopes for a
work to be correct in every detail before publication (**BerMém** XLIX,
quoted above, p. 181).   From the beginning he refused to consider a
composition finished, in another sense, until the last proofs had been
corrected; revision was inseparable from conscientious composition. The
Symphonie fantastique is a striking example of this habit: repeatedly
revised for over a decade, it was left virtually untouched after
publication.

More broadly interpreted, however, each of the five fascicles of the
autograph *is* a composing score, for each was used by the composer
himself as he settled on the mature, definitive text.   If the revisions were
inconsequential and the music no different from the published version,
then the autograph would be no more than a curiosity. But over the
years Berlioz decided on changes that affected the structure and musical
meaning of his work.   The many stages of composition evident in the
autograph reflect Berlioz's musical philosophy, his developing technique,
and even hint at aspects of his domestic life. In that sense, the
manuscript is a written factual account, on which may be based the most
far-reaching sort of speculation.

Appendix I

Unpublished Music

I. *Sur les Alpes, quel délice! (Le Chasseur des chamois; Chant suisse).* Source: **F-Pn** ms. 1188, fasc. I, pp. 35*cv*, 36*cv* (autograph).

II. *Chansonette de Mr de Wailly.* Source: **F-Pn** D 1172 (fair copy).

III. *Au bord d'une rivière* (exercise on a modal scale). Source: autograph leaf, **US–NYcu** Berlioz Collection.

SUR LES ALPES, QUEL DELICE!

2.   Dès que paraît la lumière,
        Je vais chasser des chamois;
        De ma femme la prière
        Ne peut changer ma carrière,
        Je lui dis que dans tout lieu
        Sur nous veille le grand dieu (*bis*).

3.   Là où le plus intrépide
        Craint de diriger ses pas,
        Moi, prenant le ciel pour guide,
        Nul danger ne m'intimide:
        Sans souci, le coeur content,
        Je franchis roc et torrent (*bis*)

See also **BerCG 233**: Rome, 2 July 1831; to Mme Lesueur.

CHANSONETTE DE Mr de WAILLY

AU BORD D'UNE RIVIERE

Appendix II

Libretto of *Les Francs-Juges*

(Second Version)

Source: F-Pn Papiers divers de Berlioz, no. 45.

[Remarks by Berlioz in italics; spelling modernized except when it would conflict with the metric scheme. Format edited for publication.]

Lenor, ou Les Derniers Francs-Juges
Drame Lyrique
En Trois actes

Personnages

Olmerik, Usurpateur du trône de Brisgaw et premier Franc-Juge. *Basse.*
Lenor, Neveu d'Olmerik, héritier légitime au trone. *1^{r} Tenor.*
Christiern, Grand de la Cour d'Olmerik et Franc-Juge. *2me Tenor.*
Conrad, Jeune guerrier, ami de Lenor et Franc-Juge. *Bariton.*
Amélie, Jeune princesse, amante de Lenor. *1° Soprano.*
Elmire, Confidente d'Amélie. *2° Soprano.*

    Un homme du peuple.
    Un berger.
    Nise, bergère } *soprani*
    Mery, bergère }
    Bohémiens et Bohémiennes.
    Héraults.
    Peuple.
    Soldats.
    Bergers.
    Francs-Juges.
    Le Sénéchal de l'Empire.

La scène se passe dans le Brisgaw près de la forêt noire.

ACTE I

Le théâtre représente un château antique et fortifié; il est environné d'épaisses forêts, et devant sa principale entrée s'étend une vaste place d'armes. Le soleil se lève et éclaire peu à peu le haut des tours.

Scène 1ère

(Des groupes de peuple couvrent la place et s'occupent des apprêts d'une fête; mais leur démarche et leurs gestes expriment la tristesse et l'abattement. Ils n'agissent que pressés par les satellites qui les entourent.)

(musique à faire)

Quatre hérauts

> Olmerik d'Amélie est aujourd'hui l'époux.
> Qu'il commande à jamais à son coeur comme au nôtre!
> Que l'allégresse éclate parmi vous!
> Chantez son bonheur et le vôtre!
> Olmerik d'Amélie est aujourd'hui l'époux.

(Les soldats et les hérauts se retirent.)

Un homme du peuple

(Il a dû se tenir à part pendant le récit précédent, et laisser apercevoir une indignation concentrée. Il se tourne vers le peuple qui suspend des guirlandes au château.)

Parlé

> Chantez pour égayer vos maîtres!
> Foulez au bruit des chalumeaux
> La poussière de vos ancêtres
> Qui tressaillent sous leurs tombeaux!
> De vos tyrans, filles des braves,
> Venez disputer les faveurs.
> Vierges, couronnez-vous de fleurs;
> Votre sein leur doit des esclaves!

(Pendant qu'il chante les hommes quittent peu à peu les groupes où ils étaient mêlés aux femmes, et s'assemblent autour de lui; ils s'animent en l'écoutant.)

Choeur d'hommes

> Eh! quoi!....nous taire....et trembler sur ces bords
> Où nous restent encore un vengeur et la gloire!
> Non, non...la liberté, fille de la victoire,
> Sera le prix de nos efforts.

Ensemble

Musique faite

> Lenor, entends nos fers....que leur bruit te réveille!
> Brise, brise le joug d'une honteuse loi.

Fuis l'indigne esclavage où ta valeur sommeille;
   Il est temps, lève-toi!

La première voix seule

Il est temps, amis.... l'heure sonne:
Dépouillez la honte et les fers.
Au fils de Venceslas, guerriers, rendons un trône;
Rendons des monstres aux enfers.

(Le pont-levis du château s'abaisse, et Olmerik s'avance avec Christiern. La foule qui semblait se ranimer redevient tout à coup tremblante et consternée: quelques-uns restent muets et indignés.)

Choeur général

Ah! voici le tyran.... son oeil cherche sa proie,
Et le sang tombe encor de son glaive altéré.
Malheureux!...... la terreur nous condamne à la joie.

(Olmerik s'approche,)

Qu'il vive de longs jours, et qu'il règne adoré!

(Tous se retirent excepté Olmerik et Christiern.)

Scène 2

Dialogue parlé

Olmerik, Christiern

Olmerik

(Il suit d'un oeil de mépris la foule qui le quitte.)

Ah! qu'ils sont bien faits pour leur chaîne!
Les lâches!... à ma vue ils n'osent que frémir!

Christiern

Ils tremblent... qu'importe leur haine?

Olmerik

Elle ne sait combattre.... elle saura trahir,
J'eus un frère... il régnait... tu me montras son trône,
El la route sanglante où je devais passer.
Il périt... et ta main cacha par la couronne
Les remords sur mon front ardent à s'amasser.

(Il paraît accablé d'un souvenir sinistre qu'il s'efforce d'écarter.)

Oui, je le dus... je dus verser le sang d'un frère;
Mais ses flots en coulant ne se sont pas taris:
Son fils traînant partout sa douleur téméraire
Appelle la tempête amassée à ses cris.

Christiern

> Le saint Tribunal veille... oses-tu craindre encore?
> Nulle part et partout, c'est en vain qu'on le fuit.
> Il peuple ce palais, et ce palais l'ignore;
> Son oeil puissant interroge la nuit;
> Et l'ombre vainement lui ravit sa victime.
> Si la terre à ses coups prétendait l'arracher
>> Jusqu'aux entrailles de l'abîme
>> Son regard irait la chercher.

Olmerik

> Le saint Tribunal dort, et sa foudre est éteinte;
> Dans son silence, hélas! je devine sa crainte.

Christiern

> La crainte!... il la répand, et ne la connaît pas.

Olmerik

> Et c'est ainsi qu'il a lassé le monde;
> L'éclair s'est élancé du palais des Césars.
> Au bruit lointain de l'orage qui gronde
> J'ai vu tressaillir nos remparts.
> De tous côtés hâtant leurs pas rapides
> Les soldats de l'empire entourent mes états.
> Que pourront nos guerriers et les efforts perfides
> D'un peuple qui me hait et ne combattra pas?
> Ce Lenor, tout courbé sous ses maux solitaires,
>> Ce vil proscrit, sans glaive, sans appui,
>> Tu le verras grandir à l'ombre des bannières
>> Que l'Allemagne agitera sur lui.

Christiern

> Il périra.... Demain, avant l'aurore
> J'aurai su découvrir ses pas mystérieux.

Olmerik

> Crois-tu qu'à mes regards il les dérobe encore?
> C'est au fond de ces bois, c'est non loin de ces lieux,
> Non loin de ce palais qui retient Amélie
> Qu'il cache au jour sa honte et ses ardeurs.
> Amélie!... Il l'adore... et plus que la patrie
> Elle appelle sur moi ses jalouses fureurs.
> Dès son enfance à son lit destinée,
> Il allait en parer son trône et son orgueil,
> Quand ma main renversant les flambeaux d'hyménée,
> N'alluma devant lui que des torches de deuil.
> Ami, te le dirai-je? un regard d'Amélie
> Dans mon sein palpitant éteignit ma furie:
> Je brûlai... qu'elle était belle de sa douleur!

Sur son front pâlissant j'essayai ma couronne,...
De ses mépris d'abord mon courage s'étonne....
Je fais parler la crainte à ce timide coeur;
J'ai dit que dans les fers Lenor enfin expie
Et mes tourments et ses folles amours,
Et qu'un dernier refus de la fière Amélie
Aux mains de mes bourreaux allait livrer ses jours.

Christiern

Elle a cédé; mais pour sauver la tête
De celui que toujours tu verras ton rival:
Quand la voix des hérauts commande un jour de fête,
Du bonheur est-ce le signal?
Va! de ses fiers dédains Lenor est le complice:
Ce nom parle plus haut que toi.
Il faut que la mort désunisse
Ces coeurs qu'enchaîne leur foi.

Olmerik

Eh! bien, je cède au destin qui m'entraîne!
Tout le feu des enfers bouillonne avec mon sang.
Non, jamais tant d'amour, non jamais tant de haine
Ne s'est allumé dans mon flanc.
Je cours... mais qu'aujourd'hui mon triomphe s'achève;
Et mon sceptre et mes feux s'indignent d'un rival.
Que Lenor soit en proie au glaive
De l'invisible Tribunal!

Christiern

Il suffit... le sang du perfide
Rougira l'antre de Mendor.

Olmerik

Malgré moi, je frémis encor;
Crains d'invoquer une main trop timide.

Christiern

Non, non, mon choix est fait.

Olmerik

Et quel est-il?

Christiern

Conrad.

Olmerik

Son fer lui pèserait;
Des dangers, non du crime il fit l'apprentissage.

Christiern

Que peux-tu craindre?

Olmerik

Tout, jusques à son courage.

Duo

Musique faite

Christiern

Conrad s'arma pour nous d'une sainte fureur.
Il brava les Césars, et sa jeune vaillance
Promenant dans nos camps sa superbe espérance,
Nous voua son épée et sa crédule ardeur.

Olmerik

Conrad est altéré de périls et de gloire.
Il peut dans les combats presser ses pas ardents;
Mais son bras indigné d'une lâche victoire
Servira mal ma haine et ses serments.

Christiern

Ma voix saura, si sa vertu chancelle,
Rallumer en son coeur la vengeance fidèle.

Olmerik

Garde que la pitié puisse nous le ravir!
Que les cieux évôqués consacrent la victime;
Qu'ils parlent par ta voix, qu'une clarté sublime
Montre à Conrad celui qu'il doit punir.

Christiern

Si la pitié protégeant la victime
Dans son coeur venait à gémir,
Le ciel complice armé d'une clarté sublime
Saura parler et l'éblouir.

Ensemble

Que les cieux évôqués consacrent la victime;
Que son bras soit prompt à punir.
Si sa pitié m'ose trahir,
Que son sang satisfasse au courroux qui m'anime.

(Olmerik sort: les gardes le suivent. Il fait un signe à Christiern en lui montrant Conrad qui s'avance.)

Scène 3

Dialogue parlé

Christiern, Conrad

Christiern

> Conrad, jeune héros, écoute et réponds-moi.
> Tes serments sont-ils sûrs?

Conrad

> Sûrs autant que mon glaive.

Christiern

(avec un fanatisme sombre et qui s'enflamme peu à peu)

> Ton glaive, ami!... non, il n'est plus à toi.
> N'entends-tu pas cette voix qui s'élève
> Des antres pieux de Mendor?
> Ils semblent murmurer encor.
> La foi jurée à ceux qui t'ont nommé leur frère.
> Je vais parler enfin; je le dois, il le faut.
> Ton coeur ne mentit pas, ta lèvre fut sincère;
> Il est temps d'acquitter la dette du très-haut.
> Un voile jusqu'ici t'a caché la lumière;
> Elle eût pu consumer ta débile paupière;
> Mais aujourd'hui ta main déchire le bandeau,
> Et du sein de la nuit fait poindre un jour nouveau.
> Je le vois; il se lève, il grandit, il t'inonde
> Des feux purs que les cieux font briller à ma voix.
> Ton front tout embrasé de sa clarté féconde
> Nous promet un vengeur, et menace les Rois.
> Que le sang t'initie à nos jaloux mystères.
> Prends ce fer.... Cette nuit, aux antres de Mendor,
> Une victime est due au salut de tes frères;
> Tu frapperas... mais quoi?... Conrad hésite encor?...

Conrad (avec effroi)

> Parle, qui doit tomber?

Christiern

> Que le ciel te réponde;
> C'est lui qui sur ton bras se repose aujourd'hui.
> N'attends pas que l'éclair de son courroux ait lui;
> N'attends pas que sa foudre gronde.

(Il sort.)

Scène 4

Récit et air; musique faite

Conrad seul

(Il lance des regards épouvantés sur les pas de Christiern.)

Va! je t'abhorre autant que je me fais horreur,
Monstre!... et c'est là le prix que hâtait mon ardeur!...
C'est du sang, c'est du sang qu'il faut au sacrifice;
Et l'erreur fit de moi votre hideux complice!...
Du fond des bois qui cachent tes douleurs,
Lenor, ne peux-tu voir et ma honte et mes pleurs?
Ah! si tu fus banni du trône qui t'appelle,
C'est qu'un bandeau fatal, c'est qu'un voile odieux
Me cachait un forfait que ce jour me révèle;
J'ose en prendre à témoin ta mémoire et les cieux.

(Il tombe dans une douloureuse rêverie.)

Air:

Noble amitié, ta voix, ta voix chérie
M'entraîne et retentit dans mon âme attendrie.
Quand j'accuse la vie et m'engage à mourir
Tu m'ordonnes de vivre et m'apprends à souffrir.

(Il se ranime et s'enflamme peu à peu avec enthousiasme.)

Lenor, héros trop magnanime,
Eh quoi! ne sais-tu pas que souffrir est un crime
Quand la patrie en deuil appelle son vengeur?
Ombre de Venceslas, que ton courroux vainqueur
Du haut des cieux vienne armer ma vaillance.
Mon coeur palpite encore de gloire et d'espérance:
Mon bras heureux et fier va combattre en ce jour
Pour les cieux, la beauté, les vertus et l'amour.

(A peine a-t-il fini ces derniers mots qu'il s'arrête avec effroi.)

Monologue parlé

Que dis-je? Quels transports m'entraînent?
En vain je me débats sous la main des enfers!
Mais avant d'obéir aux serments qui m'enchaînent,
    Lenor, j'adoucirai tes fers.
Je te rendrai ton Amélie,
J'en crois l'espérance et l'amour:
Peut-être encor je bénirai la vie,
Si la tienne au bonheur peut sourire en ce jour.

Scène 5

Conrad, Amélie, Elmire

(Amélie prévient les pas de Conrad qui s'éloignait.)

Amélie

> Restez, Conrad, que la triste Amélie
> Trouve du moins un coeur où verser ses chagrins.
>   Que n'ont-ils consumé la vie
>   dont m'accablent les destins!
> Lenor, hélas! Lenor dans les cachots expire....

Conrad (hors de lui)

> Que dites-vous? ô désespoir!
> N'écoutez pas un douloureux délire.

Amélie

Air à faire

> Vous le savez, Conrad, il osait chaque soir
> Braver pour moi de trop sûres alarmes;
> Chaque soir il osait visiter ces remparts;
>   Chaque soir confondait nos larmes.
> Mais qui peut d'Olmerik éviter les regards?
> Il cherchait son amie; il a trouvé des chaînes.
> Déjà brillait sur lui le poignard assassin;
> Olmerik se présente, il réclame ma main:
> Un mot a décidé mes lèvres incertaines.
> "Que Lenor, me dit-il, vive encore à ce prix."
> "Qu'il vive," m'écriai-je... et la prochaine aurore
>   Va révéler à ces vallons surpris
> Et mes nouveaux ennuis et l'hymen que j'abhorre.

Conrad

> Ainsi l'enfer triomphe!... et l'autel indigne
> Ne s'écroulera pas sur cet hymen impie.

Amélie

> Lenor, tu me devras la vie.
> A mon sort aujourd'hui j'offre un sein résigné.

Elégie

Musique faite

> La nuit voilant pour nous ces murs et nos montagnes,
> Me ramenait Lenor au pied de cette tour,
> Et tous les deux errant dans les sombres campagnes
> Sans crainte nous mêlions nos pleurs et notre amour.
> Hélas! l'ombre bientôt de ces monts va descendre:
> Mais ici mon ami ne viendra pas m'attendre.

Pourquoi, pourquoi gémir? Mes regrets superflus
Importunent en vain ces vallons solitaires.
Lenor, le souvenir des jours qui ne sont plus
    Me rend mes larmes plus amères.

Adieu! le trône en vain me dispute à la tombe:
Toi que j'ai tant aimé ne pleure plus sur moi.
Que les cieux satisfaits hélas! quand je succombe,
Te rendent le bonheur qui me fuit loin de toi.
Mon bien aimé, demain dans l'obscure vallée
Viens, viens attendre encor mon ombre consolée.
Calme, calme aujourd'hui les regrets superflus.
Nous nous plaindrons en paix sous ces bois solitaires,
Lenor, le souvenir des jours qui ne sont plus
    Rendra nos larmes moins amères.

Scène 6

Les mêmes, Troupe de Bohémiens et de Bohémiennes, parmi eux Lenor déguisé.

Musique à faire

Choeur

Pour égayer un long chemin
Il n'est rien comme un gai refrain.

Un Vieillard

Depuis cinquante ans je voyage,
Depuis cinquante ans je ne voi
Que force fous, et pas un sage;
Nous sommes frères; c'est la loi.

Une Voix

Allons, gentille Bohémienne,
Prends ta guitare, à toi l'antienne.

Bohémienne

Quand le soleil se couchera,
Bien sot l'amant qui dormira.
Le soir moins rebelle,
Fière Jouvencelle
S'attendrit parfois.
La mousse est fleurie,
Et la rêverie
Est si douce au bois.

Choeur

Merci, gentille Bohémienne,
Et du refrain et de l'antienne.

Sentinelle (au haut d'un créneau)

Coda

> Qui vive!... joyeux compagnons,
> Arrêtez, et quels sont vos noms?

Bohémien

> Ils changent ainsi que les hommes,
> Suivant les temps et les climats.

(Ils s'arrêtent sous la tour.)

Sentinelle

> Qu'attendez-vous?

Bohémien

> Que tu nous nommes:

Sentinelle

> Votre pays?

Bohémien

> Le monde.

Sentinelle

> Où se pressent vos pas?

Bohémien

> Toi, l'ami, pourrais-tu nous dire,
> Où vont les nuages errants,
> Où va l'aurore, où vont les vents,

(Il touche un arpège sur sa lyre.)

> Où s'en va la voix de ma lyre?

Sentinelle

> Passez au large... et gardez-vous
> D'approcher trop près des verroux.

Choeur

> Adieu, soldat, sur ta tourelle
> Puisse avec toi veiller l'amour.
> Sous ces vieux pins la nuit est belle.
> Nous attendrons ici le jour.

(Ils se dispersent dans les bois.)

Chef des Bohémiens

> Du fond de ces retraites sombres
> Notre oeil ne te quittera pas.

Sois prêt à suivre encor nos pas;
Nous reviendrons avec les ombres.

(Il s'éloigne.)

Scène 7

parlé

Conrad, Amélie, Elmire, Lenor

(Celui-ci [Lenor] ne s'est point encore fait reconnaitre et s'arrete un instant en contemplant Amélie.)

Lenor

D'où vient qu'à ses côtés je frémis aujourd'hui.
(Il se découvre et saisit la main d'Amélie.)

Conrad

Grand Dieu!

Lenor

Chère Amélie.

Amélie

Il est libre... c'est lui!
C'est Lenor!... qu'ai-je fait? amante infortunée!
O mon prince, à tes pieds j'expire prosternée.

Conrad (avec rage)

Horreur! horreur! exécrables destins!

Lenor (retirant Amélie)

Je revois Amélie, et dans ses yeux éteints
Je ne retrouve que des larmes.

Conrad

Il nous reste du moins nos armes!
Ecoute, et nous ferons ce que n'ont fait les cieux.
Victime d'un parjure affreux,
Elle a cru qu'Olmerik au fond de ses murailles
Sous les fers inhumains faisait taire tes droits
Et que le reste de nos Rois
Allait enfin trouver d'illustres funérailles.

Lenor

Qu'a-t-elle fait, Conrad?

Conrad

Elle a sauvé tes jours

Lenor

A quel prix?

Conrad (à Amélie)

Répondez....

Amélie

au prix de nos amours.

Lenor

Parle, qui peut briser la chaîne qui nous lie?

Amélie

Un seul voeu....

Lenor

Que fut-il?

Amélie

Te voir libre et mourir.

Lenor

Ingrate et trop chère Amélie,
C'est en mourant pour moi que tu m'osais trahir!
Ah! lève ce beau front que le chagrin consume.
    Le sacrifice est rejeté:
Mon sein brûle des feux que ton regard allume
Respire près de toi l'air de la liberté!

Amélie

Près de toi!... près de toi mon âme déchirée
Ose appeler la vie et pardonner aux Dieux.

Lenor

Oui, l'infortune fuit à ta voix adorée,
Et le ciel attendri me sourit dans tes yeux.

Ensemble

Le ciel attendri nous rassemble,
Que peuvent Olmerik, ses fers et son courroux?
Mets ta main sur mon coeur... nos coeurs battent ensemble,
Ensemble ils braveront ses coups.

Amélie

Ma fuite va bientôt lui ravir sa victoire.
Je ne te quitte plus; ta misère est ma gloire;
Ma patrie est partout où sera mon époux.

Lenor

Ton époux! Ah! paré de ce nom que j'adore
L'univers n'a plus rien que je puisse envier.

Conrad

> Donne un sceptre à l'amour: règne, un peuple t'implore,
> Et l'Etat par ma voix ose t'y convier.

Lenor

> Quand il en sera temps, héros, ami fidèle,
> Tu n'accuseras plus mon bras découragé;
> Dans ces murs, où tout me rappelle,
> Je rentrerai vainqueur ou tomberai vengé.
> Je dois les fuir encore et quitter Amélie;
> L'oeil d'Olmerik bientôt aurait surpris nos pas.
> Que ce jour qui nous luit ne nous trahisse pas!

(à Amélie)

> Dès que le soir descendra des montagnes,
> Conrad à la faveur de ces sombres forêts
> La guidera sans peine aux tranquilles compagnes
> Qui me cachent au monde et me prêtent leur paix.
> Obald est le nom qu'on m'y donne.
> Là je redoutai moins le destin adouci,
> Et là j'aurais sans peine oublié ma couronne,
> Si mon toit de roseaux t'avait couverte aussi.

(Des instruments guerriers sonnent la retraite au haut des tours.)

Conrad

(Il prête l'oreille avec effroi.)

> Quitte, ô Lenor, ces lieux funèbres,
> Et laisse à l'amitié le soin de tes amours.
> Quand l'aïrain à ces bords annonce les ténèbres,
> Malheur à l'étranger égaré sous ces tours.

Quatuor

(Musique faite)

Lenor

(Il contemple tour à tour avec attendrissement Amélie et le paysage qui l'environne.)

> Frais vallons où dorment nos pères,
> Où l'amour me promit une couche de fleurs,
> Hélas! combien de fois aux rives étrangères
> Votre doux souvenir a fait couler mes pleurs!

Conrad, Amélie, Elmire

(Le bruit des trompettes se fait encore entendre.)

> Calme ta douleur imprudente
> N'entends-tu pas l'aïrain fatal?
> Fuis ces remparts pleins d'épouvante;
> Le crime a donné le signal.

Lenor

>Adieu!... tendre assurance! Amélie est fidèle!...
>Que l'aurore pour moi se lèvera plus belle.

Conrad, Amélie

>O mon prince reçois { mon épée et ma foi.
>   { et ma vie et ma foi.

Lenor

>La vaillance s'incline et reconnaît son Roi;
>La beauté me rappelle et jure d'être à moi.

Scène 8

Les mêmes

(Les Bohémiens qui s'étaient dispersés rentrent de divers côtés sur la scène au son de mille instruments singuliers dont ils accompagnent leurs chants et leurs danses.   On entend toujours les trompettes au haut des tours.   La grande cloche du châteu tinte l'Angélus. Grand mouvement sur les remparts.)

Choeur

>Mêlons à la voix des trompettes,
>Mêlons le bruit des tambourins
>Sistres, guitares et musettes,
>Accompagnez nos gais refrains.

(Ils environnent Lenor et l'entrainent.   Leur danse augmente continuellement de vitesse, et devient d'une rapidité extrême en s'éloignant.)

>De combien d'étoiles
>Le regard nous luit.
>Qu'ils sont beaux tes voiles,
>O charmante nuit!
> Ton haleine
> Dans la plaine
> Donne aux fleurs
> Leurs couleurs
> Vite! en cadence
> Pressons la danse!
> Que le plaisir
> Ne puisse fuir!
> Ivresse! Folie!
> Le temps envieux
> S'arrête et s'oublie
> Dans nos ronds joyeux.
> Vite! en cadence
> Pressons la danse;
> Que le plaisir
> Ne puisse fuir!

(Ils disparaissent. On les entend encore dans le lointain. Amélie, Conrad, Elmire rentrent au châteu. Le pont-levis se lève.)

Fin du premier acte.

ACTE II

Le théâtre représente une vallée sauvage entourée d'épaisses forêts et dominée par de hautes montagnes dont les derniers rayons du soleil éclairent les cîmes. On aperçoit quelques châlets dans le lointain. Les Bohémiens qui ont déjà paru à l'acte précédent descendent du haut des rochers mêlés à des groupes de bergers et de bergeres. On entend les cornemuses se répondre d'une montagne à l'autre.

Musique faite

Scène 1

Lenor (déguisé en berger), Nyse, Mery, Bohémiens, bergers et bergères

Choeur

L'ombre descend dans la vallée,
Rassemblez-vous, jeunes pasteurs.
Venez sous la verte feuillée
Cueillir les plaisirs et les fleurs.
    Le bruit expire;
    Voyez-vous luire
    Le doux sourire
    Des cieux charmés?
    L'écho soupire
    Et le Zéphyre
    Semble nous dire:
    Dansez! Aimez!
Ce soir du bosquet solitaire
L'amour enchante le mystère;
Mais il fuit au rêveil du jour;
Dansez et chantez tour à tour.
Voici le son des musettes,
Et sous les ombres discrètes
Ce mois prépare aux fillettes
Des baisers des violettes.
Ah! puissent leurs rêves d'amour
Ne pas fuir au reveil du jour.
L'ombre descend de nos montagnes;
Rassemblez-vous jeunes pasteurs.
Voici vos charmantes compagnes;
Cueillez les plaisirs et les fleurs.

Ballet

Un guerrier Bohémien

Le lâche pâlit et frissonne
Quand cet arc fléchit sous mes doigts.

Il fuit en vain... le trait résonne.
Sa mort était dans mon carquois.

Second Bohémien

(Il s'élance en face du premier d'un air menaçant et ironique.)

Arrête ici, lion farouche!
Reconnais mon fer et ma main.
L'orgueil peut-il ouvrir ta bouche
Quand l'effroi soulève ton sein?

(Les choeurs se partagent. Les Bohémiens divisés en deux parties se rangent sous chacun des deux chefs précédents.)

Bohémiens

Aux armes!... la charge sonne!
L'acier résonne!
En avant!!!

(Mille drapeaux de couleurs variées s'agitent tout-à-coup dans les airs. Les femmes marquent le pas au bruit des harpes et des lyres. Les Bohémiens forment entre eux des combats simulés: Leurs attaques et leurs défenses sont tour à tour nobles et grotesques. Les bergers les admirent et s'amusent de leurs mouvements bizarres.)

Choeur de Bergers

Victoire! Victoire!
Beaucoup de gloire,
Et peu de sang!

Choeur de Bohémiennes et de Bergères

Bravo! Bravo! Voici des roses!
Des roses faute de lauriers!
Elles sont fraîchement écloses
Pour les amants et les guerriers.

(Les choeurs se couronnent de guirlandes et forment des danses en suspendant des festons aux arbres. Lenor seul, après s'être paré de fleurs, évite leurs jeux et paraît plongé dans une profonde rêverie.)

Un Berger (s'approchant de Lenor)

Obald! de nos danses légères
Tu sembles fuir les cercles gracieux.

2ème Choeur

Quoi! la douce voix des bergères
Ne parle pas à ton coeur soucieux?
De leurs yeux vois les étincelles.
Prête l'oreille à leurs accents.
Leurs sourires donnent des ailes
Aux chagrins les plus dévorants.

Lenor

>Berger, ton amitié m'est chère;
>Que ne peut-elle aussi me prêter ton repos?

1ʳ choeur, puis il reviendra en accompagnement du 2ᵈ.

Le Berger

>Etranger malheureux, pourquoi ce long mystère
>Dont ton âme attristée enveloppe ses maux?
>Depuis le jour où nos vieux chênes
>Couvrirent ton sommeil et cachèrent tes peines,
>Chacun de nous en vain interroge tes pleurs;
>Tu souffres en silence et méconnais nos coeurs.

Un Bohémien

(Il s'approche du Berger en dansant, un sistre à la main, et chante rapidement et à demi-voix.)

>Bergère naive
>Là-bas sur la rive
>Egare, pensive
>Ses feux et ses pas
>Viens tout bas, tout bas
>Saisir dans ses bras
>L'heure fugitive.

(Ils s'éloignent.)

Nise

(Elle quitte la danse et accourt près de Lenor.)

>Le ciel et les voluptés
>Sourient à nos bords tranquilles;
>Jamais plus douces clartés
>N'ont enchanté ces frais asiles.
>Toi seul, ami, mêle de pleurs
>Les dons qui parent ta jeunesse
>Ton front caché sous les fleurs
>Nous voile en vain sa tristesse.

(Mery vient se joindre à Nise tandis que celle-ci chante les derniers vers du couplet.)

Trio pastoral; musique faite

Nise, Mery

>Vois-tu le soleil s'enfuir
>De nos montagnes solitaires,
>Ainsi bientôt le plaisir
>Fuira nos chaînes éphémères.
>Pourquoi, pourquoi mêler de pleurs
>Les beaux jours que le temps nous laisse?
>Qu'Obald paré de nos fleurs
>Sourie à notre allégresse.

Lenor

> Craignez le réveil du jour:
> Dansez, ô mes jeunes compagnes;
> Pour vous la nuit et l'amour
> Parfument nos belles campagnes.
> Mais hélas! mes sombres douleurs
> Profaneraient votre allégresse.
> Parez mon front de vos fleurs
> Mais pour voiler ma tristesse.

Nise, Mery

> Craignons le réveil du jour;
> Chantons ô mes jeunes compagnes;
> Pour nous la nuit et l'amour
> Parfument nos belles campagnes.
> Pourquoi, pourquoi mêler de pleurs
> Les beaux jours que le temps nous laisse?
> Qu'Obald paré de nos fleurs
> Sourie à notre allégresse.

(Un Franc-Juge couvert d'un manteau noir et la figure voilée apparaît tout-à-coup sur un rocher du côté de la forêt.)

Bergers et Bohémiens

> Grand Dieu!

Lenor

> Ciel! (Ils veulent fuir.)

Scène 2

Les mêmes, le Franc-Juge

Le Franc-Juge

> Arrêtez!... à l'ombre de vos jeux
> Un coupable, ô Bergers, se rit en paix des cieux!!!
> Malheur, malheur à lui!... l'instant fatal s'avance.
> L'heure marche et l'accuse... il ne la fuira pas.
> Du Dieu qui l'épargna la trop lente vengeance
> L'enveloppe, le presse et gronde sur ses pas.
> Ceux dont l'oeil éternel perce la nuit profonde,
>
> Dont la voix ébranle le monde,
> Et dont le front est couronné d'éclairs,
> Ceux enfin dont le nom fait pâlir les pervers
> Citent l'impie au tribunal suprême.
> Et la terre avec moi lui répète: anathème!
> A cet appel s'il osait résister,
> A cet arrêt divin s'il osait insulter,
> Que sa présence ameute les orages,
> Qu'elle fasse écrouler le chaume hospitalier,
> Que son sommeil soit meurtrier,
> Ses songes d'horribles images!
> Que l'eau de la citerne et le lait bienfaisant
> Se changent sous sa lèvre en poison homicide;
> Que sous ses pas le sol perfide
> S'entre-ouvre en abîme brûlant!
> Comme l'écume et le reptile
> Qu'il soit vomi du sein des mers;

Que la mort soit son seul asile,
  Son seul refuge les enfers.

(Il descend du rocher et s'approche de Lenor. A voix basse et mystérieusement.)

Que minuit te retrouve en ces lieux solitaires.
Minuit!... tremble de l'oublier!
Ministre saint de nos jaloux mystères.
Un guide sera là... qu'il y soit le dernier.

(Il remonte sur le rocher, fait un signe menaçant et disparaît dans la forêt.)

Scène 3

Les mêmes, excepté le Franc-Juge.

Choeur de Bergers et de Bohémiens

O terreur! ô nuit d'épouvante
La colère céleste habite ces vallons
Et sur nous plâne, menaçante
Le sol maudit nous rejette!... Fuyons!

grand air à faire

Lenor seul

C'en est donc fait!... et ma présence impure
Contre moi dèsormais soulève la nature!
Tous les êtres vivants ont horreur de mes pas!
Comme une ombre après moi je traine le trépas!

Scène 4

Air

Tu ne me verras plus, ô ma douce Amélie,
Offrant au ciel trompeur et mes maux et ta foi,
Adorer dans tes yeux la clémence infinie,
Et m'enivrer des pleurs que tu versais sur moi!
Ah! tout ce que mon sein a conservé de vie
Prêt à s'éteindre hélas! s'exhale encore vers toi!

(Il lance autour de lui des regards enflammés.)

Mais quel soudain transport m'anime?
Quelle voix s'éveille en mon coeur?

(Il s'anime de plus en plus.)

Au sombre Dieu du mal il faut une victime,
Puisse-t-elle en tombant effrayer sa fureur!
Ah! le sang qui brûle mes veines
N'est-il pas le sang des héros?
Qu'en coulant du moins sous mes chaînes
Il fasse pâlir mes bourreaux.

Scène 5

parlé

Lenor, Amélie, Elmire, Conrad

Amélie

> Grâce à Conrad, enfin j'ai retrouvé la trace.
> Forte de mon amour, forte de tes serments
> Mes timides soupirs ont fait place à l'audace;
> D'un hymen odieux j'ai fui les fers sanglants.
> Lenor!

Lenor

> O désespoir!

Amélie

> Reçois ton Amélie.

Lenor

> Eh quoi! tu peux fouler cette terre ennemie?
> Quoi! ton coeur sur mon coeur se penche sans effroi?

(Il la repousse.)

> Ta main en me touchant s'armerait contre toi!

Amélie

> Et c'était le prix de ma tendresse.

Conrad à Lenor

> Quelle sombre fureur luit dans tes yeux brûlants?

Lenor

> Fuyez!

Conrad

> C'est l'amitié, c'est l'amour qui te presse.

Lenor

> Fuyez!

Conrad

> Sont-ce là tes serments?

Lenor

(Il éloigne Conrad d'Amélie et lui dit à voix basse:)

> Connais-tu, réponds-moi, ce tribunal terrible,
> Ce tribunal où veille un pouvoir invisible,
> Les Francs-Juges....

Conrad

> Grand Dieu!!

Lenor

> Tu frémis!...

Conrad

> Achevez!!...

Lenor

> Cette nuit devant eux ton ami doit paraître.

Conrad

> O terre, engloutis-moi!...

(Il se précipite hors du théâtre.)

Lenor

> Conrad!... Il fuit le traître!
> Lui!... Lui!... Conrad!... Ciel barbare est-ce assez!

Scène 6

Les mêmes excepté Conrad.

Lenor (se tournant vers Amélie)

> Reste du moins, ô toi, douce image d'un ange!
> Enchante mes derniers moments!
> Un seul de tes regards me venge
> Et de l'oubli du monde et de mes longs tourments.

(Il s'arrête un instant, et relève Amélie avec effroi.)

> Que dis-je?... que dis-je?... Amélie!
> Tout est danger dans ce séjour:
> Fuis un infortuné... songe, songe à ta vie.

Amélie (se relevant avec fermeté)

> Que m'importe la vie auprès de ton amour!

Duo

Musique faite

Amélie

> N'espère plus, Lenor, effrayer mon courage;
> J'osai braver pour toi l'esclavage et la mort.
> Ah! tes pleurs me sont chers; mais ton effroi m'outrage:
> Rien ne peut séparer tes malheurs et mon sort.

Lenor

>Qui? moi, de mon aspect profanant l'innocence
>J'écouterais encore nos funestes amours?
>Dépouille pour jamais ta crédule espérance:
>Si tu savais l'abîme où j'entraîne tes jours!

Amélie

>Eh bien! nous tomberons ensemble.
>Mes jours pleins de honte et d'effroi,
>Lenor, s'éteignaient loin de toi;
>La mort aujourd'hui nous rassemble.

Lenor

>Crains Olmerik!... ce nom fait frissonner ton coeur?

Amélie

>Il palpite de haine, et non pas de terreur.

Lenor

>Ton regard, ô ma bien aimée,
>Ranime mes feux abattus:
>Le noble accent de tes vertus
>Réveille mon âme enflammée.

Ensemble

>Dieu qui m'accable tour-à-tour
>Et de bonheur et de souffrance,
>Si jamais je trahis mes voeux et sa constance,
>Frappe, et venge à la fois les vertus et l'amour!

(Elmire, qui veillait au fond du théâtre, accourt avec terreur.)

Elmire

>Tout est perdu, Madame, on connaît cet asile.
>Le farouche Olmerik s'avance sur nos pas.

Amélie

>O trahison!

Lenor

>La fuite est inutile
>L'arrêt est prononcé; nous n'échapperons pas.

Scène 7

Les mêmes, Olmerik, Christiern

Quintetto

Lenor, Amélie, Elmire

(à demi-voix)

Musique à faire

Ombres de { mes / nos } aïeux, ombres de la patrie,
Ombres puissantes, levez-vous!
Allumez dans nos coeurs une sainte furie!
Détournez la tempête ou combattez pour nous.

Olmerik, Lenor	**Christiern**	**Amélie, Elmire**
Je frémis... l'amour /et la rage	Je frémis... l'amour /et la rage	Je frémis... l'amour /et la rage
Tour à tour déchirent /mon coeur	Tour à tour déchirent /son coeur.	Semblent se disputer /son coeur.
Chaque instant amasse /l'orage;	Chaque instant amasse /l'orage;	Chaque instant amasse /l'orage;
Chaque instant accroît /ma fureur.	Chaque instant accroît /sa fureur.	Chaque instant accroît /sa fureur.

Olmerik

Parlé

Courage, courage, Amélie!
A ce rival heureux cours immoler ton Roi!
Avec lui désormais dispute d'infamie;
Prononce hardiment entre un esclave et moi.
Cache-toi sous ta honte... enivrez-vous ensemble
　　De tout l'opprobre qu'il assemble
　　Et sur son front et sur ses pas;
Mon mépris satisfait ne vous trahira pas.

Lenor

Ne blasphème pas l'innocence!
Amélie a connu ton crime et mes malheurs.
Chassé du trône, objet de tes fureurs,
Il ne me restait rien, pas même l'espérance;
Mais le ciel écoutait la voix de mes douleurs,
Et l'amour d'Amélie a vengé mon offense.

Olmerik

N'arme plus contre moi tes regards impuissants;
　　Crains d'enflammer ma colère.

Lenor

Crains d'éveiller le tonnerre;
Il ne frappe que les tyrans.

Olmerik

Ce désert, le sais-tu? Ma voix y règne encore.

Lenor

C'en est assez pour qu'il t'abhorre.

Olmerik

> Qu'il se lève donc contre toi!
> Paraissez, paraissez, vengeurs de votre roi!

(D'innombrables bataillons apparaissent tout-à-coup sur les hauteurs et entrent de toutes parts en scène au bruit d'une musique farouche.)

Scène 8

Parlé

Les mêmes, Conrad

Conrad

(Il fend les rangs des soldats, et se précipite éperdu aux pieds d'Olmerik.)

> Prince, de votre sang sauvez les nobles restes!

Olmerik

> De ses vaines clameurs justement irrité,
> J'ai dû briser l'orgueil de ses projets funestes.
> Il tremble... je pardonne à sa lâche fierté.

Conrad

> Seigneur, ce n'est pas vous qu'accusent mes alarmes,
> Et je redoute peu ces guerriers et ces armes.

Olmerik

> Qu'oses-tu dire?... où sont ses ennemis?

Christiern (inquiet)

> A sa garde, Conrad, êtes-vous donc commis?

Conrad

> Une proie est promise au crime,
> Et l'assassin est près de sa victime.

(On entend des voix lugubres et solennelles sortir des profondeurs de la forêt.)

Voix mystérieuses

> Malheur au parjure!

Christiern

> Ecoutez!

Olmerik (avec une joie mystérieuse.)

> J'entends.

Conrad (Il se précipite vers Lenor.)

> Lenor, ah! pardonnez...

Christiern (à Olmerik à part, à demi-voix et très distinctement.)

>　　Vos ordres sont donnés. Jamais de tels prodiges
>　　　　N'ont assuré nos saints arrêts.
>　　Jamais d'aussi puissants prestiges
>　　　　Aux profanes regards n'ont fermé nos forêts.

Final

musique faite

(La nuit devient profonde. Un bruit sourd de tonnerre se fait entendre. Des éclairs rapides sillonnent les nues, et laissent apercevoir des groupes de bergers au haut des montagnes.)

(Conrad se rapproche de Lenor comme pour lui faire une révélation; la tempête redouble aussitôt et les mêmes voix se font entendre.)

>　　　　Malheur au parjure!

Conrad

>　　Le ciel contre moi seul s'arme de son tonnerre;
>　　Dieu! je sens sous mes pieds se dérober la terre!

Mêmes voix

>　　　Malheur au parjure!

Choeur de Bergers	**Choeur de Soldats**
Quelles clameurs sortent du fond /des bois;	Quelles clameurs sortent du fond /des bois;
Pourquoi ces bords sont-ils pleins /d'épouvante?	Pourquoi Conrad frémit-il d'épouvante?

Choeur de femmes

>　　Les cieux et les enfers mugissent à la fois;
>　　Dieu terrible! où fuira notre foule tremblante?

Olmerik, Christiern	**Conrad, Lenor, & Amélie**
Voici l'heure où ces monts déserts	Voici l'heure où ces monts déserts
Vont frémir de ma vengeance	Vont frémir de sa vengeance.
Le moment fatal s'avance;	Le moment fatal s'avance;
Mille voix grondent dans les airs.	Mille voix grondent dans les airs.

(La tempête éclate: des flammes livides s'élancent des forêts, l'on entend un horrible cliquetis d'armes.)

Ensemble

>　　O ciel la flamme et le glaive
>　　S'arment d'un horrible effort.
>　　Le nuit des enfers se lève;
>　　Ses ombres donnent la mort.

(Ils se dispersent.)

      Fin du second acte.

ACTE III

      Le théâtre conserve la décoration de l'acte précédent: l'obscurité est profonde; le vent gémit parmi les arbres. L'orchestre exprime le deuil de la nature et cette inquiétude douloureuse qui semble précéder les évènements extraordinaires.

Musique faite

Scène 1

Lenor seul

(Il s'avance à pas lents et semble accablé de fatigue.)

      Voici l'endroit fatal... vous dont l'ombre infidèle
        N'a su protéger nos amours,
      Avant que l'airain sonne et que sa voix m'appelle,
        Bois chéris, adieu pour toujours!

      (Il fait quelques pas et prête l'oreille au bruit plaintif des vents.)

      La nature se plaint et le deuil m'environne....
      La souffrance a vaincu ma paupière et mon bras....
      Arrêtons-nous ici... la force m'abandonne
        Et la terre fuit sous mes pas.
      Tu ne sais pas trahir le malheur qui t'implore,
      Dieu des infortunés; tu te plais, ô sommeil,
      A vaincre dans leurs flancs le mal qui les dévore
      Et la belle espérance enchante leur réveil.

Air

      Descends et viens rendre à mes songes
      Le calme qui fuit mes douleurs;
      Prête-moi tes riants mensonges;
      Sur mon sein efface mes pleurs.
      Ranime à l'ombre de ton aile
      Mon oeil éteint et mon bras affaibli;
      Et sur mon front qui s'incline et t'appelle
      Vers le repos et l'oubli.

(Il s'assied sur un banc de gazon et cède peu à peu au repos.)

Songe

    Son sommeil est agité et pénible. Les principales scènes des actes précédents lui apparaissent confusément en songe, et se mêlent dans son imagination. L'orchestre rappelle tour-à-tour et sans suite les motifs de la scène pastorale, la marche des gardes d'Olmerik, la fin du final du premier acte, l'anathème du Franc-Juge.

Scène 2

Lenor, Conrad

Conrad est habillé en franc-juge, le visage voilé et entièrement vêtu de noir. D'une main il tient un poignard et de l'autre une lanterne sourde. Il sort de la forêt et s'avance rapidement vers Lenor. Il contemple l'agitation de son sommeil à la lueur de son flambeau, et sa pantomime exprime l'attendrissement. Mais on entend sonner minuit dans le lointain; en ce moment une sensation pénible réveille Lenor, et il fait un geste d'effroi à l'aspect de Conrad.   Celui-ci lui fait signe de le suivre et tous deux disparaissent dans la forêt.

Scène 3

Musique faite

La décoration change et représente l'intérieur des cavernes de Mendor. Douze sièges de pierre sont disposés autour d'une vaste table tendue de noir, et couverte de poignards et d'objets symboliques. La caverne n'est éclairée que par les reflets de la lune brillant dans la partie la plus reculée. Les Francs-Juges entrent de tous côtés par les issues irrégulières des rochers, au bruit d'une marche lugubre. Ils ont ainsi que Conrad le visage voilé et sont entièrement vêtus de noir. Une large épée est suspendue à leur côté par une ceinture blanche. Ils s'approchent les uns des autres; choquent le bouclier d'airain attaché à leur bras gauche et se serrent la main. Ils se rangent près de la rampe sur une seule ligne.

Hymne

Des célestes décrets, invisibles vengeurs,
Vous dont le bras fatal est redoutable au crime,
Frappez, frappez votre victime;
A la pitié fermez vos coeurs.
De la terre et du sang étouffons les clameurs!
Nos yeux sont éclairés par un flambeau sublime;
Sans pâlir, frappons la victime
Que l'on dévoue à nos fureurs.

(Les Francs-Juges se retirent dans le fond de la caverne. Ils forment des figures mystérieuses avec leurs épées. Le sein incliné vers la terre et les bras tendus, ils chantent sur un mode sinistre et sourd l'évocation suivante:)

Accours, ô Monarque des ombres!
Viens... que ces noirs enchantements
Jusques à tes demeures sombres
Sortent nos fiers ressentiments.

(Un bruit inconnu se fait entendre. La terre tremble, et l'on voit sortir de son sein la statue de bronze, de dimension colossale, sur le pied d'estal de laquelle les Francs-Juges faisaient placer les prévenus. Ils étaient aussitôt écrasés dans ses bras au moyen de ressorts secrets que leur poids faisait mouvoir, et entraînés dans une espèce de gouffre pratiqué au-dessous d'elle. Après un moment de silence l'un des Francs-Juges s'approche de la statue, et la frappe de son épée; elle répond par un mugissement sourd. Olmerik fait un signe, et les Francs-Juges vont s'asseoir sur les sièges de pierre. Olmerik se place dans le fond, près du colosse, en face des spectateurs. Il reste debout.)

Olmerik

parlé

> Bientôt Lenor en ces lieux va paraître.
> Sur les pas de Conrad il s'avance... à la mort.
> Mon oeil enfin verra pâlir le traître,
> Et sur ces murs le sien lira partout son sort.

(Montrant la statue et élevant la voix:)

> Voici le bronze horrible, inexorable,
> Bronze vivant, mystérieux vengeur,
> Que l'enfer chaque nuit enfante avec terreur.
> Vous le savez; sitôt que le coupable
> A sur l'airain sacré posé ses pieds tremblants,
> D'une étreinte invincible enchaînant sa victime
> > Au sein enflammé de l'abîme
> Il entraîne avec lui ses membres palpitants.

(Il s'arrête un instant. Montrant les portes de la caverne:)

> Lenor est là. Voici l'heure du sacrifice,
> Si le fer de Conrad hésitait en sa main,

(Il montre la statue.)

> Dans les bras du géant précipités soudain,
> Que le même trépas à jamais les unisse.

(Il s'asseoit. Un Franc-Juge se lève, s'avance au milieu du théâtre, et chante d'un ton solennel et à haute voix.)

Le France-Juge

> Enfant de Venceslas, Lenor, Lenor, parais!
> Echos, portez ma voix du couchant à l'aurore.
> Du Dieu qui va parler publiez les arrêts!
> Ceux que le ciel chérit, ceux que la terre adore
> T'appellent par ma voix. Lenor, Lenor, parais!

(Il va reprendre sa place.)

Scène 4

Les mêmes, Conrad, Lenor

(Conrad conduit Lenor au milieu de la scène. Celui-ci a les yeux couverts d'un bandeau: Conrad se tient derrière lui le poignard à la main.)

Olmerik

> Rendez le jour à sa paupière
> Et de son front écartez le bandeau.

(Conrad ôte le voile de Lenor.)

Lenor

Où me conduisez-vous, cruels?

Olmerik

A la lumière!
Entre la terre et toi se lève un jour nouveau.
Approche... la vérité sainte
T'observe, t'interroge et belle de courroux,
Un poignard à la main vient de s'asseoir parmi nous.

Lenor

J'ai vécu sans forfaits, je répondrai sans crainte.

Olmerik

Ta bouche répandant la révolte et l'effroi
A souillé nos états de ton ignominie:
Que réclament tes cris, Lenor?

Lenor

Une patrie.

Olmerik

Proscrit ne sais-tu pas qu'il n'en est plus pour toi?
Qu' attendais-tu sur ces bords?

Lenor

La vengeance.

Olmerik

Où sont tes ennemis, insensé?

Lenor

Dans vos rangs.

Olmerik

Tes complices?

Lenor

Le Ciel!

Olmerik

Tes armes?

Lenor

L'espérance,
L'infortune du peuple et l'horreur des tyrans!

Olmerik

Ces tyrans, quels sont-ils?

Lenor

> Demandez à la terre!
> Ils ont en traits de sang partout écrit leurs noms.

Olmerik

> Va! Je lis le remords dans ta vaine colère;
> Il fait battre ton coeur.

Lenor

> Il pâlit sur vos fronts.

Olmerik

> Vil banni, tu braves tes maîtres!

Lenor

> Je brave mes bourreaux.

Olmerik

> Tremble donc sous leurs coups.

Lenor

> Je les attends sans peur.

Olmerik (avec une rage comprimée)

> Le supplice des traîtres,
> Le connais-tu? Réponds.

Lenor

> Il fut créé pour vous.

Olmerik

> O rage! ô comble d'insolence!

Lenor

> O comble de forfaits!

Olmerik

> Sacrilèges fureurs!

Lenor

> Fils des enfers.

Olmerik

> Frémis!

Lenor

> J'insulte à ta puissance!

Olmerik

> Adore là: tombe à genoux ou meurs!

Lenor

(Il hésite et cherche à reconnaitre Olmerik.)

> Je te reconnais à ma haine.
> Assouvis ta soif inhumaine,
> Olmerik, épuise en mon sein
> Le pur sang de tes rois, le pur sang de ton frère!
> Le sang de mes aïeux rougit encore ta main:
> Frappe-moi!... mais du fer dont tu frappas mon père.

Olmerik (aux Francs-Juges)

> Vous l'entendez; son vain ressentiment
> De votre tribunal souille le sanctuaire;
> Mais sur sa lèvre téméraire
> Dieu lui-même a placé son propre jugement.

> **(Récit mesuré)**

Musique faite

> Vous que le ciel chargea du soin de sa vengeance
> Que votre coeur se ferme à la clémence;
> Entendez-vous l'ombre de Venceslas?
> > De l'abîme ouvert sous vos pas,
> > Comme un horrible météore,
> > Il est tout prêt à s'élancer encore,
> > Et le foudre est dans ses regards.
> > Que votre fer hâte l'heure trop lente!
> Il est temps; et vos coups vont porter l'épouvante
> > Au palais des Césars.

(Moment de silence. Il se lève, et étendant les bras, il chante d'une voix solennelle.)

> Que l'inspiration descende en traits de flamme,
> Et vous brûle des feux allumés en mon âme!

Les Francs-Juges (debout et immobiles)

Musique faite

> Des célestes décrets invisibles vengeurs;
> Nous dont le bras fatal est redoutable au crime,
> Frappons, frappons notre victime;
> A la pitié fermons nos coeurs!
> De la terre et du sang étouffons les clameurs.
> Nos yeux sont éclairés par un flambeau sublime!
> Sans pâlir frappons la victime
> Que l'on dévoue à nos fureurs.

(Il se fait un second moment de silence. Tous à la fois lèvent leurs poignards et s'asseient.)

Le sort parle... adorons son arrêt équitable.

(à Conrad)

Glaive exterminateur, dévore le coupable.

Lenor

Puisse, Olmerik, puisse bientôt sur toi
Retomber l'anathème impie!
Mais, ô mon Dieu sauve Amélie;
Et mon dernier soupir s'exhale sans effroi.

(La lune disparaît.   On entend au dehors de la caverne un bruit terrible et toujours croissant.)

Olmerik

Quelles voix ébranlent la terre?

Christiern

Quels cris lointains?

Olmerik

Quels chants de guerre!

Choeur des Francs-Juges

Les rochers à grand bruit
S'agitent sur nos têtes,
La lune pâle fuit....
C'est la nuit des tempêtes.

(Des soldats se précipitent de tous côtés dans la caverne.)

Scène 5

Les mêmes, Amélie, le Sénéchal de l'Empire, soldats, peuple.

(Amélie se précipite dans les bras de Lenor.)

Amélie

Il est sauvé!

Lenor

C'est elle!

Amélie

O mon prince! ô Lenor!
Dieu clément, en ses bras je me retrouve encor!

Le Sénéchal (aux Francs-Juges)

Monstres qu'épargna le tonnerre,
Tombez devant nos étendards!
Cessez de profaner la terre;
Pâlissez au nom des Césars!

Francs-Juges

> Malheur, malheur au parjure!

Choeur de peuple

> Victoire! honneur à nos guerriers!
> Ils paraissent: le ciel s'épure.
> Semons leur chemin de lauriers!

Francs-Juges

> Malheur, malheur au parjure!

Lenor (à Amélie)

> Ange libérateur, qui conduisit tes pas?

Amélie

> J'ai tout su de Conrad.

Francs-Juges

> Conrad!!!

Lenor

> Ami fidèle!
> Mon coeur ici le recherche et ne le trouve pas.

Conrad (Il se découvre.)

> Regarde!

Amélie, peuple, soldats

> Il était là!!!

Lenor

> C'est lui!....vertu cruelle!
> Mon sauveur s'asseyait au rang de mes bourreaux!

(Les Francs-Juges les plus près de Conrad veulent s'élancer sur lui.)

Le Sénéchal

> Autour de lui, soldats, inclinez vos faisceaux!

(Les soldats forment autour de lui un rempart de leurs armes.)

Conrad

> Lenor, je dus sauver ta vie:
> Mais des serments affreux s'élèvent contre moi.
> Ah! puissé-je expier la tendre ignominie
> De les avoir trahis pour toi.

(Il veut se frapper. Amélie et Lenor le retiennent.)

Choeur

> Infortuné, le ciel pardonne;
> L'amitié réclame tes jours!

Le Sénéchal

> Viens au front de Lenor déposer la couronne.
> Il te devra son sceptre; il te doit ses amours.

Olmerik

(D'une voix terrible et pleine d'une majesté farouche.)

> Arrêtez!... Arrêtez!... l'Enfer attend sa proie!

(au Sénéchal)

> Ma tête sous vos coups ne s'inclinera pas.

(Il s'avance vers la statue.)

> Abîme!... tressaille de joie,
> Et ravis aux Césars l'honneur de mon trépas!

(Il monte sur le piédestal; la statue l'embrasse et disparait au milieu des flammes.)

Choeur général

(Tous se jettent à genoux.)

> Le gouffre pour jamais s'est fermé pour l'impie.
> Soldats! peuple! adorons la clémence infinie!

Final

Le Sénéchal, soldats

Musique faite

> Fier Germain, reprends ces vallons
> Qu'ont souillés tes injustes maîtres.
> Rends l'abondance à tes sillons
> Indignés de nourrir des traîtres.

Choeur de peuple

> Le bonheur aujourd'hui sourit avec l'aurore.
> Douce paix, hâte-toi d'éclore!
> Oui, la valeur et la beauté
> Ont fléchi le ciel irrité.

Choeur général

> Fier Germain, reprend ces vallons
> Qu'ont souillés tes injustes maîtres.
> Rends l'abondance à tes sillons
> Indignés de nourrir des traîtres.

Fin du troisième et dernier acte.

Appendix III

Libretto of *Le Cri de Guerre du Brisgaw*

Source: Bound with full score of *Les Francs-Juges* (**F-Pn** Rés Vm² 177). [Spelling modernized, except when it would conflict with the metric scheme. Berlioz's indications of sections complete (*musique faite*) are italicized. Format edited for publication.]

Le Cri de Guerre du Brisgaw
Intermède en un acte

Les acteurs seraient:

A. Nourrit—Lenor
Dabadie—Conrad
A. Dupont—Le Bûcheron
Mme Dorus—La Bohémienne
Mlle Jawurek—Nise
Mme Mori—Mery
Mrs Dérivis
         —Deux Bohémiens
   Massol

Le théâtre représente une vallée sauvage entourée d'épaisses forêts et dominée par de hautes montagnes. On aperçoit quelques châlets dans le lointain. Des Bohémiens descendent du haut des rochers mêler à des groupes de bergers et de bergères.

Chœur (Scherzando)

[*sic*] ~~Musique faite~~

Lenor (déguisé en berger sous le nom d'Obald)
Nyse
Mery
Bohémiens
Bergers et Bergères
Une Bohémienne, rôle de 1ère chanteuse

Mêlons à la voix des trompettes
Mêlons le bruit des tambourins,
Sistres, guitares, et musettes
Accompagnez nos gais refrains.

> De combien d'étoiles
> Le regard nous luit.
> Qu'ils sont beaux tes voiles
> O charmante nuit.
> Ton haleine
> Dans la plaine
> Donne aux fleurs

Leurs couleurs.
Vite! en cadence
Pressons la danse
Que le plaisir
Ne puisse fuir!
Ivresse! Folie!
Le temps envieux
S'arrête et s'oublie
Dans nos ronds joyeux.

L'ombre descend dans la vallée
    Rassemblez-vous jeunes pasteurs
Venez sous la verte feuillée
    Cueillir des plaisirs et des fleurs.

Le bruit expire,
Voyez-vous luire,
Le doux sourire
Des cieux charmés!
L'écho soupire,
Et le Zéphire
Semble nous dire:
Dansez! aimez!

De combien, etc.

Ballet

Un Guerrier Bohémien

Le lâche pâlit et frissonne
Quand cet arc fléchit sous mes doigts
Il fuit en vain, le trait résonne
La mort était dans mon carquois.

Second Bohémien

(Il s'élance en face du premier d'un air menaçant et ironique.)

Arrête ici, lion farouche
Reconnais mon fer et ma main
L'orgueil peut-il ouvrir la bouche
Quand d'effroi soulève ton sein?

(Les choeurs se partagent. Les Bohémiens divisés en deux parties se rangent sous chacun des deux chefs précédents.)

Bohémiens (choeur)

Aux armes!... La charge sonne
    L'acier résonne
    En avant.

(Mille drapeaux de couleurs variées s'agitent tout-à-coup dans les airs. Les femmes marquent le pas au bruit des harpes et des lyres. Les Bohémiens forment entre eux des combats simulés. Leurs attaques et leurs défenses sont tour-à-tour nobles et grotesques. Les Bergers les admirent et s'amusent de leurs mouvements bizarres.)

Bergers (choeur)

> Victoire! Victoire!
> Beaucoup de gloire!
> Et peu de sang!

Choeur de Bohémiennes et de Bergères

> Bravo, bravo! voici des roses!
> Des roses faute de lauriers!
> Elles sont fraîchement écloses
> Pour les amants et les guerriers.

(Les choeurs se couronnent de guirlandes et forment des danses en suspendant des festons aux arbres. *Lenor* seul, après s'être paré de fleurs, évite leurs jeux et paraît plongé dans une profonde rêverie.)

4 Jeunes Bergers (s'approchant de Lenor)

> Obald! de nos danses légères
> Tu sembles fuir les contours gracieux
> Quoi! La douce voix des bergères
> Ne parle pas à ton coeur soucieux?
> De leurs yeux vois leurs étincelles
> Prête l'oreille à leurs accents
> Leurs sourires donnent des ailes
> Aux chagrins les plus dévorants.

Obald (récit.)

> Bergers votre amitié m'est chère
> Que ne peut-elle, hélas, me rendre le repos!

4 Vieillards

> Etranger malheureux, pourquoi ce long mystère
> Dont ton âme attristée enveloppe tes maux?
> Depuis le jour où nos vieux chênes
> Couvrirent tes sommeils et cachèrent tes peines.

Les 4 Bergers et les 4 Vieillards ensemble

> Chacun de nous en vain interroge tes pleurs
> Tu souffres en silence et méconnais nos coeurs.
> Obald! de nos danses, etc. (Ils s'éloignent.)

Nise

musique faite

(Elle quitte les danses et accourt près de Lenor.)

Mélodie pastorale (1^rcouplet) *Andantino*

> Le ciel et les voluptés
> Sourient à nos bords tranquilles;
> Jamais plus douces clartés
> N'ont enchanté ces frais asiles.

> Toi seul, ami, mêle de pleurs
> Les dons qui parent ta jeunesse.
> Ton front caché sous les fleurs
> Nous voile en vain ta tristesse.

(Mery vient se joindre à Nise tandis que celle-ci chante les derniers vers du 1^r couplet. Au moment où elles vont commencer ensemble le second, une jeune Bohémienne s'approche d'Obald une guitare à la main et lui chante à demi-voix:)

Presto

> Bergère naïve
> Là-bas sur la rive
> Egare pensive
> Ses feux et ses pas
> Viens tout bas, tout bas
> Saisir dans ses bras
> L'heure fugitive.

Mélodie pastorale 2me Couplet à 2 voix

Nise et Mery

> Vois-tu le soleil s'enfuir
> De nos montagnes solitaires,
> Ainsi bientôt le plaisir
> Fuira nos chaînes éphémères,
> Pourquoi, pourquoi mêler de pleurs
> Les beaux jours que le temps nous laisse?
> Qu'Obald paré de nos fleurs
> Sourie à notre allégresse.

Obald   **Nise**   **Mery**   **La Bohémienne**

3me Couplet à 3 voix

avec un accompagnement de traits brillants et légers de la jeune Bohémienne

Obald (Andantino)	**Nise et Mery** (Andantino)	**La Bohémienne** (Allegro)
Craignez le réveil du /jour	Craignons le réveil du jour	Bergere naïve
Dansez ô mes jeunes /compagnes	Chantons ô mes jeunes compagnes	Là-bas sur la rive
Pour vous et la nuit /et l'amour	Pour nous la nuit et l'amour	Egare plaintive
Parfument nos belles /campagnes	Parfument nos belles campagnes	Ses feux et ses pas
Mais hélas! mes som- /bres douleurs	Pourquoi, pourquoi mêler de /pleurs	Viens, tout bas, tout /bas
Profaneraient votre /allégresse	Les beaux jours que le temps /nous laisse?	Saisir dans ses bras

Parez mon front de vos
/fleurs
Mais pour voiler ma
/tristesse.

Qu'Obald paré de nos fleurs

Sourie à notre allégresse.

L'heure fugitive.

Choeur General

Qu'Obald paré de nos fleurs
Sourie à notre allégresse.

Obald (Récitatif)

Amis, je dois répondre à votre accueil,
Connaissez les douleurs secrètes
De l'étranger qui dans vos fêtes
Porte la tristesse et le deuil.

(mouvement d'attention)

Olmerik, du Brisgaw, qui gouverne la terre,
Sur le trône est monté par de sanglants chemins;
Il a foulé le corps de Venceslas son frère,
Par ses ordres tombé sous de perfides mains.
Ce frère avait un fils, promis à l'hyménée
D'un ange, qui du ciel semble être descendu.
Par l'amour d'Amélie une ardeur couronnée
Ferait tout oublier, même un trône perdu.
Au tyran c'était peu d'un crime.
Amélie enlevée et son époux proscrit
Ont offert séparés une double victime
A sa flamme adultère, au meurtre qu'il chérit.
Mais tandis qu'il levait le poignard des Francs-Juges
D'un ami les avis secrets
Désignaient au proscrit comme assurés refuges
Le dôme hospitalier de vos sombres forêts.
Il promit que bientôt, secondant sa détresse
Il reviendrait rendre à sa foi
Un peuple libre et sa maîtresse.
Vous savez tout. Le fils de Venceslas, c'est moi.

Air

Fureur et Vengeance!
Mon impatience
Nourrit l'espérance
De finir ces maux.
Les enfants des braves
Brisent leurs entraves,
Des berceaux esclaves
Sortent des héros.
Ma voix les éclaire
Sur l'affreux mystère
Qui peuple la terre

De tant de tombeaux;
Je les vois me suivre,
Mon bras les délivre,
De l'horreur de vivre
Parmi des bourreaux.

Quelques Bohémiens

Du fond de ces retraites sombres
Notre oeil ne le quittera pas.
S'il dit vrai, qu'il guide nos pas.
Si c'est un traître... qu'il succombe.

(Tout le choeur reprenant l'expression de la joie la plus vive:)

Mêlons à la voix des trompettes, etc., etc.

(Ils sortent en dansant.)

2me Scène

Obald Seul

L'ai-je bien entendu? par des chants d'allégresse
Ils répondent encor à ma plaintive voix?
Est-ce un piège nouveau que la feinte promesse
Qui m'amena parmi ces bois?
De leurs détours l'ombrage tutélaire
A quelquefois bercé mes souvenirs d'amour:
Dois-je trouver une mort solitaire
Où du bonheur j'ai rêvé le retour....
La nature se plaint et le deuil m'environne....
La souffrance a vaincu ma paupière et mon bras....
Je me sens succomber... la force m'abandonne,
Et la terre fuit sous mes pas.

Cavatine

musique faite

Tu ne sais pas trahir le malheur qui t'implore,
Dieu des infortunés, tu te plais, ô sommeil,
A vaincre dans leurs flancs le mal qui les dévore
Et la belle espérance enchante leur réveil.

Invocation

Descends et viens rendre à mes songes
Le calme qui fuit mes douleurs:
Prête-moi tes riants mensonges;
Sur mon sein efface mes pleurs.
Ranime à l'ombre de ton aile
Mon oeil éteint et mon bras affaibli,

Et sur mon front qui s'incline et t'appelle
Verse le repos et l'oubli.

(Il s'assied sur un banc de gazon au pied d'un arbre et s'endort.)

Scène 3me

Un Bûcheron, Lenor (endormi)

Un Bûcheron entre en chantant; il travaille quelque temps dans la forêt et s'éloigne, après avoir observé Lenor endormi. (Le vent gémit tristement.) [Ed.'s note: here begins the song *Le Jeune Pâtre breton*; later it was deleted with red chalk.]

Chanson du bûcheron
(d'un caractère doux et gai)

1^r Couplet

(qu'on ne peut entendre en entier à cause de l'éloignement.)

....
....
....
....
....
....   [sic]

(Lointain;)

Oh! nenni da!
Mais j'aime la petite Anna.

(Il   entre.)

2me Couplet

A son tour Anna, ma compagne,
Conduit derrière la montagne
          Près des sureaux
Ses noirs chevreaux;
Si la montagne, ô sort bizarre
Ainsi qu'un grand mur nous sépare
          Sa douce voix
Sa voix m'appelle au fond du bois.

3me Couplet

Oh sur un air plaintif et tendre
Qu'il est doux au loin de s'entendre
          Sans même avoir
          L'heure de se voir!
De la montagne à la vallée
La voix par la voix appellée
          Semble un soupir
Mêlé d'ennuis et de plaisir.

(Il sort.)

4me Couplet chanté en s'éloignant

Ah! retenez bien votre haleine
Brise étourdie, et dans la plaine
    Parmi les blés
    Courez, volez;
Dieu! la méchante a sur son aile
Emporté la voix douce et frêle
    La douce voix
Qui m'appelait au fond des bois.

Scène 4me

Obald, Conrad (Il fait nuit.)

Lenor

Conrad habillé en Franc-Juge entre accompagné du bûcheron, qui lui montre Lenor endormi et ressort. Son visage est voilé, il est entièrement vêtu de noir. D'une main il tient un poignard et de l'autre une lanterne sourde. Il sort de la forêt et s'avance rapidement vers Lenor. Il contemple l'agitation de son sommeil à la lueur de son flambeau et sa pantomime exprime l'attendrissement. Mais on entend sonner minuit dans le lointain; en ce moment une sensation pénible réveille Lenor, et il fait un geste d'effroi à l'aspect de Conrad.

Conrad

Tu pâlis?... ne crains rien de ces voiles funèbres....
Reconnais mois....

Lenor (le reconnaissant)

Conrad!!

Conrad

Je viens à ton secours
D'un costume abhorré les fidèles ténèbres
A l'amitié servent comme aux amours.
Ecoute: il n'est que trop facile de séduire
D'un jeune sang la généreuse ardeur;
Le tribunal secret à mes yeux a fait luire
L'image des bienfaits et j'ai vu sa fureur.
Naguère son arrêt m'a dévoué ta tête:

Lenor

Dieu!

Conrad

D'un fatal serment bénissons le hasard:
Avec bonheur j'acceptai leur poignard
Loin de ton sein dans mes mains il s'arrête.
Mais ce n'est pas assez de prévenir ce mal;
Il faut un autre gage à mon pieux parjure,

> Il faut sur Olmerik réparer ton injure,
> Il faut anéantir l'odieux Tribunal.

Lenor

> Quand il en sera temps, Conrad, ami fidèle,
> Tu n'accuseras pas mon bras découragé.
> Dans ces murs où tout me rappelle
> Je rentrerai vainqueur ou tomberai vengé
> Mais comment....

Conrad (l'interrompant)

> De ces monts, lassés de tant de crimes,
> Les peuples sont unis aux peuples des vallons.
> Je commande à leur ligue; et leurs voix unanimes
> Ont dit: sans plus tarder, allons!
> Des Francs-Juges pour mieux tromper la vigilance
> Leurs affidés ont pris l'habit des Bohêmiens:
> Soupçonneux ils ont dû s'enfuir de ta présence
> Quand tu leur rappelais leurs malheurs et les tiens.

Duo

musique faite

Lenor et Conrad ensemble (Andante)

> Noble amitié, ta voix, ta chérie
> M'entraîne et retentit dans mon âme attendrie;
> Quand j'accuse la vie et m'engage à mourir
> Tu m'ordonnes de vivre et m'apprends à souffrir.

Conrad seul avec enthousiasme (Allegro)

> Lenor! héros trop magnanime,
> Eh quoi! ne sais-tu pas que souffrir est un crime
> Quand la patrie en deuil appelle son vengeur?

Lenor

> Ombre de Venceslas, que ton courroux vainqueur
> Du haut des cieux vienne armer ma vaillance!

Ensemble

> Mon coeur palpite encore de gloire et d'espérance!
> Mon bras heureux et fier va combattre en ce jour
> Pour les cieux, la beauté, les vertus, et l'amour.

Conrad (à Lenor, après le signal convenu auquel on répond de la montagne)

> A ce signal connu bientôt ils vont paraître
> Et par ma voix instruits, te proclamer leur maître.

(Les paysans et les Bohémiens entrent de tous côtés.)

Amis du jour tant désiré,
Apprêtez-vous à saluer l'aurore!
Lenor est devant vous!... son père vénéré
Vous fit heureux; vous le serez encore.
Réchauffez votre ardeur au feu de ses regards;
Reconquérez une patrie....
Et que ces bras qui l'auront affranchie
Contre l'iniquité lui servent de remparts!

Choeur et Final

Le choeur

Eh bien! qu'il nous prouve sa race!
Au danger qu'il soit devant nous!
C'est le sang qui lave la trace
Marquée au sol par les genoux.
Levons notre antique bannière;
La gloire est mortelle aux tyrans;
A son ombre l'heure dernière
N'a plus de regards déchirants.
Oui, si nous succombons, notre voix étouffée
Redira: Liberté! c'est un beau cri de mort.
Allons! le monde entier prépare le trophée
Que nous promet un si beau sort.

(Les femmes entrent en scène.)

Des sommets de nos monts à la sombre vallée
Mille échos en grondant roulent le cri de: Mort!

Tous

Partons!... le monde entier prépare le trophée
Que nous promet un si beau sort.
Aux armes! le ciel résonne....
O Lenor guidez nos pas.
Peuples! guerriers! l'airain tonne,
    Nos fers ont soif de combats.

FIN

Notes

Introduction

[1]All three works appeared between 1900 and 1914. Certain significant conclusions were thus reached simultaneously but independently by each author; Macdonald remarks that "like all good Parisians, Malherbe, Tiersot and Boschot . . . preferred to work on their own and only come together when special circumstances demanded an *entente.*" ("A Berlioz Controversy and its Aftermath," in "Hector Berlioz 1969—A Centenary Assessment," [MacCent], *Adam* 331-33 [1969], 38). Of the three, Boschot was the most systematic scholar, while Tiersot was the best musician.

[2]The bibliography of this study includes an index to *Berlioziana.*

Chapter One

[1]See Elisabeth Lebeau, "Un Mécène de la musique: Charles Malherbe," in *Humanisme actif (Mélanges d'art et de littérature offerts à Julien Cain)* (Paris, 1968), pp. 91-99. In addition to Berlioziana, which Malherbe considered his specialty, the collection included autographs of Bach, Rameau, Mozart, Haydn, Beethoven (75 items), Schubert, Mendelssohn, Schumann, Weber, Wagner, and Bruckner.

[2]*"La seule institution musicale de France dont l'avenir puisse inspirer de la confiance à un compositeur.... Peut-être plus tard ces ouvrages auront-ils pour la Société des Concerts quelque valeur"* (letter of 25 March 1863, quoted in **TierB'ana** [1910], p. 107).

[3]Briefly described by Macdonald in "Hector Berlioz 1969; Zur 100. Wiederkehr seines Todestages am 8 März," *Musica* 23 (1969), 112-15; and **MacCent**, pp. 35-47.

[4]It was thought at the time that the entire collection had reached the Bibliothèque Nationale. In 1978, however, the author identified another two dozen boxes of manuscript parts still in the orchestra's library. These parts will eventually come to the Bibliothèque Nationale. It is now clear that the total collection consists of performance material for nearly every work Berlioz is known to have presented in concert.

[5]Inscribed: *"Partition autographe offerte à mon excellent ami, Georges Kastner. Vous me pardonnerez, mon cher Kastner, de vous donner un manuscrit pareil; ce sont ses campagnes d'Allemagne et de Russie qui l'ont ainsi couvert de blessures. Il est comme ces drapeaux 'qui reviennent des guerres, / Plus beaux' (dit Hugo) 'quand ils sont déchirés.' Paris, 17 septembre 1858, H. Berlioz."*

[6]Inscribed: *"Manuscrit autographe que je prie mon excellent ami A. Morel de garder en souvenir de moi. H. Berlioz."*

[7]Inscribed: *"A Monsieur Brown, Témoignage d'un vif* [sic] *et inaltérable amitié. H. Berlioz, ce 16 avril 1839."*

[8]Inscribed: *"Je vous envoie notre ouverture du Roi Lear qui est enfin publiée, avec le manuscrit que je vous prie de garder.... La dédicace d'un morceau de musique est un hommage banal qui n'a de prix que par le mérite de l'ouvrage, mais j'espère que vous accepterez celle-ci comme l'expression de la reconnaissante amitié que je vous ai vouée depuis longtemps. H. Berlioz, 12 février 1840."*

[9]Stasov approached Berlioz with a request for the gift of a manuscript when he was visiting Paris in 1862. Berlioz wrote on 10 September 1862: *"J'ai, par bonheur, trouvé un de mes manuscripts en bon état, que je suis heureux de pouvoir offrir à la Bibliothèque publique de Saint-Pétersbourg; c'est précisément celui du* Te Deum *dont vous m'avez parlé. Si vous voulez bien me faire l'honneur d'une seconde visite demain jeudi, je vous le remettrai."*

[10]Additionally, the *Symphonie fantastique* and the *Symphonie funèbre et triomphale* were given by Berlioz to the critic Joseph d'Ortigue (1802-66) and eventually acquired by Charles Malherbe. The *Symphonie funèbre* has the following inscription: *"Puisque tu veux savoir, mon cher d'Ortigue, ce qui est de mon écriture dans cette partition, va d'ici à la septième page. Je me suis reposé là. A toi."* On page 7, a copyist took over.

[11]Berlioz has written on the cover: *"Donné à Mr Ferrand Par Mr Berlioz,"* and, at the end, *"Copié pour étude en Avril 1824."*

[12]For a possible explanation of this error, see the remarks below concerning *La Mort d'Orphée*, Table I, no. 25.

[13]Adolphe Boschot; "Berlioz, Une cantate perdue pendant un siècle," *Chez les musiciens,* 2e série (Paris, 1924), p. 50.

[14]*Catalogue des livres anciens et modernes... de feu M. Martin* (Paris, 1885), p. 150, items 1879, 1880.

[15]See J. G. Prod'homme, "Etat alphabétique sommaire des Archives de l'Opéra," *Revue de musicologie* 17 (1933), 193-205.

[16]In 1977, the Chapot family donated a hitherto unknown pocket notepad to the museum; in it is found a list of manuscripts in the composer's library in late 1845. The list is transcribed in an appendix of my *Catalogue of the Works of Hector Berlioz.*

[17]See *Collection musicale André Meyer* (Abbeville, 1960; repr. c. 1974) [CatMeyer], N. B. planches 2-5.

[18]In 1977, the Bibliothèque municipale of Grenoble acquired a partially autograph album of guitar songs (F-G Rés R 10759; see Table I, no. 60B), and in 1978 the author discovered two pages of sketches for the *Te Deum* in a manuscript which will eventually come to the Bibliothèque Nationale.

[19]Adolphe Jullien's biography of the composer, *Hector Berlioz, sa vie et ses oeuvres* (Paris, 1888) [JullHB], includes a facsimile of the title page, p. 41.

[20]Most of Spoelberch de Lovenjoul's library was willed to the Institut de France, which now administers the Bibliothèque Lovenjoul in Chantilly. His musical library, however, was dispersed. I am grateful to the Bibliothèque Lovenjoul and the Institut de France for providing information relevant to the bequest.

[21]David Cairns has recently completed the first examination of Louis' letters to his father, to appear in a forthcoming major study of Berlioz and his music. Louis eventually came to admire his father and to return his deep affection.

[22]The copies of his unreleased *Mémoires* that blocked the door were still in his office after his death, however, and his cabinet still contained some autograph material (the operas and possibly the *Requiem*).

[23]BosHB III, 646-47.

[24]TierB'ana (1911), p. 252.

[25]See Jacques Barzun, "The Latest Berlioz Finds," *Columbia Library Columns* 17 (1968), 8-12.

[26]Cecil Hopkinson, "Two Important Berlioz Discoveries," *Fontes Artis Musicae* 15 (1968), 14-16, with facsimiles, and "Berlioz Discoveries, An Open Letter," *Fontes* 16 (1969), 28-29.

[27]The existing scribal copies of orchestral scores seem to have been made either for use by assisting conductors or for presentation.

[28]*"N'est-ce pas dommage qu'il y ait des corrections, des coupures, des feuilles rapportées? Il était si bien écrit! calligraphiquement parlant.* Les Troyens *sont mieux encore; c'est moulé* [as though printed in block letters]. *Je défie mon copiste de rien faire de pareil!"* (quoted by Tiersot, in **TierB'ana** [1904], p. 300).

[29]Citations of musical passages refer to the version published in the **OBE** (or, if specified, the **NBE**) and include in addition to measure numbers a reference to the appropriate page in the **OBE**. Upper case Roman numerals indicate volume number, while those in the lower case refer to pages in the critical matter. (e.g.: **OBE** I, xvi refers to page xvi in volume I; **OBE** pp. 60/8–61/2, to the passage from the eighth measure on page 60 through the second measure on page 61.) The Choudens edition cited in reference to *Benvenuto Cellini* refers to the full score (Paris, 1886); it has been reprinted by Kalmus and included in the series of reprints of the **OBE**.

[30]See also a letter from Berlioz to his father, 14 March 1843, from Brunswick: *"Le transport de ma musique me ruine, cela pèse 500 livres sans quoi mon voyage serait assez fructueux"* (**BerCG** 820).

[31]The new call numbers are given in Table I, below.

[32]Given in facsimile by Rushton, in **NBE** 5, 107.

[33]In the autograph book of H. Bachimont, now lost. The loose leaf is now preserved in Stockholm; see Table I, no. 73. A scribal copy was made (probably for Charles Malherbe) and is now in the Bibliothèque Nationale. The song is transcribed in Appendix I.

[34]For an album of 1847 that later belonged to Charles Malherbe.

[35]Goethe-Schiller Archiv, Weimar.

[36]Julien Tiersot, ed., *Les Années romantiques (1819-1842)* (Paris, 1904), *Le Musicien errant (1842-1852)* (Paris, 1919), and *Au milieu du chemin (1852-1855)* (Paris, 1930). A portion of the remaining volume was presented in "Letters de Berlioz sur les Troyens," *La Revue de Paris 1921*, no. iv, pp. 449-73, 749-70; and v, pp. 146-71.

[37] Volume I reviewed by Holoman, *Journal of the American Musicological Society* 26 (1973), 167-71; by François Lesure, *Revue de musicologie* 58 (1972), 274-76, and by Peter Bloom, *Notes* 30 (1973-74), 51-54.   Volume II reviewed by Ralph P. Locke, "New Letters of Berlioz," *19th–Century Music* I (1977-78), 71-84.

[38] The definitive loss of the autograph letters to Humbert Ferrand must be considered tragic.   The exchange of correspondence occured over a period of forty-four years, and in it Berlioz is at his most candid and philosophical.   It is practically certain that the published version of these letters, the familiar *Lettres intimes* (Paris, 1882) [BerLI] is full of inaccuracies and omissions of every sort.

[39] The correspondence shows, for example, that both Cherubini and Fétis were kinder to Berlioz than the *Mémoires* suggest.

[40] "*Il faut que je copie des parties,*" BerCG 128; "*A présent, je ne fais que copier des parties,*" BerCG 256.

[41] "*Pour les vers je ne me suis pas amusé à courir après la rime, j'ai fait de la prose cadencée et mesurée, quelquefois rimée, c'est tout ce qu'il faut pour la musique*" (BerCG 231).

[42] "*Jamais je ne serai un amant du laid, soyez tranquille.... Il y a loin des vers* parlés *aux vers* chantés.... *Songez que les trois quarts de Shakespeare sont en vers blancs.... Tout cela est tellement l'effet de l'habitude, que les* vers *latins rimés du Moyen Age paraissent une barbarie aux mêmes personnes qui sont choquées* des vers français non rimés.*"

[43] "*P. S.–Ne faites pas attention à la malpropreté de ma lettre, je ne puis écrire san raturer horriblement, vous n'avez pas d'idée de ce que sont les manuscrits de mes articles: c'est effrayant.*"

[44] Table I as revised in 1979 is extracted and abridged from my *Catalogue of the Works of Hector Berlioz,* volume 25 of the NBE.   For the original Table I a typewritten *Draft List of Works by Berlioz,* prepared (c. 1969) by Raymond Hyatt of the British Berlioz Society, was most helpful.   Neither the table nor the catalogue could have been completed without the apparatus of the New Berlioz Edition, graciously and repeatedly extended to me by Hugh Macdonald long before I was affiliated with the edition.

[45] fp = first performance, aut = autograph, let = letter, pub = publication, ded = deduced; the abbreviations indicate the grounds for stating that the work was completed by the date given.   Dates followed by none of these abbreviations are either self-evident (e.g. pieces for the *prix de Rome,* which were submitted for competitions in July of each year Berlioz entered) or conjectures based on little firm evidence.

[46] Under this rubric are listed all known autograph sources except albumleaves and letters containing insignificant musical notation.   If there are no autographs, reference is made to a contemporaneous description of the work.   Data concerning first publication are supplied where applicable.

[47] Facsmiles of no. 8-10 in *Berlioz and the Romantic Imagination,* the catalogue of an exhibition at the Victoria and Albert Museum ([London], 1969) [CatV&A], p. 12.

[48]Shortly after arriving in Paris, Berlioz discovered that the library of the Conservatoire was open to the public (**BerMém**, chap. V), and he proceeded to go there and copy Gluck's scores. An autograph copy of excerpts from *Iphigénie en Tauride* and *Iphigénie en Aulide* was found in Paris in the mid-1960s by Richard Macnutt, who acquired it for his collection. Berlioz has written at the beginning *"copié sur la partition au Conservatoire en 1822."* Thus the manuscript, if correctly dated (as is probable, to judge from certain characteristics of the calligraphy), is among the earliest autographs of Berlioz (120 pp., facsimile of one of the title pages in **CatV&A**, p. 2). A later autograph copy of excerpts from *Iphigénie en Tauride*, dated April 1824, is now in the Pierpont Morgan Library.

[49]Two other songs with guitar accompaniment have been misattributed to Berlioz. *La Confession de la Nina* and *La Sombra de la Noche* in Grenoble (F-G R 9031) are not autographs (cf. Paul Vaillant, "Berlioz à la bibliothèque de Grenoble," *Cahiers de l'Alpe* 46 (1969) (**CatVaill**), pp. 133-36.

[50]Two copies at **F-G** of Berlioz's *Grand Traité d'instrumentation* (Paris, 1843), presumably proofs, were copiously annotated by Berlioz (F-G Rés. Vh 1036 and Rés. Vh 1960). The changes in the musical examples are of no significance to the present study and have not been included in the table.

[51]Berlioz refers to this change in his letter to Liszt of 2 July 1852 (**BerMC**, p. 5): *"Je vais m'occuper ce soir de faire le récitatif du cardinal nécessité par la scène qui suivra maintenant le sextuor."*

[52]The lithography of the chorus parts was done in April 1853; see **BerMC**, pp. 69-70 (15 April 1853; to Gye). Individual parts were published for sopranos and contraltos, tenors, and basses.

[53]C-clefs of Type III (see p. 109, above) date this fragment as no earlier than about 1845. Most probably the page was removed from the ms. piano-vocal score used as the source of Choudens' publication of 1863. There is no evidence to support Hopkinson's contention that Hans von Bülow prepared the piano reduction: not only does Meyer's fragment show that Berlioz was directly involved with the project, but there are several references to a vocal score in the correspondence before July 1854, when von Bülow arranged the overture. Indeed, in the very letter in which Berlioz expresses delight at the unexpected receipt of von Bülow's arrangement, there is also reference to a separate piano score; see **BerMC**, pp. 221-23: 28 July 1854, to Liszt; see also **BerCI** LXVII, 28 July 1854, to Hans von Bülow.

Chapter Two

[1]*"Cette écriture est celle d'Hector Berlioz: elle n'a pas changé depuis que, sûrement avant d'avoir atteint sa dix-huitième année, peut-être encore plus tôt, il nota ces airs, jusqu'au jour où il écrivit la dernière note de Béatrice et Bénédict"* (**TierB'ana** [1904], pp. 11-12). Tiersot unknowingly underscores his point; the *Recueil de romances* in question may well be from several years later than he imagines.

[2]*"Son écriture fait peine à voir. Admirable écriture, jusqu'à ce moment, artiste et décorative, impérieuse, et qui n'avait pas changé durant cinquante ans. De son premier autographe (1819) à ceux de 1868, sa main garda la même fermeté, et elle traça sur le papier, sans la moindre défaillance la preuve spontanée, réflexe, d'une organisation*

physique et d'une âme prodigieusement résistantes, d'une individualité vraiment cuirassée d'airain.... On frémit, on pleure, devant ces autographes du début de 1868, où la main qui écrivit tant de chefs–d'oeuvre se met à vaciller comme celle d'un enfant" (BosHB III, 651-52).

[3]Concerning Estelle Fornier (1797-1876), *née* Duboeuf, see the *Mémoires* in general and David Cairns's remarks (BerMemCairns, p. 542) in particular.

[4]The print of *Lélio* with forged comments is one of several cases where annotations were added to publications from the composer's own library. Copies of symphonies by Beethoven and operas by Gluck have been mutilated in this same manner.

[5]BerMém Chap. VII: *"La copie ne me coûterait rien, ce travail serait fait gratuitement et avec soin par les enfants de choeur de Saint-Roch.... Mais, après quelques instants, il faut s'arrêter à cause des innombrables fautes de copie que chacun signale dans les parties. Ici on a oublié d'écrire les bémols et les dièses à la clef; là il manque dix pauses; plus loin on a omis trente mesures.... Cette leçon au moins ne fut pas perdue."*

[6]See no. 20B in Table I, above.

[7]Boschot found a receipt for the reimbursement of copying expenses: *"4 piastres 50, pour frais de copie du premier envoi; Rome, 15 avril 1831"* (BosHB II, 60, fn. 1). Boschot is wrong, however, to attribute the manuscript of the *Resurrexit* now in Paris to Berlioz; it is in a copyist's hand with an autograph title, clearly the one referred to in the receipt.

[8]Berlioz also mentions stationing a copyist, doubtlessly Rocquemont, in the concert hall for a full day before a concert in November 1840 in order to prevent sabotage (**BerMém**, Chap. LI).

[9]*Annuaire Musical 1845* (Paris, 1845). The *copistes de musique* listed on pp. 271-72 are: Larroux, rue Marie-Stuart, 10; Maillart, rue Poissonière, 27; Potron, rue St.-Antoine, 132; Thompson, rue Dauphine, 16; Vendier, rue du Faubourg St.-Martin, 199; and Wacquez, rue du Faubourg St.-Martin, 54. An *entreprise générale de copie* was located in the offices of the short-lived *Annuaire*. Similar annual directories of 1855 and 1863 did not list copyists of music.

[10]The author of the book lived and taught classes in Rouen, and even the Paris address given in his book has no relation to the address of Berlioz's copyist. The other Rocquemont was an eminent "professor of calligraphy" and a member of the Institute. The rubber stamp of the Parisian Rocquemont specifies that his business is the copying of music.

[11]*"C'est M. Rocquemont qui surveille tout ce qui a quelque rapport à ma bibliothèque musicale."*

[12]Rocquemont's role in the copying of *Esmeralda* is limited to a few pages (vol. IV, pp. 599-600, 605-06, and 677-716), on the last of which is found the famous *air des cloches* that Berlioz was accused of ghostwriting (see **BerMém**, Chap. XLVIII).

[13]Rocquemont has a tendency when copying parts to round the lower hook of his C-clefs: 𝕂

[14]Two ledgers are preserved from the period, titled *Comptabilité*, F-Pan AJ[37], box 15 (1829-37), and box 16 (1838-48). Listed as copyists, in addition to Leborne and

Fernière, are Messrs. Roy, Chalon, Calais, Tourte, Léger, Crosilhes-Calvez, Noyrigaz, Michu, Guerville, Conteilhes, Bottée de Toulmon (later to become a librarian at the Conservatoire), Pérot, Trapp, and Chaft. In the account books at the Opéra, in addition to Leborne and Rocquemont, are listed a copyist named Pacini and the firm of Bautain et Cie.

[15]An amusing application for a position as copyist at the Opéra is found in a box at the Archives Nationales, **F-Pan** AJ^{XIII}, box 178. The applicant is one of a family of copyists, Lefebvre; a copyist named Lefebvre was still at the Opéra when Boschot began research for his biography of Berlioz. The letter of application runs as follows:

"En 1774 mon père fut nommé à la place de bibliothécaire-copiste de l'Académie R^{le} de Musique aux appointemens de 1800 f. comme bibliothécaire et par réglements de Mr Berton père, alor directeur, la copie lui fut payée comme à son prédécesseur, 4 sols la page.

"En 1810 mon père obtint 300 f. d'augmentation d'appointment pour l'entretien d'un aide. Cette augmentation ne pouvant pas se payer avec ses appointemens, à cause du budget, il fut décidé qu'elle serait portée sur ses mémoires mensuels, delà l'article, service de la bibliothèque; les choses sont ainsi restées depuis.

"En 1814, je succédai à mon père aux même conditions, lesquelles existent depuis 62 ans.

"Lefebvre."

[16]Several pages of financial records for Berlioz's concerts show his struggle to make accounts balance. He lists for each concert its personnel as well as the expense of copying, printing, and heating and lighting the hall. He even includes a list of performers he can do without in case of financial disaster. See, for example, **F-Pn** papiers divers de Berlioz, no. 9 (plans for three concerts in November and December 1835) and nos. 11-12 (plans for the *Requiem*).

[17]A number of the parts prepared by Rocquemont and his staff were evidently used by the Société des Concerts and the Conservatoire until the **OBE** was published: the original manuscript parts for *Roméo et Juliette*, for example, were filed among Breitkopf's published ones. Some of the earliest published parts, corrected by Berlioz and Rocquemont, appear to have been used in the very recent past.

[18]Berlioz appends a sharp note to proof copies of the bass drum parts for the *Symphonie fantastique* and *Roméo et Juliette*, explaining to the engraver that there are too many measures on a page for it to be legible.

[19]Dantier's advertisement, in the *Bottin* of 1840 (p. 260), reads: *Dantier fils, succ. de Charnez, rue du Temple, 106; mag. de papiers d'écriture, d'enveloppes, fourn. de bureaux, régistres perfectionnels, papiers réglés pour musique et cartons pour musique militaire, fournisseur des principaux théâtres en France et de l'étranger, reliure et cartonnage de musique, fab. encre spéciale pour la copie de musique."*

[20]Parts for the *Requiem* and *Benvenuto Cellini* are still embossed by Charnez; Dantier's seal first appears on the paper used for the score of *Roméo et Juliette*. Mlle. Lard,

presumably a daughter of the proprietor of Lard-Esnault, engraved many of Berlioz's scores.

[21]The full chorus part for *Benvenuto Cellini* (**F-Po** matériel) is simply embossed *Lard, 25, rue Feydeau, Paris*; it was used by *"Mr J. Cohen, Répétiteur des choeurs."*

[22]See H. Voorn, *De papiermolens in de provincie Noord-Holland (de geschiedenis der Nederlandse papierindustrie I)* (Haarlem, 1960); English summary on pp. 527-65. The famous collections of watermarks by Heawood (*Watermarks, Mainly of the 17th and 18th Centuries*; Hilversum, 1950); Briquet (*Les Filigraines... vers 1282 jusqu'en 1600*; Leipzig, 1923), and Churchill (*Watermarks in Holland, England, France, etc., in the XVII and XVIII Centuries and their Interconnection;* Amsterdam, 1967) are not particularly helpful for nineteenth–century papers. The automation of paper mills and increasing international trade in the nineteenth–century makes precise identification of the date and provenance of a paper on the basis of its watermark almost impossible.

[23]Ledgers and applications for employment in the archives of both the Opéra and Conservatoire are on paper watermarked with the monogram and name of D. & C. Blauw.

[24]I.e., Berlioz's manuscript of some counterpoint lessons (**F-Preboul**), and a ledger in the archives of the Conservatoire. Churchill remarks of the bell "[in the sixteenth century] the bell watermark was a French guarantee of high quality, and was eventually adopted in Holland and England, possibly for the same purpose" (p. 56).

[25]In general, it will be recalled, the autograph of a work was presented to a friend shortly after the work had been published.

Chapter Three

[1]The autograph scores are not usually the best sources for the definitive musical text because the published editions often incorporate a stage of late revisions not entered in the manuscript.

[2]Lewis Lockwood, "The Autograph of the First Movement of Beethoven's Sonata for Violoncello and Pianoforte, Opus 69," *The Music Forum*, volume II (New York and London, 1970), p. 91.

[3]*"Ces pages... ne sont donc nullement un brouillon ou une esquisse. Elles ne montrent pas le premier ou le second* état *d'une pensée qui se cherche, se corrige, se précise peu à peu, et atteint, par des retouches, à la forme définitive. On ne peut donc pas y surprendre la genèse intime et secrète d'une oeuvre qui va naître. Ce manuscrit montre seulement l'oeuvre déjà née, complètement formée et même scrupuleusement corrigée durant huit ans, au cours des auditions successives.... Le manuscrit de la* Damnation *donne le dernier* état, *le résultat, de cet effort vers la perfection. Il est une* mise au net, *une* recopie, *qui servit au graveur: il diffère donc très peu du texte édité et définitif"* (Adolphe Boschot, *Le Faust de Berlioz: Etude sur la "Damnation de Faust" et sur l'âme romantique* [BosFaust45: Paris, 3rd edn., 1945], pp. 28-29).

[4]Several orchestral works (notably the *Symphonie fantastique* and the *Grande Ouverture des Francs-Juges*) were first published in reduction for piano. The outline refers to publication in full score of those works.

[5]Jacques Barzun (**BarHB** I, 228-29) reaches the "astonishing conclusion that by the time Berlioz returned to Paris in the fall of 1832 he had sketched or conceived or been drawn to the subject of every one of his major works."

[6]Concerning the *Elégie en prose*, for example, see below, p. 116.

[7]The parenthetical identification may have been added by the editors of the *Lettres intimes*; the autograph sources, it will be recalled, have been lost.

[8]See Nicholas Temperley, "The Symphonie Fantastique and its Program" *Musical Quarterly* 57 (1971), 593-608. As early as 3 June 1829 (**BerCG** 126; to Ferrand) Berlioz had begun to think in terms of an immense orchestral work, and the *symphonie descriptive* on Faust was certainly an earlier version of the same idea. Berlioz begins to talk of an *idée fixe* in a letter to Stéphen de La Madelaine (**BerCG** 153) of early February 1830.

[9]*"C'est à ce moment [1827-28] que M. Hector Berlioz m'entretint de son projet d'une symphonie dramatique de* Roméo et Juliette.... *—La fièvre de Shakspeare était dans l'air, et je n'y avais pas nui. —Je fus heureux de ce nouvel hommage à mon divin poète, et d'une collaboration avec un grand artiste. Nous concertâmes le plan de cette oeuvre musicale et poétique; les mélodies et les vers nous arrivaient en foule, et la symphonie parut... dix ans après"* (p. xiv).

[10]*"Cette femme, je l'épouserai et sur ce drame, j'écrirai ma plus vaste symphonie."*

[11]The title page carries a date of 1828, though the publication was advertised in *Le Figaro* of 30 November 1827 (see Julian Rushton in **NBE** 5, ix). In the *Mémoires* (Chap. XXVI), Berlioz remarks about *Faust*: "*Le merveilleux livre me fascina de prime abord; je ne le quittai plus; je lisais sans cesse, à table, au théâtre, dans les rues, partout. Cette traduction en prose* [i.e. Nerval's] *contenait quelques fragments versifiés, chansons, hymnes, etc. Je cédai à la tentation de les mettre en musique.*" To Goethe, in a letter of 10 April 1829 (**BerCG** 122), he implies a longer acquaintance with *Faust* than he probably had: "*Depuis quelques années, Faust étant devenu ma lecture habituelle,...* "

[12]To be sure, a letter of 6 February 1830 (**BerCG** 152; to Ferrand), suggests that its composition was less facile: "*Après quelque temps d'un calme troublé violemment par la composition de l'*Elégie *en* prose *qui termine mes Mélodies,...* "

[13]*"C'est la seule fois qu'il me soit arrivé de pouvoir peindre un sentiment pareil, en étant encore sous son influence active et immédiate."*

[14]"The Return of the Army of Italy / military symphony in two parts. / 1. Farewell, from the summit of the Alps, to the brave men fallen in the Italian fields / 2. Victors' triumphal entry into Paris. / The idea for the symphony in two parts came to me in Turin on the 25th of May, 1832, upon seeing the Alps again, my heart full of Napoleonic memories awakened by the countryside I had just traversed." The transcription is a conflation of those by Tiersot (**TierB'ana** [1906], p. 362) and Boschot (**BosHB** II, 92). Boschot's version spells *simphonie* with *i*, as Berlioz had spelled the word in the autograph of the *Symphonie fantastique*. Tiersot's transcription of the sentence that follows is probably correct; Boschot probably added the word *"cette"* (*"L'idée de cette Simphonie..."*) to improve the construction.

[15]Maurice Bourges, in the *Revue et Gazette musicale* (6 May 1855) reported that the *Te Deum* was related to this early plan: *"Ce n'était primitivement qu'un épisode intitulé* le Retour de la campagne d'Italie.*"* This information could only have come from Berlioz himself. (See **BosHB** III, 213-14).

[16]Complete transcription and translation below, p. 229.

[17]Macdonald (in **MacSelf**, p. 30, fn. 3) and Citron (in **BerCG** I, p. 544, fn. 3) cite a manuscript draft for one more effort to resuscitate the idea, this time with Auguste Barbier as poet: *"Un prophète, un impie, choeurs d'hommes religieux, choeurs d'impies, choeurs d'anges annonçant la venue du juge suprême, choeurs de morts sortant des tombeaux.... D'abord le prophète annonçant aux croyants que les prédications vont s'accomplir.... Prière grave des croyants, suppliant le juge suprême de ne pas les confondre avec les impies. Solo de l'impie, scène voluptueuse et orgique interrompue par l'appel des trompettes célestes et la voix des archanges éveillant les morts. Choeur universel final"* (advertised in *Catalogue Charavay* #697 [June, 1957], lot 26.325, item 2).

[18]See E. Littré, *Dictionnaire de la langue française* (Paris, 1878) II, 1617, second definition.

[19]Berlioz abandoned both *Les Francs-Juges* and *Le Dernier Jour du monde* because their libretti had been rejected at the Opéra. His 1853 letters to Liszt and the *Mémoires* (Chap. XLVIII) indicate further that he was never really satisfied with the *Cellini* libretto.

[20]Notably *Robin Hood* and *Les Noces d'or d'Obéron et Titania* by Ferrand (**BerCG** 93, **BosHB** I, 110), *La Mort d'Hercule* (**BerCG** 57), probably by Stéphen de La Madelaine, and *Les Brigands* by Thomas Gounet (**BerCG** 359, 368).

[21]There is, however, a considerable correspondence with Scribe concerning plans for *La Nonne sanglante* and a project for turning *La Damnation de Faust* into an opera called *Méphistophélès;* see **BerCG** 661, 1122, 1138, 1140, 1145, and 1151.

[22]Compaignon's manuscripts of two versions of *Richard en Palestine* are preserved with the composer's letters and are quoted extensively by Citron (**BerCG**, I, 113ff).

[23]E.g. *Les Champs*, for the journal *La Romance* (12 April 1834), and *Je crois en vous*, for the fashion magazine *Le Protée* (September 1834).

[24]A poem on Beethoven by Antony Deschamps (March 1840) is now in the Berlioz collection at Grenoble (F-G N 3223); it carries an autograph note by Berlioz: *"on voit que ces beaux vers ont été inspirés à M'. A. Deschamps par le testament de Beethoven que les journaux publièrent il y a quelques années. H. Berlioz."* An autograph copy by Hugo of his *Chanson de Fabiano* (F-Preboul) includes a remark by Berlioz in the margin: *"Chanson de Fabiano écrite de la main de V. Hugo qui m'avait prié d'en faire la musique. H. Berlioz;"* this was the *Romance de Marie Tudor* (no. 66 in Table I).

[25]The relevant correspondence is cited in Chapter IV, pp. 236-37.

[26]For the concert of 1 November 1829, Berlioz had added to the *Resurrexit* (which he was then calling the *Jugement dernier*) a recitative *"accompagné par quatre paires de timbales en harmonie"* (**BerCG** 140: Paris, 30 October 1829; to Ferrand).

[27]An early sketch in the 1832-36 sketchbook carries the opening words of the scene: *"Choeur: 'A boire!' Bernardino: 'Chantons.' Cellini: 'Soit, mais pour Dieu!'"* (cf. edn. Choudens, pp. 120-24).

[28]Berlioz nevertheless fails to mention a number of the larger borrowings, notably those in *Harold en Italie*, the *Requiem*, and the *Mélologue*. And while he was quite frank with Ferrand about the borrowing from *La Mort d'Orphée* in the *Mélologue* (BerCG 234), there is no indication that Ferrand ever knew that the *Marche au supplice* came from the opera for which he had supplied the text. Berlioz also suppressed from the *Mémoires* some remarks on peasant music in Italy that included a quotation later used in *Benvenuto Cellini* (q.v. p. 144); the remarks and quotation had originally appeared in *Italie pittoresque* (Paris, 1834-36).

[29]MacSelf. In addition to a comprehensive list of the borrrowings, the study includes a brilliant analysis of the relation between literature and music in Berlioz's works (pp. 39-44).

[30]MacSelf, p. 27

[31]BosFaust45, pp. 29-30 and BosHB III, 127. The *Faust* sketch belonged to Malherbe, who planned to describe it in a published article. When he died in 1911, the sketch was not found among his papers. It is possible that he had removed a collette from *Harold en Italie* (see pp. 145-49) to show Boschot and then replaced it in the score. Boschot himself owned the sketch for *Béatrice et Bénédict*, but according to his daughter Henriette Boschot, no musical documents of Berlioz were found among his papers after his death in 1955.

[32]The term "paste-overs" is more common in studies of other composers' manuscripts, but the term *"collette,"* first used in reference to a score of Berlioz in the 1890s, was adopted by the OBE (where it is seldom correctly translated into English) and has since been adopted by most authorities, including the editors of the NBE.

[33]The vocal score and one of the separate parts (for *"Mr. Klein"*) occur as collette-versos in the first movement of the *Symphonie fantastique*. The accompaniment is missing. See Table I, no. 64, above, and the transcription in Appendix I.

[34]Chapter 5 of Hugh Macdonald's doctoral dissertation, *A Critical Edition of Berlioz's Les Troyens* (Ph.D. dissertation, Cambridge, 1968 [MacCrit]) describes these sketches at some length. See also "Sketches" in the NBE publication of *Les Troyens*, NBE 2c, 775.

[35]The author is grateful to Jacques Barzun for making his photographs of the documents in Meyer's collection available. More detailed documentation of these sketches is found in Chapter 5 of Macdonald's dissertation. A facsimile of a sketch from Meyer's collection appears in NBE 2c, 784.

[36]Punctuation mine. The date is 1857; Berlioz refers to the composition of Act II, which was finished toward the end of June.

[37]"Of this [organization] nothing is found in the sketches, but only the complete vocal lines which give the deceptive appearance of having been superimposed on the accompaniment" (MacCrit, p. 156).

[38]MacCrit, p. 176.

[39]He did intend to write the opera at a more leisurely pace than for other works he had composed. Berlioz remarks in a letter to Liszt (12 April 1856): *"J'ai besoin de beaucoup de calme d'esprit, ce dont j'ai le moins précisément. Cela viendra peut-être. En attendant je rumine,* je me ramasse, *comme font les chats quand ils veulent faire un bond désespéré. Je tâche surtout de me résigner aux chagrins que cet ouvrage ne peut manquer de me causer.... Enfin que je réussisse ou non, je ne t'en parlerai plus maintenant que quand l'affaire sera finie. Et Dieu sait quand elle sera; je ne me suis pas imposé l'obligation de faire vite"* (quoted by Tiersot in "Lettres de Berlioz sur Les Troyens," *La Revue de Paris* 1921, iv [Juillet-Août], p. 452).

[40]The following terminology for page references involving collettes has been adopted: *c*=collete, *v*=verso, *o*=original. Thus a sketch found on p. 24*cv* will be on the back of the collette on p. 24. Occasionally the pagination has been affixed to both collette and original version, in which case the notation 24(*c*) will be used, indicating that p. 24 is itself a collette.

[41]By measure number of the passage in the finished version of the work. The measure numbers are those of the movement *in which the sketch is found,* unless noted.

[42]The physical location of the sketch in the autograph, by measure number (of the **OBE** version).

[43]For this purpose, separated into three categories: sketching for experimentation (exp.), for continuity (cont.), or for revision (rev.). The categories often overlap.

[44]Citation to facsimile or transcription in the present study. Citations beginning with a Roman numeral refer to facsimiles; those beginning with an Arabic numeral, to transcriptions.

[45]Tiersot implies that the sketchbook is mostly in ink by specifically noting a few passages in pencil; here he mentions both.

[46]This sketch, if correctly identified by Tiersot, must be for one of the revisions of the song, since it had already been composed when Berlioz began using the book.

[47]There are several layers to this sketch. Berlioz first sketched the motive in tenor clef, with remarks for orchestration visible though erased; the melody was not displaced by a quarter beat. He then erased the portion in pencil (and crumbs of the erasure are still in the score) before adding the displaced line for cello.

[48]OBE XI-XII, 360-70.

[49]*"Enfin, douze pages sont remplies d'ébauches pour* Benvenuto Cellini: *deux... sont au crayon* [the first two?], *les dix autres à l'encre"* (TierB'ana [1906], p. 352).

[50]OBE VIII; the passage was deleted before publication, but appears in the autograph score.

[51]Voice parts for the recitative: *"Tels sont d'abord, tels sont les tableaux et les scènes."*

[52]TierB'ana (1906), pp. 351-52, 361-62, 367-68, and 375-76.

[53]Berlioz kept an album of *Souvenirs—Bêtises—Improvisations, etc.* during his tour of Belgium and Germany (1842-43), but none of the entries are actually sketches (though several are original melodies). Notes in the album show that Berlioz's relationship with Marie was less innocent at that time than the *Mémoires* imply: *"Quand donc irons-nous ensemble voir danser les transtévérins à la Villa Borghèse?... Marie?... "* The album is now at the Musée Hector Berlioz.

[54]A leaf at F-G (N 3298) with the incipit of *"Songe qui l'enchante"* and dedicated to Nanci Pal, September 1848, is a forgery.

[55]Berlioz mentions hearing Beethoven's oratorio at a concert in Vienna on 11 November 1845 (**BerMém** *"Deuxième Voyage en Allemagne, première lettre"*), but it seems unlikely that he had the manuscript score with him at the time.

[56]The fragment may even not be autograph, but the handwriting has several characteristics similar to the composer's own.

[57]See also an article which appeared since the original version of this study: Julian Rushton, "The Genesis of Berlioz's *La Damnation de Faust,*" *Music and Letters* 56 (1975), 129-46.

[58]The opera underwent one major and several minor revisions between its first production in Paris (1838) and its publication in vocal score nearly twenty years later (Brunswick: Henry Litolff, [1856]). Pending a definitive study of the various versions (to appear in the NBE), it is often difficult to know exactly how items like the present two relate to the complex history of the work. In brief, that history is as follows: *Benvenuto Cellini* first existed in two acts of two tableaux each. The fourth tableau contained a sequence of brief scenes concerning, among other things, a duel to take place between Cellini and Fieramosca. Unsatisfied with the many strands of unrelated action in this section, Berlioz removed scenes x through xx of Act II for Liszt's production in Weimar (March and November 1852 and February 1856) and his own (in Italian) at Covent Garden in June 1853, ultimately recasting the opera in three acts.

[59]The nineteenth century saw striking technical developments in mechanisms for brass instruments, particularly the perfection of the rotary valve. Berlioz was well aware of these developments, and eventually replaced numerous parts for natural horns and trumpets with chromatic parts (see **BerMém**, *"Premier voyage en Allemagne, septième lettre,"* as well as the other letters from Germany, and on his use of saxhorns, the *"Post-scriptum"*).

[60]Its presence in the score of *Benvenuto Cellini*, where the collette surface forms one of the 1852-53 revisions, indicates that the sketch is actually part of a major revision made in the *Te Deum* at about that time. Berlioz had hoped to perform the *Te Deum* in London in 1851; he added the third choir for children after hearing a concert that year in St. Paul's Cathedral, where a choir of 6,500 children performed (cf. *Soirées de l'orchestre, 21ᵉ soirée*).

[61]See NBE 2c, 757 ("Instrumentation").

[62]Temperley's transcription, NBE 16, 217, lacks several details.

[63]A standard classification of autograph scores analyzes their calligraphy and purpose: a manuscript is either a composing score or a fair copy, and calligraphic or non-calligraphic, and the correct permutation of those variables will describe any manuscript. Such a scheme is not useful with Berlioz's manuscripts, since none are actually "composing scores" (in the sense implied in studies of Bach and Beethoven), and few are really non-calligraphic. Among Berlioz's autographs, the only poorly copied ones are the orchestration of Weber's *Invitation à la valse*, a copy of *La Tempête*, and movement II of the *Symphonie fantastique*.

[64]Or the line in which the draft is most clearly visible.

[65]The drafts in *Harold* are commonly found in a *cue-staff*, i.e. a running series of notes reminding the composer of what is to be filled in.

[66]Page 49*o* includes a pencil draft of the part for harp (L.H.) never covered in ink.

[67]From p. 143 to p. 460, all the original pages of the autograph include pencil drafts.

[68]Pages 459-60 include a pencil draft never covered in ink.

[69]Boschot does not mention musical documents in his inventory of material destroyed, but this may simply be because he did not consider these manuscripts critical to his task as a biographer.

[70]BerCG 152: Paris, 6 February 1830. A week earlier, he had told Nanci practically the same thing (BerCG 151: Paris, 30 January 1830): *"Depuis longtemps j'ai le squelette de mon ouvrage dans la tête, il faut beaucoup de patience pour en lier les parties et bien ordonner le tout."*

[71]See BerMém Chap. LIV. Determining dates of completion is relatively easy, for Berlioz was quick to announce having finished new pieces in letters to family and professional friends.

[72]See also Berlioz's well-known statement about his methods of work on the *Symphonie fantastique* (BerMém Chap. XXVI), where he remarks that changes were made in the work over the course of several years.

[73]The second example of these deletions in OBE (I, xxiv) is mistranscribed; disregard the first measure.

[74]"Forced by a desire that no danger can arrest, Romeo, masked, dares to go to the party to speak with Juliet. And that is how the two taste the fatal intoxication of the ball. Tybalt, Capulet's ardent nephew, prepares to strike the love-deceived Romeo when old Capulet, touched by Romeo's grace and youth, stops Tybalt and disarms him. Tybalt, angered, obeys, and leaves the party shivering with rage, his face darker than the night."

[75]"These are the tableaux and scenes that before you the orchestra – searching for new paths – will try to translate into sound. May your interest support our efforts."

[76]"These are the pictures and the first tableaux that the orchestra, for new accolades, will try to translate into sound. May your interest support our efforts."

[77] Date after Nicholas Temperley in **NBE** 16, x.

[78] A copy of this version of the program is bound with the autograph score of the *Symphonie fantastique* and another, under the call number **F-Pn** 8° B pièce 265 (item 1*bis*).

[79] The *religioso* coda of movt. I, evident in the autograph; the coda of the *Bal*, mentioned in **BerMém**, Chap. XXXIV; the coda of the *Scène aux champs*, according to a guess by Edward T. Cone, in his edition (New York, 1971 [**ConeFant**]), p. 26; and the "execution" sequence at the end of the *Marche au supplice*, evident in the autograph.

[80] I am grateful to the office of Léon Constantin for granting access to this manuscript.

[81] Berlioz mentions this change in a letter to Liszt of late April 1853 (**BerMC**, pp. 72-74), reminding the pianist to revise his copy of the score accordingly: *"J'allais oublier de te dire que, depuis que ton arrangement du* Roi Lear *a été fait, j'ai changé la coda de cette ouverture. Tu en as, je crois, la grande partition. Prends donc la peine de revoir cette fin."*

[82] *"Je comptais ne la faire qu'en deux parties; mais il m'en est venu une troisième, puis une quatrième"* (**BerCG** 384: 19 March 1834; to Ferrand).

[83] See **BosFaust45**; **TierB'ana** (1904), pp. 307-08; Tiersot, *La Damnation de Faust de Berlioz* (Paris, n.d. [1924]), and A. E. F. Dickinson, "The Revisions for 'the Damnation of Faust,'" *Monthly Musical Record* 89 (1959), 180-85.

[84] "Grand final chorus of M. Berlioz (Resurrexit, announcement of the Last Judgment, the singers standing)" . . . "Chorus of fear of the people on earth, with a constantly increasing expression of terror." . . . "Stripped of wings and scythe forever, Time stands still over the destroyed planets." . . . "Annihilation of the universe."

[85] "The voice of the chosen and the angels rises and is lost in the heavens."

[86] See A. Montaux, *"Berlioz: son génie, sa technique, son caractère, à propos d'un manuscrit autographe* d'Harold en Italie (Marche des pèlerins)," *Le Ménestrel*, vol. 56 (1890), 235-36, 243-44, 259-61, 269-70, 276-77, 284-85.

[87] David Cairns, in "Berlioz, the Cornet, and the *Symphonie fantastique*," suggests that the part was written for the cornetist J. J. B. Arban. See the *Berlioz Society Bulletin* 47 (July 1964), 2-6.

[88] This passage is one of the few in Berlioz's manuscripts that is reminiscent of a typical manuscript of Beethoven.

[89] There are two complete runs of Berlioz's publications in the Bibliothèque Nationale. One belonged to Berlioz himself. The other was Georges Kastner's; most of his volumes carry an autograph dedication from Berlioz. The composer considered issuing a collected edition of his works on several different occasions. At the front of his copy of *Harold en Italie* (**F-Pn** Rés Vm⁷ 521), he notes plans for the project: *"Je voudrais que mes oeuvres complètes fussent envoyées aux chapelles ou Sociétés philharmoniques de Brunswick, Hanôvre, Carlsruhe, Berlin, Vienne, Weimar, Munich, Bremen, Hambourg, Dresden, Leipzig, Amsterdam, Londres, St. Petersbourg."* And

above, as an afterthought: *"Griepenkerl possède déjà les partitions de Roi Lear, Waverley, La Fantastique."* A prospectus for a collected edition with a list of works and their opus numbers was seen by Tiersot in a print of *Tristia* at the Bibliothèque Nationale; that copy is currently missing (see **TierB'ana** [1905], pp. 331-32). On 26 June 1854, Berlioz wrote to August Morel of still another idea: *"Je rêve une édition allemande soignée chez Kistner de Leipzig, de l'ensemble de mes ouvrages"* (**BerMC**, p. 214; cf. Malherbe's altered transcription, **OBE** I, ix).

[90]*Symphonie fantastique* (**F–Pc** Rés F 1029, **F–Pn** Rés Vm^7 528), *Huit Scènes de Faust* (**F–Pn** Rés Vm^2 172), *Harold en Italie* (**F–Pn** Rés Vm^7 521), the piano-vocal score of *Benvenuto Cellini* (**F–Po** Rés A 521c), and *Roméo et Juliette* (**F–Pn** Rés Vm^7 522). The prints of the overtures (**F–Pn** Rés Vm^7 523-27) are presumably also proofs.

[91]See **HopBib**, p. 74, no. 36A and Edward T. Cone's edition of the *Symphonie fantastique*, p. 197. The "advance edition" is copiously stamped *"Abonnement à la lecture musicale de Brandus et Cie, 97 rue Richelieu,"* a fact not mentioned by Hopkinson.

Chapter Four

[1]Berlioz tacitly approves of the term in his *Mémoires*; see, at the end of the volume, his *post-sciptum*, titled *"Lettre addressée avec le manuscrit de mes mémoires à M. *** qui me demandait des notes pour écrire ma biographie."* It is in reference to an anecdote in this letter that Edward T. Cone titled his study of Berlioz's music: "Inside the Saint's Head; the Music of Berlioz," *Musical Newsletter* 1 (1971), 3-12, 16-20; and 2 (1972), 19-22.

[2]The autographs of *Les Francs-Juges, La Nonne sanglante*, and *L'Enfance du Christ* (as well as Gluck's autograph of *Armide*) were bequeathed to the Bibliothèque Nationale by Fanny Pelletan (1830-76). Inspired by a remark of Berlioz in *Les Grotesques de la musique* ("No one in Europe dares undertake a scholarly edition of Gluck"), she began to collaborate with his executor and intimate friend Berthold Damcke (1812-75) to produce the lavish edition published by Richault between 1873 and 1889. Berlioz had willed Damcke all the miscellaneous music in his cabinet at the Conservatoire; thus it is practically certain that Fanny Pelletan in turn inherited the Berlioz autographs from Damcke.

[3]Michel Brenet (pseud. for Marie Bobillier) first described the autograph fragments in "Berlioz inédit; *Les Francs-Juges, La Nonne sanglante,"* *Le Guide musical* vol. 42, no. 4 (26 January 1896), 63-67, concerning *Les Francs-Juges*; no. 5 (2 February 1896), 83-85, concerning *La Nonne sanglante*. Tiersot develops Brenet's observations and describes the manuscript libretto as well; see **TierB'ana** (1906), pp. 199-200, 207-08, 215-16, 240-42, 246-48.

[4]**BosHB** I, 236.

[5]Even though the opera was written in 1826, the statement in the *Mémoires* is erroneous; the *Scène héroïque* was finished before Berlioz began *Les Francs-Juges*.

[6]**BerCG** 25, 33, 51, 61, 63, 111, 127, 129, 165, 174, and 179, mentioning only the letters through 1830.

[7]BerCG 55-60, 62, 64, 65, 67, 70, and 72. See also the letters to Ferrand from the period: BerCG 93, 94, 138, 140, 142, 149, 173, 182, and 189.

[8]Barzun (BarHB I, 68) says that the libretto was drawn from a booklet by François Loève-Veimars, *Précis de l'histoire des tribunaux secrets dans le nord d'Allemagne* (Paris, 1824). But this treatise cannot be "the source" of Ferrand's story; there are simply not enough details that correspond to the situation depicted in the opera. Nor could such a dry, tedious tome have much interested the young Romantic. Lamartelière's play, on the other hand, is obviously the source on which the libretto was directly based. The scene in Berlioz's Act III in which the tribunal is finally convened follows a similar passage in the play. Lamartelière has left at that point a note saying that his description, in turn, faithfully matches that of J.-N.-E., baron de Bock in his *Histoire du tribunal secret* (Metz, 1801). Berlioz and Ferrand knew the play from its revival at the Ambigu-Comique in 1823 (see BosHB I, 242) and its subsequent edition in a series called *Chefs-d'oeuvre du répertoire des mélodrames* (Paris, 1824: vol. 16). The play was first performed, incidentally, with music by the house conductor at the Ambigu-Comique, Adrien Quaisain (1766-1825).

[9]In a letter of 15 July 1828 (if Citron's date is correct; BerCG 95), Berlioz thanks Ferrand for two acts of an unspecified opera, probably *Robin-Hood.*

[10]Chapter XI was first published in *Le Monde illustré* of 4 December 1858 (p. 363), so it is possible that there are even borrowings from *Les Francs-Juges* in *Les Troyens* (1859). See also BerLI LXXII (Paris, 19 November 1858): "You will soon see the story of *Les Francs-Juges* in *Le Monde illustré*; I couldn't forget that."

[11]Actually, the inscription reads (fol. 41^r): "*A consulter et non à brûler après ma mort,*" with the "*et non*" crossed out. It must have originally read "*A consulter et non à brûler,*" with "*après ma mort*" added when he crossed out "*et non.*"

[12]Brenet attributes the name change to the fact that Rossini had introduced a character named Arnold in *Guillaume Tell* (first performance 3 August 1829). She may be right, but Berlioz would have had to know the opera well before August, since he refers to Lenor in a letter of June 1829 (BerCG 126).

[13]Citron, in BerCG I, 246, fn. 1, remarks that in the present state of the score, the Bohemians' scene is at the beginning of Act II. His interpretation is incorrect; the Bohemians' scene is indeed sc. viii of Act I (p. 446 in the transcription below, Appendix II), inc. "*Mêlons à la voix des trompettes.*" The scene at the beginning of Act II was called the "*choeur des bergers*" by Berlioz, inc. "*L'ombre descend dans la vallée*" (p. 306), though the metric structure of the two passages of poetry is similar.

[14]Berlioz may have intended to perform both overtures in December 1827. They were first performed at the concert of 26 May 1828, and again on 1 November 1829.

[15]MacCent, pp. 38-43. Macdonald traces the "Berlioz Controversy and its Aftermath" and reviews the evidence of the autograph score, though failing to note the difference in date of the two principal sources, the score and the libretto.

[16]The Breisgau flows through the Black Forest; thus the intermezzo takes place in the same region as *Les Francs-Juges.*

[17]See BerCG 356, 359, 371, 374, and 375. In the letter to Gounet of 28 December 1833, (BerCG 371), Berlioz asks him to provide the solder between the two pieces at the end.

[18]Note also the virtually direct quotation in the next section (edn. Choudens, pp. 278-306) of a passage from the *Resurrexit* (mm. 106-421, **OBE** VII, 20-48). The borrowing is apt, as it is music for monks.

[19]Boschot guessed that the *Elégie* from *Les Francs-Juges* became the *Elégie en prose* (BosHB I, p. 372, fn. 2), probably because of the similarity in titles.

[20]Metric analysis of texts is not likely to reveal borrowings, since Berlioz found it relatively easy to work words into a pre-existing musical context. Note, for example, how easily he replaced *"Et iterum venturus est"* with *"Tuba mirum spargens sonum,"* or the rest of the *Resurrexit* text with sections from the libretto of *Benvenuto Cellini*.

[21]"Strike them both with neither pity nor mercy; it's God's will." . . . "Invisible avengers, ordained by heaven, whose fatal arm is dreaded by criminals, strike your victim and close your hearts to pity."

[22]See BerCG 26, 33, 36, 40, 41, 47, 48, 50, 61, 77, 91, 93, 94, 140, and 141.

[23]BerCG 490 (Paris, 8 March 1837, to his father); BerCG 492 (Paris, 24 March 1837, to Cherubini); BerCG 493 (Paris, 11 April 1837, to Ferrand); BerCG 495 (Paris, 17 April 1837, to Adèle); BerCG 496 (Paris, 17 April 1837, to Edouard Rocher); BerCG 498 (Paris, 22 May 1837, to Liszt); BerCG 502 (Paris, 18 July 1837, to Bottée de Toulmon); BerCG 503 (Paris, [c. 20 July 1837], to Pierre Dietsch); BerCG 504 (Paris, 20 July 1837, to Liszt); BerCG 505 (Paris, 27 July 1837, to Auguste Brizeux); BerCG 506 (Paris, 29 July 1837, to his father); BerCG 507 (Paris, [c. 2 August 1837], to Rocher); BerCG 511 (Paris, 12 October 1837, to his mother); BerCG 512 (Paris, 21 October 1837, to the Director of Public Monuments); BerCG 513 (Paris, [30 October 1837], to Alexandre Dumas); BerCG 514 (Paris, 30 October 1837, to the Minister of War); BerCG 515 (Paris, 30 October 1837, to Jean Vatout); BerCG 517 (Paris, 14 November 1837, to his mother); BerCG 523 (Paris, 7 December [1837], to his father); BerCG 524 (Paris, 8 December 1837, to Jules Janin); BerCG 527 (Paris, 12 December 1837, to the Minister of War); BerCG 528 (Paris, 17 December 1837, to Ferrand); BerCG 529 (Paris, 17 December [1837], to his mother); BerCG 530 (Paris, 19 December 1837, to Bottée de Toulmon); BerCG 535 (Paris, 18 January 1838, to his mother); BerCG 538 (Paris, 8 February 1838, to Liszt); BerCG 540 (Paris, 14 February [1838], to George Sand); BerCG 544 (Paris, 17 March 1838, to Queen Victoria), BerCG 548 (Paris, 19 March 1838, to Rocher).

[24]Berlioz offered Ferrand a copy of the revised version in January 1867, remarking that it was in the press (BerLI CXXXII: Paris: 11 January 1867).

[25]Includes a printed translation of the text into French (Paris: Vinchon) with the unrevised text *"Et iterum venturus est."* There is one correction in the composer's autograph. The published score has at the top a handwritten note: *"Edition publiée en 1884."*

[26]Among the longer, numbered excerpts, Berlioz includes the end of the *Hostias* (no. 46, present mm. 33-47) to show the chords of flutes and trombones, and the beginning of

the *Tuba mirum* (no. 59, present mm. 139-78, with the words *"et iterum venturus est,"* etc., at mm. 163ff). As a minor example of part-writing for voices, he cites on p. 233 measures 9-14 of the *Lacrymosa* (see below, pp. 254-55).

[27]F-Pc D 936 is a copy of Schlesinger's edition altered by a copyist to conform to the revised second edition published by Ricordi. D 937 and L 11038 have undergone similar scribal revisions. The copy in which Berlioz entered his own corrections is lost, although all these copies may well have belonged to him. D 936 begins with an autograph note in ink (p. 1): *"Exemplaire non corrigé et non conforme à la 2ème Edition et aux parties sépareés,"* but the copyist has blotted out the two *"non"'s.*

[28]In m.99 of the *Dies irae* (OBE p. 16/9), OBE has replaced a *p* marking in violins and violas with an *mf,* which matches the dynamic of the contrabass part as well as a general marking in an earlier passage (m. 64; OBE p. 14/11; B♭'s have been restored in violins I at the end of the same movement (mm. 250-51; OBE p. 35/11-12) because Berlioz never noticed the misprint; and a note has been altered in the cornet part of the first orchestra in m. 169 of the *Lacrymosa* (OBE p. 76/6-7), since the note in Schlesinger's edition is obviously an inadvertent error.

[29]The same study of the Latin text preceded Berlioz's composition of his *Messe solennelle*; see his letter to Lesueur of July 1824 (BerCG 26).

[30]"My brain," he recalls in the *Mémoires* (Chap. XLVI), "felt as though it would explode with the pressure of ideas" (BerMémCairns).

[31]He admits the deliberate ruse, finally, in a letter to Carolyne Sayn-Wittgenstein of 16 December 1854 (BerCSW III).

[32]The reuse in *Benvenuto Cellini* of the remainder of the *Resurrexit* is similarly direct; see fn. 18. Possibly the two sections were being composed at the same time.

[33]Malherbe refers to the underlying pencil draft in passing; see OBE VII, xv.

[34]Although only the margins were left in the score, it seems likely that the pages were actually covered with musical notation, since traces of the bracket around the chorus parts can be detected. But Berlioz must have removed these pages immediately upon drafting them, or else aut. p. 35 would probably have begun with a leftover bit of the deleted section.

[35]The parts at F-Pc were placed there in February 1852 to fulfill the governmental deposition requirement. They were advertised in the *Bibliographie de la France* on 3 April 1852.

[36]See Berlioz's letter to Rocquemont outlining the necessary preparations; transcribed above, pp. 91-93. The performance was in memory of several hundred soldiers drowned during a military review at Angers when a bridge collapsed; the regiment had failed to break step. Berlioz's newly-founded Société Philharmonique came close to collapse as well; the directors could not agree whether Berlioz's *Requiem* or a Mass by the choral conductor, Pierre Dietsch, would be played *in memoriam.* The society was governed by a democratic process resembling mob rule: though the orchestra favored the *Requiem,* the chorus sided with its conductor in favor of his Mass: *"La musique de Berlioz fatigue les artistes de chant."* (See BosHB III, 237-45; his account is based

on manuscript minutes of the Society's meetings, **F-Preboul.**) Berlioz eventually won the contest, but the Société Philharmonique folded shortly thereafter.

[37]Berlioz remarks to Ricordi that the score is among the most beautifully done of any of his works (" [*Le travail du graveur*] *est admirable et aucun de mes ouvrages n'a encore été aussi bien édité"*), but the engraver had copied Schlesinger's format in practically every detail. (Facsimile of the letter in a collection published by Ricordi, *Internationale Musik- und Theater-Ausstellung, Wien, 1892*, I, 119-21.)

[38]The title *Offertoire* was changed to *Offertorium* by **OBE**.

[39]The scribe neglected to correct this measure in one of the corrected copies, **F-Pc D 936**, p. 32.

[40]Mostly changes in the size of the chorus and orchestra (e.g., p. 1, p. 48) and instructions to the performers (e.g., p. 55; *"Avec le talon de l'archet"*).

[41]One copy of Schlesinger's edition (**F-Pc D 936**) and two of Ricordi's first (**F-Pc D 937** and **F-Pc L 11038**) have been revised to agree with the definitive version.

[42]Malherbe is incorrect; the collettes are not in Berlioz's hand.

[43]One exception is the arrangement of mm. 1-45 of the *Sanctus* for tenor and soprano soloists, for which an autograph vocal part remains (**F-Pmeyer**). The manuscript was prepared for a concert at which Marie Recio and Gustave Roger were featured soloists, 6 April 1844.

[44]This quotation was included on the title page of a piano-vocal score issued by Brandus in 1882, the same year the letter was first published; see **HopBib** 20, p. 40.

[45]See *Le Ménestrel* (1906): *"Sur la Marche au Supplice"* (Tiersot, p. 153): *"La 'Marche au supplice' vient des 'Francs-Juges'"* (Boshot, pp. 160-61); *"La 'Marche au Supplice' ne vient pas des 'Francs-Juges'"* (Tiersot, pp. 169-70); *"Francs-Juges et Symphonie fantastique"* (Tiersot, pp. 240-42); *"La 'Marche au Supplice' continue à venir des 'Francs-Juges'"* (Boschot, p. 264); and letters from Tiersot (p. 264), Malherbe (pp. 271-72), Tiersot (pp. 279-80), and Malherbe again (p. 288). See also Boschot's notes in **BosHB** II, 639-41, and Michel Brenet in the *Mercure musicale* of 15 February 1906, who writes *"La Marche des gardes, des* Francs-Juges, *est devenue la Marche au supplice."* Tiersot's mistake was simple. He had seen the autograph, then owned by Malherbe, only briefly and had noted that both the fourth movement and much of the first are on 20-staff paper (see **TierB'ana** [1906], pp. 240-42). Erroneously assuming from his notes that the two papers were the same, he could not believe that the March had come from the score of *Les Francs-Juges*, which it does not resemble at all. Possibly the pasted-over title page had not been removed by the time Tiersot examined the manuscript; somewhat more likely is that Malherbe purposely withheld the crucial page. Neither Boschot nor Tiersot ever constructed the correct solution, that the *Marche des gardes* had only recently been written when Berlioz decided to use it in the *Symphonie fantastique*.

[46]Two different translations of Hoffmann's stories appeared in 1829, one by Loève-Veimars, the other by Toussend and Richard.

[47]Temperley transcribes the passages from Chateaubriand, Hugo, and De Quincey; see NBE 16, 191-93.

[48]"It's all as I thought it would be; only the *Marche au supplice* is a hundred times more terrifying than I was expecting" (**BerCG** 163: 28 May 1830; to his father).

[49]The last two movements were left generally unchanged.

[50]See **NBE**'s description of the autograph score, p. 171.

[51]See facsimiles in Chapter II.

[52]Readers referring to Cone's edition must subtract 2 from all measure numbers cited for the first movement after m. 168, since he allotted a measure number to each bar in both endings. (To find the page number in **OBE** from which Cone's edition was prepared, subtract 46).

[53]Cf. the different version of the text given by Berlioz in his *Mémoires*, Chap. XXXIV. He supposedly left the note because he intended to commit suicide (April 1831) and hoped that the revised version would be played in his memory. Note that the original copy of the score was still intact at the time.

[54]What seems to have happened is that he ran out of paper while copying the first movement, after having copied the second and fifth movements and possibly the third on 24-staff paper. Before about 1833, Berlioz did not regularly buy the same paper from one establishment (and therefore from the same manufacturer, D. and C. Blauw). If he had revised and recopied the first movement in late 1830, it would probably have been on the paper used for the score of *La Tempête*, manufactured by Laligant.

[55]Page 22*c*, covers *X*'s on p. 22*o*.

[56]Watermarks are not apparent on every page.

[57]Berlioz specifically noted, it will be recalled, that the parts for movt. II were to be completely recopied.

[58]On p. 32 appears the figure *50* preceded by a pencilled *3*. Temperley believed that it was the original measure 250, and figured that 93 bars originally went between mm. 185 and 234, i.e., in the present numeration Berlioz was using, the passage began at m. 121, plus 93 bars equals 214, plus the 36 bars to the figure, comes to "2"50. Actually the number probably is intended to be 350. Only one folio can be missing between the figure and the measure clearly marked 375 (aut. p. 35*o*), i.e., a short passage was actually added there. Thus there were 193 bars originally between mm. 185 and 234 (121 + 193 + 36 = 350). Of these bars, 21 are in the manuscript, so 170 are missing at the first cut and roughly 20 at the second.

[59]The pages of abandoned draft show why Berlioz's hand-drawn barlines always break just above the first violin staff: he generally drafted the strings parts before going back to add the winds. Moreover, he usually drafted the outer lines first before going back to add viola and second violin. (See also the abandoned page of draft in the fifth movement, p. 63*o*, transcribed **NBE**, p. 217).

[60]Temperley creates certain problems of identification by identifying only "sketches which clearly relate to part of the symphony, but which never formed part of the complex score" (p. 210). He has thus omitted several sketches and included some items best considered drafts.

[61]The figure "475" appears two measures before the cut; "525," seven measures afterwards.

[62]Neither Berlioz's autograph draft of the program, nor the versions published in 1830 (e. g. *Revue musicale*, 10 [27 November 1830], pp. 90-92) mention the phrase *"ses consolations religieuses."*

[63]See my "Reconstructing a Berlioz Sketch," *Journal of the American Musicological Society* 28 (1975), 125-30.

Bibliography

Manuscript sources

See Tables I and III.

Modern Editions of Berlioz's Music

Berlioz, Hector. *La Mort d'Orphée. Monologue et bacchanale à grands choeurs et à grand orchestre.* Facsimile. Paris, 1930.

ConeFant   Cone, Edward T., editor. *Hector Berlioz Fantastic Symphony. An Authoritative Score, Historical Background, Analysis, Views and Comments. A Norton Critical Score.* New York, 1971.

NBE   *Hector Berlioz New Edition of the Complete Works,* issued by the Berlioz Centenary Committee, London, in association with the Calouste Gulbenkian Foundation, Lisbon. Hugh Macdonald, General Editor. 25 volumes planned (some in multiple fascicles). Kassel, Paris, London, etc., 1967–.

Volumes published:

     2. *Les Troyens.* Ed. Hugh Macdonald. 3 fascicles (Vols. 2a–c). 1969-70.

     5. *Huit Scènes de Faust.* Ed. Julian Rushton. 1970.

     10. *Te Deum.* Ed. Denis McCaldin. 1973.

     13. *Songs for Solo Voice and Orchestra.* Ed. Ian Kemp. 1975.

     16. *Symphonie Fantastique.* Ed. Nicholas Temperley. 1972.

     19. *Grande Symphonie Funèbre et Triomphale.* Ed. Hugh Macdonald. 1967.

OBE   *Hector Berlioz Werke.* Ed. Charles Malherbe and Felix Weingartner. 20 vols. Leipzig, 1900-07. For numeration by series and number, see I, xvi–xix; for a list of works by Berlioz, see I, xx-xxii. Series VIII (operas) and X (unfinished works) incomplete. Volumes published:

     I. [Symphonies I] *Symphonie fantastique* (xxiii-xlv, 1-150), *Symphonie funèbre et triomphale* (xlvi-xlviii, 151-226). 1900.

     II. [Symphonies II] *Harold en Italie.* 1900.

     III. [Symphonies III] *Roméo et Juliette.* 1901.

     IV. [Overtures I] *Waverley* (v-ix, 1-38), *Les Francs-Juges* (ix, 39-86), *Le Roi Lear* (x, 87-142), *Rob-Roy* (x-xi, 143-210). 1900.

     V. [Overtures II] *Benvenuto Cellini* (v-x, 1-44), *Le Carnaval romain* (xi, 45-88), *La Fuite en Egypte* (xi-xii, 89-96), *Le Corsaire* (xii-xviii, 97-136), *Béatrice et Bénédict* (xviii-xix, 137-74), *Les Troyens à Carthage* (xix, 175-86). 1901.

VI.   [Smaller works] *Fugue à deux choeurs et à deux contre-sujets* (v, 1-9)
       [misattributed], *Fugue à trois sujets* (v, 10-12), *Rêverie et Caprice* (v-
       vi; with orchestra: 13-26, with piano: 27-32), *Sérénade agreste à la
       Madone* (vi-vii, 33-35), *Hymne pour l'Elévation* (vii-vii, 36-38),
       Toccata (viii, 39-40), *Marche pour la dernière scène d'Hamlet* (ix-x,
       41-56), *Marche troyenne* (x-xi, 57-88).   1902.

VII.   [Religious music I] *Resurrexit* (v-vi, 1-48), *Coro dei Maggi* (vii, 49-
       64), *Grande Messe des morts* (viii-xx, 65-186), *Veni Creator* (xxi, 187-
       90), *Tantum ergo* (xxi-xxii, 191-94).   1902.

VIII. [Religious music II] *Te Deum.* 1901.

IX.   [Religious music III] *L'Enfance du Christ.* 1901.

X.   [Secular vocal music I] *Scène héroïque (La Révolution grecque)* (iii-
       v, 1-106), *Huit Scènes de Faust* (v-vi, 107-214).   1903.

XI-XII.   [Secular vocal music II] *La Damnation de Faust.* 1901.

XIII. [Secular vocal music III] *Lélio, ou le Retour à la vie* (v-xxxiv, 1-
       149), *Le Cinq Mai* (xxxv, 150-75), *L'Impériale* (xxxv-xli, 176-214).
       1903.

XIV.   [Songs with orchestral accompaniment I] *Méditation religieuse* (iii, 1-
       6), *Chant sacré* (iv-vi, 7-16), *Hélène* (vi, 17-22), *Chant des Chemins
       de fer* (vi-vii, 23-74), *La Mort d'Ophélie* (vii, 75-88), *Sara la
       baigneuse* (vii, 89-126), *Hymne à la France* (vii-viii, 127-48), *La
       Menace des Francs* (viii-ix. 149-62).   1903.

XV.   [Songs with orchestral accompaniment II] *Herminie* (v-vi, 1-60),
       Cléopâtre (vi, 61-104), *La Belle Voyageuse* (vi-vii, 105-12), *Le Jeune
       Pâtre breton* (vii, 113-20), *Absence* (vii, 121-25), *La Captive* (viii-ix,
       126-39), *Zaïde* (ix, 140-59), *Le Chasseur danois* (ix, 160-67), *Villanelle*
       (x, 168-74), *Le Spectre de la rose* (x, 175-83), *Sur les Lagunes* (x,
       184-93), *Au Cimetière* (x, 194-202), *L'Ile inconnue* (x, 203-14). 1903.

XVI.   [Songs with piano accompaniment I: A. For chorus] *Le Ballet des
       ombres* (vii, 1-18), [Critical remarks concerning *Irlande* (vii-viii)],
       Chant guerrier (viii-ix, 19-26), *Chanson à boire* (ix-x, 27-34), *Chant
       sacré* (xi, Version I [1829]: 35-40; Version II [1844]: 41-46), *La
       Mort d'Ophélie* (xi: 47-58), *L'Apothéose* (xi-xii, 59-72), *Le Chant des
       Bretons* (xii-xiii, Version I [1850]: 73-78: Version II [1858]: 79-84);
       La Menace des Francs (xiii, 85-100), *Prière du matin* (xiii, 101-06);
       Hymne pour la consécration du nouveau Tabernacle (xiii-xiv, 107-18);
       Le Temple universel (xiv, Version I [1860]: 119-40, Version II [1868]:
       141-55); [B. For two and three voices] *Amitié, reprends ton empire*
       (xiv, 156-61), *Le Montagnard exilé* (xiv-xv, 162-79), *Canon libre à
       la quinte* (xv, 180-85), *Pleure, pauvre Colette* (xv, 186-93), *Héleǹe*
       (xvi, 194-99), *Sara la baigneuse* (xvi-xvii, 200-14), *Le Trébuchet* (xvii-
       xviii, 215-22).   1904.

XVII. [Songs with piano accompaniment II: C. For a single voice] *Le
       Dépit de la bergère* (v, 2-5), *Toi qui l'aimas, verse des pleurs* (v, 6-11),
       Le Maure jaloux (vi, 12-17), *La Belle Voyageuse* (vi, 18-23), *Le
       Coucher du soleil* (vii, 24-27), *L'Origine de la harpe* (viii, 28-33),

Adieu, Bessy (viii, Version I [in A$\flat$]: 34-39; Version II [in G]: 40-45), *Elégie* [*en prose*] (viii-x, 46-55), *Le Pêcheur* (xi, 56-65), *Chant de bonheur* (xi, 66-69), *Premiers transports* (xi, 70-78), *La Captive* (xi-xii, Version I [1832, contralto and piano]: 79-84; Version II [1832–not 1834–, contralto, piano, and cello]: 85-92; Version III [reduction for piano of orchestral acc., by Malherbe]: 93-100), *Le Jeune Pâtre breton* (xii-xiv, 101-06), *Les Champs* (xiv, Version I [pub. 1834]: 107-14; Version II [pub. 1850]: 115-22), *Je crois en vous* (xiv, 123-30), *Villanelle* (xiv-xv, 131-36), *Le Spectre de la rose* (xv-xvi, Version I [c. 1839–not 1834–, no introduction]: 137-42; Version II [1841, introduction of eight measures]: 143-48), *Sur les lagunes* (xvi, 149-56), *Absence* (xvi, 157-60), *Au Cimetière* (xvii-xviii, Version I [pub. 1841], 161-66; Version II [pub. 1856]: 167-72), *L'Ile inconnue* (xviii, 173-80), *La Belle Isabeau* (xviii, 181-90), *Zaïde* (xix, Version I [autograph]: 191-96; Version II [pub. 1850]: 197-204), *Le Chasseur danois* (xix, 205-10), *Page d'album* (xix-xx, 211), *La Mort d'Ophélie* (xx, 212-19), *Le Chant des Bretons* (xx, 220-26 [Versions I and II, as above, but reduced for tenor solo, after a note supplied by Berlioz], *Le Matin* (xx, 227-34), *Petit Oiseau* (xx, 235-40). 1904.

XVIII. [Arrangements] *Hymne des Marseillais* (Rouget de Lisle) (v, 2-21), *Pater noster* (Bortniansky) (v, 22-23), *Adoremus* (Bortniansky) (v, 24-25), *Plaisir d'amour* (Martini) (vi, 26-31), *Le Roi des Aulnes* (Schubert) (vi-viii, 32-51), *Invitation à louer Dieu* (Couperin) (viii, 52-57), *Invitation à la valse* (Weber) (viii-ix, 58-97), *Les Francs-Juges* [piano, four-hands] (ix-x, 98-123). Examples from *Grand Traité d'instrumentation* (Abt. II, 1-125; new pagination). 1904.

XIX-XX. *Béatrice et Bénédict.* 1907.

Writings of Berlioz

BerCSW   *Briefe von Hector Berlioz an die Fürstin Carolyne Sayn-Wittgenstein.* Ed. La Mara (pseud. for Marie Lipsius). Leipzig, 1903. (French text, German commentary).

BerCI   *Correspondance inédite de Hector Berlioz, 1819-1868.* Ed. Daniel Bernard. Paris, 1879.

            Grand Traité d'instrumentation et orchestration modernes, etc. Paris, 1843.

            Les Grotesques de la musique. Paris, 1859.

BerAR   *Hector Berlioz. Les Années romantiques, 1819-1842, Correspondance.* Ed. Julien Tiersot. Paris, 1904.

BerMC   *Hector Berlioz. Au milieu du chemin, 1852-1855. Correspondance.* Ed. Julien Tiersot. Paris, 1930.

BerCG   *Hector Berlioz. Correspondance générale.* Ed. Pierre Citron. A part of *Hector Berlioz: Oeuvres Littéraires.* Paris, 1972.

BerCG I   1803-1832 (letters 1-283). Ed. Pierre Citron. Paris, 1972.

BerCG II   1832-1842 (letters 274-775). Ed. Frédéric Robert. Paris, 1975.

BerCG III   1842-1850 (letters 776-1367). Ed. Pierre Citron. Paris, 1978.

BerME   *Hector Berlioz. Le Musicien errant, 1842-1852. Correspondance.* Ed.
                   Julien Tiersot. Paris, 1919.

                   Lettres de Berlioz sur les Troyens. Ed. Julien Tiersot. *La Revue de
                   Paris,* 1921, iv, 449-72, 749-70, and v, 146-71.

BerTG   *Lettres inédites de Hector Berlioz à Thomas Gounet.* Ed. L. Michoud
                   and G. Allix. Grenoble, 1903.

BerLI   *Hector Berlioz. Lettres intimes.* Paris, 1882.

BerMém   *Mémoires de Hector Berlioz, membre de l'Institut de France,
                   comprenant ses voyages en Italie, en Allemagne, en Russie, et en
                   Angleterre, 1803-1865,* etc.   Printed Paris, 1865; released 1870.

BerMém[Citron]   *Mémoires.* Ed. Pierre Citron. 2 vols. Paris, 1969.

BerMemCairns   *The Memoirs of Hector Berlioz.* Trans. and ed. David Cairns.
                   (Norton paperback edition, revised, corrected, and enlarged, 3rd edn.,
                   New York, 1975.)

Other Books and Articles

BarHB   Barzun, Jacques. *Berlioz and the Romantic Century.*   2 vols. 3rd
                   edn., New York, 1969.

                   Barzun, Jacques. "The Latest Berlioz Finds." *Columbia Library
                   Columns* 17 (1968), 8-12.

CatV&A   *Berlioz and the Romantic Imagination.* London, 1969. Catalogue of
                   the exhibition at the Victoria and Albert Museum.

                   Bloom, Peter. Review of *Correspondance générale I (1803-1832),* ed.
                   Pierre Citron. *Notes* 30 (1973-74), 51-54.

                   Boschot, Adolphe. "Berlioz: Une Cantate perdue pendant un siècle."
                   Chez les Musiciens, 2e série, pp. 50-56.   Paris, 1924.

                   Boschot, Adolphe. "Berlioz: Un prix de Rome réfractaire." *Chez
                   les Musiciens,* 3e série, pp. 83-94.   Paris, 1926.

BosFaust45   Boschot, Adolphe. *Le Faust de Berlioz: Etude sur la "Damnation de
                   Faust" et sur l'âme romantique.*   3rd edn., Paris, 1945.

BosHB   Boschot, Adolphe. *L'Histoire d'un Romantique.* 3 vols. Paris, 1906-1913:

BosHB I   *La Jeunesse d'un romantique.   Hector Berlioz, 1803-1831, d'après de
                   nombreux documents inédits.*   1906.

BosHB II   *Un Romantique sous Louis-Philippe.   Hector Berlioz, 1831-1842,
                   d'après de nombreux documents inédits.* 1908.

BosHB III   *Le Crépuscule d'un romantique.   Hector Berlioz, 1842-1869, d'après de
                   nombreux documents inédits.*   1913.

Brenet, Michel. (pseud. for Marie Bobillier). "Berlioz inédit: *Les Francs-Juges, La Nonne Sanglante.*" *Le Guide musical* 42 (1896), 63-67 (concerning *Les Francs-Juges*) and 83-85 (concerning *La Nonne Sanglante*).

Cairns, David. "Berlioz, the Cornet, and the *Symphonie fantastique.*" *Berlioz Society Bulletin* 47 (July 1964), 2-6.

Catalogue des livres anciens et modernes composant la bibliothèque musicale et théâtrale de feu M. Martin, ancien directeur du Conservatoire de musique de la ville de Marseille, etc. Paris, 1885.

Charlton, David. "A Berlioz Footnote." *Music and Letters* 52 (1971), 157-58.

CatMeyer   *Collection musicale André Meyer. Manuscrits autographes, musique imprimée et manuscrite; ouvrages théoriques, historiques et pédagogiques; livrets; iconographie; instruments de musique.* Abbeville, 1960. Repr. c. 1974.

Cone, Edward T. "Inside the Saint's Head." *Musical Newsletter* 1 (1971), 3-12, 16-20; and 2 (1972) 19-22.

Constantin, Léon. *Berlioz.* Paris, 1934.

Dallman, Paul J. *Influences and Use of the Guitar in the Music of Hector Berlioz.* M.A. thesis, University of Maryland, 1972.

Dickinson, A. E. F. "Berlioz's songs." *Musical Quarterly* 55 (1969), 329-43.

Dickinson, A. E. F. "The Revisions for 'The Damnation of Faust'. *Monthly Musical Record* 89 (1959), 180-85.

Holoman, D. Kern. "Berlioz au Conservatoire: Notes biographiques." *Revue de musicologie* 62 (1976), 298-92.

Holoman, D. Kern. "Les Fragments de l'opéra 'perdu' de Berlioz: Les Francs-Juges," *Revue de Musicologie* 63 (1977), 78-88.

Holoman, D. Kern. "The Present State of Berlioz Research." *Acta Musicologica* 47 (1975), 31-67.

Holoman, D. Kern. "Reconstructing a Berlioz Sketch." *Journal of the American Musicological Society* 28 (1975), 125-30.

Holoman, D. Kern. Review of *Correspondance générale I (1803-1832),* ed. Pierre Citron. *Journal of the American Musicological Society* 26 (1973), 167-71.

HopBib   Hopkinson, Cecil. *A Bibliography of the Musical and Literary Works of Hector Berlioz, 1803-1869.* Edinburgh, 1951.

Hopkinson, Cecil. "Two Important Berlioz Discoveries." *Fontes Artis Musicae* 15 (1968), 14-16, with facsimiles. Also "Berlioz Discoveries, An Open Letter." *Fontes Artis Musicae* 16 (1969), 28-29.

Hyatt, Raymond. *Draft List of Works by Berlioz.* Typewritten, c. 1969.

JullHB   Jullien, Adolphe. *Hector Berlioz, sa vie et ses oeuvres.* Paris, 1888.

Lebeau, Elisabeth. "Un Mécène de la musique: Charles Malherbe." *Humanisme actif (Mélanges d'art et de littérature offerts à Julien Cain).* Paris, 1968. 91-99.

Lesure, François. Review of *Correspondance générale I (1803-1832),* ed. Pierre Citron. *Revue de musicologie* 58 (1972), 274-76.

Locke, Ralph P. "New Letters of Berlioz," with the texts of eight unpublished letters. *19th-Century Music* 1 (1977-78), 71-84.

Lockwood, Lewis. "The Autograph of the First Movement of Beethoven's Sonata for Violoncello and Pianoforte, Opus 69." *The Music Forum,* vol. II. (New York and London), 1970, 1-109.

MacSelf   Macdonald, Hugh. "Berlioz's Self-Borrowings." *Proceedings of the Royal Musical Association* 92 (1965-66), 27-44.

MacCrit   Macdonald, Hugh. *A Critical Edition of Berlioz's Les Troyens.* Ph.D. dissertation Cambridge, 1968.

MacCent   Macdonald, Hugh. "Hector Berlioz 1969; A Centenary Assessment." *ADAM* 331-33 (1969), 35-47.

Macdonald, Hugh. "Hector Berlioz 1969; Zur 100. Wiederkehr seines Todestages am 8. März." *Musica* 23 (1969), 112-15.

Macdonald, Hugh. "The Labitte Catalogue. Some Unexplored Evidence." *Berlioz Society Bulletin* 69 (1970), 5-7. Also "More Evidence," Ibid. 70 (January 1971), 7-8.

Macdonald, Hugh. "Two Peculiarities of Berlioz's Notation." *Music and Letters* 50 (1969), 25-36.

Marshall, Robert. *The Compositional Process of J. S. Bach. A Study of the Autograph Sources of the Vocal Works.* Princeton, 1972. 2 vols.

Montaux, A. "Berlioz: son génie, sa technique, son caractère, à propos d'un manuscrit autographe d'*Harold en Italie (Marche des Pèlerins).*" *Le Ménestrel* (1890), 235-36, 243-44, 259-61, 269-70, 276-77, 284-85.

Prod'homme, J. G. "Etat alphabétique sommaire des Archives de l'Opéra." *Revue de musicologie* 17 (1933), 193-205.

Rushton, Julian. "The Genesis of Berlioz's 'La Damnation de Faust'." *Music and Letters* 56 (1975), 129-46.

Temperley, Nicholas. "Berlioz and the Slur." *Music and Letters* 50 (1969), 388-92.

Temperley, Nicholas. "The Symphonie Fantastique and its Program." *Musical Quarterly* 57 (1971), 593-608.

TierB'ana   Tiersot, Julien. *Berlioziana*. Serialized in *Le Ménestrel*, vols. 70-72
             (1904-1906) and vol. 75-77 (1909-1911). Contents:

        I.   *Au Musée Berlioz*

             Vol. 70, no. 1 (3 Jan 1904), pp. 3-4; 2 (10 Jan).
             11-12 [guitar
             books]; [*Lettres et documents inédits sur le Requiem de Berlioz*,
             interruption of series:] 3 (17 Jan), 19-20; 4 (24 Jan), 27-28; 5 (31
             Jan), 36-37; 6 (7 Feb), 44-45; [resumption of series:] 7 (14 Feb), 51-
             52 [guitar books]; 8 (21 Feb), 59-60 [Ibid.]; 9 (28 Feb), 66-68 [Ibid.];
             11 (13 March), 83-84 [documents 1805-1821]; 13 (27 March), 99-100
             [letters of Berlioz]; 14 (3 April) 107-08 [Association Nationale Hector
             Berlioz]; 15 (10 April), 116 [Meylan]; 16 (17 April), 123-24
             [Grenoble.].

        II. *Programmes, prologues, préfaces.*

             26 (26 June), 203-05 [*Symphonie fantastique*]; 27 (3 July), 210-11
             [Ibid.];   28 (10 July), 219-20 [Ibid.]; 29 (17 July), 227 [*Harold en
             Italie, Roméo et Juliette*]; 30 (24 July), 238-39 [*Roméo et Juliette*]; 32
             (7 Aug), 252-53 [*Symphonie funèbre et triomphale*]; 33 (14 Aug), 258-
             60 [*La Damnation de Faust, Te Deum*]; 34 (21 Aug), 267-68 [*Les
             Troyens, Benvenuto Cellini*].

        III. *Compositions inédites et autographes de Berlioz*

             35 (28 Aug), 275-76 [catalogue, *Requiem*]; 37 (11 Sept), 290-92
             [*Béatrice et Bénédict, Les Troyens*]; 38 (18 Sept), 299-300 [*La
             Damnation de Faust*]; 39 (25 Sept.), 307-08 [Ibid.]; 40 (2 Oct) 315
             [*L'Enfance du Christ, La Fuite en Egypte*]; 42 (16 Oct), 331-32
             [*Lélio*]; 46 (13 Nov), 363-64 [Ibid.]; 47 (20 Nov), 371-72 [Ibid.]; 48
             (27 Nov), 378-80 [Ibid.]; 52 (25 Dec), 411-12 [Ibid.].

             Vol. 71, no. 1 (1 Jan 1905), p. 4 [*Lelio*, concluded]; 3 (15 Jan), 19-20
             [*Te Deum*]; 6 (5 Feb), 43-44 [*Benvenuto Cellini*]; 8 (19 Feb), 60-61
             [Ibid.]; 9 (26 Feb), 67-68 [Ibid.]; 10 (5 March), 76-77 [Ibid.]; 11 (12
             March), 83-84 [Ibid.]; 12 (19 March), 91-92 [Ibid.]; 13 (26 March),
             99-100 [Ibid.]; 14 (2 April), 107-08 [Ibid.]; 15 (9 April), 115-16
             [Ibid.]; 23 (4 June), 180-81 [Ibid.]; 26 (25 June), 205-06 [Ibid.]; 27 (2
             July), 211-12 [Ibid.]; 28 (9 July), 220-21 ["Notes additionnelles sur
             Les Troyens et *Lélio ou Le Retour à la vie*"]; 29 (16 July), 228-29
             [*Symphonie fantastique*]; 30 (23 July), 237-38 [Ibid.]; 32 (6 Aug), 250-
             51 [*Harold en Italie*]; 34 (20 Aug), 268 [Ibid.]; 35 (27 Aug), 276-77
             [*Roméo et Juliette*]; 36 (3 Sept), 284 [*Symphonie funèbre et
             triomphale, L'Apothéose*]; 37 (10 Sept), 292-93 [Ibid.]; 38 (17 Sept),
             301 [*Ouverture de Waverley*]; 39 (24 Sept), 308 [*Ouvertures des
             Francs-Juges, du Roi Lear, et du Carnaval Romain*]; 41 (8 Oct), 324
             [*Ouverture du Corsaire*]; 42 (15 Oct), 331-32 ["Oeuvres diverses
             publiées du vivant de Berlioz:" plan for an *Oeuvres complètes*]; 43
             (22 Oct), 341 [*Irlande*]; 45 (5 Nov), 355-56 [*Le Cinq Mai, Nuits d'été,
             Rêverie et Caprice*]; 47 (19 Nov), 371 [*Sara la baigneuse, La Captive,
             Fleurs des landes*]; 48 (26 Nov), 379-80 [*Tristia*].

Vol. 72, no. 2 (14 Jan 1906), pp. 11-12 ["Oeuvres diverses publiées du vivant de Berlioz," cont'd: *Feuillets d'album*]; 3 (21 Jan), 20-21 [*Vox Populi, L'Impériale*]; 4 (28 Jan), 27-28 [*Le Temple universel*]; 5 (4 Feb), 35-36 ["Oeuvres arrangées par Berlioz:" *L'Invitation à la Valse*]; 6 (11 Feb), 43-45 [*Orphée* and *Alceste* by Gluck, *Hymne des Marseillais, Marche marocaine, Plaisir d'amour, Le Roi des Aulnes*, two choral works by Bortniansky]; 7 (18 Feb), 51-52 ["Oeuvres semi-inédites:" *Le Dépit de la bergère; Le Maure jaloux; Pleure, pauvre Colette; Le Montagnard exilé; Toi qui l'aimas, verse des pleurs; Amitié, reprends ton empire; Canon libre à la quinte*]; 8 (25 Feb), 59-60 [Ibid.]; 9 (4 March), 67-68 [*Huit Scènes de Faust, Ballet des ombres*]; 10 (11 March), 75-76 [*Je crois en vous, Hymne pour six instruments à vent, La Tour de Nice, Hymne pour la consécration du nouveau Tabernacle*]; 11 (18 March), 83-84 [*Hymne pour la consécration, Veni Creator, Tantum Ergo, Invitation à louer Dieu*]; 14 (8 April) 107-08 ["Oeuvres Inédites:" *Resurrexit*].

[Dispute over origin of the *Marche au supplice* from the *Symphonie fantastique*, interruption of series:]   20 (20 May), 153 ["Sur la Marche au Supplice"]; 21 (27 May), 160-61 [letter from Boschot: "La 'Marche au Supplice' vient des 'Francs-Juges'"]; 22 (3 June), 169-70 [Tiersot: "La 'Marche au Supplice' ne vient pas des 'Francs-Juges'"].   [Resumption of series:] 24 (17 June), 184-85 [*Resurrexit*]; 25 (24 June), 190-92 [Ibid.]; 26 (1 July), 199-200) [*Les Francs-Juges*]; 27 (8 July), 207-08 [Ibid.]; 28 (15 July), 215-16 [Ibid.]; 31 (5 Aug), 240-42 [*"Francs-Juges et Symphonie fantastique"*]; 32 (12 Aug), 246-48 [*Les Francs-Juges*]; 33 (19 Aug), 255-56 [*Scène héroïque*]; 34 (26 Aug), 263-64 [*Choeur des Mages, Oeuvres de Concours: Fugues, La Mort d'Orphée, Herminie, Cléopâtre, Sardanapale*]; [Continuation of dispute over *Marche au supplice*, interruption of series:] 34 (26 Aug), 264 [Boschot, "La 'Marche au Supplice' continue à venir des 'Francs-Juges'"]; 35 (2 Sept), 271-72 [corresp. from Malherbe]; 36 (9 Sept), 279-80 [corresp. from Tiersot]; 37 (16 Sept), 288 [corresp. from Malherbe].   [Resumption of series:] 35 (2 Sept), 270-71 ["Oeuvres de concours"]; 36 (9 Sept), 278-79 [Ibid.]; 37 (16 Sept), 287 [Ibid.]; 38 (23 Sept), 294-95 [Ibid.]; 39 (30 Sept), 302-03 [Ibid.]; 40 (7 Oct), 310-12 [*Ouverture de Rob-Roy, Erigone*]; 41 (14 Oct), 319-20 [*La Nonne sanglante*]; 42 (21 Oct), 327-28 [Ibid.]; 43 (27 Oct), 335-36 ["Appendice sur *Les Troyens* et *Béatrice et Bénédict*"]: 45 (10 Nov), 351-52 ["Pièces pour Harmonium:" *Sérénade agreste à la Madone, Hymne pour l'Elévation, Toccata; Album de notes*, "Feuilles éparses"]; 46 (17 Nov), 361-62 [sketchbook]; 47 (24 Nov), 367-68 [Ibid.]; 48 (1 Dec), 375-76 [sketchbook, miscellaneous leaves].

Vol. 75, no 14 (3 April 1909), pp. 105-06 ["Le Premier Portrait de Berlioz," article not technically in series]; 15 (10 April), 113-14 [Ibid.].

IV. *Berlioz, directeur des concerts symphoniques.*

42 (16 Oct), 332-33; 43 (23 Oct), 339-41; 44 (30 Oct), 347-48; 46 (13 Nov), 363-64; 48 (27 Nov), 379-80; 50 (11 Dec), 395-96; 52 (25 Dec), 410-11.

Vol. 76, no. 2 (8 January 1910), pp. 11-12 [Ibid.]; 3 (15 Jan), 20; 4 (22 Jan), 27-28; 5 (29 Jan), 34-36; 7 (12 Feb), 50-51; 10 (5 March), 75-76; 12 (19 March), 91-92; 13 (26 March), 99-100; 14 (2 April), 107-08; 29 (16 July), 228-30 ["Les *Huit Scènes de Faust.* Oeuvre première de Berlioz,"] not identified as part of series; 30 (23 July), 235-36; 31 (30 July), 243-44.

V. *Berlioz, bibliothécaire du Conservatoire.*

Vol. 77, no. 29 (22 July 1911), pp. 226-27; 30 (29 July), 235-36; 31 (5 Aug), 244-45; 32 (12 Aug), 252-53.

[VI.] *Berlioz à l'Institut.* [Not identified as part of series, but probably intended as Chap. VI] 33 (19 Aug), 259-61; 34 (26 Aug), 269-70; 35 (2 Sept), 276-77; 36 (9 Sept), 283; 37 (16 Sept), 291-92.

Tiersot, Julien. *La Damnation de Faust de Berlioz. Etude historique et critique. Analyse musicale.* Paris, [1924].

Tiersot, Julien. "Lettres de Berlioz sur les Troyens." *La Revue de Paris* (1921) iv, 449-73, 749-70; and v, 146-71.

CatVaill   Vaillant, Paul. "Berlioz à la bibliothèque de Grenoble." *Cahiers de l'Alpe* 46 (1969), 133-36.

Wotton, Tom. "An Unknown Score of Berlioz." *Music Review* 4 (1943), 224-28.

Index

Works in boldface type refer to the appropriate entry in Table I (pp. 23-77); index numbers are the same as for Holoman, *Catalogue of the Works of Hector Berlioz* (vol. 25 of the New Berlioz Edition).

References to musical examples and facsimiles appear at the end of each entry or subentry.